BLUE GUIDE

OXFORD & CAMBRIDGE

Geoffrey Tyack

A&C Black • London
WW Norton • New York

Sixth edition 2004
Published by A&C Black Publishers Limited
37 Soho Square, London W1D 3QZ
www.blueguides.co.uk

A CIP catalogue record of this book
is available from the British Library

ISBN 0–7136–6303–0

Published in the United States of America by
WW Norton and Company, Inc
500 Fifth Avenue, New York, NY 10110
ISBN 0–393–32586–5 USA

Published simultaneously in Canada by
Penguin Books Canada Limited
10 Alcorn Avenue, Toronto, Ontario M4V 3B2

The author and the publishers have done their best to ensure the accuracy of all the
information in Blue Guide Oxford and Cambridge; however, they can accept no responsibility for any loss, injury or inconvenience sustained by any traveller as a result of information
or advice contained in the guide.

Geoffrey Tyack was educated at St. John's College, Oxford, and received his PhD in architectural history from the University of London. He is Director of the Stanford University
Centre in Oxford. He is a fellow of Kellogg College, Oxford, and a Fellow of the Society of
Antiquaries. He is the author of *Sir James Pennethorne and the Making of Victorian London*
(Cambridge University Press, 1992); *Warwickshire Country Houses* (Phillimore and Co.,
1994); and *Oxford: An Architectural Guide* (Oxford University Press, 1998). He is also the
author, with Steven Brindle, of *Blue Guide Country Houses of England*. He lives in Oxford.

Cover pictures. Top: vault of the Divinity School, Oxford. © Collections
Bottom: details of hire punts on the River Cam, Cambridge. © P.W. Rippon, courtesy of the
Hutchison Picture Library
Title page illustration: main gateway, Clare College, Cambridge

A&C Black uses paper produced with elemental chlorine-free pulp, harvested from managed
sustainable forests

Printed and bound by M.G.I. Print, Israel

BLUE GUIDES

Albania & Kosovo

Australia

Austria   Austria
      Vienna

Bali, Java & Lombok

Belgium

Bulgaria

Czech & Slovak   Czech & Slovak
Republics   Republics
      Prague

China

Cyprus

Denmark

Egypt

France   France
      Paris & Versailles
      Loire Valley
      Provence & the Côte
        d'Azur
      Southwest France

Germany   Berlin & eastern
       Germany

Greece   Greece
      Athens
      Crete
      Rhodes & the
      Dodecanese

Hungary   Hungary
      Budapest

Southern India

Ireland   Ireland
      Dublin

Italy   Northern Italy
      Southern Italy
      Florence

Italy continued   Rome
      Umbria
      Venice
      Tuscany
      Sicily

Jordan

Malaysia &
      Singapore

Malta & Gozo

Morocco

Netherlands   Netherlands
      Amsterdam

Poland   Poland
      Kraków

Portugal

Romania

Spain   Barcelona
      Madrid

Sweden

Tunisia

Turkey   Turkey
      Istanbul

UK   England
      Scotland
      Wales
      Channel Islands
      London
      Oxford & Cambridge
      Country Houses of
       England

USA   New York
      Museums &
       Galleries of New York
      Boston & Cambridge
      Washington

Please write in with your comments, suggestions and corrections for the next edition of the Blue Guide. Writers of the most helpful letters will be awarded a free Blue Guide of their choice.

Contents

Preface 9
Acknowledgements 10
Highlights of Oxford and Cambridge 11
The history and architecture of the universities 12
Bibliography 33

OXFORD

Practical information

Getting to Oxford 35
  By air 35
  By train 35
  By bus 40
  By car 40

Where to stay 41
  Hotel listings 41
  Guest houses and bed and breakfasts 43
  Self-catering & campsites 44

Food and drink 44
  Restaurant listings 45
  Pubs 46
  Cafés and tea shops 47

Getting around Oxford 47
  Sightseeing 48

Festivals and annual events 48

Entertainment 49
  Drama 49

Music 49
Cinemas 50
  Sporting and leisure activities 50

Parks and gardens 50

Shopping 51

Museums and galleries 51

Activities for children 52

Additional information 53
  Banks and post offices 53
  Disabled travellers 53
  Emergencies and medical services 53
  Libraries 53
  Personal security 53
  Public holidays 54

The Colleges 54

Walks in Oxford

1 · The central University area 55
  St. Mary the Virgin church 55
  Brasenose College 57
  The Bodleian Library 58
  Sheldonian Theatre 62
  Wadham College 64
  New College 66
  Hertford College 69

2 · South of Carfax 70
  Christ Church 71
  Oriel College 79
  Corpus Christi College 80
  Merton College 82
  Pembroke College 86

3 • Along the High Street 88

Jesus College 88
Exeter College 89
Lincoln College 90
All Souls College 92
The Queen's College 94

St. Edmund Hall 96
Magdalen College 97
Over Magdalen Bridge 100
University College 103

4 • North and west of Carfax 105

Trinity College 106
Balliol College 108
St. John's College 110

Worcester College 113
Oxford Castle 115

5 • The Museums and the Science Area 118

Ashmolean Museum 118
Keble College 127
The University & Pitt Rivers Museums 128

St. Catherine's College 132

6 • Jericho and North Oxford 133

Lady Margaret Hall 137

The immediate vicinity of Oxford

1 • To Iffley along the river 139
2 • Port Meadow, Binsey and
        Godstow 142
3 • Osney and North Hinksey 142

4 • To Old Marston along the
        Cherwell 143
5 • Other short excursions 143

Days out from Oxford

1 • The Thames Valley, the Chilterns and Henley-on-Thames 145

Dorchester 145
The Thames Valley 147

The Chilterns 148
Henley-on-Thames 149

2 • Abingdon, the Berkshire Downs & the Vale of the White Horse 150

Abingdon 151

The Berkshire Downs 153

3 • Burford, the Cotswolds and the upper Thames 155

Witney 156
The Windrush Valley 156
Burford 157

Into the Cotswolds 158
The upper Thames 159

4 • Blenheim Palace and beyond 160

Blenheim Palace 161
Woodstock 164

The northern Cotswolds 164

5 • Rousham, Banbury and North Oxfordshire 165

Rousham House & Gardens 166

Banbury 166

6 • Waddesdon, Claydon and Stowe 168

Waddesdon Manor 168
Claydon House 170

Stowe 170

7 • West Wycombe 172

West Wycombe Park 172

CAMBRIDGE
··

Practical information
··

Getting to Cambridge 175
  By air 175
  By train 175
  By bus 175
  By car 180

Where to stay 180
  Hotel listings 181
  Guest houses and bed and breakfasts
    182
  Self-catering and campsites 182

Food and drink 183
  Restaurant listings 183
  Pubs 184
  Cafés and tea shops 185

Getting around Cambridge 185
  Sightseeing 186

Festivals and annual events 186

Entertainment 187
  Drama 187

Music 187
Cinemas 187
Sporting and leisure activities 188

Parks and gardens 188

Shopping 188

Museums and galleries 189

Activities for children 189

Additional information 190
  Banks and post offices 190
  Disabled travellers 190
  Emergencies and medical services
    190
  Libraries 190
  Personal security 191

The Colleges 191

Walks in Cambridge
··

1 • The heart of the University 193
  St. Mary the Great 193
  The Central University Buildings 194
  King's College 195
  Clare College 199
  Trinity Hall 201
  Gonville and Caius College 203
  Trinity College 206
  St. John's College 212

2 • South from King's 216
  St. Catharine's 217
  Corpus Christi College 218
  Queens' College 220
  Pembroke College 224
  Peterhouse 227
  Fitzwilliam Museum 229

3 • Southeast from Magdalene Bridge 234
  Magdalene College 235
  Jesus College 238
  Sidney Sussex College 241
  Christ's College 244
  Emmanuel College 246
  Science Area 248
  Downing College 250

4 • North and west of Castle Hill 253
  Kettle's Yard 253
  New Hall 255
  Fitzwilliam College 256
  Girton College 257
  Churchill College 258

5 • West of the Cam 260
Newnham College 260   Selwyn College 262
The Arts Faculties 261   Robinson College 264

The immediate vicinity of Cambridge
1 • To Grantchester and   3 • To the American Military
   Trumpington 265   Cemetery and Madingley 269
2 • To Stourbridge Common and   4 • The Gog Magogs 269
   Fen Ditton 268

Days out from Cambridge

1 • Ely and the Fens 270
Ely Cathedral 270   The Fens 277

2 • Newmarket and the Fen Edge 278
Newmarket 278   Anglesey Abbey 280

3 • Bury St. Edmunds and West Suffolk 281
Bury St. Edmunds 281   Ickworth 283

4 • Saffron Walden, Audley End and Thaxted 285
Saffron Walden 285   Audley End 287

5 • Wimpole Hall and beyond 289
Wimpole Hall 289

6 • Into Huntingdonshire 291
Huntingdon 293

Glossary 296
Sovereigns of England 298
Index of personal names 299
Index to Oxford 311
Index to Cambridge 315

Maps and plans

Oxford
Oxford, atlas 36–39   Christ Church Cathedral 74
Oxford, surrounding area 140–141   Christ Church: the College 77
Ashmolean Museum 120, 122   Magdalen College 99
Blenheim Palace 163   Merton College 83
Central University area 59   New College 67

Cambridge
Camrbidge, atlas 176–177   King's College 197
Cambridge, surrounding area 266–267   Queens' College 221
Ely Cathedral 273   St. John's College 213
Fitzwilliam Museum 230, 232   Trinity College 208
Jesus College 239

Preface

For most people the very names of Oxford and Cambridge are synonymous with the idea of long-established academic endeavour and achievement; indeed, some visitors assume, wrongly, that there are no other universities worthy of note in England. Yet what chiefly distinguishes Oxford and Cambridge from other, sometimes even older, university cities is not so much their intellectual prestige as their wealth of old buildings, the beauty of their settings, the quality of their art collections and their quite extraordinary institutional continuity. Here, more perhaps than in any other university cities in Europe, the past is tangible and the medieval origins of modern higher education are made manifest.

Oxford and Cambridge have much in common. Neither city is very large, and both still have strong links with the surrounding countryside, which in each case insinuates itself into the very heart of the city. Both cities retain their medieval street pattern intact, and in both the fabric of the modern city is deeply influenced by the presence of colleges and, to a lesser extent, university buildings. These buildings are integrated into the fabric of the cities in a way which those familiar with other universities sometimes find difficult to appreciate. The cry goes up: 'Where is the university?', or 'Where is the campus?', to be met with baffled expressions from the local shopper en route for Marks & Spencers, the student scurrying to a lecture, tutorial (Oxford) or supervision (Cambridge), or the scholar momentarily deflected from the pursuit of an arcane scholarly problem. The truth is that the university is everywhere and nowhere. No wonder the author of *Alice in Wonderland* was an Oxford don.

It is in their collegiate organisation that Oxford and Cambridge differ most markedly from most modern universities, and it is in their buildings that the colleges most memorably express their corporate identity. Not surprisingly, therefore, a large part of this book is devoted to the history, architecture and collections of these highly individualistic institutions. The colleges are inward-looking places, centred around enclosed courts (Cambridge) or quadrangles (Oxford) and often entered through gate towers and narrow doorways which seem intended to deter all but the most determined visitor. Visitors are in fact welcomed, or, at the very least, tolerated, but they are allowed to enter as a privilege, and not by right. Oxford and Cambridge are working universities, and people live and study in the colleges. Their interests therefore tend to come first. Having said that, many people coming to Oxford and Cambridge for the first time are surprised at how much they are allowed to see, and at how much of beauty and interest awaits those who are prepared to penetrate the sometimes formidable outer defences. As so often in English life, patience, persistence and a willingness to play the game by the rules pay ample dividends.

While retaining their ancient character, both Oxford and Cambridge changed greatly in the second half of the 20th century, and those expecting to enter a cloistered never-never land or theme park will soon be disappointed. The two universities have been among the most lavish and adventurous patrons of modern architecture in Britain, which is why modern buildings are more strongly emphasised here than in some guidebooks; even since the last edition of the Guide (1998) a number of important new buildings have been erected, and the most significant of these have been included in the text.

Many visitors come to Oxford and Cambridge for only a day or two, but those who can should stay longer in order to enjoy fully what each city has to offer: not only the colleges but also the wealth of churches, museums and gardens which help give each place its unique personality. For those obliged to stay for only a short time, a short section of Highlights is included at the beginning of the book. This edition of the Guide also contains a revised section of practical information in which details are given about hotels and restaurants, along with sections about travel, local events, and activities for children; please bear in mind that hotels and, especially, restaurants change ownership frequently and that what is true, to the best of the author's knowledge, when the book went to press may not necessarily be true even a year later.

As in previous editions of the Guide, the buildings of each city are grouped together in a series of routes which can be accomplished on foot: these have been extensively revised in this new edition, and there are now six walks for Oxford and five for Cambridge, each of them somewhat shorter and, it is hoped, less exhausting than those in previous editions. Some suggestions for short walks or excursions into the immediate vicinity are also given, and there are revised sections on the many interesting places to be seen within a day or half-day from each city centre. Those wishing to look up a particular place, either in the cities or the environs, are encouraged to use the Index. An index of artists, architects and people associated with the two universities, is also supplied, and lists of some of the more famous old members are given for each of the older colleges. There is a glossary of architectural and other terms, and the introduction outlines the history of each city and its buildings; those wishing to find out more are encouraged to use the updated bibliography.

Opening times for all major buildings have been checked, and are included at the appropriate place in the text; it should be emphasised, however, that opening times often change, and that, especially in the colleges, buildings and parts of buildings can often be closed without warning. Those wishing to see a particular place are therefore urged to telephone beforehand to avoid disappointment. When known, the closing times are those when the last visitors are admitted; when uncertain it is always worth arriving in good time. The maps and plans have also been updated. **Map references** are given in the text where appropriate; they refer to the grid squares in the detailed maps of each city.

Acknowledgments

I owe a great debt of gratitude to Mercia Mason, the author of the first three editions of the *Blue Guide Oxford and Cambridge*, who generously placed her text at my disposal for the fourth edition and passed on the relevant literature. Much of her text still remains unchanged. I am also indebted to the Bursars and other Fellows of many Cambridge colleges who carefully checked the relevant sections and excised some howlers which had crept into the text. John Ashdown was equally helpful in checking the Oxford text. I am also very grateful to friends and colleagues in both Oxford and Cambridge who have kindly given me access to parts of the colleges and university buildings not usually open to the public. The responsibility for any errors is, of course, my own.

Geoffrey Tyack, Oxford

BACKGROUND INFORMATION

Highlights of Oxford and Cambridge

In **Oxford** no visitor should miss the central group of university buildings, including the Bodleian Library, Divinity School, Sheldonian Theatre and Radcliffe Camera. Of the colleges, those most worth a visit are Christ Church (including the cathedral), Merton, Magdalen, New College, All Souls, Queen's, St. John's, Trinity, Wadham and Keble; the lover of 20C architecture should also see St. Catherine's College. Of the museums the most important are the Ashmolean and the University Museum—the latter as much for the building as for the contents—with its appendage the Pitt-Rivers Museum. Of the many groups of buildings the finest are those in Radcliffe Square and the High St, one of the most impressive streets anywhere in the world; the walk along Queen's Lane and New College Lane also gives a changing sequence of vistas of great interest and beauty. Oxford is famous for its gardens, of which perhaps the most beautiful are those of St. John's and Worcester Colleges; 'Addison's Walk' at Magdalen College and Christ Church Meadow are larger and very different in character. Of the many places of interest in the environs, **Blenheim Palace** stands out for its combination of spectacular architecture, beautiful gardens and interesting historical associations. But some of the other country houses in the area are well worth visiiting, as are the many well-preserved small villages and towns like **Burford**; the latter can be combined with a trip to the **Cotswolds**, which are easily accessible by car.

Among the buildings of **Cambridge**, King's College Chapel is supreme; indeed if only one building in either of the universities could be visited, it would have to be this. Of the older college buildings, those of Trinity (especially the Library), St. John's, Jesus, Gonville and Caius, Queens' and Emmanuel can be singled out, but those interested in 20C architecture should also seek out some of the colleges founded since the Second World War, especially New Hall, Fitzwilliam and Churchill. Many of the most interesting university buildings are also comparatively recent, notably the History and Law Faculties. The best museums, at least for the art lover, are the Fitzwilliam and Kettle's Yard. No one should leave Cambridge without walking along the Backs, and the walk from the Round Church to the Fitzwilliam Museum, or vice versa, constitutes one of the great architectural promenades of Europe. The riverside walk to **Grantchester** is also well worth making, for its literary associations as well as its intrinsic qualities. In the environs the two outstanding excursions are to **Ely Cathedral** and to the great Jacobean house at **Audley End**. For lovers of equestrianism **Newmarket** is the national mecca, and for those wishing to venture further afield a trip to Bury St. Edmunds and the beautiful small towns of west Suffolk (for example, Lavenham) is strongly recommended.

When to go

Each season has its charms and its frustrations, though the charms are perhaps more obvious and the frustrations less frustrating in late spring and early autumn. Cambridge can be very cold when the east wind is blowing in the winter and Oxford is sometimes unpleasantly humid in summer. From October to March the universities are in session for most of the time, and there are relatively few visitors. Museums and most colleges are open throughout this period, except from Christmas to the New Year (when both cities go to sleep), but it gets dark early from November to March, when the country houses in the vicinity are all shut. From April to June the evenings are longer and the universities are still functioning, but many of the Cambridge (though not Oxford) colleges are permanently closed while the students prepare for examinations. Visitors, including foreign language students, start appearing in large numbers in both cities at the beginning of July, just after most university students have departed, and the central streets and some of the colleges can then get unpleasantly crowded, especially at weekends (when many of the major buildings are shut). However, by way of compensation, there are several summer activities like concerts and open-air drama productions in both cities. The number of tourists drops off dramatically at the beginning of September, and the new academic year begins at the beginning of October.

History and architecture

Origins

Both Oxford and Cambridge are still in essence medieval towns, and both are much older than their universities. The history of Cambridge begins in Roman times, and a town was re-established by the Anglo-Saxons. Oxford, though not a Roman town, was in existence by AD 912, as the *Anglo-Saxon Chronicle* attests, and was one of the largest towns in England at the time of the Norman Conquest (1066). Both towns lie within prosperous agricultural regions in the south of England, both were important commercial centres, and both became county towns after the Norman Conquest. Even without their universities they would still be important provincial towns today.

Low-lying and damp, **Oxford** is situated at the meeting place of two rivers, the Thames or Isis, and the Cherwell (pronounced Charwell). Their waters join to the south of the old city centre, from which point they flow on southeast towards London, and a settlement grew up, probably in the 8C, on a gravel terrace to the north of a 'ford for oxen', near the present Folly Bridge. Here, according to legend, **St. Frideswide** (d. c 735), probably a noblewoman, founded a priory on the site of the place where a well-aimed thunderbolt rescued her from the undesired attentions of a Mercian King. Nothing remains of her church or convent buildings, but fragments of her shrine can still be seen in Christ Church Cathedral.

In the 10C Oxford became both an important road junction and a defensive strong point for the Kings of Wessex, commanding some of the main means of communication between the south of England and the Midlands, and between the southeast and Wales. Even today it is an important crossroads, as the constant heavy traffic around the ring-road attests. It was surrounded by a stockade, which was later rebuilt in stone as the **town wall**, and is still visible in places. Inside the walls there was a grid of streets, with the two main thoroughfares crossing at **Carfax**, still the centre of the city. Trade flourished in the 11C and 12C, and the boundaries were extended to the east, almost as far as the Cherwell; as a result of this expansion the **High Street** acquired its famous curve. In 1155 the town received its charter, with the earliest municipal seal in England.

Cambridge, on the southern edge of the Fens, also owes its existence to a river crossing, but it has a definitely East Anglian character, compounded of wide skies, flat expanses—it is nowhere more than 50ft above sea level—and light reflected by the waters of river, brooks, channels and winter-flooded fields. And often an icy east wind blows 'straight from the steppes of Russia' (it is often asserted that the nearest high ground to the east is the Urals). Excavations on the higher ground north of the river (Castle Hill area) have revealed evidence of pre-Roman settlement, and it was here that the Romans established a **camp**, close to the Colchester–Huntingdon road.

The River Cam was navigable northward to the sea, and good road connections to the south and west made Cambridge a natural entrepôt for local traders. In Anglo-Saxon times a prosperous town grew up south of the river, with a **market place** between the old Colchester road (the present Sidney St and St. Andrew's St) and a High St which ran parallel to the river (Trinity St, King's Parade and Trumpington St); the warehouses of merchants lined the river bank. The two streets merged next to the present Round Church, and crossed the river by a 'Cam bridge' (Magdalene Bridge); the town's Anglo-Saxon name was Grantabrycge (Granta-bridge), and through a number of variations this eventually developed into Cambridge. At some stage in the 12C the defences were strengthened by the construction of the **King's Ditch**. This artificial 'moat' enclosed the south and east sides of the town, and followed roughly the line of Mill Lane, Pembroke St, Lion Yard, Hobson St and Park Parade, where it rejoined the river.

When **William the Conqueror** arrived in 1066, Oxford was handed over to one of his followers, Robert d'Oilly. He built a **castle** to the west of the town centre, the artificial motte or mound of which survives, along with a massive tower built of the local 'coral rag' rubble stone. The Normans also built a castle at Cambridge, near the old Roman camp, of which now only the mound remains; like Oxford Castle it became the centre of county administration.

Monasteries were established in both towns after the Norman Conquest, although there was nothing on the scale of the cathedral priory at Ely, 16 miles north of Cambridge, which still retains its magnificent Romanesque nave, transepts and west tower, or the great Benedictine abbey at Abingdon, 6 miles south of Oxford, all but destroyed in the 16C. There were two large monastic establishments in Oxford: the Augustinian priory of St. Frideswide (the patron saint of the town), whose late 12C church later became Christ Church Cathedral; and Osney, demolished after the Reformation. Godstow and Rewley abbeys followed, and there was also a flourishing college of secular canons in the castle. At Cambridge there was the nunnery of St. Radegund, whose church (rebuilt in the

1 3C) later became Jesus College Chapel, and the Augustinian priory at Barnwell, to the east of the town, of which little survives; both were established outside the King's Ditch in the 12C.

Various orders of **friars** established themselves in the two towns, starting in Oxford in 1226, when the Franciscans built a friary in the low-lying marshy ground to the south of the town wall. In the 1 3C a Franciscan friary was founded in Sidney St, Cambridge, and a Dominican house just outside the King's Ditch in St. Andrew's St; Sidney Sussex and Emmanuel Colleges now occupy their sites. But by this time the character of both towns had already begun to be transformed by the existence of the universities.

The oldest **parish churches** date from slightly before the Norman Conquest: St. Bene't, Cambridge, and St Michael at the North Gate, Oxford, both of which have plain stone towers dating back to the 11C. More churches were built after the Conquest in the Anglo-Norman version of Romanesque architecture; of these the most interesting are St Sepulchre's (the 'Round Church') in Cambridge, and St Peter-in-the-East (now St Edmund Hall library) and the village church at Iffley in Oxford.

The richest merchants lived in stone **houses**, but the vast majority of the citizens of both towns lived in wooden houses, and continued to do so for many generations. Timber-framed houses were still being built in Oxford as late as the 19C, and the townscape, like that of Cambridge, still owes much to the survival of old merchants' houses, some of them of medieval origins.

The universities in the Middle Ages

The universities are two of the oldest in Europe, although neither is so old as was once believed. The foundation of Oxford University has been attributed at different times to a mythical King Memphric, to Brutus—an equally mythical grandson of Aeneas who came to England after the fall of Troy—and to Alfred the Great; Cambridge countered with Prince Cantaber of Spain, in the 'year of the world' 4321, and in 1820 a guide book could state that 'its establishment as a place of instruction for youth, probably soon followed the introduction of Christianity into this island, in the fourth century, during the Saxon heptarchy'.

In fact neither university was 'founded'. Both grew up in the 12C, and began with groups of scholars congregating around famous teachers of the day. In 1167 English students were expelled from Paris, the second oldest university in western Europe (Bologna is the oldest), and it is probable that many migrated to **Oxford**, a conveniently accessible place. By 1200 Oxford was providing a regular course of study, similar to that followed in the University of Paris, and in 1214 the university received its first charter. There must also have been famous teachers at **Cambridge** at this time, probably connected with monastic schools, for when in 1209 a number of students fled from Oxford after a quarrel with the townspeople (the first of many), it was chiefly in Cambridge that they settled.

The arrival of the mendicant orders (Franciscans and Dominicans) in the 13C gave a further impetus to scholarship. Both universities grew rapidly in reputation and numbers, and received the protection and patronage of the King and the Pope. Both favoured the infant institutions because they could supply an elite of trained clerics ('clerks', like Chaucer's 'clerk of Oxenford'—the academic gowns of today are the descendants of their clerical robes) to administer both the Church and the embryonic State, a function which has remained constant down to modern times. An intimate connection with the religious and political establishment has thus remained a marked feature of both universities down to the present day.

In the early days there were no colleges. Students lived in lodgings, or, as time went on, in licensed **Academic Halls** (Oxford) or Hostels (Cambridge) presided over by a Master. Architecturally, these buildings differed little from the larger merchants' houses of the period, and most had ceased to exist as independent institutions by the 16C, but a few Halls continued to flourish in Oxford and one (St Edmund Hall) survived into the 20C, when it became a college. Lectures were held in '**schools**' close to the parish churches of St. Mary (Oxford) and Great St. Mary (Cambridge), both of which were rebuilt in the 15C and both used for ceremonial occasions and meetings. Thus each town acquired a distinct 'university quarter' which has remained a main focus of academic life down to the present day.

Students entered at about 16 for a seven-year course in the Liberal Arts, divided into the Trivium—Grammar, Rhetoric, and Logic—and the Quadrivium—Arithmetic, Geometry, Astronomy and Music. After taking his Bachelor of Arts degree the student had to study and teach for at least a further two years to qualify for his Master's degree. To achieve a doctorate required in all about 16 years; most doctoral students were in the faculty of theology—'the queen of the sciences'—but, as in most other European universities, it was also possible to gain a doctorate in the two other 'higher faculties' of Law and Medicine. In days when books and writing materials were scarce and expensive, both teaching and examination (of which the 'disputation' was an important part) were oral. Latin was spoken throughout. This pattern continued little altered until the mid-16C.

Until the 16C most undergraduates continued to be taught through the medium of university **lectures**. But it was not until the 14C, when Oxford built the Convocation House next to St. Mary's church (1320s), and the Old Schools in Cambridge were started (c 1350), that either university had any buildings of its own. The building of the Divinity School, in 1423–83, gave Oxford a magnificent lecture room for theology with a new university **library** above, containing the books bequeathed by Henry V's younger brother, Duke Humfrey of Gloucester. In Cambridge the architecturally modest Old Schools remained the centre of the university's teaching and administration down to recent times.

Oxford gradually became one of the intellectual centres of medieval Europe, playing a leading part in the development of **scholastic philosophy**, the revived study of Aristotle (albeit in Latin translation) and the beginnings of experimental methods of enquiry. Its members included Robert Grosseteste (the first Chancellor), Roger Bacon, Duns Scotus and William of Ockham. But in the mid-14C the university was torn by the controversies surrounding the teaching of John Wyclif and his followers. Regarded as heretical by conservative church authorities, they came under severe episcopal displeasure, and for a time Oxford was in considerable disfavour, and suffered some decline. Cambridge meanwhile waxed as Oxford waned, and the 14C saw considerable growth. By 1500 both universities were of approximately the same size and of comparable academic prestige.

The story of the universities throughout the Middle Ages is punctuated with conflicts, often bloody, between **town and gown**. These conflicts were aggravated by the exemption of members of the university, who came under ecclesiastical law, from lay jurisdiction, and by attempts by the universities to enforce their authority over the two towns. Antagonism reached its climax in Oxford in 1355 with the Massacre of St. Scholastica's Day, when townsmen, summoned by the bells of St. Martin's, and students, summoned by the bells of St. Mary's, joined battle till the streets allegedly 'ran with blood'. Although triumphant in the field, the townspeople later paid dearly for their victory, in fines and a yearly penance before the Vice Chancellor in St. Mary's church. This ceremony was discontinued only in 1825.

At Cambridge a somewhat similar event took place in 1381 during the feast of Corpus Christi, which was an occasion for the display of much collegiate wealth. Rioters attacked colleges, seized the treasures of Great St. Mary's, raided the university chest, and made a bonfire of documents outside the church. University and college authorities were forced to sign away their rights and privileges. But, as at Oxford, the university soon triumphed. The townsmen were severely punished with loss of rights, while the university's were all restored, and in addition the university was given control over the town trade in food and drink, a control exercised until 1886. In both towns animosity between the citizens and what is sometimes perceived as an overweening and arrogant university remains a feature of modern life.

Medieval colleges and their buildings

The architectural and institutional distinctiveness of Oxford and Cambridge derive from their colleges which, unlike those of other European universities, have retained their independence and endowments down to modern times. The **first colleges** appeared in the mid- to late 13C, and followed a pattern already established at the Sorbonne in Paris. Merton, University and Balliol Colleges in Oxford were in existence by the 1260s, and Peterhouse in Cambridge was founded in 1284. Seven more followed in the first half of the 14C. All were established by rich benefactors—often, but not always, high-ranking ecclesiastics—who wished to provide a sheltered environment for 'godly learning'. None of the first colleges housed more than a handful of members, or 'fellows', who were almost all graduates, and celibate; there were also servants, and at the top of the hierarchy was the 'head of house', variously described as Master, Warden, Rector, President or Provost. Until the foundation of King's Hall, Cambridge (1337) and New College, Oxford (1379) there were very few undergraduates in any college.

Compared with the academic halls or hostels, or even to a great extent with the universities, the colleges had one enormous advantage: they were endowed with lands by their founders, enabling them to provide scholarships and sustenance to the fellows, and enabling them to construct permanent and, in due course magnificent, buildings. And as inward-looking, self-governing establishments, protected by their legal independence, they fostered a communal *esprit de corps*, not unlike that of contemporary monasteries, which they in many ways resembled. This helped attract later benefactions, and has indeed continued to do so down to the present day. Simple and austere in their inception, many of the colleges eventually became both wealthy and powerful. Indeed, their influence, as great landowners and as ecclesiastical patrons, extended far beyond the confines of their respective universities.

The earliest colleges consisted of collections of disparate buildings arranged around an open space known in Oxford as a **quadrangle** (or 'quad'), and in Cambridge as a **court**. The first buildings were constructed of rubble stone, of which there was much to be quarried within easy distance of Oxford. Stone was much less plentiful around Cambridge, and from the 15C onward (e.g. Queens' College) brick began to be used instead, except where the decision was taken (as at King's College Chapel) to import high-quality ashlar stone from further afield (usually Ketton in Rutland or Weldon in Northamptonshire). In the 15C the Oxford masons began facing their buildings with a smooth ashlar stone from Headington, to the east of the town. This was easy to carve but turned out to be disastrously liable to crumble, and has had to be replaced by stone from elsewhere. The differences in building materials remains one of the greatest differences between the architecture of the two places.

The centre of a college's secular life was the **Hall**, a large single-storeyed structure with an open timber roof, like the hall of a castle or gentleman's country house. Here the fellows and their guests dined communally, with a 'high table' for the leading dignitaries at one end and the rest of the company sitting at long tables in the body of the room. At the 'lower' end, opposite the high table, was the entrance, and close to it were doorways leading to the pantry and buttery, where the food and drink was served, and the kitchen, which at first was detached from the rest of the buildings because of the risk of fire. Heating was by a central brazier, with the smoke escaping through a hole in the roof, protected by a louvre. To an extent unmatched by almost any other secular institutions in Europe, the colleges have retained their medieval dining customs down to modern times, an extraordinary example of institutional continuity.

The spiritual counterpart of the Hall was the **Chapel**, where the services were performed day by day, with prayers being offered for the souls of the founder, his or her kinsfolk, and departed members. There was a division between the antechapel—used at first for subsidiary altars, later as a place of assembly and college meetings—and the chancel, or main body of the chapel, where the main services took place; here the seating faced inwards, as in the chancel of a monastic church or cathedral. In medieval colleges the Chapel was invariably the most richly decorated part of the college, and it was usually the largest too; the chapels of Merton, Oxford, and King's, Cambridge, still tower over the rest of the buildings. Even after the Reformation the college chapels continued to be used for regular daily services, albeit according to the reformed rite, and some (King's and St. John's, Cambridge, and New College, Magdalen and Christ Church, Oxford) retained their choral foundations, another example of the continuity which is so striking a feature of both universities.

The fellows of medieval colleges lived and slept in shared **rooms**, four or more to a room, with separate study cubicles next to the bedroom. Like the lodgings of late medieval country houses, these rooms were arranged on two storeys and were entered from the courtyard by doorways which gave access to staircases leading to the upper-floor rooms: an arrangement which can still be seen in Mob Quad at Merton, Oxford and Old Court at Corpus Christi, Cambridge, both of them dating from the 14C. Heads of colleges had their own accommodation, and the **Library** was invariably placed on the upper floor, as can still be seen at Merton College, Oxford.

The first college to be planned as a single entity on a grand scale was New College, Oxford (1379). The college was much larger than earlier colleges, with 70 members, including undergraduates, and its foundation involved the demolition of houses deserted after the Black Death (1346) and the realignment of streets. In this respect it marks a significant stage in the gradual takeover of the centre of the city by the university. The layout of New College not only influenced later Oxford colleges like All Souls, Magdalen and Christ Church, it also influenced the original plans for the two most important 15C establishments in Cambridge—King's and Queens'—and through them many of the later colleges there.

New College was the first building in either university to be designed in the **'Perpendicular' Gothic style**. This peculiarly English version of late Gothic prevailed in both Oxford and Cambridge for the next 150 years, and continued to influence local architects and master masons down to the early 18C. Marked by soaring buttresses, profusely decorated pinnacles and large windows filled with repetitive tracery patterns, it left an indelible mark on Oxford and, to a lesser extent, Cambridge. At Cambridge it produced one of the supreme masterpieces of European architecture: King's College Chapel, begun in 1446.

The urban fabric 1300–1800

While **Oxford** University flourished in the later Middle Ages, the town suffered badly from the Black Death in the 14C, and by the 16C it had become a middle-ranking market and county town, drawing much of its revenue and employment from supplying goods and services to the university. Henry VIII carved a new Diocese of Oxford out of the unwieldy Diocese of Lincoln in 1542, but plans to turn the former Augustinian priory church of Osney into the cathedral came to nothing, blighting the area to the west of the River Thames and condemning the great church to destruction; instead, the priory church of St. Frideswide became the cathedral, doubling up as chapel to the King's new collegiate foundation of Christ Church. The university eventually recovered from the disruption caused by the Reformation and the Dissolution of the Monasteries, but from 1642 to 1646 Oxford was once more thrown into turmoil when it was adopted by Charles I as his capital during the Civil War. Traces of the earthworks raised to defend the city can still be seen (many of the townspeople, meanwhile, sided with Parliament).

The city recovered much of its prosperity in the late 16C and early 17C, the population increasing from about 3000 in the mid-16C to 10,000 in the 1660s. This led to the growth of housing both inside the walls, where former gardens were filled with densely packed buildings—some of which can still be seen in the yards and alleys to the south of the High St—and outside, in areas like Holywell and St. Ebbe's. Many of these picturesquely gabled timber houses still survive, but others were given a Georgian refacing in the 18C, and still more have been demolished. The 18C also saw a major programme of urban improvements, first with the creation of Radcliffe Square in the heart of the 'university quarter' and later, in the 1760s, with the expulsion of the market from Carfax and the demolition of the old town gates which impeded traffic along the main streets. The walls, which had confined the city, for centuries meanwhile fell into disrepair until only a few sections remained.

The prosperity of **Cambridge** also declined after the Black Death, as the trade along the River Cam dwindled. But the university, like that of Oxford, flourished during the 15C, and Henry VI's foundation of King's College in 1441 led to the acquisition of a large block of land alongside the river, where there had previously been busy wharves and warehouses. The academic takeover of central Cambridge continued in the 16C with the foundation of St. John's and Trinity Colleges, both of which extended west from Trinity St to the banks of the river. By 1600 the colleges controlled virtually all the land along the river from Bridge St south to Silver St, and had begun to acquire land on the west bank. The towns-people were compensated for the loss of land by the acquisition of the open space known as Parker's Piece, to the south-east of the centre; together with Christ's Pieces, Jesus Green and Midsummer Common to the north, this formed part of a belt of open common land to which they had free access.

Cambridge, like Oxford, revived as a commercial centre in the 16C, and the great annual fair held on Stourbridge Common, east of the town, attracted traders not only from all over England, but from the Continent as well. The dues from this fair were granted to the town by Henry VIII; from then on, the conduct and revenues of the fair became one of the many points of dispute between the town and university authorities. In the 16C and 17C it was the great event of the Cambridge year, formally visited by both Mayor and Vice-Chancellor with their entourages, and it continued until well into the 19C.

A matter of common concern was the frequent outbreaks of plague, which attacked citizens and scholars alike. 'Miasma' from the fens was regarded as the cause, but the true source of infection was the water supply from the polluted river, and the filthy King's Ditch, used as an open sewer and as a repository for the town's rubbish. Dr Perne of Peterhouse suggested a scheme (in fact mooted by Matthew Parker of Corpus Christi some years earlier) for a fresh water supply which would also flush out the ditch, and this was eventually carried out in 1610, in a rare instance of co-operation between town and university. Further improvements followed in the 18C, and the clearing of houses in King's Parade led in time to the creation of one of the great architectural ensembles of England.

The Universities 1500–1800

Interest in the **New Learning** began in the 15C, stimulated by contact with the Italian universities where the Renaissance was already in full flower. At Oxford the movement towards humanistic (Classical) studies and away from medieval scholasticism was led by John Colet (who strongly influenced Erasmus during his sojourn in Oxford in 1498), and by William Lily, Thomas Linacre and William Grocyn, who first taught Greek publicly in the early 1500s; one of the latter's pupils was Sir Thomas More. In Cambridge the way was led by John Fisher (Vice-Chancellor and later Chancellor of the university, and Bishop of Rochester, mar-tyred in 1535). At his invitation Erasmus came to Cambridge, where he was the first to teach Greek, and in 1511 became Professor of Divinity. His presence much enhanced the university's European standing. New colleges like Corpus Christi (Oxford) and St. John's, Christ's and Gonville and Caius (Cambridge) emphasised humanist studies from the beginning, and they gradually worked their way into the general curriculum.

The religious upheavals of the 16C greatly affected Oxford and Cambridge. The monasteries, monastic colleges and houses of the mendicant orders were closed down, and heads of colleges who would not recognise Henry VIII's supremacy (1534) were ejected. Oxford suffered more severely; the university library lost all its books, and for many years the very existence of the university as a place of scholarship was threatened.

Cambridge came under the influence of Thomas Bilney, Hugh Latimer, Nicholas Ridley, and the German protestants Martin Bucer and Paul Fagius, and was in the forefront of the **Reformation**. After the execution of Bishop Fisher, Thomas Cromwell became Chancellor, and royal favour was shown in the establishment of five new professorships and also of the university's largest college: Trinity. Henry VIII also showed his confidence in Oxford by founding new professorships, and establishing a new college—Christ Church—out of an abortive foundation begun by Cardinal Wolsey on the site of St. Frideswide's Priory. The former priory church, shorn of its three western bays, became both the chapel of the college and cathedral of the new Diocese of Oxford, with the Dean serving as head of the college—a unique arrangement.

In 1555–56, when, under Mary Tudor, attempts were being made to restore the old faith, Oxford was the scene of the trial for heresy, and death at the stake, of the three bishops Cranmer, Latimer and Ridley (the 'Oxford Martyrs', though all Cambridge men). At Cambridge, John Hullier endured the same terrible death on Jesus Green. A more positive result of the 'Marian reaction' was the foundation of two new Oxford colleges, St. John's and Trinity, on the site of recently suppressed colleges for Cistercian and Benedictine monks, something which had already happened in Cambridge with the establishment of Magdalene College in 1542.

After these storms **Elizabeth I's reign** provided a period of relative tranquillity. Protestantism was gradually accepted, and from 1581 all members of the universities had to assent to the Thirty-nine Articles; Roman Catholics and (later) Nonconformists remained excluded until the 19C. The Queen took a close interest in both places, visited them several times, and provided Cambridge with new statutes, which remained in force until the 19C and were in many respects imitated in the statutes promulgated in Oxford by William Laud, Archbishop of Canterbury under Charles I, in the 1630s. These cemented the power of the colleges within the two universities. All students now had to belong to a college or to one of a very small number of approved academic halls. The universities continued to offer lectures and examine, but important decisions were made by the heads of the colleges meeting together in council, and much of the teaching also took place in the colleges.

During the late 16C and the 17C the number of **students** increased greatly, and the range of studies was widened to prepare young men for the professions and public life as well as the Church. Several more new colleges were founded, some of them, like Emmanuel and Sidney Sussex (Cambridge) and Wadham (Oxford) on abandoned monastic sites, others, like Jesus and Pembroke (Oxford) on the sites of academic halls; Emmanuel and Sidney Sussex were intended to train a 'godly preaching ministry', and in the early 17C Cambridge developed a pronounced Puritan character.

There were considerable social distinctions between the various types of student: gentlemen or fellow commoners, who paid high fees and wore special gowns and tasselled caps; commoners (Oxford) and pensioners (Cambridge), who paid lower fees; scholars, paid for by the foundation; and servitors (Oxford) and sizars (Cambridge), who received free board and lodging and some tuition and in return acted as servants to fellows and fellow commoners.

The **Civil War** of 1642–46 had damaging effects. Oxford, always royalist and High Church, naturally supported Charles I. Cambridge did likewise, though, owing to its strong Puritan elements, with less enthusiasm. Almost all the colleges surrendered their plate to provide funds for the royalist cause. Both towns became deeply embroiled in the war, Oxford as the King's headquarters, Cambridge as a Parliamentary military stronghold. At Cambridge those Masters who were suspected of High-Church or royalist leanings were expelled, and chapels were stripped of their ornaments by the notorious iconoclast William Dowsing (though some, anticipating this purge, prudently removed or concealed their treasures). During the Interregnum similar treatment was meted out to Oxford, though fortunately it escaped the activities of Dowsing. At the Restoration of Charles II to the throne in 1660 the whole process was, of course, reversed.

Both Oxford and Cambridge played an important part in the intellectual and **scientific discoveries** of the late 17C. A Botanic Garden was laid out at Oxford in the 1630s, and in the 1650s an important group of young scientists, including Christopher Wren, the Savilian Professor of Astronomy Robert Boyle and Robert Hooke, met regularly at Wadham College, Oxford, forming the nucleus of the Royal Society, founded in 1660. Trinity College, Cambridge, numbered among its fellows the man who perhaps did more than anyone else to lay the foundations of modern science: Isaac Newton. The philosopher John Locke was a student (fellow) of Christ Church, Oxford, but he was expelled for unorthodoxy in 1684.

During **the 18C** both universities sank to a low ebb; there are many contemporary comments on the idleness, heavy drinking and lack of scholarship among dons and undergraduates alike. Examinations deteriorated into a farcical repetition of stereotyped questions and answers; any change or reform was obstinately opposed. According to Sydney Smith, the universities were like 'enormous hulks confined within mooring chains, everything flowing and progressing around them', while Edward Gibbon said that his 14 months at Magdalen College, Oxford, were 'the most idle and unprofitable of my whole life'. The colleges became more and more the preserve of the wealthy and privileged, as numbers dwindled and expenses increased; most fellows were more interested in ecclesiastical preferment than scholarship. Even so, the intellectual torpor can be exaggerated. Oxford in the 18C was the intellectual nursery of Samuel Johnson and John Wesley, and Cambridge that of William Wordsworth.

Architecture 1500–1800

In matters of collegiate planning, and also to some extent in architecture, Oxford and Cambridge remained remarkably conservative for much of this period. New colleges continued to be built with open-roofed communal halls long after they had been abandoned in noblemen's houses and in the royal palaces. Chapels were still provided with the inward-facing seating of monastic chancels. Above all, collegiate buildings continued to be disposed around quadrangles or courts in the medieval fashion.

The new colleges of the **first half of the 16C**—Brasenose, Corpus Christi and Christ Church in Oxford; Christ's, St. John's and Trinity in Cambridge—are still largely medieval in appearance. All are entered through gate towers, all employ the Perpendicular style of architecture. The influence of Renaissance architecture is first seen in decorative details, above all in the chapel of King's, Cambridge, completed by Henry VIII; here the architecture is Perpendicular, but the wooden screen and stalls are covered with ornament derived from Renaissance Italy, and the magnificent stained-glass windows have a three-dimensional quality absent from earlier decorative art in Oxford or Cambridge.

Renaissance ideas were taken further in Gonville and Caius College, Cambridge, founded in 1557. Here Classical detail was introduced on two of three new gateways, the Gate of Virtue and the Gate of Honour, and one of the courts was left with one end open. The open-ended, or three-sided, court appeared in several 16C and 17C Cambridge colleges (e.g., Sidney Sussex, founded in 1596), but did not arrive in Oxford until the 1660s, with the building of the Garden Quad at Trinity.

Medieval courts and quadrangles had been two storeys high, with the rooms unheated and those on the upper floors open to the roof. In the 16C it became usual to introduce fireplaces and tall chimneys, and from the **early 17C** onwards, to accommodate the growing numbers of students, the rooms began to be arranged on three floors, as in the Fellows' Quad at Merton, Oxford (1610), and also at Wadham, Oriel and University Colleges, and at Clare, Cambridge (1638). Most of the detailing in these colleges was still Gothic, as it is in Oxford's new Schools Quad, begun in 1613 next to the refounded university library (the Bodleian). But Classicism made a tentative appearance in the form of 'frontispieces', or towers of the orders, ultimately derived from French Renaissance architecture and proclaiming the triumph of humanistic learning in tangible form.

Classical and Gothic architecture coexisted in Oxford and Cambridge for much of the 17C and even into the 18C. Gothic was used when the builders wished to emphasise continuity with the medieval past, as in the façade of the Bodleian, the library at St. John's, Cambridge (1623–25) and the fan-vaulted hall staircase and gate tower at Christ Church, Oxford (1638 and 1681–82 respectively). Continuity with the past was especially marked in the chapels, and above all in the painted glass windows, many of them by the Van Linge brothers from Germany, which appeared in large numbers in the Oxford chapels of the 1620s and 1630s: a reminder of the Laudian High-Churchmanship which flourished in Oxford under Charles I. But there are round-arched Italianate loggias in the Canterbury Quad at St. John's, Oxford (1631–36), financed by Archbishop Laud himself, and in Nevile's Court at Trinity, Cambridge. The free-standing Fellows' Building at Christ's, Cambridge (1640–45) shows something of the influence of the rigorous Italian Renaissance style introduced to England by Inigo Jones and promoted by Charles's Court.

The Restoration of 1660 brought about a decisive shift towards Classical architecture. Until then buildings in both universities had been both designed and built by master masons, working in close collaboration with the patrons. Now, for the first time, the learned amateur architect made his appearance, and with him came a more rigorous form of Renaissance-inspired Classical architecture from which traditional elements were totally excluded. The first such architect was **Sir Christopher Wren**, nephew of the ejected Master of Peterhouse, Cambridge, and Fellow, first of Wadham College, Oxford, and then of All Souls. He was responsible for the Sheldonian Theatre in Oxford and for the chapels at Pembroke and Emmanuel, Cambridge; he also designed the library at Trinity, Cambridge, the finest 17C building in either university. Through these buildings he succeeded in imbuing a new generation of master masons, men like William Byrd and Bartholomew Peisley in Oxford, and Robert Grumbold in Cambridge, with the principles of Classical design.

The 80 years or so following the Restoration saw a concerted effort to impose a degree of Classical grandeur onto what were still for the most part medieval towns. Although student numbers were beginning to decline, the number of fee-paying commoners was going up, and it was regarded as important to house them in a suitably dignified manner. Such students did not wish to share rooms; instead, like their teachers, they now demanded suites of rooms in which they could entertain guests. Several colleges therefore embarked on lavish building schemes, especially in Oxford, resulting for instance in the complete rebuilding of Queen's, a medieval foundation, and the building of new quadrangles like Peckwater at Christ Church (begun 1707).

The architect of Peckwater was **Henry Aldrich**, Dean of Christ Church, who acted as an informal architectural adviser to Oxford in the late 17C and early 18C. When he died his place was taken by **George Clarke**, a fellow of All Souls, who was responsible, together with the master mason William Townesend, for the design of the magnificent library on the south side of Peckwater Quad, as well as for much of Queen's and for Worcester, a new college founded on the site of a decayed academic hall in 1720.

Mainly as a result of benefactions from wealthy donors, Oxford also succeeded in converting the central academic area near the Bodleian Library and Schools' Quad into an impressive series of linked open spaces surrounded by magnificent buildings. The process began with the building of the Sheldonian Theatre, and continued with the Old Ashmolean—England's first public museum and also the university's first purpose-built scientific laboratory—the Clarendon Building, and finally the library now known as the Radcliffe Camera, built out of the munificent bequest of John Radcliffe, the most fashionable physician of his day.

In the later stages an important role was played by Wren's pupil **Nicholas Hawksmoor**, who worked with Sir John Vanbrugh at Blenheim Palace, the magnificent Baroque house built with public funds for the Duke of Marlborough at Woodstock, a few miles to the north of Oxford. Hawksmoor designed the Clarendon Building and was involved in the conception of Radcliffe Square, overlooked on the east side by his Gothic north quad of All Souls College. The Radcliffe Camera, however, Oxford's finest Classically-inspired building, went up after his death to the designs of **James Gibbs**.

Cambridge was less active in building during this period. Although there were plans, by Hawksmoor and others, for creating a central university 'campus' near, and on the site of, the Old Schools, the only buildings actually constructed were the new Senate House (1722–30), designed by Gibbs (whose work can also be seen at Wimpole Hall, a few miles away), and the rather later library front to the Old Schools quadrangle (1754–58), by the Palladian architect Stephen Wright. The Senate House serves, like the Sheldonian in Oxford, as a stately setting for the academic ceremonial to which both universities have always been addicted.

The rebuilding of the Cambridge colleges generally took place rather later than in Oxford, and, with the exception of Gibbs's monumental Fellows' Building at King's, in a rather less grandiose manner. Here the equivalent figure to Aldrich and Clarke was **Sir James Burrough**, Master of Gonville and Caius from 1754. He played a part in the building of the Senate House, and was the guiding spirit behind the refacing of several of the older colleges—Gonville and Caius, Peterhouse, Trinity Hall—in smooth ashlar stone, with Classical details in place of their old mullioned windows and Gothic arches. He also designed some complete buildings, including the chapel at Clare, and trained **James Essex**, the son of a Cambridge carpenter, who became the leading architect in Cambridge in the second half of the 18C. Essex's Oxford counterpart was **James Wyatt**, a brilliantly inventive if somewhat mercurial architect whose most important building was the Radcliffe Observatory (1776–94), with its tower based on the Hellenistic Tower of the Winds in Athens.

It was in the 18C that the distinctive landscape of the Cambridge '**Backs**' achieved its present form. When the banks of the Cam ceased to be extensively used for river trade in the 17C, the colleges closest to the river began to acquire the land and to lay out gardens, and build handsome bridges. As early as 1662, Thomas Fuller had remarked in his *Worthies of England* that 'Oxford is a university in a town, Cambridge a town in the university: where the colleges are not surrounded by the offensive embraces of streets, but generally situated on the outside, affording the better convenience of private walks and gardens about them'. Lancelot ('Capability') Brown, whose work can be seen at Wimpole Hall and, on an even larger scale, at Blenheim Palace in Oxfordshire, made plans in the 1770s for merging the gardens along the 'Backs' into a single landscape. They came to nothing, but enough landscaping and tree-planting took place on a piecemeal scale to ensure the creation of one of the most beautiful natural settings for any university: in its way as great an aesthetic experience as King's College Chapel and Trinity Library, both of which look out onto it.

Oxford's colleges, meanwhile, developed their **gardens** behind high stone walls, all but invisible to outsiders. They too date back for the most part to the 17C, but most were landscaped in the 18C, with lawns surrounded by plantations of trees and herbaceous borders.

The nineteenth and twentieth centuries: urban growth

Large-scale growth outside the walls of **Oxford** did not begin until the early 19C, with the rise of working-class districts to the south and west of the city centre, following the opening of the Oxford and Coventry Canal in 1790. It was with this in mind that the poet Gerard Manley Hopkins later lamented the existence of Oxford's 'base and brickish skirt'. The canal linked Oxford by water to the industrial Midlands, and communications were further improved with the opening of the railway, again to the west of the city centre, between 1844 and 1852. But plans to establish the Great Western Railway's carriage works in Oxford were vetoed by the university, and until the 20C the main industrial employer remained the University Press; even in the early 19C, grass was said to grow in the middle of the High St during university vacations.

Meanwhile, with the growing desire for suburban residence among the professional and mercantile classes, smart suburbs of brick-built villas grew up to the north of the city centre on land owned, and profitably developed, by St. John's College, starting in the 1860s. As the middle classes decamped for north, and, later, parts of east Oxford, land was freed in the centre of the city for more building by the university and colleges, a process which has continued down to the present day.

Large-scale manufacturing industry came to Oxford with the motor car. William Morris, later Lord Nuffield (not to be confused with the writer, socialist and designer of the same name), established his first car works in Oxford in 1912–13, and after the First World War the firm moved to Cowley, east of the city, where it flourished as Morris Motors. The Cowley works provided employment for thousands of people during the 1920s and 1930s, many of them migrants to Oxford from the older industrial districts devastated by the Depression. Inter-war Oxford was one of the fastest-growing towns in England; one wit called the old city 'the Latin quarter of Cowley'. The establishment of a Green Belt after the Second World War saved the city from further expansion, but, with a population of over 130,000, Oxford remains a town of substantial size.

Since the Second World War—which fortunately left it virtually unscathed—Oxford has had to cope with a rising student population, mass tourism, chronic traffic problems, and an inexorable growth in the demand for shopping. A large area to the south and west of the historic centre was flattened during the heyday of 'comprehensive redevelopment' in the 1960s and 1970s in order to provide a new shopping centre, car parks and access roads. A scheme to drive a road across one of the main open spaces, Christ Church Meadow, was mercifully quashed, but there was a severe environmental cost in the form of excessive and growing traffic in the city centre. This was until recently most noticeable in the High St where pedestrians jostled with cars, lorries and squadrons of buses belching out noxious fumes; now, however, the cars and lorries have departed, at least during the daytime, and Cornmarket St, the city's main shopping street, is completely traffic-free. Despite the pressures of modern life, the city remains one of the most beautiful in Europe, its skyline unaffected by the late 20C mania for high building, its ancient buildings and peaceful gardens jealously preserved and awaiting exploration by the patient and persistent visitor.

Urban expansion in **Cambridge** was made possible by the enclosure of the open fields to the south and east of the city in 1811. The railway arrived in 1845, fuelling further growth towards the east and southeast. But the areas to the north and, especially, the west of the river remained largely undeveloped until the second half of the 19C, when they were spaciously laid out with comfortable houses for the professional middle classes, including married dons; much of this area was turned over to university use in the 20C.

With the development of scientific studies in the university and the building of research laboratories, new science-based industries grew up to supply their needs, and such industries, later widely diversified, became an important source of employment and prosperity in late 20C Cambridge. The town grew to envelop several surrounding villages, and now has a population of about 100,000. In 1951 it was granted the status of city. As in Oxford, there was some fairly disastrous redevelopment in the central area in the 1960s and '70s, but the effects have been less intrusive and the city centre is now almost completely traffic-free. Happily too, the 20C expansion of Cambridge has taken place round the perimeter, so that the many open spaces in the centre, which are such a distinctive and attractive part of the Cambridge scene, remain, as from time immemorial, common pasture land. Horses still graze on Coe Fen and Lammas Land, and cattle browse on Midsummer Common. *Rus in urbe* indeed.

The reformed universities ~ 1800 to the present

At the beginning of the 19C Oxford and Cambridge were still in many respects medieval institutions. The colleges were closed corporations, responsible to no one but themselves, often admitting only handfuls of students per year (half of all undergraduate admissions in mid-19C Cambridge were to just two colleges, Trinity and St. John's), and then often only those who had been to particular schools, or who came from particular parts of the country, or could claim to be 'founder's kin'. Roman Catholics, Non-conformists and women were excluded. Fellows, many of them young men awaiting ecclesiastical preferment, rarely pursued research, and many university professors treated their posts as sinecures.

Many undergraduates 'went down' without taking a degree, and those who did graduate, most of them would-be Anglican clergymen, were examined in the most cursory manner. The curriculum had changed little in the previous 200 years, lectures were often poorly attended and poorly delivered—a problem still not unknown today—and undergraduate teaching languished.

Many of these abuses were reformed during the 19C, but change came slowly, and often reluctantly. Some improvements were made in the examination system and some new subjects were introduced in the early 1800s. As early as 1748 Cambridge undergraduates could read for an honours degree in mathematics; in Oxford the most ambitious students focused on the Classics. But new ideas were still strongly resisted both by students and dons, and Oxford in particular got immersed in the 1830s and 1840s in the often arcane religious controversies which raged round the **Oxford Movement**, the aim of which was to rediscover the Catholic roots of the Anglican Church.

The leader of that movement, which was centred on Oriel College, was John Keble, and among its members was the immensely influential John Henry Newman. To conservative churchmen the Oxford Movement appeared danger-ously Papist (Newman did in fact join the Church of Rome in 1845, and eventu-ally became a cardinal), but the Oxford reformers nevertheless left a permanent mark on Anglican worship and spirituality. Cambridge, meanwhile, always more Puritan in inclination, produced a series of Evangelical clergymen like Charles Simeon, whose influence was probably just as great, if not so controversial.

Reform was forced on the universities through the Parliamentary Commissions of 1850 and 1874. There were widespread changes in administra-tion, finance, subjects of study and examination requirements. Religious tests were abolished in 1871, and from 1877 fellows of colleges were allowed to marry; many of them did so with alacrity, converting large areas of north Oxford and west Cambridge into high-minded intellectual ghettos in the process.

The new, characteristically 19C, emphasis on written examinations led to a marked improvement in undergraduate teaching. The much-vaunted **tutorial system**, under which undergraduates are taught individually by college tutors, dates in its present form from the late 19C, when most of the remaining sinecure fellowships were abolished and university teaching became a lifelong career. This process was pioneered by colleges like Balliol, Oxford, which, under the charis-matic mastership of Benjamin Jowett (d. 1893), stressed the ideal of an Oxford or Cambridge education as a preparation for a life of public service, whether at home or in the expanding Empire. For men like Jowett, an Oxford education still meant primarily an education in the Classics (in Cambridge, mathematics was more heavily stressed).

But subjects such as history, modern languages, English literature and the social sciences gradually gained a foothold in the curriculum. **Science** also received a boost in Oxford with the opening of the University Museum and its associated library and laboratories in 1860; soon after its opening the famous Huxley/Wilberforce debate took place there, in which the traditional 'creationist' view of the origin of man was openly challenged by the new Darwinian beliefs. In Cambridge the Cavendish Laboratories were established after 1871, providing a centre for research which soon made the university a byword for scientific excellence, far surpassing Oxford's achievements, at least until the second half of the 20C. No fewer than 29 Nobel prizewinners came from Cambridge in the 20C, all of them scientists.

The late 19C also saw the first tentative emergence of university education for women. The first **women's colleges** at Cambridge date from the 1870s: Girton (1873) and Newnham (1878). In Oxford, Lady Margaret Hall and Somerville were both established in 1879. These new colleges were built outside the city centres, where land was available for building, but members were able (very much on sufferance and closely chaperoned) to attend university lectures, and from 1881 (1894 in Oxford) to take examinations.

In the controversies surrounding the women's campaign for recognition, the most extraordinary arguments were brought against them, ranging from the theory that the female brain could not survive long periods of study, to objections that female hats obscured the view during scientific demonstrations. Women became full members of Oxford University in 1920, but it was only in 1948 that they were fully admitted to Cambridge. In 1952 (1959 in Oxford) their colleges achieved equal status with men's, and in the 1970s and 1980s the men's colleges opened their doors to women, followed, more reluctantly, by all but three of the women's colleges (St. Hilda's in Oxford; Newnham and New Hall in Cambridge) admitting men, the biggest change in undergraduate collegiate life in the 20C. Meanwhile the clubby masculine ambience of the Senior Common Rooms was subtly changed by the slow and piecemeal appointment of female fellows. In 1994 three of the older Oxford colleges elected female heads and in 2003 a woman took up office as Cambridge's vice-chancellor (the chief executive of the university).

The rising status of women was just one of the changes that affected both Oxford and Cambridge after the **Second World War**. State aid for higher education brought a huge increase in the number of undergraduates, especially from less privileged backgrounds than before, and of graduates reading for advanced degrees, many of them from abroad. As a result the character of the student body changed dramatically. There was a new emphasis on research, especially in the sciences, also encouraged by central government. This led to a proliferation of institutes and libraries. It also led to a growth in the power and influence of the universities—the main recipients of government grants—relative to the colleges, reversing a trend which went back to the 16C.

Despite the growing importance of government funding, which reached a high-water mark in the 1960s and has recently been severely restricted, both Oxford and Cambridge had much help from munificent private and corporate **benefactors**; colleges, individual buildings, professorships, fellowships, scholarships and research programmes bear witness to their names. At Oxford, Lord Nuffield, who made a fortune in motor manufacture, poured the benefits of his wealth onto the university, in spite of his well-known aversion to academics, and his low opinion of the value of academic education; one result was Nuffield College, the first all-graduate college (with the exception of All Souls, always *sui generis*) and also the first to have a clearly defined subject emphasis, in this case on the social sciences.

A Frenchman who had made a fortune in the Middle East, M. Antonin Besse, had such a high opinion of Oxford graduates that he gave a complete new college (St. Antony's), to foster the study of international relations, and handsome endowments to a number of others. Yet another Oxford college (Green College) has been largely funded by Dr and Mrs Cecil Green of Dallas (Texas), two of many American benefactors, while the Nissan Motor Company of Japan has established and endowed a Centre for Japanese Studies attached to St. Antony's College. Prominent among Cambridge benefactors are David Robinson, a local businessman, who has given the college of that name, and the Cripps family, donors of new buildings at Queens', St. John's and Selwyn.

Nineteenth and twentieth century architecture

After 50 years or so of relative inactivity, both universities began building extensively in the **early 19C**. For many years Cambridge took the lead. It had largely escaped the building boom which transformed much of Oxford in the early 18C, and now felt a growing need for more student accommodation and more public university buildings. Some of the new Cambridge buildings were Classical in character; others were built in a Tudor-Gothic style which, in one form or another, soon became the norm in both universities down to the mid-20C.

Downing College, a new foundation, begun in 1807, was an important pioneer both of Greek Revival architecture and of a new, more spacious, form of collegiate planning which, at least in the short term, was more influential in the USA than in either Cambridge or Oxford. Its architect, **William Wilkins**, a fellow of Gonville and Caius College, had travelled extensively in the eastern Mediterranean, but was also capable of designing in the Tudor-Gothic manner when the occasion demanded, as it did at Corpus Christi, in New Court at Trinity, and, above all, in the completion of the Front Court at King's with its screen to King's Parade (1824–28): one of the finest pieces of urban scenery in either university. Tudor-Gothic was chosen here partly because, with its array of pinnacles and turrets, it was deemed more picturesque than Classical architecture; partly because it made a strong emotional appeal to the Romantic sensibility. Both impulses explain the choice of Tudor-Gothic for New Court at St. John's (Rickman and Hutchinson 1826–31), deliberately designed to form part of the landscape of the Backs, while at the same time visually alluding to the period of the college's foundation.

The last great monumental Classical buildings in Oxford and Cambridge were public art museums. At Cambridge the impulse came from the bequest of a collection of Old Masters of international importance to the university by Viscount Fitzwilliam in 1816. The Fitzwilliam Museum was finally begun, to the designs of George Basevi, in 1837, four years before the building of University Galleries (now the Ashmolean Museum) in Oxford, designed to hold the university's collections of art and antiquities. The Oxford building was designed by **C.R. Cockerell**, one of the most accomplished Classical architects of his generation; he had earlier made extensive plans for new university buildings on the site of the Old Schools in Cambridge in the eclectic Classical style of which he was a master, but they were only partially realised, and the remains of the medieval Schools have, against all expectation, survived down to the present day.

By the time the Ashmolean Museum was finished in 1845, both Oxford and Cambridge were coming under the influence of an architectural movement which condemned Classical architecture as 'pagan' and argued for the universal validity of Gothic, and, what is more, a purer form of Gothic than the 'debased' Tudor used by Wilkins and Rickman. The **Cambridge Camden Society** (later the Ecclesiological Society) was founded in 1839, and exerted an immense influence on church architecture and furnishing, not only in Oxford and Cambridge but throughout England. It drew much of its inspiration from the example of A.W.N. Pugin, some of whose exquisitely detailed craftsmanship can be seen in Jesus College Chapel, Cambridge, restored after 1845; Pugin also made designs for a complete rebuilding of Balliol College, Oxford, only to see them quashed because of the anti-Catholic beliefs of the then Master (the college was eventually rebuilt, but by other architects).

The influence of Pugin and the Camden Society can be seen in numerous restorations of medieval churches and chapels in both Oxford and Cambridge. It can also be seen in several new buildings of the mid-19C, starting with the Martyrs' Memorial in Oxford, designed in the approved English 'Middle Pointed' (Decorated) style by the young Gilbert Scott in 1841.

By the 1850s architects attracted to the Middle Ages were beginning to incorporate ideas derived from the Gothic of the Continent, and the result was the powerful and vigorous style sometimes called **High Victorian Gothic**. The prophet of this movement was the Oxford-educated John Ruskin—though he, characteristically, disclaimed any responsibility for the results—and his influence lies behind the design and detailing of the Oxford University Museum (Benjamin Woodward, 1855–60). Equally impressive, though very different in its purpose and architectural character, is the museum's neighbour, Keble College, begun to the designs of William Butterfield in 1868; with its polychromatic brick walls and spiky skyline, it still retains its power to startle. A more sober form of French Gothic was employed by Gilbert Scott in his majestic chapels at Exeter College, Oxford (1856–59) and St. John's, Cambridge (1866–69).

High Victorian Gothic enjoyed only a short vogue, and by the 1870s, when a large increase in student numbers was necessitating further expansion of accommodation, architects were turning to a more eclectic style in which medieval and Renaissance motifs were mixed. In Cambridge the leading architect in this manner was **Alfred Waterhouse**, who had already worked extensively in the Gothic style at Balliol College, Oxford; his main works in Cambridge were at Gonville and Caius College (1868–70) and Pembroke (1874–77), both of them drawing on the architecture of early 16C France, and at Girton, starting in 1873, where he introduced neo-Tudor detailing.

In Oxford the shift from Gothic to 'free-style' eclecticism took place with the building of the Examination Schools in 1876–82 to the designs of **Thomas Graham Jackson**, a fellow of Wadham College. An architectural magpie of the first order, Jackson designed buildings all over Oxford in virtually every conceivable combination of late medieval or early Renaissance styles (for example, at Hertford, Trinity and Brasenose Colleges); he also did some work in Cambridge (for example, the Museum of Archaeology and Anthropology). He also played a crucial part in the movement to restore Oxford's older buildings, whose smoke-blackened Headington ashlar façades were rapidly crumbling in the polluted atmosphere. He pioneered the use of stone from Clipsham (Rutland), later used widely in the great refacing of the 1950s and 1960s, and in his own buildings he employed a durable form of rubble stone from Bladon, near Woodstock, later much used in inter-war Oxford buildings.

The buildings of Jackson and his contemporaries are often enlivened by excellent craftsmanship influenced by the burgeoning **Arts and Crafts movement**, whose mentor William Morris, educated at Exeter College, Oxford, had his summer residence at Kelmscott Manor, not far away on the Upper Thames. As a young man Morris had been involved in the decoration of the Oxford Union, and the firm of Morris, Marshall, Faulkner & Co. was later employed in the decoration of All Saints church, Cambridge, and the redecoration of the halls at Queens' College and Peterhouse. The firm also completed the restoration of Jesus College chapel and supplied stained-glass windows of great beauty for Christ Church Cathedral, Oxford, and the chapel of Manchester College. Work of this calibre supplied the inspiration for a tradition of craftsmanship which lasted down to the mid-20C.

The **late 19C and early 20C** was a period of great architectural creativity and extraordinary stylistic diversity in both Oxford and Cambridge. Some architects worked in the eclectic 'free style' pioneered by Jackson; Oxford Town Hall (H.T. Hare 1893–97) is an excellent example. Others remained faithful to Gothic, notably George Frederick Bodley (e.g., St. Swithun's Quad at Magdalen College, Oxford, 1881–85; All Saints church and the chapel at Queens', Cambridge, 1889–91). At Newnham, Cambridge, one of the first women's colleges, Basil Champneys, another architect widely employed in both universities, evolved a collegiate version of the domestic 'Queen Anne' style, distinguished by red-brick walls, white-painted sash windows and 'Dutch' gables. Meanwhile, the neo-Georgian style was employed successfully by Reginald Blomfield at Lady Margaret Hall, Oxford, starting in 1896, and it can be seen in many of the prosperous middle-class houses built in west Cambridge and the further reaches of North Oxford during the same period.

Architecture between the wars was dominated by the universities rather than the colleges. This was chiefly because of the expansion of scientific research, necessitating the building of laboratories which only the universities could finance. Architecturally, the results were not very distinguished, either on the New Museums and Downing sites in Cambridge, south of the city centre, or in the Science Area in Oxford, to the east of the University Museum.

At the same time, the inexorable growth of printed matter forced the two university libraries to expand, the Bodleian onto an adjacent site in Parks Road, the Cambridge University Library onto a virgin site to the west of the Cam, to which all the collections were moved; the architect of both buildings was Giles Gilbert Scott, grandson of the great Victorian Gothic architect of the same name. Scott also acquired several collegiate commissions, notably for the neo-Georgian Memorial Court for Clare College, Cambridge, aligned on the new University Library.

Of the buildings of this period in Oxford, perhaps the most impressive are Herbert Baker's Rhodes House, built out of the South African fortune of the Rhodes Trust, and Campion Hall, a Jesuit college designed by Edwin Lutyens.

The expansion of the universities after the Second World War, and especially during the 1960s, led to another spate of building comparable in quantity with that at the turn of the century. Its architectural character was, however, very different. The **Modern Movement** made relatively little impact on Oxford and Cambridge before the 1950s, but then there was an almost instantaneous conversion to a style of architecture based on the principles of Le Corbusier and other luminaries of 'International Modernism'. The new style made a tentative appearance at first, but in the 1960s a large number of modernist buildings were commissioned which put Oxford and Cambridge in the vanguard of architectural patronage nationwide.

Many of these structures were commissioned by the older colleges, sometimes on pockets of empty land near their existing buildings, sometimes—especially in Cambridge, where there was less available space in the city centre—further afield. Others were new colleges built from scratch, like St. Catherine's and Wolfson in Oxford, or Churchill, New Hall and Fitzwilliam in Cambridge. Still more were commissioned by university departments, such as the vast complex of

Arts Faculty buildings in Sidgwick Avenue, Cambridge, or the St. Cross building for the English, Law and Economics faculties in Oxford.

The buildings of the **1960s and 1970s** will probably never be as popular with visitors to Oxford and Cambridge as those of previous eras. They deliberately turn their back on the architecture of the past, often in the interest of making a 'statement', and in so doing they eloquently represent the spirit of those iconoclastic times. Also, though strongly influenced by the so-called functionalist aesthetic, some of them have weathered badly, especially those influenced by the 'new brutalist' love of concrete surfaces. But, for all their obvious shortcomings, some Oxford and Cambridge buildings are among the most adventurous of their time, and can give unexpected pleasure to those who approach them with an open mind.

Among those that can be singled out in Cambridge are Churchill College (Richard Sheppard, Robson and Partners, 1959–68), the Cripps Building at St. John's (Powell and Moya, 1964–67), James Stirling's quite extraordinary History Faculty building of 1964–68, and Robinson College (Gillespie, Kidd and Coia, 1977–80), with its beautiful stained-glass windows by John Piper in the chapel. In Oxford a comparable list would include St. Catherine's College (Arne Jacobsen, 1960–64), the St. Cross building (Leslie Martin & Colin Wilson, 1961–64) and the Hayward and de Breyne buildings at Keble (Ahrends, Burton & Koralek, 1970–77), admirably complementing, without competing with, Butterfield's passionate red-brick Gothic.

But perhaps the most attractive monument to the Modern Movement in either university is the Kettle's Yard gallery at Cambridge, in which the collection of 20C art amassed by Jim Ede is housed in a row of old cottages and an extension deftly designed in 1969–70 by Leslie Martin, the university's Professor of Architecture. Here, modern art and architecture reveal a human face which is so often lacking in larger and more pretentious structures.

As so often in the history of Oxford and Cambridge, a boom in building was followed by a lull, but that lull came to an end in the boom years of the later 1980s, when colleges and university departments expanded onto the steadily diminishing reserves of available open space, driven partly by the growing scarcity of student accommodation for rent and partly by the insatiable demands of research, especially in the sciences. Modernism gave way to **post-modernism** in the 1980s, and some of the buildings of that era were both more elaborately ornamented, and designed with more respect for their surroundings, than those of the previous decades: an indication both of a revived interest in the past and of a growing concern with the urban environment which has also manifested itself in a spate of excellent and popular conservation projects (for example, the Golden Cross in Oxford, involving the conversion of an ancient inn).

Important harbingers of the new style were the Sainsbury Building at Worcester College, Oxford (MacCormac, Jamieson and Pritchard, 1979–83) and the Howard Building at Downing, Cambridge (Quinlan Terry, 1987), the first an essay in a picturesque neo-vernacular style with references to Japan and to Frank Lloyd Wright, the second neo-Georgian in deference to the Classical character of the rest of the college. MacCormac adopted a more monumental approach in his new buildings of the 1990s at Wadham and St. John's Colleges, Oxford, and at Trinity, Cambridge, but at Gloucester Green, Oxford (Kendrick Associates 1987–90), the City Council carried out a major redevelopment of a public space in a manner which recalled the 'free style' of the turn of the 20C. In Cambridge, the most impressive examples of 'post-modern' architecture were the Judge Institute for Management Studies (John Outram), the Queen's Building at Emmanuel College (Michael Hopkins) and the Library at Jesus College (Evans and Shalev), all dating from the 1990s.

Architectural post-modernism later became somewhat *passé*. Some of the most impressive buildings of the **past 20 years** have reasserted the continuing appeal of the modernist idiom, among them the Schlumberger Research Laboratories (Michael Hopkins, 1984), Norman Foster's Law Faculty at Cambridge (1995), the Centre for Mathematical Sciences at Cambridge (Edward Cullinan, 2001), and the Rothermere Institute for American Studies at Oxford (Kohn, Pedersen and Fox, 2001). Now, judging from the projects currently (2003) under way in both universities, modernism is once more firmly in the saddle. Whatever the style adopted, it is clear that Oxford and Cambridge are continuing to make an important contribution to new architecture, as they have done throughout their long existence.

University life and organisation

In both Oxford and Cambridge the colleges have for the last 700 years co-existed with the university, which has always retained the all-important power to grant degrees. Each college is still a residential community consisting of the head of house, fellows, research fellows and lecturers, graduate students, undergraduates and staff. With only one or two exceptions, the head is known as Master in Cambridge, but in Oxford he or she may equally well be called Warden, Principal, Provost, Rector, Dean (at Christ Church), or President. The Fellows are usually selected on a competitive basis, and collectively form the governing body and do most of the college teaching.

Colleges also employ lecturers and junior research fellows, usually younger people on short contracts. All those in senior positions in both college and university are popularly known as Dons (from the Latin *dominus*, meaning lord). Undergraduates, and many graduate students, live in their college or one of its satellite buildings for most of their time at the university and are expected to have meals in hall regularly. The college, therefore, is the main focus of their loyalties.

In theory the ultimate governing authority of both universities is made up of all MAs (Masters of Arts) who have kept their names on the college books; it is known as Convocation at Oxford and the Senate at Cambridge. In the past these bodies had wide voting rights, but since 1926 their function has been limited to formal matters, such as the election of the Chancellor, who is elected for life and is usually an eminent public figure. His role nowadays is purely ceremonial, and in practice his executive duties are carried out by the Vice-Chancellor. The highest legislative authority now rests with Congregation (Oxford) and Regent House (Cambridge), made up of all resident MAs and recipients of higher degrees who hold teaching or administrative posts in the university or colleges. But in practice both universities are administered by boards and committees, bewildering not only to outsiders but also to many of the resident members.

In the past the main functions of the universities, as distinct from the colleges, were to award the final degree, to set the curriculum, to organise examinations and to arrange lectures. But with the growth of research, especially into the sciences, in the late 19C and 20C, the role of the university in both Oxford and, especially, Cambridge has inexorably increased, both as a dispenser (and recently raiser) of funds and, through its faculties, sub faculties and departments, as a forum of senior members. Each faculty is headed by one or more Professors; professorships are university, not college, appointments, though they carry college fellowships with them. Faculties have their own specialist libraries, supplementing the libraries of the colleges and the central university libraries.

Most undergraduates stay at the university for three (sometimes four) years and 'read' just one subject or group of subjects. Formal teaching only takes place during university terms, of which there are three, lasting eight weeks each: Michaelmas, Hilary and Trinity at Oxford; Michaelmas, Lent and Easter at Cambridge. Each college arranges for students to receive individual instruction (in tutorials at Oxford, supervisions at Cambridge); specialist teaching is also given outside the student's own college and all students are entitled to attend university lectures. For many undergraduates, however, especially those reading for arts (humanities) degrees, lectures are not compulsory, and the weekly tutorial or supervision is a far more important means of instruction, involving the writing of essays which form the basis of discussion with the tutor. These provide the main preparation for the all-important university examinations on which the student's academic fate depends. In Oxford, the examinees still have to wear 'Sub Fusc'—dark suit, white shirt, white bow tie for men, dark skirt, white blouse, dark stockings for women, and academic gowns. Sub Fusc is also worn for matriculation (formal admission to the University) and degree ceremonies.

There has been a great growth in recent years in the numbers of graduate students, many of them on scholarships, of which the most famous are the Rhodes Scholarships to Oxford, founded under the will of Cecil Rhodes (d. 1902); Bill Clinton, the ex-President of the USA, is a former Rhodes Scholar. Among postgraduate degrees, some, like the Doctorate of Philosophy (PhD, or DPhil in Oxford), are awarded as a result of research leading to a book-length thesis; others involve examinations and a shorter thesis.

Sport plays a large part in university life, although its position has somewhat declined as the importance of examination results has grown. Inter-collegiate boat races are hotly contested, and most colleges have their own sports grounds. Music and drama flourish at both universities, and there are also informal university and college clubs for virtually every conceivable interest, serious and not so serious.

Many aspiring politicians have served their apprenticeship in the Oxford and Cambridge Unions. But many of the most seductive amusements, like punting, are not susceptible to organisation. Drifting in a flat-bottomed boat down the willow-lined Cherwell or Cam on a sunny afternoon or twilit evening in early summer is one of the most agreeable ways in which to fritter away one's undergraduate days. But even here the universities have to differ: Oxford punts from the sloping end, Cambridge from the flat.

Bibliography

A good, scholarly and beautifully illustrated historical introduction to both universities is C. Brooke, R. Highfield & W. Swaan, *Oxford and Cambridge*, Cambridge University Press 1988. This contains a detailed bibliography. The books listed below include those which have been most useful in the preparation of this edition of the Blue Guide.

Oxford

Batey, Mavis. *Oxford Gardens*, Avebury, 1982
Colvin, H.M. *Unbuilt Oxford*, Yale University Press, 1983
Green, V.H.H. *A History of Oxford University*, Batsford, 1974
Hibbert, C. & E. *The Encyclopedia of Oxford*, Macmillan, 1988
Kersting, A.F. & John Ashdown. *The Buildings of Oxford*, Batsford, 1980
Morris, Jan. *Oxford*, OUP, 1978
Morris, Jan. *The Oxford Book of Oxford*, OUP, 1978
Pevsner, Nikolaus & Jennifer Sherwood. *The Buildings of England: Oxfordshire*, Yale University Press, 1974
Opher, P. *Oxford Modern: A Guide to Recent Architecture*, Heritage Tours Publications, 2001 is very useful; it is on sale in most Oxford bookshops, and there is also a good guide to stained glass in Oxford in the same series
Prest, J. (ed.). *The Illustrated History of Oxford University*, OUP, 1993
Rowse, A.L. *Oxford in the History of the Nation*, Weidenfeld, 1975
Tames, R. *A Traveller's History of Oxford*, Interlink Publishing, 2002
Tyack, G. *Oxford: an Architectural Guide*, OUP, 1998

The Oxford University **website** is www.ox.ac.uk. The Oxford City Council's website for tourist information is www.visitoxford.org. See also www.oxfordcity.co. uk.

Cambridge

Gray, R. & E. Frankl. *Cambridge Gardens*, Pevensey Press, 1984
Leedham-Green, E. *A Concise History of the University of Cambridge*, Cambridge University Press, 1996
Pevsner, Nikolaus. *The Buildings of England: Cambridgeshire*, Yale University Press, 2002
Rawle, Tim. *Cambridge Architecture*, André Deutsch, 1993
Ray, N. *Cambridge Architecture: a Concise Guide*, Cambridge University Press, 1994
Royal Commission on Historic Monuments. *City of Cambridge*, HMSO, 1959
Taylor, A. *Cambridge: the Hidden History*, Tempus, 1999
Taylor, N. & P. Booth. *Cambridge New Architecture*, Leonard Hill Books 1970 and 1972
Willis, R. & J.W. Clarke. *The Architectural History of the University of Cambridge*, 1886, reprinted Cambridge University Press, 1988
Cambridge Architecture post 1945 (Cambridge, 2000) lists and illustrates the most important modern buildings.

The **website** www.cambridge2000.com has comprehensive and accurate information about the city's buildings. The University website is www.cam.co.uk, and the Tourist Information Centre website is www.tourismcambridge.com.

Environs

Scarfe, N. *Cambridgeshire: a Shell Guide*, Faber & Faber, 1983
Sherwood, J. *A Guide to the Churches of Oxfordshire*, Oxfordshire Historic Churches Trust, 1989

Nearly all the houses and churches described in the Environs sections have their own guide books or leaflets. See also the volumes on Oxfordshire, Cambridgeshire, Berkshire, Buckinghamshire, Essex and Huntingdonshire in Nikolaus Pevsner's *Buildings of England* series (Yale University Press).

OXFORD

Practical information

 Getting to Oxford

By air

From London's **Heathrow Airport**, take the airline bus service, operated by the *Oxford Bus Company*, to the Gloucester Green bus station, with intermediate stops at Thornhill park-and-ride, Green Road roundabout, Headington, Gypsy Lane, St. Clements and Queen's Lane. Buses leave the Central Bus Station (serving Terminals 1–3) every half hour 06.30–23.00, and at two-hourly intervals 23.50–04.00, and Terminal 4 every half hour from 06.10–22.40 (☎ 01865 785400, ✉ www.theairline.info); the adult fare is £13 single, £16 period return. The journey from the Central Bus Station normally takes 70 minutes (90 minutes from Terminal 4). The airline bus service also runs from **Gatwick** south terminal to Gloucester Green hourly from 07.00–23.00, and two-hourly from then to 05.00 (five minutes later from the north terminal); the adult fare is £20, £23 period return. The journey takes about two hours. It is also possible to go by train from Gatwick to Oxford, with a change at Reading.

National Express bus services run every two hours throughout the day from **Stansted** and **Luton** airports (☎ 08705 757747, ✉ www.nationalexpress.com), the journey to Stansted taking about 3 hours and that to Luton 2½ hours. The single fare to Luton is £10 and to Stansted £15.

By train

The railway station is in Park End St (10 minutes' walk from the city centre, or 5 minutes by bus or taxi). Trains run to and from **London Paddington** every half hour Mon–Sat, every hour Sun, with a usual journey time of just under an hour (☎ 08457 484950 for recorded information, or ☎ 0845 330 7182 for National Rail Enquiry Service, ✉ www.thamestrains.co.uk or ✉ www.nationalrail.co.uk). The single adult fare is £16.30, but cheap day returns are available in off-peak hours for £14.30.

Trains also run regularly to and from Reading, Banbury, Stratford-upon-Avon, Worcester, Birmingham and Southampton, and there are less frequent services to other parts of Britain (☎ 0345 484950). Unfortunately, the service to Cambridge was axed in the notorious 'Beeching cuts' of the 1960s and, despite repeated promises to restore it, nothing has yet been done.

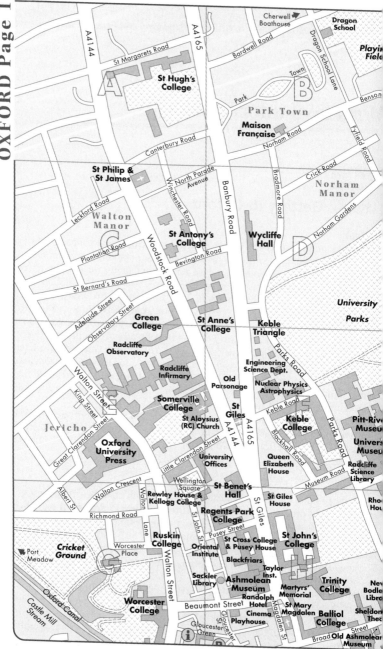

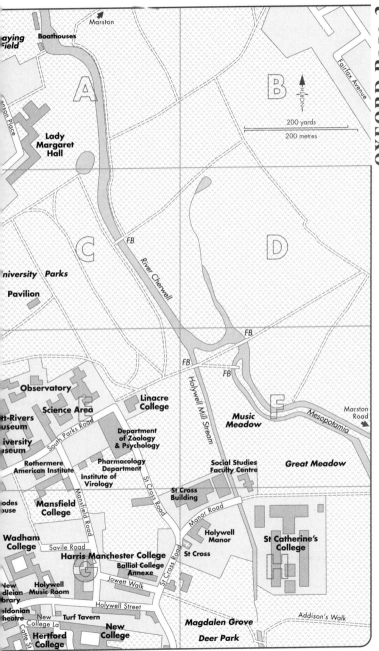

aying Field

Boathouses

Marston

A

B

N NORTH

200 yards

200 metres

Lady Margaret Hall

nson Place

FB

C

River Cherwell

D

niversity Parks

Pavilion

FB

FB

FB

Holywell Mill Stream

Observatory

Science Area

Linacre College

Music Meadow

E

Marston Road

Mesopotamia

tt-Rivers useum

South Parks Road

Department of Zoology & Psychology

iversity useum

Rothermere American Institute

Pharmacology Department Institute of Virology

Social Studies Faculty Centre

Great Meadow

odes ouse

Mansfield Road

St Cross Road

St Cross Building

Mansfield College

Manor Road

Holywell Manor

St Catherine's College

Wadham College

Savile Road

Harris Manchester College

St Cross

New dleian brary

Holywell Music Room

G

Balliol College Annexe

Jowett Walk

eldonian heatre

Holywell Street

Addison's Walk

New College La

Catte St

Turf Tavern

New College

Magdalen Grove

Hertford College

Deer Park

Port Meadow

Worcester College

Castle Mill Stream

Hythe Bridge

Saïd Business School

A420

Station

Bus Station

New Theatre

St Michael at the North Gate

Broad St

Old Ashmol Museum

Gloucester Green

Gloucester St

Ship Street

Exeter College

Cinema

George St

Politics & Sociology Library

Jesus College

Divi

St

Hythe Bridge Street

Old Fire Station

Wesley Memorial Church

St Michael's St

New Inn Hall Street

Cornmarket Street

Market Street

Turl Street

Lin Co

Park End Street

Nuffield College

Oxford Union Soc.

Covered Market

Tidmarsh La

New Road

St Peter's College

Clarendon Shopping Centre

All Saint (Library

St Thomas Street

Castle Mound

Castle

Paradise

St Martin's Tower

Golden Cross

Carfax

Bann Square

Queen Street

Bear Inn

Blue Boat

St Peckw

Former Prison

Westgate Shopping Centre

Town Hall City of Oxford Museum

Paradise Square

Paradise Street

Castle Street

St Ebb's St

Modern Art Oxford

GPO

Ch Chu

College of Further Education

St Ebbe's

Pembroke Street

St Aldate's

Tom Quad Tower

Oxpens Road

Norfolk Street

Old Greyfriars St

Turn Again Lane

Pembroke College

Brewer Street

Campion Hall

Faulkner Street

Catholic Chaplaincy

St Aldate's

Music Faculty

Ice Rink

A420

Speedwell Street

Cromwell Street

Crown and County Courts

Pol Stat

Recreation Ground

Thames Street

Sadler Walk

Trinity St

Friars Wharf

Folly Bridge

Osney Lock

Sir Geoffrey Arthur Building

Cobden Cres

Buckingham Street

Brook St

Hertfor College Annex

Abingdon Road

Marlborough Road

Western Road

Grandpont

White House Road

White House Road

Kineton Road

Marlborough Road

Chiswell Road

Newtor

Edit

Cricket Ground

Reservoir

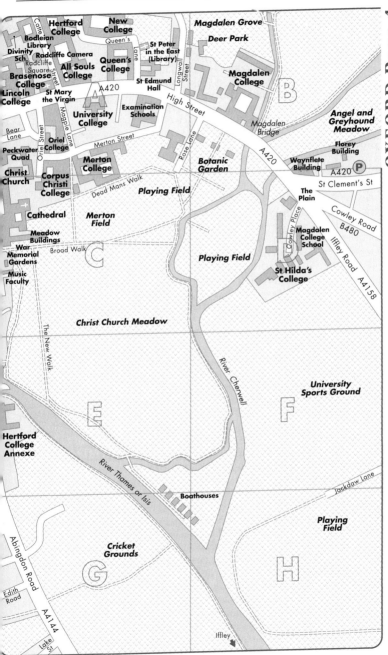

Hertford College
New College
Bodleian Library
Divinity Sch
Radcliffe Camera
Radcliffe Square
All Souls College
Brasenose College
Lincoln College
St Mary the Virgin
University College
Oriel College
Peckwater Quad
Christ Church
Corpus Christi College
Cathedral
Meadow Buildings
War Memorial Gardens
Music Faculty
Bear Lane
Merton College
Merton Street
Dead Mans Walk
Merton Field
Broad Walk
Cattle St
Magpie Lane
Oriel Street
Queen's Lane
Queen's College
St Edmund Hall
St Peter in the East (Library)
Longwall Street
Examination Schools
High Street
Rose Lane
Botanic Garden
Playing Field
Christ Church Meadow
The New Walk
River Thames or Isis
Boathouses
Cricket Grounds
Abingdon Road
Edith Road
A4144
Lake St
A420
Magdalen Grove
Deer Park
Magdalen College
Magdalen Bridge
A420
Angel and Greyhound Meadow
Florey Building
Waynflete Building
A420
St Clement's St
The Plain
Cowley Place
Magdalen College School
St Hilda's College
Cowley Road
B480
Iffley Road
A4158
Playing Field
River Cherwell
University Sports Ground
Jackdaw Lane
Playing Field
Hertford College Annexe
Iffley

A
B
C
E
F
G
H
P

By bus

The main bus station is at Gloucester Green. Express buses to and from **London** are operated by two rival companies whose tickets can be bought on the bus but are not interchangeable. They are cheaper than the train—£9 adult single fare, £10 day return, £12 period return—but the journey takes longer (90–100 minutes) and there are often delays in the morning and evening rush hours. The *Oxford Bus Company*'s X90 Oxford express service operates at 20-minute intervals daytime (15 minutes Sat), half-hourly in the evenings and also more irregularly through the night (☎ 01865 785410, ✉ www.oxfordbus.co.uk). Buses leave from Victoria Coach Station in London and pick up passengers at Grosvenor Gardens (Victoria Railway Station), Marble Arch (Speakers' Corner), Gloucester Place (Baker Street) and Hillingdon Underground Station.

The *Oxford Tube* service (☎ 01865 722250, ✉ www.oxfordtube.com), operated by the *Stagecoach* company, runs every 12 minutes during the day (20 minutes evening, half-hourly or hourly at night) from Grosvenor Gardens, London (close to Victoria Railway Station), picking up passengers at Marble Arch, Notting Hill Gate, and the west end of Holland Park Rd (*Kensington Hilton*). Both companies' buses stop in Oxford at Thornhill park-and-ride, Green Rd roundabout, Headington, Gipsy Lane, St. Clements and Queens Lane before or after leaving Gloucester Green.

Oxford (Gloucester Green) is linked to **Cambridge** via Bedford by an hourly service operated by *Stagecoach* Express X5 (✉ www.stagecoachexpress.co.uk); the journey takes about three hours. There is an hourly service from Gloucester Green to Stratford-upon-Avon and Birmingham operated by *Stagecoach Midland Red*. *National Express* buses also link Oxford to many other places in England, Wales and Scotland (☎ 01865 791579, ✉ www.nationalexpress.com: detailed information at the booking office at Gloucester Green).

A comprehensive network of local buses is operated by the *Oxford Bus Company* (☎ 01865 785400, ✉ www.oxfordbus.co.uk) and *Stagecoach* (☎ 01865 772250, ✉ www.stagecoach-oxford.co.uk: information also available at Gloucester Green).

By car

From London take the M40/A40; about 1¼ hours from central London, longer at busy times. Oxford is also easily accessible from the south by the A34, from the west by the M4/A34 or A40, and from the north by the M40/A34.

Parking Car parks are shown on the map; the largest number of spaces is at St. Ebbe's, close to the main shopping centre. There is also a limited amount of street parking in or near the centre (buy ticket from machine; expensive), but the High Street is closed to through traffic between 07.30 and 18.30 daily, including Sundays, and the congestion in the surrounding streets is considerable. Visitors by car are therefore strongly recommended to use the frequent and efficient **Park and Ride** bus service (☎ 01865 785400, ✉ www.parkandride.net). It operates daily at frequent intervals to the city from: **Thornhill**, on the A40 London road; **Pear Tree**, Woodstock Road, off northern ring-road (A34); **Seacourt**, Botley Road, off western ring-road (A34); **Redbridge**, Abingdon Road, off southern ring-road; and **Water Eaton** (not Sundays), on the A4260 Kidlington road. Journey times vary from 10 to 20 minutes, and passengers are deposited at various points in the city centre.

Where to stay

Many visitors to Oxford spend only a day in the city, but this is not nearly long enough to explore it properly, and a stay of at least one or two nights is strongly advised. Because so much of the centre of Oxford is taken up by college and university property there are fewer hotels than in comparable historic cities elsewhere in Europe, though more than there were a few years ago, so booking ahead is recommended, especially in the summer holiday season (July and August). Accommodation can be booked through the *Oxford Information Centre*, 15/16 Broad St (open all year Mon–Sat 09.30–17.00, also Sun & bank hol. summer only 10.00–13.00 and 13.30–15.30; ☎ 01865 726871).

The main city centre hotels are listed here, together with a few that are further away. They are arranged in two price categories, £££ for the more expensive and ££ for the cheaper establishments. Hotels in Oxford are quite expensive, but special offers are often made, especially by those hotels which form part of chains, and it is worth checking the relevant websites for these. There is also a plethora of guest houses and bed and breakfast establishments (£), of which only a few are listed; some are some distance away from the city centre, though nearly all are on or near bus routes. All hotels, guest houses and bed and breakfast establishments are listed, according to price category, in the *Oxford City Council's* annual leaflet *Staying in Oxford* (obtainable from the *Oxford Information Centre*, 15/16 Broad St, Oxford OX1 3AS); information is also available on the *Oxford City Council* website (✉ www.visitoxford.org) and on the website of the *Oxford Association of Hotels and Guest Houses* (✉ www.stayoxford.co.uk).

Hotels

£££
Bath Place Hotel, 4/5 Bath Place, OX1 3SU, ☎ 01865 791812, 🖷 01865 791834, ✉ www.bathplace.co.uk. Hidden away in an alley just outside the town wall to the south of Holywell St, this intimate, centrally located hotel occupies two old houses. There are 14 well-appointed bedrooms; the neighbouring **Turf Tavern** is one of Oxford's most popular pubs and can be noisy at times, but for those of a more peaceful disposition the Holywell Music Room is just over the road.

Cotswold Lodge Hotel, 66A Banbury Road, OX2 6JP, ☎ 01865 515121, 🖷 01865 512490, ✉ www.cotswoldlodgehotel.co.uk. A large Victorian-Gothic North Oxford house with 50 bedrooms (several in an extension) and a restaurant. The city centre is not far away on foot or by a short bus ride, and chic North Parade, with shops and restaurants, is on the other side of the main road.

Eastgate Hotel, High St, OX1 4BE, ☎ 0780 400 8201, 🖷 01865 791681, ✉ www.eastgate-hotel.com. Marking the ancient eastern entrance to the city, this sensitively detailed building of 1899–1900 was designed by the brother of the then President of the nearby Magdalen College; like the Randolph, it is now part of the Macdonald chain. There are 64 rooms, a restaurant and a bar/brasserie. The hotel is well placed for the city centre and for the Botanical Garden and Christ Church Meadow.

Hawkwell House Hotel, Church Way, Iffley Village, OX4 4DZ, ☎ 01865 749988,

01865 775175, www.corushotels.co.uk/hawkwellhouse. A much-extended stuccoed early Victorian villa standing in spacious grounds at the Oxford end of the quiet village street of Iffley, close to the famous 12C church and a short walk from bus stops with frequent buses into the city centre. There are 51 rooms, and there is a restaurant.

Old Bank Hotel, 92–4 High St, OX1 4BN, ☎ 01865 799599, 01865 799598, www.oxford-hotels-restaurants.co.uk. The 18C headquarters of one of Oxford's oldest banking firms, this centrally located group of buildings has been well restored as a comfortable though expensive hotel with 42 rooms. Downstairs is the *Quod*, one of Oxford's best new restaurants.

Old Parsonage Hotel, 1 Banbury Rd, OX2 6NN, ☎ 01865 310210, 01865 311262, www.oxford-hotels-restaurants.co.uk. This attractive 17C stone building is conveniently situated just to the north of the city centre, within easy walking distance of the colleges and museums. It was once the parsonage for the neighbouring St. Giles church and subsequent residents have included Oscar Wilde. There are 30 comfortable bedrooms and a well-furnished bar/restaurant where good meals are served.

Oxford Spires Four Pillars Hotel, Abingdon Rd, OX1 2LN, ☎ 01865 324324, 01865 324325, www.four-pillars.co.uk. Recently-built complex with 115 rooms in pseudo-Cotswold farmhouse style next to the genuine Eastwyke Farm. It is close to the River Thames and handily situated for the city centre. Restaurant, sauna, fitness room, etc.

Randolph Hotel, Beaumont St, OX1 2LN, ☎ 0780 400 8200, 01865 791678, www.therandolphhotel. com. This massive Victorian Gothic behemoth, facing the Ashmolean Museum in the heart of the city, has become an Oxford institution and those staying here are treading in the footsteps of generations of eminent guests. There is a good restaurant, a comfortable bar and a newly refurbished brasserie in the basement. Many of the 109 rooms are large and well appointed but some of those on the top floor are quite small.

Royal Oxford Hotel, Park End St, OX1 1HR, ☎ 01865 248432, 01865 250049, www.royaloxfordhotel.co.uk. This long-established and recently refurbished hotel with 25 rooms is situated close to the railway station and next to the new Saïd Business School.

££

Head of the River, Folly Bridge, St. Aldates, OX1 4LB, ☎ 01865 721600, 01865 726158. A converted warehouse next to a former boatyard next to the river and Folly Bridge, this popular and sometimes noisy pub offers 12 rooms in a convenient and attractive location.

Linton Lodge Hotel, Linton Rd, OX2 6UJ, ☎ 01865 553461, 01865 310365, www.lintonlodge.com. A short bus ride along Banbury Rd, this 69-room hotel, now part of the *Best Western* chain, stands in the North Oxford estate developed by St. John's College in the late 19C. The older part of the building contains a bar, lounge and restaurant; most guests are housed in a modern extension.

Old Black Horse Hotel, 102 St. Clements, OX4 1AR, ☎ 01865 244691, 01865 242771. Small but picturesque old inn with 10 rooms and a restaurant, on a busy street on the far side of Magdalen Bridge but within very easy walking distance of the city centre and close to eating places in Cowley Rd.

Oxford Travel Inn, Oxford Business Park, Garsington Rd, OX4 2DZ, ☎ 08701

977204, ✉ www.travelinn.co.uk. One of the more reasonably priced hotels in Oxford, providing standardised basic accommodation. The drawback is that it is situated near the ring road 3 miles from the city centre, but there are frequent buses, and for car-drivers the location could be an advantage.

Parklands Hotel, 100 Banbury Rd, OX2 6JU, ☎ 01865 554374, 📠 01865 559860, ✉ www.oxfordcity.co.uk/hotels/parklands. Victorian North Oxford house with 18 rooms, set back from road and well situated on bus route into city centre.

River Hotel, 17 Botley Road, OX2 0AA, ☎ 01865 243475, 📠 01865 724306, ✉ www.riverhotel.co.uk. Riverside hotel with 18 rooms in converted Victorian houses close to Osney Lock and the railway station, on the main road leading west out of Oxford. Just a short walk to the city centre and good too for strolls on the towpath to Port Meadow, etc.

Tower House, Ship St, OX1 3DA, ☎ 01865 246828, 📠 01865 247508, ✉ www.scoot.co.uk/towerhouse. A recently-opened hotel with only 7 comfortable rooms in an old house in a quiet street just inside the old town wall and very conveniently placed for the colleges, bookshops in Broad St, etc.

Guest houses and bed and breakfasts

£

Burlington Guest House, 374 Banbury Rd, Summertown, OX2 7PP, ☎ 01865 513513, 📠 01865 311785, ✉ www.burlington-house.co.uk. An especially well-appointed B & B near the northern edge of the city, but on bus route.

Chestnuts Guest House, 45 Davenant Rd, OX2 8BU, ☎ 01865 553375, 📠 01865 311785. Another up-market establishment on the outer fringes of prosperous North Oxford; city centre easily accessible by bus.

College Guest House, 103/5 Woodstock Rd, OX2 6HL, ☎ 01865 552579, 📠 01865 311244, ✉ www.collegeguesthouse.oxfordpages.co.uk. Large Victorian house on one of the main routes leading north out of the city, within walking distance of centre. 12 rooms (not all en suite), car parking available.

Gables Guest House, 6 Cumnor Hill, OX2 9HA, ☎ 01865 862153, ✉ www.oxfordcity.co.uk/accom/gables. Comfortable accommodation for those who do not mind staying on the outer suburban fringe of Oxford.

Heather House, 192 Iffley Rd, OX4 1SD, ☎/📠 01865 249757. 5-room B&B on main road on far side of Magdalen Bridge. City centre within walking distance, and also easily accessible by frequent buses. Other B&Bs further along Iffley Rd if this is full.

Isis Guest House, 43–53 Iffley Rd OX4 1ED, ☎ 01865 205333, 📠 01865 711544. Student accommodation close to city centre on far side of Magdalen Bridge. Only open July–Sept.

Newton House, 82–4 Abingdon Rd, OX1 4PL, ☎ 01865 240561, 📠 01865 244647. 10 rooms in two Victorian terrace houses on main road just south of Folly Bridge and within easy walking distance of city centre. Other B&Bs nearby if this is full.

Old Mitre Rooms, 4B Turl St, OX1 3DR, ☎ 01865 279921, 📠 01865 279963. Very reasonably priced but spartan student accommodation in old houses belonging to Lincoln College behind Mitre Hotel in heart of city. 40 single, 16 twin-bedded and three family rooms, most of which do not have private bathrooms. NB: this establishment is only open in July, August and the first week of

September. No car parking.

Oxford Youth Hostel, 2A Botley Rd OX2 0AB, ☎ 01865 727275, 🖷 01865 251182, ✉ www.yha.org.uk. Spartan but conveniently located next to railway station.

St. Michael's Guest House, 26 St. Michael's St, OX1 2EB, ☎ 01865 242101. Very conveniently situated in the heart of the city, in attractive street off Cornmarket St opposite Oxford Union, this is a basic 9-roomed establishment with no frills attached. Car parking virtually impossible.

Self-catering accommodation and campsites

Ambassadors Oxford, Rowland Hill Court, Osney Lane, OX1 1LE, ☎ 01865 849530, 🖷 01865 849533 ✉ www.ambassadorsoxford.co.uk. 16 luxury apartments not far from new business school.

Other self-catering accommodation can be found through *OxfordShortlets*, ☎ 01865 376772, ✉ www.OxfordShortlets.co.uk.

Oxford's main **camp site** is close to the Redbridge park-and-ride car park at the southern end of Abingdon Rd.

Food and drink

Oxford has an excellent selection of restaurants covering the whole gamut of cuisines and varying greatly in price. Booking is in general advisable in the more expensive places, especially at weekends. Most of the smarter restaurants do not start serving meals in the evening before about 18.30 (sometimes later), and close at 23.00 or thereabouts; lunch (which is often considerably cheaper and just as good) is usually served from about 12.00 to 14.00. Meals are served throughout the day at some of the cheaper restaurants and good food at modest prices can also be had in the some pubs in the city centre. Tips of about ten per cent are expected (but not insisted upon) when food is brought to your table, but not, as in pubs, where it is collected from a counter.

Some restaurants popular with the young get very crowded at certain times of the year (for example, after examinations), and some of the city centre pubs are unpleasantly noisy, crowded and smoky in the evenings. Good draught beer can be sampled in most pubs, along with bottled beer from abroad (also available in cafés and restaurants), and most restaurants serve an adequate house wine as well as several more sophisticated wines, though prices are often high. Pubs are increasingly open throughout the day, but it is not always possible to get food before about 12.30 or between 14.00 and 18.00. Cafés and tea shops usually close at about 17.00.

A selection of restaurants is listed in two price categories; preference has been given to those in or near the city centre over those further away. As a rough guide **£** = £15–£30, **££** = £30 and above, for a three-course meal in the evening. There is also a short selection of pubs, tea shops and sandwich bars.

Restaurants

££

Aquavitae, Folly Bridge, ☎ 01865 247775. Outstanding, stylish restaurant serving modern Italian food in beautiful riverside location just south of city centre. Art gallery above.

Cherwell Boathouse, Bardwell Rd, ☎ 01865 552746. Very good restaurant on banks of River Cherwell, where punts can be hired: *la dolce vita* Oxford-style, especially on a summer evening. Varied, carefully planned menu; rather a long way to walk from city centre.

Fisher's, 36–7 St. Clement's, ☎ 01865 243003. An up-market fish restaurant on the east side of Magdalen Bridge serving fresh fish and shellfish, with outstanding variations on fish and chips as well as more innovative dishes.

Gee's, 61A Banbury Rd, ☎ 01865 553540/558346. Excellent restaurant serving international cuisine of high standard in a glazed former conservatory about a mile north of the city centre in North Oxford. Top-quality service.

Old Parsonage, 1 Banbury Rd, ☎ 01865 310210. Described in the latest Oxford student handbook as 'the kind of place you simply must bring your parents to when they come to Oxford', the restaurant is attached to the eponymous hotel and offers good, varied food in very comfortable surroundings. The teas (served from 15.00–17.30) are quite exceptional.

Le Petit Blanc, 71 Walton St, ☎ 01865 510999. Stylish French cuisine from the family of Raymond Blanc, owner of the ***Manoir aux Quat Saisons*** at Great Milton, one of England's most celebrated restaurants (and a good place to stay near Oxford for those for whom money is no object). Walton St is about 1½ miles from the city centre, on the edge of Jericho in a trendy area. Set lunch menu is excellent value given the high quality of the food.

Quod, 92–4 High St, ☎ 01865 202505. Popular restaurant in central location offering good international cuisine in somewhat minimalist setting enlivened by 20C art on the walls. Sometimes crowded, especially at lunchtimes.

Restaurant Elizabeth, 82 St. Aldate's, ☎ 01865 242230. One of Oxford's oldest-established restaurants, situated in former medieval academic hall just north of Folly Bridge and within easy walking distance of the city centre. Good international cuisine and a superb setting in ancient candle-lit panelled rooms.

£

English/Eclectic

Brown's, 7 Woodstock Rd, ☎ 01865 311415. Large and popular restaurant, especially with young people, so somewhat noisy at times. Varied, somewhat pricy, international cuisine. A short walk from city centre.

Next Door, Holywell St. Stylish café-bar in former Blackwell's Music Shop run as extension of adjacent ***King's Arms***.

Nosebag, St. Michael's St, ☎ 01865 721033. A mainly vegetarian establishment with varied menu, close to Cornmarket St.

French

Bistro Je T'Aime, 11 Wheatsheaf Yard, Blue Boar St, ☎ 01865 722473. Newly-opened restaurant situated just south of the High St, near Carfax.

Pierre Victoire, 9 Little Clarendon St. ☎ 01865 316616. Part of a chain and not dissimilar to the adjacent ***Café Rouge***, though without the café-style frills. Good value.

Italian/Mediterranean

Café Co-Co, 23 Cowley Rd, ☎ 01865 200232. Good and varied food in a relaxed and lively ambience on the far side of Magdalen Bridge.

Pizza Express, Golden Cross, Cornmarket St, ☎ 01865 790442. Part of the well-known chain, serving excellent pizzas in the upper floor of a former 16C inn with well-preserved wall paintings (in the two far rooms to the left at the top of the stairs) at the very heart of the city. Sometimes crowded but well worth visiting for the setting as well as the food.

Middle Eastern

Al Shami, 25 Walton Crescent, ☎ 01865 310066. Friendly, long-established Lebanese restaurant in a quiet street north of Worcester College, this is the best place in central Oxford for lovers of east Mediterranean cuisine (kebabs, etc.); good Lebanese wine too.

Indian

Aziz, 228–30 Cowley Rd, ☎ 01865 794945. Probably the best of Oxford's many Indian restaurants, and a short bus or taxi ride from the city centre, *Aziz* specialises in Bengali cuisine.

Chutneys, 36 St. Michael's St, ☎ 01865 724241. Good, reasonably priced, mainly south Indian food quickly and efficiently served in city-centre location, popular with students.

Moonlight, 58 Cowley Rd, ☎ 01865 240275. Not far from Magdalen Bridge and The Plain, this restaurant specialises in south Indian cuisine, with an emphasis on vegetarian dishes.

South-East Asian

Chiang Mai Kitchen, 130A High St, ☎ 01865 202233. Excellent Thai food in a timber-framed merchant's house of the 1630s in an alley to the south of High St near Carfax.

Chinese

Opium Den, 79 George St, ☎ 01865 248680. Good and long-established Chinese restaurant close to Nuffield and Worcester Colleges.

Wok 23, 4–6 Woodstock Rd, ☎ 01865 554996. Basic Chinese restaurant, popular with students; quick service and very good value for money.

Japanese

Endaname, 15 Holywell St, ☎ 01865 246916. Excellent, reasonably-priced but small restaurant in attractive city-centre location opposite New College. NB: open lunchtimes (exc. Mon) and Thur–Sat evenings 15.00–20.30. Sushi Thur evenings only.

Pubs

Bear, Blue Boar St. Small, picturesque and often crowded.

Eagle and Child, St. Giles. 1980s retro interior, full of Tolkien enthusiasts.

King's Arms, Parks Rd—archetypal student/donnish pub, good solid food.

Turf Tavern, Bath Place between Holywell St and New College Lane—in the shadow of the city wall and very popular in summer, but with lots of space outside, food variable.

White Horse, Broad St. Also small, picturesque and often crowded.

For those prepared to venture out of the city centre, the *Perch* at Binsey, the *Trout* at Godstow (be prepared for crowds and slow service), the *Isis Tavern* at Iffley, the *Fishes* at North Hinksey, the *White Hart* at Wytham and the *Victoria Arms* at Marston all offer food at all times of day in pleasant surroundings. See entries in text.

Cafés and tea shops

Grand Café, High St. Up-market establishment serving good food in sumptuously refurbished former coffee room of what was once Oxford's main coaching inn.
Mortons, Covered Market. Excellent café and sandwich bar, either to take away or eat on premises, often crowded.
Museum of Modern Art, Pembroke St. Basement café under museum, with solid wholesome lunches, etc.
Queen's Lane Coffee House, High St. Claims to be one of the oldest in England, even Europe; good sandwiches, etc.
The Rose, High St. Good lunches and teas, recently remodelled in elegant minimalist style.
Vaults and Garden, Radcliffe Sq. In the former Congregation House (14C) next to University Church, offering food using organic ingredients.

Coffee can also be had in *Blackwell's* and the other city centre bookshops as well as at the usual *Starbucks* and similar establishments. Teas are usually available during the summer at St. Edmund Hall, but those who wish to experience English tea at its best—and at a price—should try the *Old Parsonage* hotel or the *Randolph*.

The **Covered Market** is the best place in which to buy the components of a **picnic**, and the best place to have a picnic is Christ Church Meadow, ideally by the banks of the River Cherwell on a balmy spring or autumn day if you are lucky enough to be in Oxford then. Sandwiches can be bought both in the Market and at *Harvey's* in the High St, opposite the *Eastgate Hotel*, but Harvey's is very popular with students and the queues are often long.

Getting around Oxford

Since the city centre is quite small, most excursions can be undertaken on foot. For longer journeys, Oxford is liberally served by **buses** run by two competing companies (*Stagecoach* and the *Oxford Bus Company*) whose tickets are not interchangeable; journeys within the city cost between 50 pence and £1.

    Taxis are reliable and reasonably cheap (£3 approx for a journey of 1½ to 2 miles); you can hail a taxi on the street, hire one at a cab rank (e.g., at the railway station or Carfax) or phone a cab firm (eg, *001 Taxis*, ☎ 01865 240000).

    If you can cope with (or avoid) the traffic on the main roads, Oxford is an excellent **cycling** city. There are cycle tracks alongside most main roads, and many good excursions on car-free paths, eg, the river and canal towpaths. Cycles can be hired from *Bikezone*, Market St (☎ 01865 728877).

Tours of the Cotswolds and further afield are offered from April to October by *Cotswold Roaming* (✉ www.oxfordcity.co.uk/cotswold-roaming, ☎ 01865 308300) and, twice a week, by *City Sightseeing* (☎ 01865 790522, ✉ www.citysightseeingoxford.com).

Car hire can be arranged from *Avis* (☎ 01865 249000), *Budget Rent-a-car* (☎ 01865 724884), *National Car Rental* (☎ 01865 240471) and *Thrifty Car Rental* (☎ 01865 250252).

Sightseeing

The centre of Oxford is quite compact, and it is possible to see a lot in a relatively short time. By far the best way to see it is on foot, though there are tours on **open-top buses**, operated by *City Sightseeing Oxford* (☎ 01865 790522, ✉ www.citysightseeingoxford.com) and *Full Circle*, tickets for which can be bought on the bus (£9 approx per head). Buses leave from the railway station and from outside the Sheldonian Theatre and elsewhere. If you want a guided tour, the **walking tours** by trained members of the Oxford Guild of Guides can be recommended; they leave at regular intervals from the Oxford Information Centre, Broad St, encompassing some of the colleges and university buildings (£6.50 per head). Inspector Morse tours and Ghost Tours are also offered: contact the Information Centre for details. Themed tours are also offered by *Blackwell's* and start at their Bookshop, 53 Broad St (☎ 01865 333606). But many, perhaps most, visitors will get more enjoyment from exploring the city and the colleges on their own.

Oxford does not go out of its way to make life easy for visitors. Normal **opening times** of colleges and other buildings are given in the relevant sections of the book, but it should be borne in mind that colleges and university buildings are parts of a working academic community, and can often be closed unexpectedly. All but a handful of colleges are closed during the morning, and many are also closed during parts of the Christmas, Easter and summer vacations. Some nowadays never seem to be open to the public at all, though determined visitors can usually gain access by asking permission in advance from the Domestic Bursar, or by speaking nicely to the porter. The central University buildings (Bodleian Library, etc.) are also infuriatingly closed on Saturday afternoons, and for the whole of Sundays and some Bank Holidays, and the Ashmolean Museum is closed on Mondays. But despite these restrictions, and despite the formidable array of high walls, narrow gateways and surly porters with which the university and colleges sometimes choose to confront the outer world, it is possible, with patience and sometimes persistence, to see almost all of what you want to see, and also much that the average visitor misses.

 ## Festivals and annual events

The main festivals and events peculiar to Oxford are:
Torpids college boat races, held late Feb. The races can be watched from the river towpath between Folly Bridge and Iffley Lock.
Oxford Literary Festival held for a week in early April (✉ www.sundaytimes-

oxfordliteraryfestival.co.uk).

May Morning: singing from the top of Magdalen College tower and associated festivities, starting at 06.00 on 1 May, though some students will be *en fête* for all the previous night, and the choir will probably be inaudible.

Eights Week: college boat races, held late May.

Encaenia: the awarding of honorary degrees in the Sheldonian Theatre, held on the first Wednesday after the end of Trinity term (late June), including processions of dons and dignitaries to and from the Sheldonian.

St. Giles Fair: held in St. Giles on the first Monday and Tuesday after the Feast of St. Giles (1 Sept), this is the main festival of the Town as opposed to the Gown, and attracts large crowds to the often terrifying rides and roller coasters (there are also merry-go-rounds for the more timid or sedate). The Ashmolean is closed during this period.

NB Oxford's academic terms run from mid-October to early December (Michaelmas), mid-January to early March (Hilary) and late April to mid-June (Trinity).

Entertainment

For a town of its size Oxford is well supplied with entertainments of all kinds, and they are often of a very high artistic quality. The monthly publication *In Oxford* (✉ www.inoxfordmag.co.uk), available free of charge from numerous outlets, gives listings.

Drama

The main theatres are the recently refurbished **New Theatre**, George St (☎ 01865 244544), a vast 1930s building which presents visiting professional opera (Welsh National and Glyndebourne) and ballet from time to time, as well as musicals, pantomimes, etc.; and the **Oxford Playhouse**, Beaumont St (☎ 01865 798600, ✉ www.oxfordplayhouse.com), where there is a good programme of professional plays as well as student and amateur productions. There are also numerous **student productions** of varying quality in colleges and elsewhere during term time (open-air in college gardens in early summer). **Open-air Shakespeare productions** are mounted during the summer months by the Creation Theatre Company in Headington Hill Park (☎ 01865 245745, ✉ www.creationtheatre.co.uk) and by the Oxford Shakespeare Company in Wadham College garden (☎ 01865 305305, ✉ www.oxfordplayhouse.com).

Music

Concerts are regularly put on, often in historic venues (eg, college chapels and the **Sheldonian Theatre**), by Music at Oxford (☎ 01865 242865, ✉ www.musicatoxford.com), which brings in nationally and internationally known performers; by Oxford University's orchestra in residence, the Oxford Philomusica (☎ 01865 305305, ✉ www.oxfordphil.com); and also by the City of Oxford Orchestra (☎ 01865 744457, ✉ www.cityofoxfordorchestra.co.uk). Chamber concerts, often of excellent quality, are performed regularly in the **Holywell Music Room**, Holywell St, including Coffee Concerts held on Sunday mornings throughout the year (☎ 01865 305305, ✉ www.coffeeconcerts.com); tickets include a cup of coffee before or after the concert in the *King's Arms* nearby. Concerts by professional performers are also regularly held throughout the year in the **Jacqueline du Pré Music Building** at St. Hilda's College (☎ 01865 276821, ✉ www.sthildas.ox.ac.uk/jdp). There are also many musical performances by good amateur choirs—in which Oxford abounds—and by student choirs and orchestras during term time, and concerts of Baroque music are put on regularly during the summer in Exeter College Chapel.

The three ancient choral foundations (New College, Magdalen and Christ Church) sing **choral services** in their respective chapels in term time (for details, see the entries on the colleges) and put on concerts from time to time. Details of concerts are prominently posted throughout the city centre and in the Information Centre.

Cinemas

The *Odeon* cinemas in George St and Magdalen St (☎ 0780 505050 007, ✉ www.odeon.co.uk) offer the usual films on general release. The *Phoenix*, Walton St (☎ 01865 512526, ✉ www.picturehouses.co.uk) and the *Ultimate Picture Palace*, Jeune St, off Cowley Rd (☎ 01865 245288), have a more *recherché* repertoire, with some classics. The *Ozone Multiplex Cinema* (☎ 0870 444 3030, ✉ www.ozonemultiplex.com) is in Grenoble Rod, on the edge of the city next to the new Oxford United football stadium, and offers a large and varied programme.

Sporting and leisure activities

Boating Punts and rowing boats may be hired at Folly Bridge, the Magdalen Bridge Boathouse (☎ 01865 202643) and the Cherwell Boathouse in Bardwell Rd, off Banbury Rd in North Oxford. Punting is not as difficult as it looks; the first principle is to use the pole as a rudder, keeping it as close as possible to the side of the boat.

There are frequent **boat excursions** in the summer along the Thames from Folly Bridge to Iffley Lock and twice a day to Abingdon, operated by *Salters Steamers* (☎ 01865 243421, ✉ www.saltersteammers.co.uk).

Swimming The main indoor pools are the Temple Cowley Pool, Temple Rd, Cowley (☎ 01865 749449) and the pool at the Ferry Sports Centre, Marston Ferry Rd (☎ 310978). There is a refurbished outdoor pool in Hinksey Park, Abingdon Rd (open late May–Sept, ☎ 01865 247737).

Skating There is a modern Ice Rink, designed by Nicholas Grimshaw, designer of London's Waterloo International Station, in Oxpens Rd (☎ 01865 247676).

Parks and gardens

The centre of Oxford is surrounded by open space and the close proximity of so much of it gives the city a lot of its character. Much of the space is privately owned and jealously preserved. To the south of the city centre is **Christ Church**

Meadow (entered from St. Aldate's, Merton Street or Rose Lane), where cattle still graze and boys from the nearby schools practise their sports; visitors are restricted to the walks and paths, which meander alongside the Rivers Thames and Cherwell. The **University Parks**, to the north of the centre, were landscaped in the mid-19C and offer a contrasting landscape interspersed by clumps of trees and shrubs, with a path by the River Cherwell; in the middle is the University's cricket ground, where it is easy to fritter away an early summer afternoon among the somnolent spectators. Of the **college gardens**, those at St. John's, Worcester, Wadham, New College and Magdalen (Addison's Walk) are regularly accessible and particularly worth visiting (for times, see entries on the colleges), as is the University's **Botanic Garden** (☎ 01865 286690, ✉ www. botanic-garden.ox.ac.uk). Further afield is the vast expanse of **Port Meadow** (best reached from Walton St and Walton Well Rd), an area of common land where animals roam freely; this merges into genuine countryside.

Shopping

Oxford is a large and busy shopping centre, but many of the main shops (in Cornmarket and Queen Streets) are the branches of chain stores found in any English town, and the pressure of crowds, especially at weekends, often makes shopping an exhausting and not very satisfying experience. There are, however, some exceptions to this general rule. The **Covered Market** is not only good for food but also contains several boutiques, and the clientele is worth observing for its own sake. There are some good **clothes shops**, especially for women. There are also some excellent **bookshops**. *Blackwell's* is one of the most famous, and best-stocked, bookshops in the English-speaking world; it has offshoots in the form of Blackwell's Art and Poster Bookshop and Blackwell's Music Shop on the opposite side of Broad St. *Waterstone's*, at the corner of Broad St and Cornmarket St, and *Border's*, in Magdalen St, have a smaller stock. There are also some secondhand and remainder bookshops, though they tend to be somewhat expensive compared with those in some other towns.

Museums and galleries

Even if it had no university and college buildings, Oxford would be worth visiting for its museums alone. They cater for a wide range of interests, from western art to old musical and scientific instruments, and are often surprisingly quiet, especially outside the peak summer tourist season. What is more, they are, with a handful of exceptions, free of charge.

Ashmolean Museum, Beaumont St (☎ 01865 278000, ✉ www.ashmol. co.uk), open Tues–Sat 10.00–17.00 (closes 19.30 on Thur in summer), Sun 14.00–17.00. Oxford's main art museum, with outstanding Egyptian, Greek and Roman, Middle-Eastern, south and east Asian and western art collections, as well as silver, ceramics and coins and special exhibitions.

Bate Collection of Musical Instruments, St. Aldates (☎ 01865 276139, ✉ www.ashmol.ox.ac.uk/BCMIPage), open Mon–Fri 14.00–17.00, Sat 10.00–13.00 term-time only.

Christ Church Picture Gallery, Christ Church (☎ 01865 276172, ✉ www.chch.ox.ac.uk/gallery), open Mon–Sat 10.30–13.00, 14.00–17.30, Sun 14.00–17.30. Closes 16.30 Oct–March. Excellent collection of Old Master paintings and drawings. Adm. charge.

Modern Art Oxford, Pembroke St (✉ www.modernartoxford.org.uk, ☎ 01865 722733), open Tues–Sun 11.00–18.00, closes 21.00 Thur. Temporary exhibitions, often of avant-garde contemporary art.

Museum of the History of Science, Broad St (☎ 277280, ✉ www.mhs.ox.ac.uk), open Tues–Sat 12.00–16.00, Sun 14.00–17.00. Old scientific instrumenst housed in the Old Ashmolean, Oxford's first museum building.

Museum of Oxford, St. Aldates (☎ 01865 252761), open Tues–Fri 10.00–16.30, Sat 10.00–17.00, Sun 12.00–16.00. The history of the city. Adm. charge.

Pitt Rivers Museum, Parks Rd (☎ 01865 270927, ✉ www.prm.ox.ac.uk), open Mon–Sat 13.00–16.30, Sun 14.00–16.30. Extraordinary collection of objects of anthropological interest from all over the world, displayed in late-Victorian setting, reached through University Museum.

University Museum, Parks Rd (☎ 01865 272950, ✉ www.oum.ox.ac.uk), open daily 12.00–17.00. Natural history collections displaying in stunning mid-Victorian building.

Activities for children

Though many of the best-known 'sights' of Oxford do not make many concessions to children, there are some places which are almost certain to be popular. They include the University Museum with its dinosaurs, the adjacent Pitt-Rivers Museum (the shrunken heads near the entrance will appeal to some and horrify others) and the Oxford Story, 6 Broad St (☎ 01865 728822, ✉ www.oxfordstory.co.uk) where there is a special children's commentary. The Ashmolean Museum is also intimate and unintimidating enough to be enjoyable for many children, especially perhaps the Egyptian section. The University Parks and Christ Church Meadow are good places in which to relax, as is the open-air swimming pool in Hinksey Park. Many children will also enjoy the boat trips from Folly Bridge, and, for those prepared to try their hand, there is also punting.

Outside the city, Cogges Manor Farm, the Didcot Railway Centre, the caves at West Wycombe and the Cotswold Wildlife Park near Burford are all excellent places to take children. There are plenty of children's attractions, including a miniature railway, boats and an adventure playground, at Blenheim Palace. For those with a car, Shotover Country Park, on the edge of Oxford, is an excellent place for children to let off steam.

Additional information

Banks and post office

There are branches of all the major **banks** in the centre of Oxford, all of which have cash machines and bureau de change facilities. Banks are usually open from 09.00–17.00 Mon–Fri; some branches are also open on Sunday mornings. The main branches are *Barclay's*, 54 Cornmarket St; *HSBC*, 65 Cornmarket St; *Lloyds-TSB*, 1–5 High St; *Natwest*, 32 Cornmarket St and 121 High St; and *Royal Bank of Scotland*, 32 St. Giles. There are also **bureaux de change** at *Thomas Cook*'s and *American Express* in Queen St, and at the main **post office**, at 102–4 St. Aldate's, open Mon–Fri 09.00–17.30, Sat 09.00–18.00 (☎ 01865 223344).

Disabled travellers

Most of the college quads are accessible to the disabled, but there are sometimes flights of steps to be negotiated to halls, etc. There is also disabled access to the ground floor at least of most of the larger museums (e.g., the Ashmolean, the University Museum), but for smaller museums and for the country houses in the Environs of Oxford section it is worth making a telephone call first; see also the *Museums and galleries of Oxfordshire* leaflet produced by the Oxfordshire Museums Council. Most buses in Oxford now have low floors, and there are slopes on many kerbs, making it easier for wheelchairs and parents with pushchairs to traverse the streets. For questions about disability issues, call Oxfordshire County Council (☎ 01865 375515).

Emergencies and medical services

The main casualty departments are at the **John Radcliffe Hospital** (☎ 01865 741166) and the **Radcliffe Infirmary** (☎ 01865 311188; eye, ear, nose and throat emergencies only). Dial 999 for an ambulance.

Libraries

The **Central Library** is in the Westgate Centre (☎ 01865 815509), and there is an excellent collection of books on the history of Oxford in the Centre for Oxfordshire Studies on the top floor. Other libraries, including those of the university and colleges, are only open on written application, supported by a letter of recommendation.

Personal security

Oxford is not a dangerous city, but neither is it crime free. Car crime is common, so make sure cars are always locked and valuables removed or at least hidden. The city centre, like most others in England, is sometimes beset with drunken youths late at night, but with normal prudence they will not present a problem. If you are unfortunate enough to be a victim of crime, contact the **Police Station** in St. Aldate's (☎ 01865 266000).

Public holidays

Many Oxford buildings are closed on **bank holidays** (New Year's Day, Good Friday, Easter Monday, the first and last Mondays in May, the last Monday in August, Christmas Day, 26 December and often some of the days between it and New Year's Day.

The Colleges

Oxford University has (2004) just over 17,000 resident students, of whom about 11,000 are undergraduates and the remainder graduate students, many of the latter coming from overseas. There are 39 colleges, of which nine are for graduates only. Five colleges were initially founded for women but of these only St. Hilda's is still for women only. There are also six Permanent Private Halls through which it is possible to read for a university degree: Blackfriars, Campion Hall, Greyfriars, Regent's Park College, St. Benet's Hall and St. Stephen's House. The names of the colleges, in order of foundation, are:

University, 1249
Balliol, 1263
Merton, 1264
Exeter, 1314
Oriel, 1326
Queen's, 1341
New College, 1379
Lincoln, 1427
All Souls, 1438 (fellows only)
Magdalen, 1458
Brasenose, 1509
Corpus Christi, 1517
Christ Church, 1546
Trinity, 1555
St. John's, 1555
Jesus, 1571
Wadham, 1612
Pembroke, 1624
Worcester, 1714
Hertford, 1740
Keble, 1868

Lady Margaret Hall, 1878
Somerville, 1879
St. Hugh's, 1886
St. Hilda's, 1893 (women only)
St. Anne's, 1952
St. Antony's, 1953 (graduates)
St. Edmund Hall, 1957 (formerly an academic hall)
Nuffield, 1958 (graduates)
St. Peter's, 1961
St. Catherine's, 1963
Linacre, 1965 (graduates)
St. Cross, 1965 (graduates)
Wolfson, 1966 (graduates)
Green, 1977 (graduates)
Kellogg, 1990 (graduates)
Templeton, 1995 (graduates)
Mansfield, 1995
Harris Manchester, 1996

Walks in Oxford

1 ~ THE CENTRAL UNIVERSITY AREA

Historic Oxford has two centres. The centre of the city is the crossroads called Carfax, while the heart of the University is the area between the University Church of St. Mary and Broad St. This walk explores this second area, starting at the University Church.

St. Mary the Virgin church

History

St. Mary's has from earliest times been closely linked to the University. Until the 17C, meetings of Convocation, examinations, learned disputations and degree ceremonies all took place here and in the distant past the church bells summoned scholars to do battle with the townspeople. In 1555 St. Mary's witnessed the trial of the Oxford Martyrs and in the following year Cranmer's repudiation of his recantation; one of the grooves cut to support the platform on which he stood can be seen on a pillar to the left of the Vice-Chancellor's throne. John Wesley worshipped and preached here (the last time in 1744), as did the leaders of the Oxford Movement, including John Keble and John Henry (later Cardinal) Newman, who was vicar from 1828–43. A University sermon is still delivered by a 'select preacher' on Sunday mornings in term in the presence of the Vice-Chancellor, as are the famous Bampton lectures, endowed by Dr John Bampton (d. 1751).

The church (plan 4, A; open Mon–Sat 09.00–17.00, Sun 11.30–17.00, ☎ 01865 279111) is a largely 15C building in the Perpendicular Gothic style, but the tower is of c 1270 and the elaborate pinnacled spire, encrusted with ballflower ornament, dates from c 1310–20. There have been several restorations, and the statues on the pinnacles are replacements of the originals, which can now be seen in the cloister of New College.

The church is best entered through the ornate **south porch** (1637), facing the High St. It was probably designed by the master mason John Jackson and given by Archbishop Laud's chaplain Morgan Owen, Bishop of Llandaff. It is flanked by twisted columns like those used by Bernini in his baldachino in St. Peter's, Rome (believed at the time to echo those in Solomon's temple), and over the entrance there is a statue of the Virgin and Child; for 17C Puritans this was tantamount to popery, and the statue was part of the indictment against Laud in his trial in 1644.

The **nave** was built by the University in 1487–1503, but the **Brome Chapel** (named after the founder of Oriel College) to the north (far side) survives from the previous church; the nave furnishings, including the screen and the pulpit from which Keble preached his famous Assize Sermon on 'national apostacy' in 1833, date from 1827–28.

The east window of the **south aisle** (right) has glass by A.W.N. Pugin and so does the third window from the east: the latter is an excellent example of Victorian stained glass at its best. The **chancel** dates from 1462–63; the tall Perpendicular windows are now filled with clear glass, but the 15C stalls and reredos survive in a truncated state. The painting of the *Angel appearing to the Shepherds* over the altar is by Francesco Bassano; a floor slab nearby records the burial place of Amy Robsart (d. 1560), neglected wife of Queen Elizabeth's favourite, the Earl of Leicester.

The north porch leads out into Radcliffe Square; note the Gothic Revival monument on the ground floor of the lobby (now a shop) commemorating the Countess of Pomfret (d. 1762), who gave the Arundel Marbles to the University (now in the Ashmolean Museum). From here, stairs lead up to the **tower**, which affords excellent views of the central University area (adm. charge).

The unpretentious building on the north-east side of the church is the medieval **Congregation House**, probably the oldest surviving purpose-built university—as opposed to collegiate—building in Europe. It dates from the 1320s, and the vaulted ground floor (now a coffee shop) was originally used for meetings of the University's legislative body. The upper floor (no adm.) was used in the early 15C as the University's first library, housing books donated by Thomas Cobham, Bishop of Worcester (d. 1327).

The north porch of the University Church leads into **Radcliffe Square**, one of the great urban spaces of Europe. Bounded by the Bodleian Library and Schools Quadrangle (north), All Souls College (east), Brasenose College (west) and St. Mary's church (south), it was formed in the early 18C by the clearance of houses in Catte St and School St. At the centre is Oxford's finest Classical building, the domed rotunda now known as the **Radcliffe Camera**. Originally called the Radcliffe Library, it was built in 1737–48 out of the munificent bequest of Queen Anne's physician Dr John Radcliffe (d. 1714). Its circular shape echoes the form of ancient Roman mausolea, but it has always been used as a library, concentrating at first on medical books and now on literature and history.

The architect was the Italian-trained James Gibbs—who also designed the Senate House in Cambridge—but the concept of a domed circular library originated with Nicholas Hawksmoor, who saw Radcliffe Square as a 'Forum Universitatis'. The arches of the rusticated ground floor were unglazed until 1863, when the library was incorporated into the Bodleian system and given its present name; above is the main reading room or *camera*, articulated outside by pairs of giant Corinthian columns.

The noble interior (no adm.), encircled by round arches supporting the drum of the dome, is embellished with beautiful plasterwork by Giuseppe Artari, Charles Stanley and Thomas Roberts; there is a statue of Dr Radcliffe by Rysbrack in a niche over the entrance doorway.

On the west side of Radcliffe Square, facing the Radcliffe Camera and Hawksmoor's North Quad of All Souls College, is Brasenose College.

Brasenose College

Plan 4, A; open 14.00–17.00 or dusk if earlier: adm. charge; ☎ 01865 277830, 🖾 www.bnc.ox.ac.uk.

History

Founded in 1504 by William Smythe, Bishop of Lincoln, and Sir Richard Sutton, both of them Lancashire men, Brasenose (officially the 'King's Hall and College of Brasenose': colloquially B.N.C.) was the direct successor to an academic hall of the same name on the site, whose last Principal became the first head of the new college. The curious name probably derives from the 12C or 13C brazen knocker—possibly a handle or sanctuary ring, with a lion-like mask—of the original Hall. This was carried off to Stamford (Lincolnshire) in 1333 by a group of Oxford dons and students who wanted to found a rival university there and was only recovered in 1890. The original early Tudor quadrangle still survives, with alterations, but a new Chapel and Library were built to the south during the Interregnum of the 1650s. Further changes occurred in the 1880s with the construction of New Quadrangle, giving the college a façade to the High St. Brasenose has recently had to expand away from its cramped central site, and today many of the students live in Frewin Hall, New Inn Hall St (see p 117) and elsewhere.

The **Old Quadrangle** was begun in 1509; the gables, together with the battlements on the outside walls, were added 100 years later. On the north wall (right) is an attractive sundial (1719); instructions on how to read it correctly appear on a new aluminium panel at the entrance to the Hall. The **Hall** itself was panelled in 1684 (by Arthur Frogley) and there is an excellent carved representation of the royal coat of arms at the far end; a plaster ceiling of 1754 hides the original wooden roof. The brass door-knocker or 'brazen nose' which gives the college its name hangs above the high table.

In the small **Chapel Quadrangle**, reached through a passage in the southeast corner of Old Quad, are the Library and Chapel of 1656–63, the most ambitious Oxford buildings constructed during the Interregnum. They were designed by the mason John Jackson in an unusual hybrid style, part Gothic and part Classical, best savoured on the east front, which faces onto Radcliffe Square.

The **Chapel**, the last in Oxford to be built on the T-plan, replaced an earlier chapel alongside the Hall, now the Senior Common Room. The chapel roof is made of 15C timbers brought from the old Augustinian College of St. Mary in New Inn Hall St, but most of the medieval work is concealed by the spectacular plaster fan vault of 1659, colourfully painted by C.E. Kempe in 1895 as part of T.G. Jackson's restoration of the building. In the antechapel is a memorial to Walter Pater (Fellow, 1864–94), flanked by figures of Leonardo da Vinci, Michelangelo, Plato and Dante.

Beyond Chapel Quad is **New Quadrangle** (T.G. Jackson, 1882–1911), a good example of his eclectic style: for the High St front see Walk 3. A doorway on the west side of the quad (no adm.) leads to an unashamedly modernist block of rooms cunningly inserted into a very confined space by Powell and Moya in 1959–61: the first, and one of the best, of their many buildings in Oxford and Cambridge. It can be glimpsed from the southern end of Turl St.

Famous members

John Foxe, martyrologist, 1517–87
Robert Burton, author of *The Anatomy of Melancholy*, 1577–1640
Elias Ashmole, founder of the Ashmolean Museum, 1617–92
Thomas Traherne, mystic and poet, 1636–74
Walter Pater (see also Queen's College)
Field-Marshal Earl Haig, 1861–1928
John Buchan, statesman and novelist, 1875–1940
William Golding, novelist, 1911–93

Robert Runcie, Archbishop of Canterbury, 1921–2000
Michael Palin, writer and broadcaster, b. 1943
John Middleton, a Lancashire giant known as 'The Childe of Hale', visited Brasenose, then full of Lancashire students, in about 1613. A life-sized portrait of him was painted, and his huge hand carved on a stone (which Samuel Pepys paid two shillings to see on his visit in 1668). The college boat is always named *Childe of Hale* after him

The eastern side of Radcliffe Square is taken up by the Gothic-turreted north quadrangle of All Souls College, begun to the designs of Nicholas Hawksmoor in 1716 (see Walk 3). On the north side is the impressive complex of buildings now housing the Bodleian Library.

The Bodleian Library

The Bodleian is a complex of libraries rather than a single library, and at its heart lies the **Schools Quadrangle** (open Mon–Fri 09.00–17.00, closes 18.00 summer, Sat 09.00–12.30, ⌨ www.bodley.ox.ac.uk), built in 1613–19 by the Halifax masons Akroyd and Bentley (see Merton College) to house new lecture rooms arranged on two floors, with a gallery and book store on the third floor (the present Upper Reading Room of the Library); here the University's collection of portraits was originally displayed, thus making it England's first public art gallery.

The quadrangle was built in a highly conservative style of architecture, but the **Tower of the Five Orders** on the east side—an afterthought—is ornamented with paired Classical columns arranged in their proper hierarchy: in ascending order, Tuscan, Doric, Ionic, Corinthian and Composite. On the penultimate floor is a statue of James I, 'the wisest fool in Christendom' (by John Clark, 1620), giving a donation of his books to the University and attended by Fame blowing a trumpet. The royal coat of arms on the parapet is all but smothered by riotous strapwork ornament, incongruously placed between two Gothic pinnacles of different sizes; the larger of these pinnacles is over a spiral stairway which gave access to a room housing the University Archive. Over the Gothic-arched doorways in the courtyard are the Latin names of the former schools in which teaching and examinations took place. Since the opening of the Examination Schools in 1882 the whole building has been occupied by the Bodleian Library. Changing displays of some of the library's treasures are mounted in the

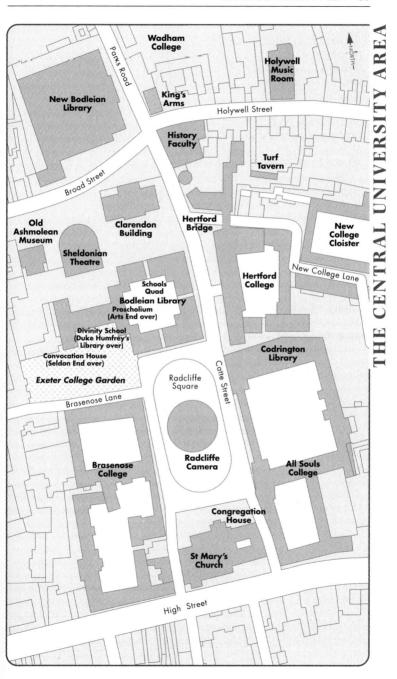

THE CENTRAL UNIVERSITY AREA

Oxford's university library

Oxford's first university library was housed in a room above the the early-14C Congregation House (see above), but after a large gift of books from Henry V's younger brother Humfrey, Duke of Gloucester (1391–1447), it was rehoused in 1488 in a larger room above the newly-constructed Divinity School. This still survives, but the books were dispersed in a spate of anti-Catholic frenzy after the Reformation and in 1602 the university library was refounded by, and named after, Sir Thomas Bodley, Fellow of Merton College and former Ambassador to the Netherlands. One of the oldest and most important libraries in the world, the Bodleian started with 2000 books, but it now now contains over six million, including about 6500 incunabula and 161,000 MS books of incalculable value.

The Bodleian is one of the six libraries which receive a copy of every book published in the UK, a right negotiated with the Stationers' Company by Sir Thomas Bodley himself. No book may be taken out, no matter how exalted the status of the would-be borrower (Charles I was refused, as was Cromwell). Readers are admitted by ticket and must be members of the University or suitably sponsored.

Exhibition Room in the former School of Natural Philosophy, on the south side of the Quad (for information about exhibitions ☎ 01865 277213/277216, ✉ www.bodley.ox.ac.uk/users/jd/exhibitions).

The entrance to the library is on the west side of the Schools Quadrangle, in a range of buildings (1610–12) covered with blind Gothic arcading in deliberate imitation of the 15C façade of the Divinity School and Duke Humfrey's Library behind; in front is a bronze statue by Hubert Le Sueur of the Earl of Pembroke, Chancellor of the University in the early 17C, brought here from Wilton House in 1722.

To visit the Library a guided tour must be taken (see below). Visitors are, however, admitted free of charge into the vestibule known as Proscholium, and also into the Divinity School which occupies the ground floor under the oldest part of the Library. (Open Mon–Fri 09.30–16.45, Sat 09.30–12.30, exc. some days at Christmas and Easter, ☎ 01865 277224.)

The **Proscholium** was built onto the 15C Divinity School in 1610–12 and now contains the Bodleian shop as well as the readers' entrance to the library. Opposite the entrance, in the middle of a wall which retains its 15C carved stone panelling is the doorway into the **Divinity School**. This magnificent room, one of the triumphs of late Gothic architecture in Europe, was begun in the 1420s, but the progress of the work was often interrupted due to lack of funding and the main feature, the exquisite stone-vaulted roof, was not introduced until 1480–83, probably by the local master-mason William Orchard. It is enriched with 455 carved bosses, some of them with with religious emblems, others bearing the arms or initials of King Edward IV, the University officers, the master mason and donors, the most important of whom was Thomas Kemp, Bishop of London; his emblem of three sheaves is repeated many times. Pendants with tiny carved figures of the Evangelists and Doctors of the Church hang down like stalactites from the transverse arches which bear the main weight, allowing the walls to be almost entirely given over to traceried windows letting in floods of light.

The Divinity School was the scene in 1555 of the examination of Cranmer, Latimer and Ridley, the 'Oxford Martyrs'; later, in 1669, it was renovated by Wren, who inserted the doorway on the north side and reinforced the buttresses to support the growing weight of books in Duke Humfrey's Library above. The wooden fittings at the far (west) end also date from 1669. They include two pulpits in which students and their examiners stood for the oral degree examinations which were the norm in Oxford before the 19C; the central pulpit for the moderator, which stood against the far wall, has been destroyed. The Divinity School ceased to be used for teaching and examinations in the 19C, and it is now a venue for receptions and a place of assembly before degree ceremonies (when it is closed to the public). Among the objects on view are Sir Thomas Bodley's chest, with its elaborate threefold lock mechanism, and a chair made out of timbers from Sir Francis Drake's ship the *Golden Hind*, given to the library in 1662.

Tickets for **guided tours** of the library are sold in the Divinity School (Apr–Oct Mon–Sat at 10.30, 11.30, also Mon–Fri 14.00 and 15.00, Nov–March Mon–Fri 14.00, 15.00, Sat 10.30, 11.30, University ceremonies permitting, ☎ 01865 277224, ✉ www.bodley.ox.ac.uk/history; adm. charge). They include the **Convocation House**, entered through a door at the west end of the Divinity School. It was built in the Gothic style in 1632–37, and retains its original dark wood fittings, including the canopied throne for the Vice-Chancellor which stands against the south window; the stone fan-vaulted roof dates from 1759. The Convocation House was given over to the House of Commons in Charles II's last Parliament (1681); on the King's arrival Parliament, to its intense dismay, was instantly dissolved. The room is still used for meetings and university ceremonies, including the annual admission of the proctors and assessor. Elections to the offices of Chancellor and Professor of Poetry, the franchise for which remains in the hands of Oxford MAs who are on the books of their colleges, are held either here or in the Divinity School.

The oldest parts of the Bodleian Library proper are **Arts End**, above the Proscholium, and **Duke Humfrey's Library**. The bookshelves of Arts End (1610–12) are arranged floor to ceiling against the walls—an innovation in the early 17C—and the upper shelves are reached by galleries supported on wooden columns. The University's coat of arms is painted on the wooden ceiling panels, with Thomas Bodley's arms at the intersections of the timbers; arabesques of Renaissance inspiration are painted on the cross-beams beams. At the entrance to Duke Humfrey's Library—now used by readers of manuscripts and early printed books—there are busts of Bodley (1605) and Charles I (1636, by Le Sueur). From here there is a vista of the library itself, built above the Divinity School in 1444, but dating in its present form from Bodley's restoration of 1598–1602. The shelves, which project from the walls in the traditional manner, are loaded with venerable and immensely weighty volumes, with high wooden benches and sloping reading desks calculated to keep the sleepiest scholar awake; the panelled ceiling is profusely decorated with painted coats of arms of the University, and some of the oldest of the University's collection of portraits hang on the walls. At the far end is **Selden End** (no adm.), built over the Convocation House to house books bequeathed by the lawyer John Selden (d. 1654).

To the north of the Schools Quadrangle is a paved courtyard which straddles the site of the northern city wall (a diagonal line on the paving slabs marks its position). Straight ahead is Nicholas Hawksmoor's monumental **Clarendon Building** (no adm.). It was built as a printing-house and offices for the Oxford University Press (formerly housed in the Sheldonian Theatre) in 1712–13, and was largely financed by the profits of Lord Clarendon's *History of the Great Rebellion* (1702–04); Clarendon's statue, by Francis Bird, is in a niche on the west side, and the lead statues of the Muses on the balustrade are by Sir James Thornhill (two are modern fibreglass replacements). The building was intended to evoke the grandeur of ancient Rome—though Hawksmoor never travelled abroad—and its grandeur owes much to the massive temple-like porticos of the Doric order, framing the north-south passage which originally separated the Learned and Bible Presses and which now serves as a public route from the Bodleian to Broad St. The Press moved to new premises in Walton St in 1830, and after many years of use as University offices, the Clarendon Building is now used as administrative offices by the ever-expanding Library.

The Hertford College bridge (popularly but incorrectly known as the Bridge of Sighs: see below) and the tower of New College can be seen to the east of the courtyard in front of the Clarendon building. To the west is the somewhat ungainly side elevation of the Sheldonian Theatre.

Sheldonian Theatre

Plan 1, H; open Mon–Sat 10.00–12.30 and 14.00–16.30 summer (closes 15.30 in winter); adm. charge; liable to close without notice for concerts, degree ceremonies or other functions; ☎ 01865 277299, ✉ www.sheldon.ox.ac.uk.

History

The Sheldonian Theatre was built in 1664–69, at the expense of Gilbert Sheldon, former Warden of All Souls and Archbishop of Canterbury. Its purpose was to provide a venue for University degree ceremonies, up to that time held in St. Mary's church and sometimes marred by rowdiness. The annual conferment of honorary degrees or Encaenia is held here at the end of the summer term (late June), the stately and complicated ceremonies made richly colourful by the full academic dress of the participants; the proceedings are still conducted in Latin (though nowadays translations are provided). The Theatre is also used for large public lectures and concerts.

The Sheldonian was the first major building designed by Christopher Wren, then Savilian Professor of Astronomy, and was inspired by the Theatre of Marcellus in Rome, which Wren only knew from pictures. As in all the theatres of Classical antiquity, the seating is arranged in a banked semicircle. The curved end faces Broad St; the straight end, facing the Divinity School to the south, where the stage would have been in a true classical theatre, is the formal entrance used only on ceremonial occasions. Its façade is accordingly more richly embellished than the rest of the building, with two orders of engaged Classical columns and two interlocking pediments; the Latin inscription on the lower frieze commemorates Sheldon's generosity, and his coat of arms is carved over the doorway.

On the Broad St side there are railings interrupted by stone plinths with busts of bearded men (renewed in 1868 and again in 1972), popularly called emperors' heads, but in fact herms, i.e. Roman boundary markers. The rather strangely proportioned exterior is dominated by the octagonal cupola added by Edward Blore in 1838; it replaces Wren's smaller cupola.

The splendid, galleried **interior** has been little altered since the 1660s. There is outstanding woodwork by Richard Cleer (for example, on the Vice-Chancellor's throne and the two rostra for the proctors with their projecting *fasces* symbolising authority). On the flat ceiling is a large allegorical painting (by Robert Streeter, Charles II's serjeant-painter, 1669) of the *Triumph of Truth* (in the centre), descending on the Arts and Sciences, and casting out Envy and 'brutish scoffing ignorance' (over the organ)—appropriate sentiments for a university whose belief in the cause of 'Church and King' had been vindicated by the Restoration of Charles II. A portrait of Wren hangs high on the wall to the right of the organ case.

It is well worth ascending to the cupola, from which there is a superb **view** of central Oxford. The roof timbers are not Wren's but date, like the cupola itself, from the restoration of 1838.

To the west of the Sheldonian is the Old Ashmolean, which contained the first purpose-built public museum in England and is now the home of the **Museum of the History of Science** (plan 1, H; open Tues–Sat 12.00–16.00, Sun 14.00–17.00, closed Christmas week & bank hols, ☎ 01865 277280, ✉ www. mhs.ox.ac.uk). It was built in 1679–83, probably to the designs of the local mason Thomas Wood, to house Elias Ashmole's collection of 'rarities' (now in the Ashmolean Museum in Beaumont St), as well as a lecture room for the Natural Sciences and a chemical laboratory, which occupied the basement. The formal entrance is through a superbly carved porch of paired Corinthian columns supporting a curved pediment, facing the Sheldonian, but nowadays visitors enter through the north entrance onto Broad St.

The nucleus of the museum is the Lewis Evans Collection of scientific instruments (given 1925), ranging from the world's largest collection of astrolabes—including an Islamic example from the 9C—to clocks and chemical apparatus, recently redisplayed. Also shown are items relating to the history of pharmacy and medicine, including the development of penicillin, and a blackboard used by Einstein.

On the opposite side of Broad St is the entrance to **Blackwell's** famous bookshop, the nucleus of which is in a pair of much-rebuilt early-18C houses. Next door, to the right, is the massive and graceless **New Bodleian Library**, (no adm.), built in 1937–40 to the designs of Sir Giles Gilbert Scott, architect of the Cambridge University Library and partly paid for by the Rockefeller Foundation. Of its 11 bookstacks, providing storage for some five million volumes, three are underground and connected with the old library across the road by a passage and conveyor-belt; there are also reading rooms for politics and economics, a map room and the library of the Indian Institute.

Opposite the entrance to the New Bodleian in Parks Road is the *King's Arms*, popular with students, dons and assorted Oxford eccentrics, where good, reasonably priced food can be had at most times of day. Immediately to the north, in Parks Rd, is Wadham College.

Wadham College

Plan 2, G; open term time 13.00–16.15, vacations 10.30–11.45, 13.00–16.15, Sun 09.00–16.15, ☎ 01865 277900, ✉ www.wadham.ox.ac.uk.

History

Founded in 1610 on the spacious site of the long-suppressed monastery of the Augustinian Friars by Dorothy, widow of Sir Nicholas Wadham, a west-country landed gentleman, Wadham was the last completely new Oxford college to be established before Keble in 1868 and it is now the most complete example of an early 17C college in either Oxford or Cambridge. The main buildings were erected by the Somerset mason William Arnold and remain almost exactly as they were when completed in 1613. Wadham's most illustrious phase was during the Interregnum, when many founder members of the future Royal Society, including the young Christopher Wren and Thomas Sydenham ('the English Hippocrates'), gathered round the scientifically minded Warden John Wilkins, Cromwell's brother-in-law. In more recent times the college acquired a reputation for radical politics and also some distinguished modern buildings.

Wadham is set back from the road and entered through a fan-vaulted gateway. The somewhat dour **Front Quad** is laid out on strictly symmetrical lines, with three-storeyed residential ranges to the north and south, and the hall and chapel on the east side, facing the entrance. Between them is a portal or 'tower of the orders' like that in the Fellows' Quad at Merton, enclosing doll-like statues of the founders (Sir Nicholas is dressed in armour), with the figure of James I above them. The **Chapel**, lit like the Hall by Gothic windows—a deliberate archaism—is entered from a passage in the northeast corner (left) of the quad, and follows the (for Oxford) traditional T plan. Apart from alterations at the east end by Edward Blore in 1832, it remains largely in its original state, with its superb Jacobean screen by Thomas Bolton, bristling with strapwork ornament, and much of the original stained glass, including the east window by Bernard van Linge (1622). The antechapel contains a splendid monument to Sir John Portman (d. 1624). The spacious **Hall** (often locked) is also largely unaltered, with the original hammerbeam roof (also by Bolton), and another exuberantly carved Jacobean screen; there are portraits of the founders and also of the architects Sir Christopher Wren and Thomas Graham Jackson, both members of the college.

To the north is the **Garden**, among the loveliest in Oxford, with sweeping lawns, stately copper beech and cedar trees and a glorious herbaceous border. Remains of Oxford's Civil War earth fortifications survive in the Fellows' Garden, behind the wall on the north side. In the part of the garden which lies behind the Hall and Chapel is an extraordinary statue of Sir Maurice Bowra (Warden, 1938–70), by John Doubleday, 'monumental but emergent in rather ectoplasmic style from the back of an armchair' (David Piper); Bowra, who described himself as 'a man more dined against than dining', was for many years a central figure in the social life of Oxford, and appears in the memoirs of countless *literati*. The Library (1978), to the east, is a somewhat graceless building in glass and concrete with a massive lead-clad roof (architects, Gillespie, Kidd and Coia).

Further south is the turreted Bowra Building (MacCormac, Jamieson and

Pritchard, 1990–92), one of the most impressive new collegiate buildings in Oxford; it contains an 'internal street' aligned on the tower of New College. The college's property extends south to Holywell St and includes the ingeniously planned former Blackwell's Music Shop (Gillespie, Kidd and Coia, 1970), now the *Next Door* restaurant.

Famous members

Robert Blake, admiral, 1599–1657
Christopher Wren, architect, 1632–1723
John Wilmot, 2nd Earl of Rochester, poet, 1648–80
T.G. Jackson, architect, 1835–1924
Francis Kilvert, diarist, 1841–1930
F.E. Smith (Lord Birkenhead), statesman, 1872–1930

C.B. Fry, cricketer and journalist, 1872–1956
Sir Thomas Beecham, conductor, 1879–1961
C. Day Lewis, poet, 1904–72
Michael Foot, Labour politician b. 1913
Melvyn Bragg, writer, broadcaster and Labour life peer, b. 1939

Facing the King's Arms at the corner of Catte St and Holywell St, to the south of Wadham, is the former Indian Institute (Basil Champneys, 1882–84), currently the home of the **History Faculty**; heads of tigers and an elephant are carved on the circular corner tower, which closes the view east from Broad St, and there is another elephant on the weathervane. **Holywell St**, which leads east from here, grew up as an extramural suburb, and contains a number of attractive 17C and 18C houses, though much of the south side is dominated by Gilbert Scott's gloomy Holywell Building for New College (1872–74), through which the college must be entered in the winter months (see below). The building on the north side which looks like a nonconformist chapel is the **Holywell Music Room** (plan 2, G; opened 1748, later remodelled), the first room in England to be built solely for musical performances; the chandeliers were given by George IV and were made for his coronation banquet in Westminster Hall. Almost opposite is Bath Place, from which a very narrow passage threads its way past the *Turf Tavern*—the most picturesque of Oxford's pubs—to New College Lane; the northern city wall looms impressively over the garden, which is much frequented by summer visitors.

A tortuous alleyway (St. Helen's Passage) leads from the Turf to **New College Lane**, from which the Sheldonian Theatre can be seen framed by **Hertford Bridge** (T.G. Jackson, 1913), reminiscent not so much of the Bridge of Sighs as of another well-known Venetian bridge, the Rialto. No. 7 New College Lane (turn left from St. Helen's Passage) was the home of the astronomer Edmund Halley (d. 1742) and his unpretentious observatory can be seen on the roof; opposite are the stone buildings of the former Hart Hall, now part of Hertford College (see below). Ahead, after two right-angled turns, is the gateway to New College, with the Warden's Barn (1402) on the right-hand side of the street and the south wall of the college's cloister opposite: a view which has not changed in its essentials since the early 15C.

New College

Plan 2, G; open Easter–mid-Oct 11.00–17.00: adm. charge; Oct–Easter 14.00–16.00, when entrance is through the lodge in Holywell St; ☎ 01865 249555, ✉ www.new.ox.ac.uk.

History

New College was founded in 1379 by William of Wykeham, Bishop of Winchester and former Chancellor of England, to provide for the advanced studies of young men educated at his other great foundation, Winchester College. His object was to repair the ravages of the Black Death among the ranks of the clergy, and to produce a supply of 'men of learning, fruitful to the Church ... the King, and the Realm'. From the beginning undergraduates were an important part of the foundation and in this as in many other respects New College set an important precedent. Entry was restricted to Wykehamists (pupils of Winchester College) up to the 19C; until 1834 its members were exempt from taking University examinations and received degrees on the Warden's word alone (a system clearly open to abuse). Although New College played a prominent part in the 16C revival of learning, its wealth and privilege afterwards led to a period of decline which was not reversed until the University reforms of the 19C. It then became well-known as a nursery of civil servants and other public figures.

The buildings stand just within the old town wall, on land bought by Wykeham after the original population had been decimated by the Black Death. The wealth and prestige of the founder enabled his designs to be carried out in full and the buildings and layout exercised a great influence on later collegiate architecture and planning in both Oxford and Cambridge. They are echoed on a smaller scale in the sister foundation at Winchester; the master mason in both colleges was almost certainly William Wynford, who also worked for Wykeham at Winchester Cathedral.

The **gate tower**, in New College Lane, the oldest in Oxford, carries statues of the Virgin, the angel Gabriel and William of Wykeham; the first floor has always formed part of the Warden's lodgings. The **Great Quadrangle**, inhabitable by 1386, was the first in Oxford to be planned as a single entity and it remains one of the most impressive, despite the visually unfortunate addition of a third storey and battlements to the west, south and east ranges in 1674 and 1711. The south side of the quad is made up of residential accommodation arranged around staircases, but the formidably impressive north side (left on entry from New College Lane) is made up of the Hall and Chapel, placed side by side, with a Muniment Tower for the college treasures in the north-east corner. This arrangement was followed in many later colleges.

The **Chapel**, the first major example of Perpendicular architecture in Oxford, is entered through a dark passageway in the north-west corner of the quad (left on entering). It is planned in the shape of a letter T, with the antechapel separated from the choir by a 19C wooden screen. The tall, spacious antechapel retains its late 14C **stained glass**, except in the west window, which was painted with representations of the *Nativity* and the *Seven Virtues* by Thomas Jervais to designs by Sir Joshua Reynolds (1777); some of the glass it displaced is in York

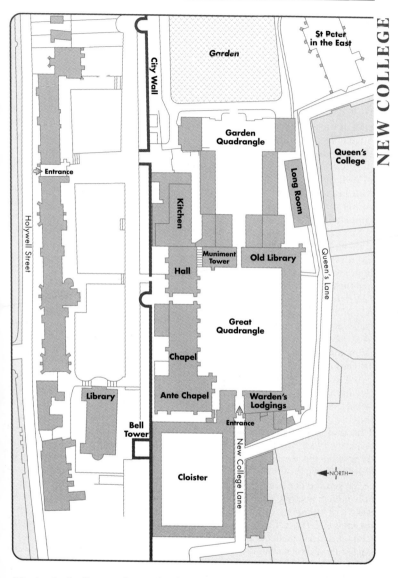

Minster. In the floor on the north side are several 15C and 16C brasses, some of fine quality, and high up on the south wall two 'squints', from which the Warden could observe services and disputations. Below are memorials, by Eric Gill, to members of the college, both English and German, killed in the First World War, and under the west window is Jacob Epstein's compelling and somewhat disturbing stone figure of *Lazarus Rising from the Dead* (1948). Opposite, on either side of the screen, are two large late 15C panels of the *Annunciation* by Bartolomeo

Montagna, and above is the organ, by Grant, Degens and Bradbeer (1969), in a modernistic case by George Pace.

The **choir** has suffered from the loss of most of its original medieval glass in the 18C; the present windows, by William Price and William Peckitt (1736–71) are a poor substitute. Otherwise, most of what can be seen dates from 1877–81, when Gilbert Scott carried out a thorough remodelling, including the construction of a new roof with a steeper pitch than the original (a stipulation of the college fellows, not the architect); the reredos, occupying the whole of the east wall, with its ranks of anaemic saints and prophets, was designed by J.L. Pearson. The original armrests and misericords of the upper row of seating survive, however; the **misericords** are of excellent quality, and include representations of a lecture, scholars fighting with daggers, and one traditionally said to show William of Wykeham welcoming scholars to Oxford. On the north (left) side of the **sanctuary** is a painting of *St. James* by El Greco. Next to it, William of Wykeham's crozier of silver-gilt set with jewels and enamelwork is housed in a glass case; opposite is a posthumous portrait of the founder.

New College boasts the oldest choral foundation in either Oxford or Cambridge, with 16 boy choristers augmented by choral scholars and lay-clerks; the services, continuing a tradition inaugurated by Wykeham himself, are of a very high musical quality (term-time only: Sun 18.00, weekdays exc. Wed 18.15), and the choir has issued many superb recordings.

A right turn from the chapel doorway leads to the **Cloister**, an afterthought whose building necessitated the right-angled kink in New College Lane. The walkways shelter some of the original early 14C figures of saints from the tower of St. Mary the Virgin church, removed following a restoration of 1894, and there are memorial tablets to many old members; on the north side is the **Bell Tower** (1396–97), built onto the town wall.

The **Hall**, reached by a staircase in the Muniment Tower in the Great Quadrangle, has a screen and linenfold panelling of 1533–35, and a roof by Gilbert Scott (1862–65). An archway under the Old Library on the east side of the Great Quad leads into the open-ended **Garden Quadrangle**, added between 1682 and 1707; hidden away behind its south range is the late 14C Long Room or latrine block which backs onto Queen's Lane. The Garden Quad—in fact a three-sided space, not a true quadrangle—is separated from the garden by a beautiful wrought-iron screen of 1711, substantially repaired in 1894.

The **garden** is enclosed on the north and east sides by the best-preserved section of the 13C **town wall**, complete with ramparts and semicircular bastions (it is even more impressive when viewed from the north). The large artificial viewing mound in the middle of the garden dates from the late 16C; the steps leading up it are a recent creation, the formal arrangement of the rest of the garden having been long swept away.

To the north of the Chapel is the architecturally unremarkable Library (by Hubert Worthington, 1939). The buildings facing north onto Holywell St were erected to the designs of Gilbert Scott and Basil Champneys between 1872 and 1896; in the centre is the Robinson Tower, through which the college is entered when the gatehouse in New College Lane is closed.

Famous members

Henry Chichele, founder of All Souls College, 1362?–1443
William Waynflete, founder of Magdalen College, 1395?–1486
William Grocyn, scholar and humanist, 1446–1519
Thomas Ken, one of the Seven Bishops imprisoned by James II in 1688, 1637–1711
Sydney Smith, writer and wit, 1771–1845
W.A. Spooner (Warden), originator of the spoonerism, 1844–1930
H.A.L. Fisher, historian, 1865–1940
Gilbert Murray, classical historian, 1866–1957

John Galsworthy, novelist and playwright, 1867–1933
Maurice Bowra, classicist and later Warden of Wadham, 1898–1971
Lord David Cecil, literary critic, 1902–86
Hugh Gaitskell, leader of the Labour Party, 1906–63
Richard Crossman, Labour politician, 1907–74
Tony Benn, Labour politician, b 1925
John Fowles, novelist, b. 1926
Hugh Grant, actor, b. 1960
Also numerous bishops and Whitehall mandarins

New College Lane continues to the east as Queens Lane, eventually reaching the High St (see Walk 3). Those who wish to return to the starting point of the walk should walk back along New College Lane to **Catte St**. At the junction of the two streets is is one of Oxford's best architectural views, with the box-like bulk of the Bodleian Library, the circular Radcliffe Camera and the spire of the University Church juxtaposed in sharp perspective. Immediately on the left in Catte St is the entrance to Hertford College.

Hertford College

Plan 2, G/4, A; open 10.00–12.00, 14.00–dusk, ☎ 01865 279400, ✉ www.hertford.ox.ac.uk.

History

One of the more recent college foundations, Hertford stands on the site of an academic hall known as Hart Hall, which traced its origins back to the 13C, but it was not granted collegiate status until 1740. The new college was poorly endowed, and in 1816 it was amalgamated with the more flourishing Magdalen Hall (see Magdalen College), which moved into its buildings six years later. But in 1874, following a generous benefaction from the banker Thomas Charles Baring, the college was refounded, and it was subsequently greatly enlarged by the ubiquitous T.G. Jackson in a fascinating pot-pourri of architectural styles. Because of its cramped site, Hertford has recently had to expand on the south side of the River Thames, close to Folly Bridge.

The Catte St front is made up of three sections, with Jackson's first-floor Hall (1887–88), lit by three Venetian windows, sandwiched between two much plainer blocks of 1818–22 (architect E. Garbett). The entrance, under the Hall, leads into the main quadrangle, with the unremarkable (and much remodelled) late 16C and 17C buildings of Hart Hall opposite on the north and east sides. Much more interesting are Jackson's contributions: the **Hall** (no adm.), reached by a spectacular staircase loosely modelled on one in the chateau at Blois in France, and the surprisingly spacious **Chapel** (1906–08; sometimes locked), based on Italian quattrocento models, but with some excellent craftsmanship (eg, the stalls) in the Arts and Crafts manner. It completely dwarfs the former Chapel of 1716 (now the Library) to the west.

The Bridge (Jackson, 1913), spanning New College Lane, connects the core of the college to the buildings of the **North Quadrangle**. They too were designed by Jackson (1901–03 and later), this time in a loosely neo-Jacobean style, and incorporate the much-rebuilt octagonal **Chapel of Our Lady**, built c 1520 adjoining one of the gates in the town wall; a somewhat mutilated carving of the Annunciation of this date can be seen over the doorway to Catte St.

Famous members
John Donne, poet and divine, 1572–1631 (Hart Hall)
Charles James Fox, Whig states-
man, 1749–1806 (Hertford College)
Evelyn Waugh, novelist, 1903–66 (Hertford College)

A left turn out of Hertford College leads back into Radcliffe Square.

2 ~ SOUTH OF CARFAX

This walk starts at Carfax, the busy heart of the city (see p 88). The street known as **St. Aldate's** leads south from here to Folly Bridge, the site of the 'oxen ford' which gave Oxford its name. On the east (left-hand) side is the **Town Hall**, built to the designs of H.T. Hare in 1893–97. The façade is a splendidly ornate exercise in the neo-Jacobean style and there is a dramatic staircase leading up to the Main Hall, which is richly adorned with decorative plasterwork. A copy of Pietro da Cortona's *Rape of the Sabines* hangs in the Assembly Room, overlooking the street, and a selection of the civic plate, going back to the 17C, is kept in a vaulted 15C undercroft, formerly part of the medieval Knapp Hall (open on request, ☎ 01865 249811); the former police court has formed the backdrop to many films. Though not normally open to the public at the time of writing, there are currently plans to turn the building over to community uses and to allow more public access.

The southern part of the Town Hall building, formerly the Public Library, houses the excellent, though somewhat cramped, **Museum of Oxford** (plan 3, B; open Tues–Fri 10.00–16.30, Sat 10.00–17.00, Sun 12.00–16.00; entrance in Blue Boar St; adm. charge; ☎ 01865 252761, ✉ www.oxford.gov.uk/ museum). This tells the history of Oxford through pictures, models, old maps, prints, etc. and gives proper weight to the town as well as the gown. The displays include (in the downstairs galleries) a Roman pottery kiln from the site of Churchill Hospital in Headington; the town's charter with its seal of 1191 (the oldest of any English town); objects from excavated medieval houses; the original 16C wooden figures from Carfax clock tower; part of the Jacobean screen of Exeter College Chapel (see p 90); and Jan Wyck's retrospective bird's-eye view of the siege of Oxford in the Civil War. Upstairs there is a large late 17C view of the city from the south-west; a reconstruction of an 18C gentleman commoner's study from Christ Church; rooms from 19C and 20C houses; part of the Keble College barge (1898); and the counter of a draper's shop from 26 St. Ebbes.

To the south, past Blue Boar St, is the impressive façade of **Christ Church**, physically Oxford's largest, and architecturally its most impressive, college. It dates mainly from 1525–29, and the ornate lower portion of the gateway is an excellent example of Tudor-Gothic work; the tower above (Tom Tower, one of Oxford's most famous landmarks) was added to the designs of Sir Christopher Wren in 1681–82, and there is some very early Renaissance carving of the the 1520s underneath the first-floor oriel at the southern end of the façade, opposite Brewer St. The visitor's entrance (except for those attending Cathedral services) is further south and is approached through the wrought-iron gateway into the **War Memorial Garden** (1925), commemorating members of Christ Church killed in the First World War; note the inscription from John Bunyan's *Pilgrim's Progress* set into the paving at the entrance and also the excellent view of the Hall, begun in 1525. Beyond is the Broad Walk of Christ Church Meadow and on its north side is the Meadow Building through which the college is normally entered.

Christ Church

The entrance to Christ Church (plan 3, B/D; 4, A/C; open Mon–Sat 09.30–17.30, Sun 12.00–17.30, closes 16.30 in winter; adm. charge; ☎ 01865 286573, 🖾 www.chch.ox.ac.uk) is through the ponderous Victorian Gothic **Meadow Building** (T.N. Deane, 1863–66). It gives access to an irregular courtyard, from which a dark passage leads into the vaulted Perpendicular **cloister** of the former St. Frideswide's Priory, dating in its present form from c 1499. On the upper floor of the south side was the refectory, later the college library, now divided into undergraduate rooms.

The Catheral
To the east was the dormitory and chapter house and to the north the priory church, now the Cathedral; the west side was pulled down in 1525. It was in the cloister that Archbishop Cranmer was formally 'degraded' in 1556, being publicly insulted, stripped of his vestments and having his hair shorn. From the west side a passageway leads past the hall staircase and into Tom Quad (see below, p 75), on the right-hand side of which is the entrance to the cathedral.

History of the Cathedral
Christ Church Cathedral is the smallest of England's ancient cathedrals, but is the mother church of the largest diocese, encompassing the counties of Berkshire, Buckinghamshire and Oxfordshire. Many additions and alterations have been made since the original construction, which took place c 1160–1200, and the result is a highly idiosyncratic building in which most of the main phases of medieval church architecture can be seen in close prox-

imity. The rather squat spire, one of the oldest in England, was added in the early 13C; it is best viewed from the cloister. The chapels on the north side of the choir followed in the 13C and 14C, the superb late Perpendicular choir vault is usually reckoned to date from c 1500, and the remodelled neo-Norman east end from the time of Sir Gilbert Scott's restoration in 1870–76; the three western bays of the nave were destroyed by Wolsey to make way for the quadrangle of his college. There are outstanding stained and painted glass windows and there is also a good collection of fittings and monuments. Christ Church has a choral foundation dating back to Wolsey's time and **choral services** are held throughout the year (Sun 11.15 and 18.00; weekdays, exc. Mon, 18.00), with the excellent Cathedral choir singing during University term and for some weeks on either side of it, and at major festivals.

The **west entrance** was constructed to the designs of G.F. Bodley in 1872–73, and occupies the site of the western bays of the nave which were pulled down by Cardinal Wolsey when he laid out Tom Quad in 1525–29; had he not fallen foul of Henry VIII the rest of the building would quickly have followed suit. The eastward vista through the screen to the high altar shows the basic Romanesque structure of the building, but you can also see some of the effects of the later alterations which have made Christ Church such a fascinating compendium of ecclesiastical art and architecture over eight centuries: notice especially the elaborate late Gothic vault over the chancel and the splendid Victorian floors, woodwork and stained glass. The massive piers of the late 12C **arcades** are alternately round and octagonal and an illusion of height is given by the unusual—and visually not altogether satisfactory—placing of the triforium inside the main arches, with a secondary arch below (as at Romsey Abbey, Hampshire).

The **nave** has a restored early 16C timber roof and a pulpit and organ screen of c 1630; the organ case dates in part from 1680, but the organ itself is by Rieger (1979). There are monuments on the piers to the philosopher George Berkeley, Bishop of Cloyne (d. 1753; epitaph by Alexander Pope) and to Dean Henry Aldrich, architect of Peckwater Quad (d. 1710: monument by Henry Cheere 1732—note the grinning skull). The seating in both nave and choir faces inwards, collegiate-fashion, and dates from Gilbert Scott's restoration, as does the excellent marble floor and the ironwork (by Skidmore).

The normal visitors' route starts in the **north aisle**, with its 12C rib vault and its spectacular painted glass west window by Abraham van Linge (c 1630) depicting Jonah contemplating Nineveh from underneath a gourd tree.

The original Romanesque character of the church can most easily be appreciated in the **north transept**, but the chapels leading out of it to the east are Gothic. To the left (north) is the **Latin Chapel**, built in the early 14C to house the tomb of St. Frideswide. The early 16C oak stalls were originally in the chancel and the north wall has early 14C (Decorated) windows with flowing tracery and well-preserved stained glass of the same date; the window (third from the left) depicting the saint marks the position of her shrine, the fragmentary remains of which were dug up in the 19C and 20C and were reconstructed on this site in 2002. Overlooking it is a richly carved 15C oak watching-chamber or chantry, from which guard may have been kept on the treasures of the shrine, and between the piers to the south are three 14C tomb-chests with effigies, one of which retains its original colouring. The east window was designed in 1858 by

A college and cathedral

Known familiarly as 'the House', from its Latin name, *Aedes Christi*, Christ Church is physically the largest and architecturally the most magnificent college in Oxford. It was founded by Thomas Wolsey as Cardinal College in 1525, on the site of the Priory of St. Frideswide, a 12C foundation of Augustinian canons which stood near the place where Frideswide, Oxford's patron saint, established a community of nuns in the 8C. Her cult attracted a local following, but the priory was never one of England's major monasteries and, when Wolsey suppressed it, it housed only a handful of canons.

Wolsey's original intention was to raze the buildings to the ground and to replace them with a vast new quadrangle containing a new Hall and Chapel facing each other and a gatehouse on the street façade. But only the Hall and the lower part of the gatehouse were built in Wolsey's lifetime and much of the old Priory, including most of the church, was allowed to survive after his fall from favour in 1529. Henry VIII refounded the college in 1532, but it did not prosper and it was refounded yet again, in 1546, under its present name, with a larger endowment derived mostly from the lands of suppressed monasteries, including Osney Abbey to the west of the city. The old priory church, shorn of its three western bays, now became both the cathedral of the new diocese of Oxford and the college chapel—a unique arrangement—and the Dean became head of both the college and cathedral chapter, some of whose members were and still are holders of regius professorships (in divinity, etc) founded by the King. The Dean is appointed by the Crown; the reigning sovereign is also the college Visitor. The royal connection was strengthened during the Civil War, when Charles I made the deanery his residence.

Wolsey's quadrangle (Tom Quad) remained unfinished until after the Restoration of 1660 and his chapel—intended to rival that of King's College, Cambridge—was never built. But the college flourished and developed strong links with some of the older public schools, notably Westminster and Eton, attracting generations of often well-connected undergraduates, some of whom went on to become famous in the annals of British history and politics and in the cultural and religious life of the nation. Substantial additions to the original buildings were made in the Classical style in the 18C (Peckwater and Canterbury Quadrangles), and there were further extensions in the 19C and 20C. Christ Church also attracted generous donations of books, manuscripts and pictures from its old members, and now boasts the finest art collection of any Oxford or Cambridge college, beautifully displayed and regularly open to the public.

Benjamin Woodward, the architect of the University Museum, and contains brilliantly coloured stained glass by the young Edward Burne-Jones depicting scenes from the life of St. Frideswide, quite different in character from his other, later, windows in the Cathedral. Against a pier at the west entrance to the chapel is a monument to Robert Burton, author of *The Anatomy of Melancholy* (d. 1640).

The **Lady Chapel**, to the right of the Latin Chapel, dates from the mid-12C and is a good example of Early English Gothic; its unusual placing is explained by the fact that the the canons could not expand the church to the east because of the proximity of the city wall. The east window, designed by Burne-Jones and exe-

CHRIST CHURCH CATHEDRAL

10   10   10

Latin Chapel   5   9

North
Transept   11 11   8

Lady Chapel   7

North Choir Aisle   6

12

Entrance
from   13   Nave   Tower   Choir   4
Tom Quad

1   South   South Choir Aisle   3
Transept

Visitors' exit   St Lucy's
Chapel   2

Slype

Chapter House
(shop)

Cloister

1 Three Virtues window (Burne-Jones)
2 Becket window (14C)
3 Edith Liddell window (Burne-Jones)
4 High Altar
5 St Frideswide Shrine
6 St Cecilia window (Burne-Jones)
7 Vyner Memorial window (Burne-Jones)
8 Watching Chamber (15C)
9 St Frideswide window (Burne-Jones)
10 14C stained glass windows
11 14C monuments
12 Jonah window (Van Linge)
13 Organ loft

cuted by Morris & Co, commemorates Frederic Vyner, who was murdered by brigands in Greece in 1870. Burne-Jones also designed the equally beautiful St. Cecilia window (1874) at the east end of the **north choir aisle**, each of the main lights occupied by an elegantly swaying angel holding a musical instrument.

The east end of the **sanctuary** dates from Scott's restoration (his round-arched windows, based on tenuous archaeological evidence, replace a large late medieval window); the excellent stained glass is by Clayton & Bell, and the reredos is by Bodley. But the main feature of the chancel is its glorious **vault**, a *tour de force* of late medieval inventiveness, with stone pendants hanging down with no visible means of support from the intricately carved lierne ceiling; the designer may have been the local mason and quarry owner William Orchard.

The **south choir aisle** contains a bust commemorating the high-church Anglican divine Edward Bouverie Pusey, a canon of the cathedral (d. 1882), and the Burne-Jones window at the east end (1878) commemorates Edith Liddell, daughter of the then Dean and sister of Alice in Wonderland. The painted glass window just before the south transept (attributed to Bernard van Linge, c 1630) shows Robert King, first Bishop of Oxford (d. 1557) in full regalia. King's monument is on the north side of **St. Lucy's Chapel**, which leads out of the south transept and which contains some excellent 14C stained glass in the Decorated east window; in the upper lights are the arms of England and France, in the central light the martyrdom of Thomas à Becket and to the right St. Martin dividing his cloak to give to a beggar. The chapel and south transept contain several monuments to cavaliers killed in the Civil War, including one to Viscount Grandison (d. 1643), father of Charles II's notorious mistress Barbara Villiers. A doorway at the end of the **south aisle**, next to Burne-Jones's west window depicting the *Three Virtues* (1870), leads back into the cloister.

Before exploring the college proper it is worth seeing the early 13C **Chapter House** (now the cathedral shop and treasury), entered from the east walk of the cloister through an impressive mid-12C Romanesque doorway. The graceful interior is lit by tall lancet windows and some restored fragments of medieval painting can be seen on the rib-vaulted roof; the once-uncluttered interior has been filled with display cases containing specimens of plate from the cathedral and diocese.

The College

It is best to begin the tour of the college in the Hall, which is entered under the handsome **Bell Tower** (by Bodley, 1876–79) at the southeast corner of Tom Quad. It is on the first floor, and is reached by a spacious stone **staircase**, built by James Wyatt in 1805; the splendid fan vault, of 1638, is one of the best examples of the survival of medieval building traditions in post-Renaissance Oxford. Under the staircase is the entrance to Wolsey's vast kitchen, which is still in use (no adm.); an election slogan of 1829 reading 'No Peel' is burned into a doorway at the stair foot, referring to Sir Robert Peel, the future Prime Minister and an old member of the college. In the ante-hall at the top of the stairs is a seated statue of Dean Jackson, a major university reformer, by Chantrey (1820).

The **Hall**, the largest in Oxford (115ft by 40ft), was completed in Wolsey's time and has a sumptuously carved and gilded hammer-beam roof of timber, possibly altered after a fire in 1720. The central bosses bear the arms of the see of Winchester, of which Wolsey was bishop, encircled by the Garter; the arms of five more of Wolsey's sees appear, along with his cardinal's hat, in the heraldic glass (partly original) of the west window. The remaining stained-glass windows date from the 1880s (Burlison and Grylls) and contain portraits of members of the college, including Charles Dodgson (Lewis Carroll), along with characters from the *Alice in Wonderland* books (south wall). The Hall features in the recent *Harry Potter* film.

The **pictures** constitute a miniature National Portrait Gallery; note especially (north wall: right on entering) the philosopher John Locke (after Kneller), Sir John Skynner (by Gainsborough), W.E. Gladstone (by Millais); (west wall, behind the high table) Henry VIII (17C copy after Holbein), flanked by Elizabeth I and Wolsey, Dean Fell (after Lely), Dean Simpson (by Graham Sutherland); (south wall) Richard Robinson, Bishop of Armagh (by Reynolds), George Canning (by Lawrence), Dean Liddell (by Watts); (east wall, on either side of entrance) Charles Dodgson (by Herkomer), William Penn, John Wesley (by Romney) and W.H. Auden. A bust of Queen Elizabeth II is placed beneath Henry VIII over the high table.

Tom Tower, Christ Church

Tom Quad was laid out by the master masons Henry Redman and John Lubyns in 1525, but was left unfinished when Wolsey fell from power; the springing of the vault of the unbuilt cloister can still be seen along the walls. The north side, where the chapel was to go, contains houses built for the canons of the Cathedral in the 1660s and **Tom Tower**, one of Oxford's main landmarks, followed in 1681–82. It was designed by Sir Christopher Wren, who wrote that he had 'resolved that it ought to be Gothic, to agree with the founder's work', but that he had 'not continued so busy as he began'—a reference to the ornate late Gothic work visible on the St. Aldate's front. The tower derives its name from the huge bell (Great Tom, 6¼ tons, last recast 1680) taken from Osney Abbey. It rings 101 times every evening at 21.05 (21.00 by the Oxford meridian), once for each member of the original foundation, and was formerly the signal that all undergraduates should be within their colleges and the gates closed. The statue of Wolsey was carved by Francis Bird in 1719.

The sunken **courtyard** was made in 1668, the spoil being used to create Broad Walk, and in the centre of the pool, originally the college reservoir, is a 1928 copy of Giovanni da Bologna's *Mercury* on a pedestal by designed by Sir Edwin Lutyens; the statue replaces one toppled from its plinth by the future Prime Minister Lord Derby in 1817.

In the northeast corner of Tom Quad is **Fell's Tower**, named after John Fell, Dean 1660–86, and the subject of the rhyme: 'I do not like thee Dr Fell/The reason why I cannot tell/But this I know, and know full well/I do not like thee Dr Fell'. Fell completed the building and layout of Tom Quad in the late 17C, but the upper stages of the tower were added to Bodley's designs in the time of Dean Liddell; the tower displays statues of both Deans. Beneath it, Kill Canon Passage (so called for its draughty cold) leads into **Peckwater Quad**, built on the site of the older Peckwater Inn to the designs of Dean Aldrich in 1707–14. Aldrich had travelled in Italy and the palazzo-like façades of the west, north and east ranges, built for sons of noblemen and gentleman commoners, apply the Italian Renaissance idiom to the design of an Oxford quadrangle with calm assurance.

The south side is taken up by the magnificent **Library** (no adm.), begun in 1717 but not finished internally until the 1760s. Described by one contemporary as 'the finest library that belongs to any Society in Europe', it was designed by George Clarke, Fellow of All Souls, after Aldrich's death, and has a monumental façade articulated by giant Corinthian columns enclosing an Ionic order on the ground floor—an arrangement which echoes Michelangelo's mid-16C *palazzi* on the Capitol hill in Rome. The ground floor was formerly an open arcade, but was enclosed as an art gallery in 1769 (it is now part of the library). The vestibule is lined with busts of past royal Visitors and distinguished members of the college (one of J.L. Lowe, Dean 1939–59, is by Epstein), and leads to the staircase, presided over by a statue of John Locke (by Rysbrack, 1757) and a bust of Dean Aldrich.

The spacious **Upper Library** is notable for its exuberant Rococo plasterwork (by Thomas Roberts of Oxford) and for the splendid woodwork of 1756–63, by John Phillips and George Shakespear. The Library houses a priceless collection of books and MSS, and such interesting relics as Wolsey's cardinal's hat (acquired from Horace Walpole) and his chair, John Evelyn's diary, Edward Gibbon's miniature travelling library and Lewis Carroll memorabilia.

To the west of Peckwater Quad is **Blue Boar Quad** (Powell and Moya,

1964–67), one of the more attractive manifestations of Modern Movement architecture in Oxford, with striking elevations of Portland stone; it is not open to visitors, but the north elevation can be seen from Blue Boar St. **Canterbury Quad**, to the east of Peckwater, was built in a restrained Classical manner by James Wyatt in 1775–78 on the site of Canterbury College, a monastic establishment dissolved after the Reformation. It is entered from the east by Wyatt's imposing **Canterbury Gate** (1775–78), the east front of which is treated as a triumphal arch—a most effective contribution to the Oxford townscape—and on the south side of Canterbury Quad is the entrance to the Christ Church Picture Gallery.

Famous members

Sir Philip Sidney, poet and soldier, 1554–86

William Penn, Quaker, founder of Pennsylvania, 1644–1718

John Locke, philosopher, 1632–1704

John Wesley, founder of Methodism, 1703–91, and his brother Charles, hymn-writer

George Canning, Prime Minister, 1770–1827

Sir Robert Peel, Prime Minister, 1788–1850

Rev. E.B. Pusey, theologian, 1800–82

W.E. Gladstone, three times Prime Minister, 1809–98

John Ruskin, art critic and social philosopher, 1819–1900

Lord Salisbury, Prime Minister, 1830–1903

C.L. Dodgson (Lewis Carroll), 1832–98

Edward VII as Prince of Wales

Lord Halifax, Foreign Secretary at the outbreak of World War II, 1881–1959

Sir Anthony Eden, Lord Avon, Prime Minister, 1897–1977

W.H. Auden, poet, 1907–73

H.R. Trevor-Roper, historian, 1914–2003

Christ Church Picture Gallery

Open Mon–Sat 10.30–13.00, 14.00–17.30, Sun 14.00–17.30, closes 16.30 Oct–Mar; separate adm. charge; ☎ 01865 276172, ✉ www.chch.ox.ac.uk/gallery. Entry can be made directly through Canterbury Gate.

The bulk of the collection comprises three main bequests: from General John Guise (d. 1765), W.T. Fox-Strangways (in 1828 and 1834) and from the family of the writer Walter Savage Landor in 1897. Italian medieval, Renaissance and Baroque art is especially well represented, but there are also good examples of the Flemish and Dutch schools and there is a superb collection of Old Master drawings, selections of which are shown on rotation. The gallery was ingeniously fitted into a piece of ground to the north of the Deanery Garden by Powell and Moya in 1968 and, despite the modern style of architecture (invisible from the outside), it retains the agreeable air of a well-displayed and not over-frequented private collection.

The Fox-Strangways pictures are mostly in the **Primitives Room**, to the right of the well-lit passageway which looks out onto a garden. They include Italian altarpieces of the 13C, 14C and 15C, a panel with four angels playing musical instruments (Florentine School c.1340–50), a *Calvary* by Giovanni di Paolo, a *Wounded Centaur* by Filippino Lippi, a *Virgin and Child* by a follower of Piero della Francesca, paintings of Sybils by Filippino Lippi and (possibly) Botticelli, a fragment of a *Lamentation* by Hugo van der Goes, and a late 15C profile portrait of Beatrice d'Este.

The **Great Room** contains the bulk of the Guise pictures and some others (Guise himself is represented in the form of a bust and a portrait by Reynolds, to the left of the entrance from the Primitives Room); taken together they give an admirable picture of 18C and early 19C artistic taste. Particularly noteworthy are Bassano's Titian-esque *Christ crowned with thorns*, Tintoretto's powerful *Martyrdom of St. Lawrence* and a portrait of an unknown man, Annibale Carracci's *Butcher's Shop* and picture of a man drinking (Guise's collection contained no fewer than 12 paintings and 43 drawings by the Carracci brothers), Van Dyck's early *Continence of Scipio*, a work of great Baroque brio, and Bernardo Strozzi's *Judith with the Head of Holofernes*; there are also works by Palma Giovane, Lorenzo Lotto, Veronese and Salvator Rosa (two rocky landscapes and a picture of a hermit). Outside in the passageway usually hangs a classical capriccio by Sebastiano and Marco Ricci.

The **South Room** contains smaller 17C and 18C pictures, including a tiny portrait by Frans Hals and a picture of one of the college servants by Riley; there are also works by or attributed to Jan van Scorel, Domenichino and Girolamo da Treviso. But the greatest strength of the collection lies in the drawings, mostly from the Guise bequest, including works by Leonardo, Raphael, Michelangelo, Titian, van der Goes, Rubens, Rembrandt and Claude; changing exhibitions of these are regularly shown in the **Print Room**.

The Canterbury gate leads into Oriel Square, on the far side of which is Oriel College.

Oriel College

Plan 4, A; usually closed to visitors, ☎ 01865 276555, ✉ www.oriel.ox.ac.uk.

History

One of the oldest Oxford collegiate foundations, Oriel was founded as St. Mary's College in 1324 by Adam de Brome, almoner to Edward II, and rector of St. Mary the Virgin church, which was used at first as the college chapel. Two years later, in 1326, the college was refounded by the King himself, who gave it the Hospital of St. Bartholomew in Cowley Rd (see p 101) as a source of income. Thereafter it was known officially as the King's College; the name Oriel—meaning an upper-floor bay window—derives from a house on the site named La Oriole acquired in 1329. The medieval buildings were replaced by the present front quadrangle in 1620–42; a new library was built in 1788–89 and in 1902 the college took over one of the last surviving academic halls, St. Mary Hall, on the south side of the High St. Oriel enjoyed a formidable reputation for theological scholarship in the early 19C and was the main nursery of the Oxford (Tractarian) Movement, which transformed the Anglican Church.

The **Front Quadrangle** (1620–42, and little altered) is a hybrid part-Gothic, part-Renaissance ensemble, with Gothic elements predominating. Ornamental gables of Flemish derivation line the roof and the Hall and Chapel are lit by

Gothic-arched windows too. A flight of steps leads up to the **Hall**, which has a handsome hammerbeam roof; over the porch, with its inscription 'Regnante Carolo' (In the reign of Charles I), are statues of Edward II and James I (or possibly Charles I), and above them is the Virgin and Child: a provocatively high-church statement for its time. The **Chapel** (right) has a plain interior with its original 17C furnishings intact, including the richly carved communion rails and a recently restored lectern; the painting of *Christ Carrying the Cross* is by Bernard van Orley, and there is good late Victorian stained glass of 1885 by Wooldrich and Powell.

The **Back Quadrangle** (left) is on the site of the original garden. On the north side is the **Library**, a handsome palazzo-like building by James Wyatt (1788–89), with an engaged Ionic order over a rusticated base. A passage to the right of the library leads into **St. Mary's Quad**, incorporating the buildings of the former St. Mary Hall. The quad is approached through the screens passage of the former (1639–40), now the Junior Common Room, above which is the former chapel. The homely looking timber-framed building on the east side dates from 1743, and opposite is a Tudor-Gothic range by Daniel Robertson (1826).

The north side of St. Mary's Quad is taken up by the imposing **Rhodes Building**, designed by Basil Champneys in 1909–11 in an eclectic style, part Baroque, part neo-Jacobean (best seen from the High St: see Walk 3). Cecil Rhodes had already made a fortune from diamond mining when he came up to Oriel in 1873, and owing to frequent absences in Southern Africa he took eight years to get his degree, but he left the college £100,000 at his death.

Famous members

Sir Walter Raleigh, explorer, poet, 1552?–1618

Gilbert White, naturalist, 1720–93; John Keble, divine, 1792–1866

Thomas Arnold, headmaster of Rugby, 1795–1842

Samuel Wilberforce ('Soapy Sam'), Bishop of Oxford, 1805–73

John Henry (later Cardinal) Newman, 1810–90

Thomas Hughes, author of *Tom Brown's Schooldays*, 1822–96

A.H. Clough, poet, 1819–61

Matthew Arnold, poet, 1822–88

J.A. Froude, historian, 1818–94

Cecil Rhodes, 1853–1902

The south range of Oriel looks out onto **Merton St**, which still preserves its cobbled road surface for most of its length, to the hindrance of cyclists and the bewilderment of tourists. On the south side of Merton St, facing Oriel, is the much-refaced front of Corpus Christi College.

Corpus Christi College

Plan 4, A/C; open 13.30–16.00, ☎ 01865 276700, ✉ www.ccc.ox.ac.uk.

History

The college was founded in 1517 by Richard Foxe, bishop in turn of Exeter, Bath and Wells, Durham and Winchester, and Lord Privy Seal to Henry VII and Henry VIII. Foxe was a great benefactor not only to Oxford but also to Cambridge, where he was Chancellor and Master of Pembroke College. He was responsible for implanting a strong tradition of Classical learning at Corpus, which has continued to the present day, expressing the wish that the college should be like a beehive, where 'the scholars night and day may make wax and sweet honey to the honour of God, and the advantage of themselves and all Christian men'. Provision was made for lectures in Greek, Latin and Hebrew, causing Foxe's friend Erasmus to call it a 'bibliotheca trilinguis'.

The buildings occupy the site originally intended for the nave of Merton College chapel, just inside the southern town wall, and they survive largely intact. Unlike the other Oxford colleges Corpus did not surrender its plate to Charles I in 1642 and therefore has many priceless early pieces, including Foxe's gilt and enamelled pastoral staff. Always one of the smaller Oxford colleges, Corpus has had little room to expand, and it still retains an intimate character, especially in comparison with Christ Church and Merton on either side.

The **Front Quadrangle** still retains its early Tudor dimensions. In the centre is a tall **sundial** (1581) topped by the college emblem, a pelican (a modern replacement); the perpetual calendar round the plinth dates from 1606. A room in the gate tower, originally part of the President's lodgings (no adm.), has a rich late-16C plaster ceiling. On the east side (left) is the **Hall**, with its original hammerbeam roof by Humphry Coke, who was also responsible for the Hall roof at Christ Church; the panelling and screen date from 1700–05. A passage in the southeast corner leads to the **Chapel**, with handsome late 17C stalls and screen, an altarpiece after Rubens and a pre-Reformation brass eagle lectern, the earliest to survive in Oxford. Some of the bookcases in the **Library**, in the south range (no adm.), still have the rods with locks to which books were formerly chained.

Corpus is a place of small enclosed spaces. To the east of the Front Quad is a tiny quadrangle dominated by the **Gentlemen Commoners' Building** of 1737 on the east side, and south of it is the narrow **Cloister Quad**, so called from the covered walkway on the north side (1706–12), lined with memorial tablets to old members and embellished with fine plasterwork. Opposite is the **Fellows' Building**, also built in 1706, possibly to the designs of the master mason William Townesend. Its handsome pedimented south front looks out onto the diminutive garden, from which there are views across Christ Church Meadow and to the Cathedral; a fragment of the town wall also survives, with steps leading up to the rampart, and a semicircular bastion.

Famous members

Nicholas Udall, scholar, teacher and dramatist, 1505–56

Richard Hooker, theologian, 1554?–1600

General Oglethorpe, founder of Georgia, 1696–1785

John Keble and **Thomas Arnold** as undergraduates (see Oriel)

Sir Henry Newbolt, poet, 1862–1938

Robert Bridges, poet, 1844–1930

Isaiah Berlin, philosopher, 1909–97

Vikram Seth, novelist, b. 1952

At the corner of Merton St and **Magpie Lane** is an exuberantly detailed block of buildings designed by T.G. Jackson for Corpus in 1884–85, and to the north of it in Magpie Lane is a block of rooms for Corpus students by Powell and Moya.

The impressive 15C crossing tower of Merton College chapel closes the view south from Magpie Lane; notice also the 15C statuary on the north transept front over the doorway through which parishioners used to enter the building (unlike other Oxford college chapels Merton's once served as a parish church). Facing Merton College in **Merton St**, Beam Hall is a rare survival of one of the academic halls in which most Oxford students lived during the later Middle Ages; it dates largely from the 15C, and a plaque on the wall records the residence of Thomas Willis who did research on the anatomy of the brain in the 1660s. Postmasters' Hall, next door, was the birthplace and home of the antiquary Anthony Wood (1632–95), who is buried in the north transept of Merton chapel; the adjacent barn has recently been shown to be a rebuilding of a 12C stone house. Next to it, through a courtyard, is a rare survival of a covered 'real tennis' court—one of three known in Oxford—dating from the 17C and recently restored.

Merton College

Plan 4, A; open 14.00–16.00; ☎ 01865 276310, ✉ www.merton.ox.ac.uk.

History

Merton College is in all essentials the oldest in Oxford or Cambridge, although both University College and Balliol were endowed a few years earlier. It was founded in 1264 by Walter de Merton, Chancellor of England and subsequently Bishop of Rochester; the original deed, complete with seals, is in the college archives, and by 1300 there were 30 fellows in residence. The statutes of 1274, and the whole organisation, served as a model for subsequent colleges at both Oxford and Cambridge. In 1380 a former fellow, John Wyliott, provided scholarships whose recipients were known as *portionistae*, corrupted to 'postmasters'.

The buildings are among the oldest and most interesting in Oxford. There was no attempt at first to plan them as an integrated whole and the college is still dwarfed by the chapel, which takes up much of the frontage to Merton St. The choir, with its large Decorated windows, was built at the end of the 13C next to the site of the parish church of St. John, which was subsequently demolished. The transepts were added in the 14C and 15C; the magnificent Perpendicular tower, by Robert Janyns, dates from 1448–51, but the projected nave was never built (Corpus Christi College occupies its intended site). Major expansion of the college took place in the 17C and 20C, and now it extends as far as the Botanic Garden to the east.

The entrance is through the **gatehouse** of 1418, rebuilt in the 19C; over the door is a curious reset 15C carving of St. John the Baptist in the Wilderness with a figure of Walter de Merton wearing a mitre (notice the unicorn in attendance). On the south side of **Front Quad**, facing the entrance, is the **Hall** (usually closed), in existence by 1277 but virtually rebuilt by Gilbert Scott in 1874; the door, however, with its elaborate 13C ironwork, is original. The east front of the Chapel stands to the right (west), detached from the other buildings, and on the north side (left), on the site of houses purchased by Walter de Merton when he founded the college, are the original Warden's Lodgings, extended 1299–1300, the hall of which survives in part as a common room.

A passage between the Hall and Chapel leads to **Mob Quad**, the oldest in Oxford. In the north-east corner is the Treasury or Muniment Room (1288), with its unusual high-pitched stone roof; it is flanked by residential ranges of c 1304–11. The south and west sides of the quad were not built until 1371–78. Their upper floor is taken up by the **Library** (guided visits weekdays on the hour at 14.00, 15.00 and 16.00; adm. charge. Closed for six weeks at Christmas and New Year), one of the most interesting medieval libraries in England. It was the first to house the books upright on shelves, instead of lying flat in chests (one of which can be seen near the stairway); one volume is still chained to the shelves, which are fitted with reading boards. The furnishings, panelling, plasterwork and dormer windows are late 16C to early 17C; in some of the small side windows are fragments of 15C stained glass originally in the chapel. In addition to MSS, the Library's historic treasures include two 14C astrolabes, an early Welsh Bible, and a massive chest with a complicated threefold locking mechanism in the lid. The original floor level was lower than the present one, so the traditional ghost can be seen only from his knees up.

Leading off the Library are two rooms devoted to Max Beerbohm, author of *Zuleika Dobson*, one of the classic Oxford novels; several of his cruelly witty cartoons of late 19C celebrities are on display.

A passage in the west range of Mob Quad leads to the **Chapel**, entered through the south transept of 1367–68. To the right is a 14C piscina, curiously set high on the wall, and opposite on the west wall is a fine monument to the Classical scholar

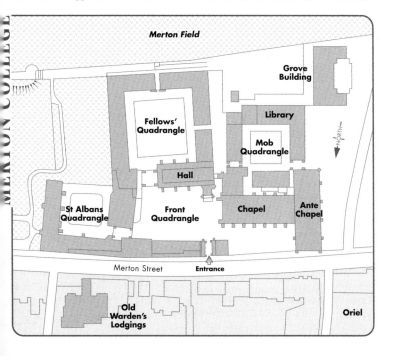

Bodley Memorial,
Merton College Chapel

Sir Henry Savile (d. 1622), Warden of Merton and founder of two University professorships. The crossing tower rests on tall arches supported by clustered shafts, framing the vista to the early 15C north transept; the organ stands where the opening to the nave would have been. The impressive marble and alabaster monument on the west wall of the north transept is to Sir Thomas Bodley (d. 1613), founder of the Bodleian Library, by Nicholas Stone, and is replete with symbolism (note the Classical pilasters in the form of piled books). The lower part of the large Perpendicular north window has recently been re-glazed with early 18C painted glass removed in an earlier restoration, and set in the floor underneath are two magnificent memorial brasses, of c 1420 and 1471.

The **choir** (c 1290–97) is entered through a handsome late-17C wooden screen, removed in the 19C and restored in 1960. The exquisite Decorated tracery of the east window contains late 13C or early 14C **stained glass** and the well-preserved stained glass in the side windows, given by Henry de Mamesfield, a fellow of the college, is of the same date; he is depicted as the donor in each window. Over the altar is a *Crucifixion*, of the school of Tintoretto. The beautiful brass lectern is of c 1500, and the seating and roof date from William Butterfield's restoration of 1849–51.

Returning to the Front Quad, the **Fitzjames Gateway** (1497) on the southeast side gives access to the **Fellows' Quad**, built in 1610. The rooms above the gate formed part of the original Warden's lodgings; they are now known as the **Queen's Rooms**, from their occupation by Queen Henrietta Maria during the Civil War. The austere buildings of the Fellows' Quad were designed by two Halifax masons, John Akroyd and John Bentley, brought in by Warden Savile, a Yorkshireman, in order to avoid the exorbitant charges of the Oxford craftsmen. This was the first quadrangle in Oxford to be built to three storeys throughout and it was also the first to incorporate a Classical frontispiece, or 'tower of the orders', of the kind later to be seen at Wadham and in the Old Schools quadrangle.

To the east of the Front Quad is **St. Alban's Quad** (Basil Champneys, 1904–05). It stands on the site of St. Alban Hall, incorporated into the college in 1881; the 1599 doorway to the Hall can still be seen on the south side of Merton St, embedded in the newer building. To the east and south is the **garden**, laid out inside the medieval town wall (not normally open to visitors).

The huge neo-Jacobean house opposite St. Alban's Quad, on the north side of Merton St, was built by Champneys as the **Warden's Lodgings** in 1908; the present Warden lives in less grandeur (but possibly more comfort) in the nondescript brick house which closes the view at the end of the street.

An iron gateway immediately to the west of Merton chapel leads to a path alongside the outer walls of Mob Quad, at the far end of which is a gate into **Christ Church Meadow** (open 07.00 to dusk; the meadow can also be reached by turning right from Merton St onto the High St and then right again into Rose Lane). From here the path continues between Christ Church and Merton Field,

> ## *Famous members*
> **John Wyclif**, translator of the Bible, 1329?–84
> **Sir Thomas Bodley**, founder of the Bodleian Library, 1545–1613
> **Anthony Wood**, antiquary, 1632–95
> **William Harvey**, physician and anatomist, 1578–1657
> **Cardinal Manning**, 1808–92
>
> **Lord Randolph Churchill**, politician, 1849–96
> **Max Beerbohm**, writer and caricaturist, 1872–1956
> **T.S. Eliot**, poet, 1888–1965
> **Frederick Soddy**, scientist, 1877–1956
> **J.R.R. Tolkien**, writer, 1892–1973
> **Louis Macneice**, poet, 1907–63
> **Keith Douglas**, poet, 1920–44

now a playing field, and allows an excellent view of the east end of Christ Church Cathedral through a wrought-iron gate to the right. A left turn from the meadow gateway follows the north side of the playing field next to one of the best-preserved stretches of the medieval town wall; it is popularly known as **Dead Man's Walk**, allegedly because the Jews of early medieval Oxford took the bodies of their dead along it for burial in their extramural cemetery on the site of the present Botanic Garden.

Both paths lead to **Broad Walk**, first laid out in 1668, which narrowly escaped being turned into part of Oxford's inner relief ring-road in the 1960s—a fate avoided, it is said, because of the presence of large numbers of Oxford graduates in the Government at the time. From its east end a path meanders along the banks of the Cherwell to the Thames and the college boathouses; in summer the air is heavy with the scent of the enfolding lime trees, and in winter the meadows are sometimes flooded (normally, strange varieties of long-horn cattle can be seen grazing there). At the western end of the Thames-side path an inconspicuous gate gives access to the bottom of St. Aldate's, where refreshment can be had at the *Head of the River* pub (a former boatyard); if the gate is closed, New Walk leads back to the Meadow Building of Christ Church, and thence to the Memorial Garden and St. Aldate's .

At the foot of St. Aldate's is **Folly Bridge**, where punts can be hired in the summer. The late 11C bridge was replaced by the present bridge in 1825–27, but some old masonry encasing the causeway to the south—a major feat of Norman engineering—can still be seen from the footpath on the far side. Until 1779 a tower and gatehouse stood on the bridge, where the Franciscan friar Roger Bacon, scientist and astronomer (c 1214–94) was traditionally said to have had his study; near the site of these structures is a curious crenellated flint and brick house of 1849.

On the south side of the bridge, next to Salter's boat office (from which trips along the river are organised), is a new block of student rooms for **Hertford College** (Oxford Architects Partnership, finished 2000); it is best seen from the towpath, where the brick-clad blocks of student rooms enclose a diminutive 'harbour'. From here the towpath can be followed southeast to Iffley Lock (see p 139), giving excellent views of Christ Church Meadow. To the right of Folly Bridge the towpath continues west to Pembroke College's fortress-like **Sir Geoffrey Arthur Building** (Maguire and Murray, 1986–89)—the first college residence to be erected on the south, or Berkshire, side of the Thames—and thence, after about a mile, to Osney (see p 142).

From Folly Bridge **St. Aldate's** leads back to Carfax. The southern end, formerly lined with picturesque old houses, was uninspiringly rebuilt in the 1930s; the large building on the left, formerly the Morris motor showroom, is now the Crown Court. On the right-hand side past the police station is the rubble-faced, hipped-roofed **Music Faculty**, built to the designs of Sir Hubert Worthington in 1936 for the non-collegiate students belonging to St. Catherine's Society (later transformed into St. Catherine's College, see Walk 5). It houses the **Bate Collection of Historical Instruments** (open Mon–Fri 14.00–17.00, Sat during term 10.00–12.00, ☎ 01865 276139, ✉ www.ashmol.ox.ac.uk/ BCMIpage). This is best known for its splendid collection of brass, woodwind and percussion instruments, including the oldest playable Javanese gamelan in England. There are also some important early keyboard instruments, including a harpsichord played by Handel in 1720.

Nos 82–83 St. Aldate's, opposite, began life as an academic hall called Littlemore Hall in the 15C, but were much rebuilt in the early 17C and mid-20C; **Alice's Shop** (no. 83) has long been famous as the sheep's shop in Lewis Carroll's *Alice Through the Looking Glass*. Next door to the north is the so-called **Old Palace**, a timber-framed building erected by a local merchant in 1622–28 and said to stand on the site of a house occupied by Robert King, the last Abbot of Osney and first Bishop of Oxford. The building was extended to the west along Rose Place in 1970–71 and now houses the University's **Roman Catholic Chaplaincy** with an austere but numinous Chapel.

A left turn along Brewer St, a little to the north, leads along the line of the city wall past the Cathedral Choir School to **Campion Hall**, a Permanent Private Hall for Jesuit students, named after Edmund Campion, the Roman Catholic martyr executed in 1581. The main buildings (1935–37) were designed by Sir Edwin Lutyens and are clad in the Bladon rubble stone much employed in Oxford in the 1930s; the barrel-vaulted chapel, on the first floor (open by appointment, ☎ 01865 286100), contains some of Lutyens's characteristically quirky light fittings, with tassels alluding to cardinals' hats, along with Stations of the Cross by Frank Brangwyn.

The north side of Brewer St is occupied by the buildings of Pembroke College, which also include the much-remodelled early 16C former **Wolsey Almshouses**, now the Master's Lodgings, facing Christ Church. The college is entered from the south side of St. Aldate's churchyard.

Pembroke College

Plan 3, D; usually closed to visitors, ☎ 01865 276444, ✉ www.pembroke.ox.ac.uk.

History

Pembroke was founded in 1624 by two local men, Thomas Tesdale and Richard Wightwick, and was named after the 3rd Earl of Pembroke, Chancellor of the University at the time. One of the smaller Oxford colleges, it stands on the site of the medieval Broadgates Hall, part of which was incorporated in the buildings of the new foundation. The college has never been a very wealthy one, and the buildings have grown piecemeal, with representative examples of the architecture of all centuries from the 17C to the 20C.

The gateway, surmounted by a pretty Gothic oriel window (Daniel Evans, 1829–30) leads into the 17C **Old Quad**, remodelled 1829–30; the northwest corner (right on entering) was part of Broadgates Hall. From here a passage to the right gives access to the largely 19C **Chapel Quad**, built around the former 17C garden. The **Chapel** (William Townesend, 1728–32) is to the left, a rectangular early Georgian box with a boldly rusticated front. The interior was colourfully embellished by the stained-glass artist C.E. Kempe in the Italian Renaissance taste in 1884; Kempe also designed the windows, and the altarpiece is a copy of Rubens's *Risen Christ*. At the far end, approached up a flight of steps, is the handsome **Hall** (John Hayward, 1847–48), with a hammerbeam roof and tall Perpendicular windows. The **North Quad** (1965) is made up of a heterogeneous collection of buildings, of which the most attractive is a row of mainly 17C houses whose front doors look out onto Pembroke St. On the south side are three bronze statues of *Mourning Women* by J.W. Harvey (1946), commemorating members of the college who died in the Second World War.

Pembroke's most famous son was Dr Johnson, who studied here for four terms in 1728–29 till poverty forced him to leave. He occupied the second-floor rooms over the gateway. Johnson retained a great affection for Oxford in spite of his brief and not always happy sojourn. His portrait by Reynolds hangs in the Senior Common Room; his teapot, cider mug, one of his 'themes' (essays) and some books are displayed in the library, and the college possesses various other Johnson memorabilia.

Famous members

Francis Beaumont, playwright, 1584–1616 (Broadgates Hall)

John Pym, parliamentarian, 1584–1643 (Broadgates Hall)

Sir Thomas Browne, author of *Religio Medici*, 1605–82

Samuel Johnson (see above), 1709–84 (Pembroke)

William Shenstone, poet, 1714–63 (Pembroke)

George Whitefield, leading Methodist, 1714–70 (Pembroke)

Sir William Blackstone, author of *Commentaries on the Laws of England*, 1723–80 (Pembroke)

James Smithson, founder of the Smithsonian Institution in Washington, 1765–1829 (Pembroke)

Michael Heseltine, former Conservative politician, b. 1933 (Pembroke)

St. Aldate's church is a hotbed of Oxford Evangelicalism. First recorded in the 12C, it was almost entirely rebuilt in the Decorated style by J.T. Christopher, a cousin of the then incumbent, in 1862–73, and has recently been refurbished internally. It still contains a fine early-16C alabaster monument to John Noble (d. 1522) of Broadgates Hall. For many years the south aisle of the old St. Aldate's church housed the library and chapel of Pembroke College.

From here it is a short walk back to Carfax.

3 ~ ALONG THE HIGH STREET

This walk proceeds along the north side of High St, crosses the River Cherwell at Magdalen Bridge, and returns on the south side, exploring some of the attractive streets leading off it on the way.

It starts and finishes at **Carfax**, the name of which derives from the Latin *quadrifurcus* (four forks), or the French *quatre voies* or *carrefours* (four ways). The oldest structure here is the much-restored early 14C **tower** of St. Martin's church, demolished in 1896 as part of a street-improvement scheme; the composer Orlando Gibbons (1583–1625) was baptised here. There is a good view over the city—best in the afternoon—from the top of the tower (open Apr–Oct 10.00–17.15, Nov–Mar 10.00–15.30; adm. charge), whose clock has jacks which strike at each quarter-hour (the originals are in the Museum of Oxford). Opposite, at the corner of Cornmarket St and High St, is the curvaceous, almost Art Nouveau façade of Lloyd's Bank (Stephen Salter, 1901).

The north side

The first point of interest on the north side of the street is the **Covered Market** (plan 1, D), which contains an excellent collection of shops selling food, clothes, gifts and much else; the plain Classical façade (John Gwynn, 1774) survives above the modern shop-fronts, but the attractive interior, with its open timber roofs, dates mainly from the late 19C. Beyond, on the corner of Turl St, is the *Mitre Hotel*, a former coaching inn of the 17C and 18C; it is now a restaurant, with students' rooms above.

Turl St (the Turl) leads north from the Mitre, its unusual name probably deriving from a revolving ('twirling') gate in the long-demolished town wall at the northern end. The southern end of the street is flanked on the west side (left) by tall 17C timber-framed houses and on the east by Lincoln College (see below). After the junction with Market St on the left is Jesus College.

Jesus College

Plan 3, B; usually open 14.00–16.30, ☎ 01865 279700, ✉ www.jesus.ox.ac.uk.

History

> The first college to be established in Oxford after the Reformation, Jesus was founded in 1571, nominally by Elizabeth I, but in reality by Hugh Price, treasurer of St. David's Cathedral, who persuaded the Queen to lend it her prestige. The college took over the sites of former academic halls and expanded to the west of its cramped original site in the 17C. It has always had a very close connection with Wales, which even as late as the early 1900s supplied over half its members.

Part of the Turl St front dates from the founder's time, but it was drastically remodelled in the 18C and again (by J.C and C.A. Buckler) in 1854–56. The attractive, irregular **First Quadrangle**, however, still retains its late 16C and 17C character. On the north (right) side is the **Chapel**, built in 1621 and extended eastwards in 1636; it has a barrel-vaulted roof, late 17C screen and early 17C pulpit, but was otherwise remodelled by G.E. Street in 1864; his vigorously carved reredos and colourful tiled floor have recently been uncovered after being hidden from public view for many years. There is a good monument to Sir Eubule Thelwall (Principal 1621–30) on the north wall of the chancel, and on the south wall (right) is a picture of *St. Michael overcoming Satan* by Guido Reni (formerly over the altar); in the antechapel is a bust of T.E. Lawrence (a replica of one in St. Paul's Cathedral), an undergraduate at the college in 1907–10.

The **Hall**, opposite the main entrance, dates from the early 17C, but the plaster ceiling with its Rococo embellishments dates from 1741. There are portraits of Queen Elizabeth I (along with a carved wooden bust over the fireplace); of the architect John Nash, by Lawrence, given after he had carried out minor repairs in 1815; of T.E. Lawrence (of Arabia); and of Harold Wilson, twice Prime Minister. The heavily carved Jacobean screen is decorated with dragons, perhaps a reminder of Welsh loyalties.

The **Second Quadrangle** was built between 1646 and 1713, and remains largely unchanged. It was mainly the work of Leoline Jenkins (Principal 1661–73), the college's 'second founder', and, with its array of small mullioned windows and rows of tiny gables on the roof-line, is a good example of the conservative style of architecture adopted by so many Oxford colleges in the 17C. The college has subsequently expanded to fill all the available space outside this quad, but architecturally the results are unremarkable.

Famous members

Henry Vaughan, poet, 1622–95
Richard ('Beau') Nash, social mentor of 18C Bath, 1674–1762
J.R. Green, historian, 1837–83

T.E. Lawrence (see All Souls)
Harold Wilson, Labour Prime Minister and politician, 1916–95

On the other side of Turl St is Exeter College, the long-standing rival of Jesus.

Exeter College

Plan 3, B; open 14.00–17.00, ☎ 01865 279600, 📷 www.exeter.ox.ac.uk.

History

Exeter College was founded in 1314 as Stapeldon Hall by Walter de Stapeldon, Bishop of Exeter. From 1405 it was known as Exeter College, and in 1566 it was handsomely re-endowed by a former member, Sir William Petre, whose portrait hangs in the Hall. Like the founder, Bishop Stapeldon, Petre came from Devon and made his fortune through service to the Crown; for many years the college maintained strong links with the West Country. In 1994 Exeter became the first of the former men's colleges to elect a woman as Head of House (Rector).

The college has a complicated architectural history and successive rebuildings have meant that it retains hardly any of its medieval buildings. But, by way of compensation, there is a splendid 17C Hall and a 19C Chapel which is one of the finest Victorian buildings in Oxford.

The 17C entrance range was remodelled by the local architect H.J. Underwood (1834–35), but some 17C buildings survive in the **Front Quadrangle**, notably the **Hall** (no adm.), built in 1618, with large, light, Perpendicular-style windows, a fine open timber roof and a richly carved Jacobean screen; over the high table is a splendid retrospective portrait of the founder by the Rev. Matthew Peters (1780).

Opposite is Gilbert Scott's magnificent **Chapel** of 1856–59, the finest building in Oxford by that unfairly maligned architect. It replaces a less grandiose 17C predecessor, part of whose screen can still be seen in the Museum of Oxford (Walk 2), and its great height overwhelms the rest of the quadrangle. Loosely based, like Scott's chapel at St. John's, Cambridge, on French Gothic precedents, its dark vaulted interior is an intact High Victorian period-piece, richly adorned with carved wood and stone, ironwork, mosaics and stained-glass windows (by Clayton and Bell). On the south side of the chancel is a tapestry of *The Adoration of the Magi* (1890) by Edward Burne-Jones and William Morris, who first met when undergraduates here in the early 1850s.

The only medieval building to survive at Exeter is **Palmer's Tower**, the original gatehouse of 1432, situated beyond the apsidal east end of the chapel, just within the long-vanished town wall. A passage in the east range of the front quadrangle leads into the pleasant, secluded **garden** (usually open 14.00–16.00), from which there is a good view of the Bodleian Library's Selden End and the Divinity School; on the north side is Gilbert Scott's neo-Gothic Library (1855–56).

Famous members

Anthony Ashley-Cooper, 1st Lord Shaftesbury, politician, 1621–83

Charles Lyell, geologist, 1797–1875

Edward Burne-Jones, artist, 1833–98

William Morris, artist, poet, social philosopher, 1834–96

C.H. Parry, composer, 1848–1918

J.R.R. Tolkien, philologist, author, 1892–1973

Richard Burton, actor, 1925–84

Martin Amis, novelist, b. 1949

The southern side of Exeter College is flanked by Brasenose Lane, which leads to Radcliffe Square (Walk 1) and still retains its medieval-type open gutter for rainwater. On the south side of Brasenose Lane is Lincoln College.

Lincoln College

Plan 4, A; usually open Mon–Sat 14.00–17.00, Sun 11.00–17.00, ☎ 01865 279800, ✉ www.lincoln.ox.ac.uk.

History

Founded in 1427 by Robert Fleming, Bishop of Lincoln, as a counterblast to the Wycliffite Movement, Lincoln College was intended 'to defend the mysteries of Scripture against those ignorant laymen who profaned with swinish snouts its most holy pearls'. The religious conservatism of its foundation persisted, and during the Reformation three successive Rectors and many fellows were expelled. Always one of the smaller Oxford colleges, Lincoln counts among its members John Wesley, the founder of Methodism, who was elected to a fellowship in 1726.

The original 15C buildings survive largely intact, though, as so often in Oxford, there has been much refacing of the stonework. Alterations took place in the early 17C, and the Chapel is a particularly good example of the architecture and decorative art of that period. Because of its confined site, Lincoln has had to expand by swallowing up neighbouring buildings, including the houses on the west side of the Turl, many of the properties on the south side of the High St, and, most notably, the 18C church of All Saints which now serves as an unusually grand and spacious library.

The **Front Quad** retains much of its intimate 15C character, despite internal refacing in the 18C and the addition of battlements to the outer façade in 1824. The **Hall** (opposite the gateway) dates from 1437. Its open timber roof survives intact and the restored louvre, through which smoke escaped from the central hearth, can still be seen. A fireplace was installed in 1699 (replaced by T.G. Jackson in 1891), and the excellent wood panelling dates from 1701. In the south range of the quad are what are thought to be Wesley's rooms, restored in 1928 with gifts from the American Methodist Church.

To the south is early 17C **Chapel Quad**, with the Gothic-windowed **Chapel** (1629–31) on the south side. The main features are the beautifully carved 17C woodwork, including the pulpit from which Wesley preached, the panelled roof decorated with shields, swags and crowns and a superb set of painted glass windows by Abraham van Linge of 1629–30, depicting prophets and apostles on either side and Old and New Testament scenes over the altar.

Further south, at the corner of Turl St and High St, is the **Library** (open only by special arrangement). This was built as **All Saints church** in 1706–08, replacing an older church, and was almost certainly designed by Henry Aldrich, Dean of Christ Church; the noble tower and spire which punctuates the vista along High St was not completed until 1718, after Aldrich's death, by an unknown architect who was clearly influenced by Wren's City of London churches. When the library was created a new raised floor was inserted and a basement reading-room created. The interior is light and lofty, the ceiling decorated with elaborate plasterwork and the walls with giant Corinthian pilasters. There are several reminders of the building's ecclesiastical past, notably the funeral hatchments, the memorial tablets, and the tomb of William Levins, alderman, who died in 1616 aged 100.

Famous members

William Davenant, poet and playwright, 1606–68
John Wesley, founder of Methodism, 1703–91
Dr John Radcliffe, 1652–1714
Mark Pattison, University reformer, 1813–84

Edward Thomas, poet, 1878–1917
Dr Seuss, writer of children's books, 1904–91
Osbert Lancaster, cartoonist, 1908–86
John Le Carré, thriller writer, b. 1931

A short way down the High St from Turl St is the south front of Brasenose College (see Walk 1), a sensitive example of Tudor-Gothic architecture by T.G. Jackson (1882–1911), with excellent carved detail in the Arts and Crafts manner. Beyond it is the 15C University Church of St. Mary, with its extraordinary porch of 1637 (see Walk 1). Past the east end, and across the pedestrianised Catte St, the High St begins to curve down towards the crossing over River Cherwell. Immediately on the left is the entrance to All Souls College.

All Souls College

Plan 4, A; open Mon–Fri 14.00–16.00, ☎ 01865 279379, 🖂 www.all-souls. ox.ac.uk.

History

Founded in 1438 by Henry Chichele, Archbishop of Canterbury, with Henry VI as co-founder, the college commemorated those who had died in the Hundred Years' War and served both as a chantry (the full title is 'The College of All Souls of the Faithful Departed, of Oxford') and as an institution for the study of theology and law. Uniquely in Oxford or Cambridge colleges, it has a Warden and fellows only, their number augmented by visiting scholars from outside Oxford; there are no students reading for degrees. The college is in essence an institute of advanced study, with a long-established reputation for scholarship in history and law, though many other academic disciplines are now represented.

The college owed much in its original design and layout to New College, and 15C buildings survive largely intact, save for the Hall, which was replaced when a large new quadrangle was built to the north, on the site of the original cloister, in 1716–34. This was designed by Nicholas Hawksmoor and its Gothic windows, pinnacles and spires set it apart from the normal run of architecture in early Georgian England. Since then there have been no significant alterations, and today the college retains a character of cloistered undergraduate-free calm which recalls an earlier and more peaceful age.

The entrance gateway is in High St; the statues of the founders and relief of the Resurrection on the gateway date from 1940. It leads into the **Front Quadrangle**, which has changed little since it was built in 1438–43, though the original library, on the upper floor of the east (right-hand) range has been turned into a lecture room.

The **Chapel**, immediately opposite the entrance gateway, is reached through a fan-vaulted passage (entrance to left). Modelled on the chapel of New College, of which Archbishop Chichele was a graduate, and well restored by Gilbert Scott in 1872–76, it is entered through the antechapel, lit by large Perpendicular windows. Some of the original stained glass of the 1440s survives here and there are also good monuments to Warden Hovenden (d. 1614) and to George Clarke (d. 1736), a fellow of the college and designer of Christ Church Library and several other early 18C buildings in Oxford.

The main body of the chapel is approached through a splendid wooden screen of 1664, beautified by Sir James Thornhill in 1716. It retains its 15C hammer-beam angel roof, stalls with misericords and also the framework of the magnificent carved stone reredos. But the figures in the niches are Victorian, some of them modelled on contemporary members of the college; the originals were destroyed during the Reformation. In 1664 the reredos was obscured by a fresco of the *Last Judgement* by Isaac Fuller (since removed), with accompanying painted ceiling panels above, some of which now hang in the antechapel. Later in the 18C the college commissioned a large *Noli me Tangere* by Anton Raphael Mengs to serve as an altarpiece, but this has now also been removed.

The **North Quadrangle** is reached through a passage in the northeast (right) corner of the Front Quad. It stands on the site of the original cloister and was built in 1716–34 in Nicholas Hawksmoor's idiosyncratic version of Gothic, chosen by the fellows in preference to a Classical design submitted by the same architect. The telescope-like towers on the east side were designed to close the vista from Radcliffe Square, from which the quad is separated by a screen wall with a bizarre ogee-capped gatehouse in the centre.

The north side is formed by the **Codrington Library** (no adm.), replacing the old library in the front quad, and donated by the sugar plantation owner Christopher Codrington (d. 1710), Governor of the Leeward Islands and former fellow of the College. It contains some 120,000 volumes, including over 350 incunabula, and many manuscripts, including drawings from the office of another fellow, the 27-year-old Christopher Wren, who reputedly designed the sundial on the south front (previously on the chapel wall) in 1659.

Though Gothic outside, the 200ft-long Library has a spacious Classical interior, finally completed in 1751, largely at the instigation of the great legal commentator Sir William Blackstone, whose seated marble effigy (by John Bacon, 1782) presides over it still. Classical too, albeit with more than a tinge of Baroque drama, are Hawksmoor's **Hall** and **Buttery** (no adm. to either), on the southeast side of the quad, the latter containing a portrait bust of the architect by Henry Cheere, the only known image of him.

Famous members

Thomas Linacre, founder of the Royal College of Physicians, c 1460–1524

Jeremy Taylor, Anglican divine, 1613–67

Christopher Wren, architect, 1632–1723

Sir William Blackstone, lawyer, 1723–80

T.E. Lawrence, Lawrence of Arabia, 1888–1935

Lord Curzon, politician and viceroy of India, 1859–1925

A.L. Rowse, historian, 1903–96

Sir Isaiah Berlin, philosopher 1909–97

Lord Hailsham, lawyer and Lord Chancellor, 1907–2001

A left turn out of All Souls leads past the **Warden's Lodgings**—designed by George Clarke as his private residence but externally remodelled—and some attractive timber-framed houses to the impressive Classical façade of Queen's College.

The Queen's College

Plan 4, A; adm. only on tours organised by the Oxford Guild of Guides; apply to the Information Centre, ☎ 01865 726871; college ☎ 01865 279120, ✉ www.queens.ox.ac.uk.

History

The college was founded in 1341 by Robert de Eglesfield, chaplain to Queen Philippa, consort of Edward III; she was the first of a long line of queens to take an interest in the foundation. The statutes provided not only for a Provost and 18 fellows but also for a number of 'poor boys', the first undergraduates specifically included in the foundation of an Oxford college.

Strict rules of discipline were laid down: no bows and arrows, no dogs, no musical instruments except on special occasions, no playing of marbles on the steps. Several old customs remained until recently: the college was summoned to dinner by the sound of the trumpet; on feast days the founder's drinking horn—an aurochs horn mounted on eagle's feet and banded with silver gilt—was used as a loving-cup; at Christmas a 'boar's head dinner' was celebrated (many of the original scholars were north-country men who could not get home for Christmas). At New Year the bursar presented to each guest at the 'Gaudy' (a celebratory college dinner) a needle and thread (*aiguille* and *fil*, a pun on Eglesfield's name), with the words 'Take this and be thrifty'. The college was entirely rebuilt between 1671 and 1765, making it architecturally the most consistently classical of all Oxford colleges. Since then there have been few additions or alterations and, as numbers of students have grown, new accomodation has had to be found away from the main site (e.g. Florey Building, below).

The **Front Quadrangle** was built on the site of the medieval buildings by the local mason-contractor William Townesend with the advice of George Clarke, fellow of All Souls; work started in 1710 but was not finished until 1756. Unlike the traditional Oxford quadrangle, but like the contemporary North Quad at All Souls, it is in fact three-sided, with only a blank wall (1733–36) separating it from the street, as in a Parisian nobleman's house. The screen wall, together with the central gateway and domed cupola, was designed by Nicholas Hawksmoor; the cupola shelters a statue (by Henry Cheere) of George II's consort Queen Caroline, who contributed £1000 towards the building. The Hall and Chapel (1714–19), are on the north side of the quad, separated by a passage, with an engaged temple front in the centre and a cupola on the roof, echoing Sir Christopher Wren's earlier Chelsea Hospital in London.

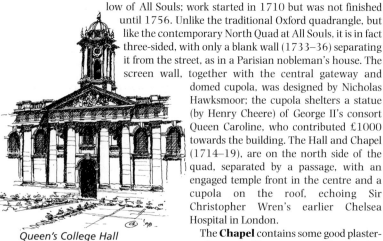

Queen's College Hall and Chapel

The **Chapel** contains some good plasterwork, a magnificent screen and a painting of the *Ascension* by Sir James Thornhill (1716) over the altar. The windows, unusually for a building of this date, are filled with stained and painted glass, much of it taken from the previous chapel, including four windows on each side by Abraham van Linge (1635), and others with glass of 1518 (the east window, by Joshua Price, is of c 1717); there is also an excellent Baroque-style organ of 1965, by the Danish builder Frobenius, on which public recitals are given each Wednesday lunchtime during term.

The **Hall**, with its barrel-vaulted plaster ceiling, is a powerful example of English Baroque design, with echoes of Vanbrugh; it contains portraits of Joseph Addison by Kneller, and of Jeremy Bentham, one of the College's most famous members.

The **North Quadrangle** was built piecemeal between 1671 and 1721. Behind the east range (right on entering) is the remodelled Williamson Building of 1671–72, designed by Wren, and facing it on the west side is the **Library** (no adm.), a grand Classical structure of 1692–95 (architect unknown), supported on a rusticated arcade which was open until 1841. The interior, one of the finest in Oxford, retains its original beautifully carved bookcases, and the ornate ceiling was further embellished with Rococo plasterwork (by Thomas Roberts) in 1756. From its south end a narrow high-walled passage leads past the old brew-house into a tiny formal garden opening out on to a lawn, behind a row of timber houses in High St.

Famous members

Thomas Middleton, playwright, 1570–1627
William Wycherley, playwright, 1640–94
Edmund Halley, astronomer, 1656–1742
Joseph Addison, who both migrated to Magdalen

Jeremy Bentham, legal and social philosopher, 1748–1823
Walter Pater, critic and essayist, 1839–94
Rowan Atkinson, comedian, b 1955
John Wyclif (see also Merton and Balliol) lived in the college as a lodger from 1363 to 1381

On leaving Queen's, it is worth making a brief detour along **Queen's Lane**, which runs alongside the eastern and northern sides of the college and allows good views of Queen's Library, the towers of All Souls to the west and, to the north, the gaunt external walls of New College, enlivened by grotesque carvings on the string-course (1958–67). Just before the second right-angled bend is the **Provost's Lodging** of Queen's, an accomplished Classical villa by Raymond Erith (1958), and around the corner is the entrance to New College (see Walk 1). Returning from here, at the far end of Queen's Lane, just before the High St, is the former church of St. Peter in the East (see p 100) with its 15C tower and, immediately to the south of it, St. Edmund Hall, the longest-lasting survivor of Oxford's once-numerous academic halls.

St. Edmund Hall

Plan 4, A; open 09.00–dusk, ☎ 01865 279000, ✉ www.seh.ox.ac.uk.

History

Familiarly known as Teddy Hall, St. Edmund Hall is dedicated to St. Edmund of Abingdon, Archbishop of Canterbury, who taught at Oxford c 1195–1200. Undergraduates were housed on the site from at least the 13C, but there was no endowment and the hall was controlled first by Osney Abbey and then by Queen's College from 1557, of which it became a virtual appendage. The Hall survived until 1937, when it became self-governing, and it finally achieved full collegiate status in 1957. It is now numerically one of the largest Oxford colleges, though on one of the smallest sites.

The oldest part of the picturesque **Front Quadrangle** is the east part of the north range (left); it dates from the late 16C. The rest of the quad was built piecemeal, the south range (right) not being finally completed until 1927–34. In the centre of the quad is the old well (the well head is modern), and on the north range is a painted sundial.

The handsome ashlar-faced block on the east side, opposite the entrance, was built by the local mason Bartholomew Peisley in 1680–82. The two giant Corinthian columns at the centre mark the entrance to the tiny panelled **Chapel** (usually locked), the doorway to which is surmounted by a curved pediment resting on piles of books. The intimate interior has 17C stalls and screen by the local joiner Arthur Frogley, glass by Burne-Jones (1865), made by the William Morris firm, and a striking painting of *The Supper at Emmaus* by Ceri Richards (1958) over the altar. Over the antechapel is the cosy **Old Library** (no adm.), with its original woodwork intact.

To the east of the chapel, and ingeniously squeezed into a constricted site between the High St and New College gardens, is a quadrangle of 1968–70 (architect Gilbert Howes), providing common rooms, a spacious Hall (the old Hall is in the entrance range of the Front Quad), and sets of students' rooms.

The college Library is now housed in the former church of **St. Peter in the East**, to the north of the Front Quad. It dates from the early to mid-12C, and the shadowy groin-vaulted **crypt** (apply for key at the Porter's Lodge) survives intact from that period (note the three carved capitals). This is one of the most impressive and least altered survivals of Oxford before the arrival of the University. Some Norman features are also visible outside at the east end of the church, but the interior (no adm.) is a medley of Norman and Gothic work of different dates, and the tower is of the 14C and 15C.

Returning to High St, refreshments can be had at the *Queen's Lane Coffee House*, one of the oldest in England, or at one of several nearby eateries. The city's East Gate stood near here until the 1770s and beyond its site is **Longwall St**, which passed between the east wall of the city—a substantial part of which survives in New College garden—and the 15C stone wall erected by Magdalen College to enclose its extensive holdings of land. A short distance along Longwall St, on the right, are the stone-built (not merely stone-clad) **Grove Buildings** (no adm.) by Dmitri Porphyrios, including an auditorium, opened in 1999, which is based on the idea of an ancient Greek 'Odeon' and is entered through a curious octagonal structure alluding to the Tower of the Winds in Athens; the style of the complex is both eclectic and backward-looking. At the corner of High St and Longwall St is the former hall of Magdalen College School, a Tudor-Gothic building by J.C. and C.A. Buckler (1851) now serving as the **Library** of Magdalen College, whose buildings extend from here down to the River Cherwell.

Magdalen College

Plan 4, B; open Oct–Mar 14.00–17.00 or dusk if earlier, Apr–Sept 14.00–18.00; adm. charge; ☎ 01865 276000, ✉ www.magd.ox.ac.uk.

History

Magdalen (pronounced 'Maudlin') College was founded in 1458 by William Waynflete, a graduate of New College and in turn headmaster of Winchester, Provost of Eton, Bishop of Winchester and Lord Chancellor; the buildings occupy the site of the former Hospital of St. John, which stood outside the east gate of the city. The scholars were traditionally known as 'demies' (because in the past they received only half the allowances of a fellow); from the earliest days there were also places for commoners, or fee-paying students. There was also a choral foundation, which still flourishes, as does Waynflete's grammar school, Magdalen College School, which occupied premises to the west of the college, later shared with Magdalen Hall, one of the longest lasting of Oxford's academic halls; the school has since migrated to the opposite side of the River Cherwell, and Magdalen Hall moved to the site of the present Hertford College in 1816.

In its early days Magdalen College was in the forefront of the revival of Classical learning and it was strongly Puritan for a time in the early 17C. Nevertheless, it loyally supported Charles I in the Civil War, giving him nearly all its silver. James II rewarded this sacrifice by attempting to force upon the fellows a President, Anthony Farmer, who was unacceptable in morals, qualifications and churchmanship. Their determined resistance both to Farmer and to a subsequent nominee, Samuel Parker, Bishop of Oxford, led to their expulsion. Eventually, however, the King had to bow to public opinion and reinstate them; Restoration Day, 5 October 1688, has been celebrated ever since.

The original quadrangle was planned and largely completed by Waynflete and his master mason William Orchard in 1474–80, the tower on the High St front following in the 1490s; James I thought that Magdalen was 'the most absolute building in Oxford'. The college's position outside the town wall gave it plenty of room and the grounds were beautifully landscaped in the 18C. Since then the college has greatly expanded, but Waynflete's buildings still survive virtually intact (though much-restored) and even today Magdalen remains a place in which the 'last enchantments of the Middle Ages' can be strongly felt by the visitor.

The most notable external feature of Magdalen College is the beautiful Perpendicular Gothic **tower**, built in 1492–1505 when Thomas Wolsey, the future founder of Christ Church, was bursar of the college; it serves both as the chapel bell tower and as a sentinel announcing the presence of the university to travellers approaching from the London direction across Magdalen Bridge. A hymn is sung from the top at 06.00 on May morning, usually inaudible to the debauched revellers at ground level; since the late 18C the hymn has been the college grace.

The college is entered through an inconspicuous porter's lodge on the High St front, which leads into the irregular St. John's Quad. A gate tower to the west (left) gives access to **St. Swithun's Quad** (Bodley and Garner 1881–85), standing on the site of Magdalen Hall, a small portion of which still survives as the much-remodelled early 17C **Grammar Hall** to the north of the gate. The north side of St. John's Quad is occupied by the neo-Tudor President's Lodging, also by Bodley and Garner; like their St. Swithun's Quad, its style matches that of the original 15C collegiate buildings.

Founder's Tower and Cloisters

The original college buildings are to the east (right) of St. John's Quad. They include the gate tower or **Founder's Tower**, a splendid example of Perpendicular architecture, which leads directly into the main quadrangle, and, to the south, the Muniment Tower, also of the late 15C, through which a passage leads to the Chapel. In the south-east corner (right) is the **outdoor pulpit**, from which a university sermon used to be preached on St. John the Baptist's Day (24 June; the sermon is now preached on the nearest Sunday). Originally the quadrangle was strewn with rushes (to represent the wilderness) for the occasion. Beside the pulpit another passage leads to **Chaplain's Quad**, overlooked by the south wall of the Chapel, with a bronze sculpture of Christ and St. Mary Magdalene by David Wynne (1964); the buildings to the right, flanking High St, incorporate some of the masonry of the former St. John's Hospital.

The **Chapel** (completed c 1480) has gone through many vicissitudes since it was first built, and the interior owes much of its present character to a sensitive restoration by L.N. Cottingham in 1830–35. Hanging over the entrance in the antechapel is a near-contemporary copy of Leonardo da Vinci's *Last Supper* (c 1510–14), on loan from the Royal Academy, its vivid colouring recapturing something of the original effect of that faded masterpiece.

Some of the medieval stalls, with carved misericords, are arranged around the walls of the **antechapel**; the monuments include one (on the northeast wall) to Waynflete's father, brought from the church at Waynflet (Lincs) in 1833, and one by Nicholas Stone to the Lyttleton brothers (1635) above it. The unusual grisaille glass is by Richard Greenbury, 1632, and the west window, divested of its Perpendicular tracery in the 17C, is filled with an impressive 18C painted glass version of Michelangelo's *Last Judgment*, recently rescued from a cellar. The **organ screen** and choir stalls are by Cottingham, but the organ itself is by Noel Mander and the case by Julian Bicknell (1986). The sculptures on the altar

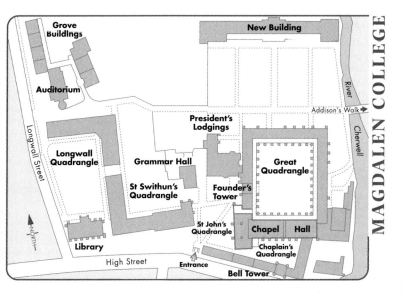

Grove Buildings
New Building
Auditorium
River
Addison's Walk ➡
Cherwell
President's Lodgings
Longwall Street
Longwall Quadrangle
Grammar Hall
Great Quadrangle
St Swithun's Quadrangle
Founder's Tower
NORTH
St John's Quadrangle
Chapel
Hall
Library
Chaplain's Quadrangle
High Street
Entrance
Bell Tower

MAGDALEN COLLEGE

screen are all of 1864 (by Earp), and the painting of *Christ Carrying the Cross* over the altar is by the 17C Spanish artist Valdes Leal. Choral services are held at 18.00 daily (exc. Tues) during term time, and the musical standard is very high.

The **Great Quadrangle**, unlike any other in Oxford or Cambridge, is encompassed by a covered walkway or cloister, giving the college a compelling sense of quasi-monastic seclusion. The north range and the roofs were largely rebuilt in the 1820s and, as so often in Oxford, the stonework has been replaced on several occasions. There are splendid carved bosses in the vault under the Founder's Tower and on the buttresses within the quad are grotesque figures called 'hieroglyphs' whose symbolic significance, if any, is obscure.

Up a flight of stairs in the southeast corner (right), next to the Chapel, is the **Hall** (usually locked), which retains its early 16C linenfold panelling and a set of ornate early Renaissance carvings, five of which depict the life of St. Mary Magdalene. The **Old Library** (no adm.), on the west side, contains illuminated MSS, Wolsey's copy of the Gospels and Waynflete's stockings, buskins and cope.

A narrow passage through the north side of the Great Quadrangle leads across a wide lawn to the country-house-like **New Building** of 1733, originally intended as part of a vast Classical quadrangle planned by one of the college's fellows, Edward Holdsworth, with the help of George Clarke and William Townesend, but never completed. Behind, and to the left, is Magdalen Grove, where deer have grazed since 1700. To the right, a bridge leads to a meadow by the Cherwell, famous for the snake's-head fritillaries which bloom there in spring. The meadow is enclosed by **Addison's Walk**, named after Joseph Addison, the early 18C essayist and poet; for part of its length the pathway follows the line of defensive earthworks laid out by the Royalists during the Civil War. The circuit takes about 20 minutes, and gives superb distant views of the college, as well as glimpses of the River Cherwell flowing alongside.

Famous members

Richard Foxe (see Corpus Christi)
John Colet, humanist scholar,
1467–1519
Cardinal Wolsey, 1475–1530
Sir Thomas Bodley, founder of the
Bodleian Library, 1545–1613
John Hampden, parliamentarian,
1599–1643
Joseph Addison, essayist and poet,
1672–1719
Oscar Wilde, dramatist, 1854–1900
C.S. Lewis (see University College)
John Betjeman, poet, 1906–84

Duke of Windsor (Edward VIII),
1894–1972
Dudley Moore, comedian,
1935–2002
William Hague, former leader of
the Conservative Party, b. 1961
Edward Gibbon, historian
(1737–94), left after only 14
months
William Tyndale (d. 1536) and
Thomas Hobbes (1588–1679)
were among the famous graduates
of Magdalen Hall

Those who would like to continue the walk into east Oxford should now cross **Magdalen Bridge** (John Gwynn, 1771–79). Otherwise, cross the road outside Magdalen College to the Botanic Garden (see p •••), from which the elegant arches of the bridge itself can best be viewed. Those wishing to go under the bridge on a boat can hire a punt at the boatyard on the north side of the bridge.

Over Magdalen Bridge

On the far side of the bridge is a traffic nexus known as **The Plain** (plan 4, D), created after the demolition of the medieval St. Clement's church in 1830. St. Clement's St, to the left, gives access, via a car park, to Queen's College's extraordinary **Florey Building** (1968–71: no adm.), a futuristic extravaganza of red tiles and glass on concrete stilts designed by James Stirling (cf. History Faculty Building in Cambridge); the students' rooms are arranged in the form of a grandstand or theatre, looking west across the Cherwell towards Magdalen.

A little further along St. Clement's St is **Stone's Almshouses**, built by the local builder Bartholomew Peisley in 1700. Beyond here, Marston Rd diverges to the left, on the left-hand side of which is the neo-Norman **St. Clement's church**, built in 1826–30 (architect Daniel Robertson) as a replacement for the demolished church at the Plain. Beyond is the site of the **Centre for Islamic Studies**, with its own mosque, currently being built to the designs of Professor Abdul Wahid El-Wakil, and due to be completed in 2005.

Returning along Marston Rd to the traffic lights at the bottom of Headington Hill, the open spaces on either side (**Headington Hill Park** and **South Park**) once formed part of the extensive property of the Morrell family, successful local brewers (their brewery, near the Castle, has recently been closed). Headington Hill Park, to the left of the road leading up the hill, was the pleasure garden of Headington Hill Hall (John Thomas, 1856–58), now occupied by **Oxford Brookes University**, most of which is housed in a collection of mediocre 1960s' buildings in Gipsy Lane at the top of the hill. The university started life as an art school and subsequently became Oxford Polytechnic; it became a full university in the 1990s.

It is worth walking to the top of South Park, where there is an excellent, and much-photographed, view of the 'dreaming spires'. From here a gate leads across Morrell Avenue—the original main road from London—and into Divinity Rd, lined with late-Victorian middle-class houses. At the bottom is **Cowley Road**, Oxford's most cosmopolitan street, with an interesting variety of restaurants (especially Indian), food shops and people. A left turn from Divinity Rd leads past the large Victorian church of **St. Mary and St. John** to almost rural enclave containing the small 14C **Bartlemas Chapel** (for adm. apply to nearby house), built by Oriel College to serve the inmates of a leper hospital; the college still owns the surrounding land.

*Magdalen Tower
and Bridge*

Returning about half a mile along Cowley Rd, a left turn into Marston St leads to St. Stephen's House, an Anglican theological college formerly occupied by the Cowley Fathers, an Anglican monastic order founded in the 19C; its chapel is the beautifully proportioned late Gothic-style **St. John's church** (G.F. Bodley 1894–96; apply for adm to St. Stephen's House). Its west tower looks out onto Iffley Rd, a left turn into which leads to **Greyfriars**, a private Hall for Franciscan students, attached to the large flint Roman Catholic church of St. Edmund & St. Frideswide (Benedict Williamson 1911). Iffley Rd returns to the Plain past the **University Sports Ground**, where Sir Roger Bannister ran the first four-minute mile in 1954.

At the end of Cowley Place, leading left from the Plain past Magdalen College School, is **St. Hilda's College** (☎ 01865 276884), founded for women in 1893 by Miss Dorothea Beale, one of the great pioneers of women's education, and now the only surviving women's college in Oxford. Miss Beale, the famous and formidable principal of Cheltenham Ladies' College, was immortalised by the rhyme: 'Miss Buss and Miss Beale/Cupid's darts do not feel./How different from us,/Miss Beale and Miss Buss'.

The college was named after St. Hilda, the 7C Abbess of Whitby who was one of England's first women scholars, and achieved full collegiate status in 1926. Its first home was Cowley House, an elegant Georgian villa by the Cherwell, built for Dr Sibthorpe, Professor of Botany, c 1780. Since its foundation the college has extended south in linear fashion along the banks of the River Cherwell, incorporating a large Victorian house and later neo-Georgian additions. In 1968–70 the **Garden Building** was built in a modernistic idiom to the designs of Alison and Peter Smithson. Nearby is the brick-clad **Jacqueline du Pré Music Building** (van Heyningen & Haward, completed 1995), commemorating the cellist Jacqueline du Pré (1945–87), who was an honorary fellow of the college; an extension with a glass foyer was opened in 2002. Concerts are held here throughout the year.

The south side

Returning to the High St over Magdalen Bridge, Magdalen tower dominates the view. On the left is the **Botanic Garden** (plan 4, B; open daily Oct–March 09.00–16.30, Apr–Sept 09.00–17.00; adm. charge Apr–Aug, ☎ 01865 286690, ✉ www. botanic.garden.ox.ac.uk).

Originally the Physick Garden, linked with the Faculty of Medicine, Oxford's Botanic Garden is the oldest in Great Britain. It was founded in 1621 by Lord Danby on the site of the former Jewish burial ground outside the town wall. The original three-acre garden is enclosed by a high wall and Danby's bust is over the impressive Classical portal (built, and probably designed, by Nicholas Stone, 1632–33), flanked by statues of Charles I and Charles II.

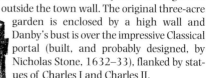

The common wasteland weed Oxford ragwort was first grown here from seed brought from Mount Etna and it was here too that the London plane tree was first grown in England by the first Keeper of the Garden, Jacob Bobart. The garden now contains 7000 types of plant, including some 150 trees of botanical interest, among them a yew planted c 1650. Cacti, lilies, palms and

Gateway to the Botanic Garden

other exotic plants can be found in the greenhouses. There is also an excellent rock garden to the south of the original walled area, constructed in 1926 and replanned in 1996–97, and a recently-replanted water garden.

The rose garden facing Magdalen College, at the entrance to the Botanic Garden proper, was created by Sylvia Crowe after the Second World War to commemorate the university's contribution to the discovery of penicillin.

Rose Lane leads to the left past the Botanic Garden into Christ Church Meadow (see Walk 2). A short distance to the west the *Eastgate Hotel* announces the position of the demolished East Gate. To the left, a little way down Merton St, is the grandiose east façade of the **Examination Schools** (no adm.), built by the university on the site of Oxford's premier coaching inn, the *Angel*, to the designs of T.G. Jackson in 1876–82; its exuberant eclecticism heralded a new era in Oxford architecture. The Schools are used not only for examinations but also for lectures during the university term and for conferences at other times of the year. The main entrance is in the High St (notice the carvings of a viva-voce examination and the conferment of a Master's degree over the porch). The building at the corner of Merton St and the High St is the **Ruskin School of Drawing**, housed since 1975 in buildings designed by Jackson for non-collegiate students in 1887–88.

Just past the Examination Schools is the former coffee room of the Angel Inn, now an up-market restaurant called the *Grand Café*. Beyond it, facing Queen's College, is University College.

University College

Plan 1, A; open only on application by prior arrangement with the Domestic Bursar, ☎ 01865 276602, ✉ www.univ.ox.ac.uk.

History

One of the three oldest Oxford colleges (the others are Merton and Balliol), University College (colloquially 'Univ.') long claimed primacy on the grounds of a fictitious belief that it was founded by Alfred the Great. This claim, invented to support a lawsuit in 1381, was upheld as late as 1727, and the college celebrated its millennium in 1882, when the Regius Professor of Modern History presented it with a gift of burnt cakes. It was in fact endowed by William of Durham in 1249, and was at first administered by the University (hence its name). The first statutes as an independent foundation were granted in 1280. In its early days University was a small and relatively poor college.

The medieval buildings were swept away in a complete rebuilding which began in 1634. A new quadrangle (Radcliffe Quad) was added in 1716–19, and there have subsequently been piecemeal additions and alterations which extend over the public footpath known as Logic Lane, linking High St and Merton St, and the college has also taken over several of the adjoining houses.

The long frontage, with its two gate towers, dates from the 17C and early 18C and testifies to the quite extraordinary conservatism of many Oxford dons and builders of that time. The **main gateway** carries a statue of a pugnacious-looking Queen Anne (a generous benefactor) on the outer face, replacing one of King Alfred, and a statue of James II in a Roman toga inside. The latter is a reminder of the late 17C Master, Obadiah Walker, who became a Roman Catholic but managed to retain his post through a dispensation granted by the King. James II's daughter Queen Mary II presides over the gateway to the Radcliffe Quad, further east, built after a bequest by the wealthy physician Dr Radcliffe in 1719.

The **Front Quadrangle** was built slowly between 1634 and 1677 and has been little altered, except for the south range (facing the entrance), which was Gothicised in 1802 and altered again in 1957. The **Hall**, in the south range, was extensively remodelled inside in 1766 and again in 1904. It contains portraits by Sir Thomas Lawrence, Graham Sutherland and others. The **Chapel** was much altered by Gilbert Scott, who added the heavy timber roof in 1862. But the screen, stalls and reredos are late 17C and there are fine windows by Abraham van Linge (1641). There are also four monuments by John Flaxman, one of them to the orientalist Sir William Jones (d. 1794) creator of a 'digest of Hindu and Mohammedan laws'.

Radcliffe Quad (1716–19) is reached by a passage to the east (left), of the Front Quad (doorway 7). Radcliffe, whose statue (by Francis Bird, 1717) is on the gate tower, wanted the building to be 'answerable to the front already built', and these instructions were carried out faithfully, down even to the fan vault in the porch.

A passage (doorway 3) in the northwest (right) corner of the Front Quad leads to the **Shelley Memorial** (1893), with the effigy of the drowned poet, by Onslow Ford, resting on a marble slab in an eerily top-lit domed chamber (by Basil Champneys)—a captivating example of *fin de siècle* sensibility. Shelley was 'sent down' from Oxford in 1811 for producing, with his friend Hogg, a pamphlet on 'The Necessity of Atheism'. Outside, facing the High St, is a plaque marking the site of the house where the scientist Robert Boyle (1627–91) and his assistant Robert Hooke worked while in Oxford. To the west of this is the **New Building**, by Sir Charles Barry (1842), and to the south-west the **Library** by Gilbert Scott.

Famous members

Lord Herbert of Cherbury, philosopher, 1583–1648
Dr John Radcliffe, 1650–1714
Sir Roger Newdigate, founder of the Newdigate Poetry Prize, 1719–1806
Percy Bysshe Shelley, Romantic poet, 1792–1822
William Beveridge, economist, 1879–1963
Clement Attlee, Labour Prime

Minister, 1883–1967
C.S. Lewis, author and literary critic, 1898–1963
Bob Hawke, former Prime Minister of Australia, b. 1929
Stephen Hawking, physicist, b. 1942
V.S. Naipaul, writer, b. 1932
Bill Clinton, former President of the USA, b. 1946

Returning west towards Carfax, past the Old Bank—now the trendy *Quod* restaurant and hotel—it is worth looking down **Magpie Lane** towards the 15C tower of Merton College (see Walk 2); on the left are some late-16C attractive fronts of former merchants' and tradesmen's houses. In Kybald St, a cul-de-sac leading off Magpie Lane to the left, are the former John Parsons Almshouses (1814), now part of University College. Between Magpie Lane and Oriel St is the rather gloomy north front of Oriel College's **Rhodes Building** (Basil Champneys 1909–11), with a besuited Cecil Rhodes gazing down from a lofty height above statues of Edward VII and George V. Behind it, on the left of Oriel St, is the inconspicuous entrance (now closed) to **St. Mary Hall**, a 15C academic hall incorporated into Oriel College (see Walk 2).

Back in High St, behind no. 107 High St (currently occupied by A-Plan Insurance) is the hall of **Tackley's Inn**, an academic hall built c 1320 by the vicar of Tackley; the 16C timber roof survives intact, as does the original early 14C vaulted cellar of the shops in front. Beyond is **King Edward St**, cut through a maze of old houses belonging to Oriel College in 1871–75 and leading to Oriel Square; a plaque on one of the houses on the west side marks the rooms occupied by Cecil Rhodes.

A block of timber houses follows on the south side of High St, stuccoed in the 18C but retaining earlier features behind the façades. After the National Westminster Bank, a Gothic Revival building of 1866, is Alfred St, which leads to the *Bear*, a small and often crowded pub notable for its collection of cut-off ties. The block between Alfred St and Carfax contains more old merchants' houses, notably no. 126 High St, a well-preserved 15C gabled house refronted in the late 17C. Three alleys lead south from this part of the street, containing pubs, a useful and long-established ironmonger's shop and, in the alley next to no. 130, **Kemp Hall**, a particularly well-preserved house of 1637 (now a good Thai restaurant, the *Chiang Mai Kitchen*).

4 ~ NORTH AND WEST OF CARFAX

This walk is another circuit from Carfax, taking in the northern and western parts of the city centre. It starts in **Cornmarket Street** (plan 3, B), one of Oxford's main shopping streets, but now mercifully traffic-free. Despite the encroachments of modern commerce, some interesting older buildings survive here. They include no. 3, just north of Carfax, formerly the Crown Tavern, which was leased from c 1592 to 1614 by John Davenant, whose son William, also a playwright, was Shakespeare's godson; according to John Aubrey, Shakespeare 'was wont to go into Warwickshire once a yeare, and did in his journeye lye at this house in Oxon where he was exceedingly respected'. Behind the unremarkable façade, on the second floor, is **The Painted Room** (adm. by appointment only, ☎ 01865 793003), so named from the well-preserved wall paintings of c 1560–80, depicting stylised bunches of fruit and flowers.

Immediately to the north is the entrance to the *Golden Cross*, the best preserved of Oxford's ancient inns, sensitively converted in 1986–87 into shops and a restaurant. The oldest buildings, on the north side of the courtyard, probably date from the early 16C; the rooms on the first floor (now part of the *Pizza Express* restaurant) contain excellent 16C wall paintings, some of them with Renaissance-inspired arabesque designs. Opposite is an impressive range of 17C timber buildings with projecting bay windows, and in the northeast corner there is an entrance to the Covered Market (see Walk 3).

Further north, at the corner of Ship St (nos 26–28) is finest of Oxford's medieval timber buildings: the former New Inn, built c 1386 and now occupied by the *Laura Ashley* shop; a small courtyard can still be seen inside the shop. The northern part of the three-gabled jettied façade to Cornmarket St was restored in 1951 and the rest was reconstructed in an architecturally accurate style in 1986–87.

On the opposite side of Ship St is the rugged mid-11C tower of **St. Michael's church**, Oxford's oldest building. Built of local corallian ragstone, it stood next to the North Gate and originally formed part of the town's fortifications. The church (open weekdays 10.00–17.00, Sun 12.00–17.00, closes 16.00 Nov–Mar; adm. charge for climbing tower) was rebuilt in the 13C and has been extensively restored several times since, most recently after a fire in 1953. Some good late-13C stained glass survives in the east window, and another 15C panel in a north aisle window shows Jesus crucified on a lily. St. Michael's is now the City Church and contains the 14C font originally in the demolished St. Martin's, Carfax, as well as the door of the town prison over the North Gate, known as Bocardo, where Latimer, Ridley and Cranmer were held before their deaths at the stake in 1556.

From here **Ship Street** runs east just inside the town wall, some fragments of which survive behind the attractive 17C and 18C stuccoed house fronts on the north side; most of

Ship Street, with Exeter College Chapel in the distance

the south side is occupied by the buildings of Jesus College, and the view is satisfactorily terminated by the west gable and spire of Gilbert Scott's Exeter College chapel (see Walk 3).

A left turn from Ship St into the northern end of Turl St leads to **Broad Street**. Originally known as Horsemonger St, and then as Canditch—a reference to the town ditch outside the walls—its wide expanse was long used for market carts; it has recently been partly pedestrianised. The shops are mostly devoted to University needs, notably books, with the most famous of all Oxford bookshops, **Blackwell's**, occupying a row of houses on the north side and outposts of the Blackwell's empire elsewhere in the street. The view east from towards the Sheldonian Theatre, Clarendon Building and the former Indian Institute (see Walk 1) is one of the finest in Oxford.

Straight ahead from Turl St, behind 18C iron gates, is Trinity College.

Trinity College

Plan 1, H; open 10.00–11.30, 14.00–17.00 or dusk if earlier; adm. charge; ☎ 01865 279900, ✉ www.trinity.ox.ac.uk.

History

Trinity College was founded in 1555 by Sir Thomas Pope, a wealthy civil servant during the reign of Mary Tudor. It stands on the site, and occupies some of the buildings, of Durham College, established in the late 13C for students from the Benedictine cathedral priory of Durham, but suppressed at the Dissolution of the Monasteries. Trinity traditionally drew many of its members from the landed gentry, and has a long list of distinguished members. It also, in the 17C, had two remarkable and eccentric Presidents, Ralph Kettell and Ralph Bathurst. Kettell had a particular dislike of long hair; John Aubrey records that he would come into the hall with 'a pair of scissors in his muffe, and woe to them that sate on the outside of the table'.

The buildings have a small-scale, intimate character which sets them in sharp contrast to those of the larger and grander colleges. They date back to the 15C, but there have been additions and alterations in most centuries since then. Much of the charm of the college derives from its setting, with large open lawns separating it from the busy streets around, inculcating a sense of seclusion among the fortunate inhabitants.

The oldest parts of Trinity lie, unusually, some distance back from the street; they were originally approached along a narrow high-walled lane, like that which still survives in front of Jesus College, Cambridge. The beautiful iron gate onto Broad St is a 1737 copy of the one at the eastern end of the garden, but the normal entrance is alongside a row of modest cottages taken over for college rooms in the 19C and largely rebuilt c 1970; to their right is the gabled, stone-built **Kettell Hall**, built by President Kettell as his own residence in 1618–20. The neo-Jacobean building of 1883–85 along the east side (right) of **Front Quadrangle** is one of the most exuberant and successful of T.G. Jackson's contributions to Oxford and he also designed the slightly later President's Lodging on the north side, next to the Chapel; his plans to demolish the cottages on the Broad St front were fortunately abandoned after vehement protests from, among others,

William Morris. The west side of the quad belongs to Trinity's neighbour and long-standing rival, Balliol.

The **Chapel**, of 1691–94, is approached from the Front Quadrangle through a passageway under the gate tower of the same date, adorned with statues of Geometry, Astronomy, Theology and Medicine. It was built at the expense of the President, Ralph Bathurst, but although the design was shown to several 'able judges in architecture', including Sir Christopher Wren, the architect remains unknown. The exterior, with its large round-arched windows between Corinthian pilasters, is a pleasing Classical design in the manner of Wren's City churches, but the real glory of the building is the interior, entered through a doorway in Durham Quadrangle and almost untouched except for the insertion of inoffensive stained glass in 1885.

The gorgeous plaster ceiling has as its centrepiece a painting of the *Ascension* by Pierre Berchet; note also the plaster panel of the Instruments of the Passion in the cove over the east end. The reredos is embellished with limewood carvings of flowers, fruit, etc., in the style of Grinling Gibbons and possibly by the master himself; it is well matched by the beautiful panelling, stalls and screen, by Jonathan Maine and Arthur Frogley. On the north side (left) of the altar, hidden behind Oxford's first sash windows, is the tomb of the founder and his third wife (1567) transferred from the former chapel.

The Chapel forms the southern side of **Durham Quadrangle**, the east range of which (right), survives from the medieval Durham College; it contains the **Old Library** (no adm.), whose windows contain some 15C glass. The **Hall** (left) is one of the smallest and most intimate in Oxford. It was built in the 15C and remodelled in 1620, but the interior is largely of 1772; it was repainted in the late 1980s by Alec Cobbe. Its chief interest lies in the splendid collection of portraits, with representations of the founder, several Presidents of the college, and old members including Oliver Cromwell's general Henry Ireton, the elder William Pitt, Lord North and Cardinal Newman.

A passage next to the Hall leads into the **Garden Quadrangle**: in fact a three-sided space, opening out on the east side to the garden, whose well-kept lawns are a poor substitute for the elaborate formal layout shown in early 18C views. The buildings on the north side, originally a single isolated block, were designed by Wren in 1668, but have been much altered since; on the side next to the garden is a bust of Cardinal Newman.

To the south of the garden is the drab **Library Quad** with the Classical War Memorial Library (1925–27) and the charmless Cumberbatch Building (Maguire and Murray, 1964–68). The quadrangle adjoins Blackwell's bookshop, whose large underground Norrington Room (named after a former President of Trinity) extends beneath it.

Famous members

Lord Baltimore, one of the founders of Maryland, 1580–1632

Archbishop Sheldon, builder of the Sheldonian Theatre, 1598–1677

Henry Ireton, Cromwell's son-in-law, 1611–51

John Aubrey, antiquary and biographer, 1626–97

William Pitt the elder, first Earl of Chatham, statesman, 1708–78

Lord North, Prime Minister at the time of the American Revolution,

1732–92	critic, 1863–1944
John Henry Newman as an undergraduate, theologian and cardinal, 1801–90 (see also Oriel) **A. Quiller-Couch**, author and	**James Elroy Flecker**, poet, 1884–1915 **Terence Rattigan**, playwright, 1911–79

Immediately to the west of Trinity is Balliol College.

Balliol College

Plan 1, H; opening times variable; sometimes open afternoons, ☎ 01865 277777, ✉ www.balliol.ox.ac.uk.

History

Balliol, now one of the largest and most illustrious Oxford colleges, began life c 1263 as a hostel or hall established on this site by John de Balliol, a powerful northern nobleman and father of a future King of Scotland, as a penance imposed by the Bishop of Durham for his frequent disputes with the Church. It thus boasts the longest continuous occupation of any Oxford college, though University College was founded earlier and Merton has older buildings. The first statutes date from 1282, by which date Balliol had died and his wife Dervorguilla had taken on the role of patroness.

The college, though small at first, played an important part in the spread of the New Learning in the 15C, when a number of leading Greek scholars were among its members, notably William Gray, afterwards Bishop of Ely, who bequeathed to it his superb collection of books, most of which the college still possesses. However, it rose to its greatest academic prominence in the 19C, when it was blessed with a series of outstanding Masters, the best known of whom was Benjamin Jowett (1870–93). Through his teaching and his brilliant pupils he had a far-reaching influence on Victorian thought and public life. He is commemorated in the contemporary rhyme: 'Here come I, my name is Jowett;/There's no knowledge but I know it./I am the Master of this college;/What I know not isn't knowledge.' Since Jowett's time, Balliol has continued to produce many leading academics and politicians, as well as the last three Chancellors of Oxford University, and still retains something of its 20C reputation as a hotbed of left-wing politics.

Balliol was substantially rebuilt and enlarged in the 19C, and the formidable Gothic **front** to Broad St dates mainly from 1867–68 (architect Alfred Waterhouse); the Classical Fisher Building to the west (left) was built to the designs of Henry Keene in 1768 but was altered in the 19C. Waterhouse's impressive, if somewhat overbearing, buildings so dominate the **Front Quadrangle** that it is easy to ignore the modest 15C Old Hall (now part of the Library) and Old Library on the west and north sides, the latter placed on the first floor in the usual manner.

Next to the Old Library, and impossible to ignore, is William Butterfield's pink and white striped **Chapel** of 1856–57, Oxford's first taste of the high Victorian 'constructional polychromy' later used to great effect at Keble College (see Walk 5). Some stained glass of 1529–30 from the former chapel was installed in 1912 and other windows are by Abraham van Linge (1637).

The interior is now alas less colourful than it once was, much of Butterfield's polychromatic alabaster-work having been plastered over, and his Gothic furnishings removed, in a fit of 'good taste' in 1937, when the reputation of Victorian architecture was at its nadir. The splendid silver-gilt repoussé-work altar front by Bainbridge Reynolds is a First World War memorial, and on the north wall is a monument to Jowett by Onslow Ford, creator of the Shelley Memorial at University College.

A passage in the northwest corner of the Front Quad (left) leads to **Garden Quadrangle**; the ancient wooden gates, now hung on the wall, were originally at the Broad St entrance and were to be sold for firewood in the 1860s, but were rescued by the Rev. T. Harling Newman, who 'deemed it a pity that gates which had witnessed so many deaths by burning (see below) should themselves end in flames'. Garden Quad is open, spacious and covered with lawns and trees. The buildings present a rather random appearance, due largely to the piecemeal expansion of the college in the 18C and 19C.

At the north end is Waterhouse's ponderous Gothic **Hall** (1877, usually locked), approached by a long steep flight of steps; the organ was given by Jowett, by whom a tradition of regular concerts was established. The quintessentially 1960s buildings on either side are by the Oxford Architects Partnership (1966–68).

Famous members

John Wyclif, Master in 1360, religious reformer and Bible translator, 1329?–84

John Evelyn, diarist, 1620–1706

Adam Smith, economist and political philosopher, 1723–90

Robert Southey, poet, 1774–1843

Cardinal Manning, 1808–92

Both **Archbishops Temple**, father 1821–1902, and son, 1881–1944

Matthew Arnold, poet, 1822–88

Algernon Swinburne, poet, 1837–1909

Gerard Manley Hopkins, poet, 1844–89

Lord Curzon, Viceroy of India, 1859–1925

Lord Milner, statesman, 1854–1925

Hilaire Belloc, writer, 1870–1953

William Beveridge, economist, 1879–1963

Aldous Huxley, novelist, 1894–1963

Graham Greene, novelist, 1904–91

Adam van Trott, executed as one of the leaders of the conspiracy against Hitler in 1944

Three 20C Prime Ministers, **H.H. Asquith**, 1852–1928; **Harold Macmillan**, 1894–1986; and **Sir Edward Heath**, have been Balliol men, and so too have been the last three Chancellors of Oxford University: **Harold Macmillan**; **Roy** (Lord) **Jenkins**, Labour politician (1920–2003); and **Chris Patten** (b. 1945), Conservative politician and the current (2003) Chancellor. One of the most famous fictional English detectives, **Lord Peter Wimsey**, was also educated at Balliol

A cross in the roadway opposite the old Master's Lodgings at Balliol marks the place where Cranmer, Latimer and Ridley were burnt at the stake in 1556. On the south side of Broad St, at nos. 15–16, is the **City Information Centre** and nearby, at no.6, is the **Oxford Story** (open Jan–June, Sept–Dec Mon–Sat 10.00–16.30, Sun 11.00–14.30; July–Aug daily 09.30–17.00, ☎ 01865 728822, or 790055 for facilities for disabled visitors, ✉ www.oxfordstory. co.uk), in which the history of the University is painlessly explained in a series of tableaux; part of the 'experience' is an unexpected glimpse of a tower of the town wall.

At the end of Broad St is the churchyard and church of **St. Mary Magdalen** (usually locked), one of the main centres of Anglo-Catholicism in Oxford. The largely 14C building was restored by Gilbert Scott, who added an extra aisle to the north in 1842; the incense-laden interior has since been embellished with Baroque statuary and other aids to devotion, and in the south chapel there is a memorial tablet to John Aubrey (d. 1697), the biographer and antiquarian.

Immediately to the north of the church is the **Martyrs' Memorial**, designed by Gilbert Scott in 1841 in the style of the late 13C Eleanor Cross at Waltham (Essex). It commemorates Cranmer, Latimer and Ridley, whose statues (by H. Weekes) now gaze out onto the heavy traffic of Oxford's inner ring road. To the east (right) are the Warren and Salvin Buildings of Balliol College, the latter with a neo-Tudor gate tower of 1852–53 (architect Anthony Salvin).

The Martyrs' Memorial is at the southern end of **St. Giles**, a wide tree-lined thoroughfare. From medieval times a great two-day fair has been held here, on the Monday and Tuesday following the first Sunday in September; the road is closed and all traffic diverted for this annual bacchanalia. Behind the walled forecourt on the east side is St. John's College.

St. John's College

Plan 1, H; open 13.00–17.00, or dusk if earlier, ☎ 01865 277300, ✉ www.sjc. ox.ac.uk.

History

St. John's was founded in 1555 by Sir Thomas White, a rich clothier and former Lord Mayor of London, on the site of the old College of St. Bernard, established by Archbishop Chichele for Cistercian monks in 1437 and closed at the Dissolution of the Monasteries. The object was to 'strengthen the orthodox faith' and the statutes were strongly religious in character. White was a Merchant Taylor and a number of places were reserved for boys from Merchant Taylors' School; St. John the Baptist, the dedicatee, is patron saint of tailors. Shortly after the founder's death the college acquired estates which included what is now the residential area of North Oxford; after being developed in the late 19C, this became an important source of income.

Elizabeth I visited St. John's in 1567 and was welcomed with a Latin speech by the young Edmund Campion, later executed for his alleged complicity in a Roman Catholic plot; later royal vistors were James I (who was entertained by a play which went on till one in the morning), Charles I, Charles II and George III. William Laud, later Archbishop of Canterbury and one of Charles I's chief advisers, was President in 1611–21; a great benefactor, he gave the college the Canterbury Quadrangle, architecturally its main claim to fame, and after

his execution he was buried in the chapel between the founder and his successor as President, William Juxon, who, as Bishop of London ministered to
Charles I in his last moments on the scaffold. In the 18C St. John's was
staunchly Jacobite in its loyalties and for a long time it remained an unusually conservative institution, even by Oxford standards.

The **Front Quadrangle**, though much remodelled, incorporates the 15C buildings of St. Bernard's College; the attic rooms with dormer windows were added
in the late 16C and early 17C to relieve overcrowding and the sash windows were
inserted in the 18C. On the outer face of the gate tower, completed in the 1470s,
is a statue of St. Bernard flanked by the two founders, Archbishop Chichele and
Sir Thomas White; on the inner side is a statue of St. John the Baptist by Eric Gill
(1936). The north range (left) is taken up by the Chapel and Hall.

The **Chapel**, though consecrated in 1530, owes its present appearance to a
drastic remodelling, in a somewhat insensitive Perpendicular Gothic style, by
Edward Blore in 1843; the reredos and east window are both by Kempe (1892).
The **Baylie Chapel** of 1662, to the left of the altar, is more attractive; it has a
plaster fan vault and contains some interesting monuments, some of them
removed here from elsewhere in the chapel, along with a late 15C altar frontal.

The early 16C **Hall** (not usually open to visitors) was enlarged in 1616 and
largely remodelled inside in the 18C; the plaster ceiling of 1730 hides the original timber roof and the stone screen at the west end is by James Gibbs (1742). An
18C scagliola (imitation marble) version of Raphael's *St. John the Baptist* is
incorporated into the upper part of the handsome marble fireplace (by William
Townesend, 1731), and portraits of Laud, Juxon and Sir Thomas White hang
over the high table. Another painting depicts Dr William Paddy, physician to
James I, and a great benefactor to the college.

The **North Quadrangle**, beyond the Chapel and Hall, grew up piecemeal and
only achieved its present appearance in the 1950s. To the right on entering is a
block housing the Senior Common Room (Bartholomew Peisley, 1676), one of
the first purpose-built common rooms in Oxford, and to the left, beyond the
kitchen, is a well-detailed neo-Tudor range of rooms designed by the younger
G.G. Scott in 1881. But by far the most striking building is the '**Beehive**' on the
east side, a series of interlocking hexagons creating a honeycomb effect, topped
by polygonal lanterns (Architects Co-Partnership, 1958–60). Beyond, a passage
in the northeast corner of the North Quad leads to the extensive **Sir Thomas
White Building** (Philip Dowson of Arup Associates, 1970–75), its grid-like
appearance determined by the prominent concrete frame.

Back in the Front Quad, a fan-vaulted passage opposite the main gateway leads
underneath the President's Lodgings to the **Canterbury Quad**, built in 1631–36
by Laud when Archbishop of Canterbury and Chancellor of the University, and
architecturally the most distinguished ensemble of its period in Oxford. It incorporates the plain Library block, of 1596–1601, on the south side, imitated in the north
range (note the splendid metal rainwater heads). But to the east and west there are
Renaissance-inspired Tuscan arcades with busts of the Virtues and Liberal Arts in
the spandrels and at the centre of each side is a Classical 'frontispiece' under a
curved pediment, richly adorned with Mannerist detail and sheltering bronze statues of Charles I (east range) and Henrietta Maria (west range), both of them by
Hubert Le Sueur (1633). There were extravagant entertainments when the King

Canterbury Quad, St. John's College

and Queen opened the new buildings, including 'an invention of Pyes walking, the one half representing English bishops ... th'other forraine Cardinalls with the Pope leading them, and both came to the king at table'.

The **Library**, on the south and east sides of the quad (no adm.), contains the founder's chest and several memorabilia relating to Laud, including the staff he carried on his way to the scaffold, his skullcap and his diary. There is also a painting of Charles in which his features are delineated in minutely written psalms; when Charles II visited St. John's he asked for this picture of his father, but later, on offering the hospitable Fellows whatever they wished, returned it.

The east front of the Canterbury Quad overlooks the **garden**, laid out in its present landscaped form in 1770–78, and now among the most beautiful in this city of beautiful gardens; George III thought that 'his dominions did not afford another example of gardening skill to match it'. On the north side, and largely obscured by trees, is the **Garden Quadrangle** (MacCormac, Jameson and Pritchard, completed 1990–94), the most ambitious and in many ways the most impressive of Oxford's architectural projects of the 1990s, with numerous visual references to the work of earlier architects, including Sir John Soane. On the ground floor is an auditorium in which concerts are given from time to time.

Famous members

Edmund Campion, Jesuit martyr, 1540–81
William Laud, Archbishop of Canterbury, 1573–1645
William Juxon, Archbishop of Canterbury, 1582–1663
Jethro Tull, agricultural improver, 1674–1741
A.E. Housman, poet and classical scholar, 1859–1936
Gilbert Murray, classical historian, 1866–1959
Robert Graves, poet, 1895–1985
Philip Larkin, poet, 1922–1985
Kingsley Amis, novelist, 1922–95
The current (2004) Prime Minister, **Tony Blair** (b. 1953), is an old member of the college

---

Opposite St. John's at the southern end of St. Giles is the Ashmolean Museum (see Walk 5). Its southern façade looks out onto **Beaumont Street**, laid out in 1823–28. The street takes its name from the long-vanished Beaumont Palace, built by Henry I and the birthplace of two kings, Richard I and John; in 1318 it was abandoned and the remains given to a Carmelite Friary which vanished at the Dissolution. The spacious street is lined with well-proportioned houses faced in Bath stone, but the clumsy *Randolph Hotel* (William Wilkinson, 1864), opposite the Ashmolean, destroys the scale at the eastern end, Further west on the south side is the neo-Georgian **Oxford Playhouse**, sympathetically designed in 1938 by Edward Maufe—an old member of St. John's—and used both by the Oxford University Dramatic Society and by professional companies.

Gloucester St leads south from the Playhouse to **Gloucester Green**, a large residential and shopping development on the site of the former cattle market, with whimsical turreted façades in ornamental brick (Kendrick Associates, 1987–91); here each Wednesday and Thursday a lively open-air market is held. At the southwest corner is the entrance to the **Old Fire Station** arts centre. The development incorporates the **Bus Station**, to the north of which is the former Central Boys' School (Leonard Stokes, 1900), now a pub.

The view west along Beaumont St is terminated by the façade of Worcester College.

Worcester College

Plan 1, G; open Mon–Fri 14.00–17.00 or dusk if earlier, ☎ 01865 278300, ✉ www.worcester.ox.ac.uk.

History

The college was founded in 1714 on the site of Gloucester College (1283), established for monks of the Benedictine order studying at Oxford, each parent abbey being responsible for its own 'house'. The Dissolution in 1539 brought the college to an end, but it was later re-established as Gloucester Hall, partly dependent on St. John's College, which by then owned the site. The present foundation was made possible through the benefaction of a wealthy Worcestershire landowner, Sir Thomas Cookes, aided by the substantial benefactions of George Clarke, former Joint Secretary to the Admiralty, Fellow of All Souls and amateur architect. Comparatively remote from the ancient city centre, the college displays some fascinating architectural contrasts, and boasts one of the most beautiful gardens in Oxford.

The entrance is through an open courtyard flanked by the Hall and Chapel, each lit by a Venetian window, with the Library on the first floor of the main block to the west: a unique plan for Oxford. The buildings were begun in 1720, to the designs of George Clarke, aided by his protégé Nicholas Hawksmoor and the mason William Townesend, but work proceeded very slowly and the Hall and Chapel were not decorated until the later 18C.

The entrance leads into a Classical loggia, looking west to the open-ended **Main Quadrangle**. The south (left) range consists of the picturesque 15C houses, or *camerae*, of Gloucester College; the arms of the abbeys which maintained them can be seen over some of the doors (Glastonbury, Malmesbury, St. Augustine's Canterbury, Pershore), though not all are in their original positions. The north range, opposite, is a complete contrast, built in a plain Classical style to Clarke's designs (but after his death) in 1753–59, with the **Provost's Lodgings** at the west end added by Henry Keene in 1773–76; proposals to construct matching buildings in place of the medieval south range foundered, fortunately perhaps, for lack of money.

The **Hall** (left on entering: usually locked) was decorated by James Wyatt in 1776–84 and lavishly redecorated by William Burges in 1877. In a fit of neo-Georgian good taste, the fellows chose to return it to its original chaste Neo-classical appearance after World War II, but Burges's sideboard was saved and can now be seen at Knightshayes Court, Devon.

The **Chapel** (right: key in Porter's Lodge) presents a strong contrast: too strong perhaps, even now, for some tastes. It was also designed by Wyatt, and, like the Hall, is entered through a screen of columns; but it was completely redecorated by Burges in 1864–65 in the most exuberant High Victorian Renaissance manner. There is a wealth of ornament, with heavily carved woodwork full of naturalistic carving (including an elephant and a dodo on two of the bench ends), a patterned floor, a superb alabaster lectern and candlesticks (by W.G. Nicoll), and richly painted wall surfaces; the stained-glass windows, by Henry Holliday, complete the ensemble.

Between the Hall and the Chapel, above its loggia, is the light and spacious **Library** (no adm.), completed internally in 1736; it contains an outstanding collection of architectural books and drawings bequeathed by Clarke.

The **gardens**, reached by passages through the south range, were laid out in the early 19C by the Bursar, Richard Gresswell, with tree-studded lawns and an ornamental lake, reinforcing the impression of the college as a large and elegant country house. Buildings of varying 20C styles and aesthetic quality overlook the lawns to the south and east, but to the north, reached by the lakeside path, is the one 20C building of real distinction at Worcester, the **Sainsbury Building** (so named from its benefactor, of supermarket fame). Built in 1979–83 to the designs of MacCormac, Jamieson and Pritchard, it rises romantically from the edge of the lake in a picturesque arrangement of cubes and pitched roofs, with much external wood and rubble stone, calling to mind Japanese and English vernacular architecture, as well as that of Frank Lloyd Wright.

The Sainsbury Building, Worcester College

Famous members
Richard Lovelace, Cavalier poet, 1618–57 (Gloucester Hall)
Thomas de Quincey, essayist and author of *Confessions of an Opium Eater*, 1785–1859 (Worcester College)
Rupert Murdoch, media tycoon, b. 1931

To the north of Worcester College in Walton St are the red-brick buildings of **Ruskin College** (no adm.), founded in 1899 by Walter Vrooman and Charles Beard, American admirers of John Ruskin, to enable working men to study history, sociology and economics in Oxford. Walton St continues north to the Oxford University Press, Jericho and Port Meadow.

Worcester St, the southern continuation of Walton St, passes alongside the Gloucester Green development; a right turn at the corner of Hythe Bridge St leads to the towpath along the **Oxford Canal**, from which Port Meadow can be reached (see p 142). At the far end of Hythe Bridge St, next to the **railway station**, is the **Saïd Business School**, designed by the Dixon Jones partnership and opened in 2001. It stands on the site of the iron-framed former London and North Western Railway station, designed by the contractors for the Great Exhibition of 1851 and re-erected at the Buckinghamshire Railway Centre at Quainton Rd (see p 170). The entrance is through a glazed façade flanked on the western side by a low tower surmounted by a peculiar ziggurat-like turret clad in copper, possibly inspired by Hawksmoor's equally odd tower of St. George, Bloomsbury, London. Behind the entrance block is an impressive courtyard flanked by long wings punctuated by tall rectangular openings, with a Classically-inspired theatre-like arrangement of stone seating at the far end.

From still-unnamed space in front of the Business School the dreary late 19C **Park End Street** leads over the Castle Mill Stream—one of several channels into which the River Thames splits to the west of the city centre—to the huge grassy motte or mound of Oxford Castle.

Oxford Castle

History

Oxford Castle was built by Robert d'Oilly in 1071, its construction necessitating the destruction of many houses. Queen Matilda was besieged here in 1142 during her struggle for the throne with King Stephen, eventually escaping, according to the romantic story, through the snow camouflaged in white. The castle ceased to have a military function in the 14C, but it continued to be used as the county gaol and assize court and the buildings remained in repair until 1652 when, in the words of Anthony Wood, 'they were in four dayes' space in a whimsey quite pulled down and demolished'. New Rd was cut through the circular courtyard or bailey in 1776 and a Prison built next to it in 1785; it was subsequently enlarged and was closed in 1997. The buildings are currently empty and plans for turning the whole complex into a hotel and heritage centre, with restaurants and some public access to the historic portions, were about to be implemented at the time of writing, with a view to completion in 2005. The rest of the castle site is occupied by county administrative buildings and by Nuffield College.

There are two main survivals of the medieval castle: the Norman motte or **mound**, an artificial earthwork which still retains its hexagonal 13C well-chamber; and the starkly impressive late 11C **St. George's Tower**, best seen at the time of writing from Quaking Bridge, first recorded in 1294 (turn right from Park End St into Tidmarsh Lane). The tower was built of local rubble stone and served both as part of the castle's outer defensive walls and as the tower of the chapel of the collegiate foundation of St. George, founded in 1074, one of whose canons was the historian Geoffrey of Monmouth. The chapel has disappeared, but its much-altered Norman crypt survives underneath one of the Prison buildings. Next to the tower was the Castle Mill, demolished in 1930.

The **Prison** is entered from New Rd through a forbidding castellated gateway. The main block dates from the 1850s and its gloomy galleried interior has changed relatively little since then; since closure it has featured in several films. A late-18C cell block links it to St. George's Tower. To the east of the prison in New Rd is the former **County Hall** and Assize Court, built in a neo-Norman style in 1841 (architect John Plowman); it still forms part of the county administrative complex, which was extended in the 1970s.

On the opposite side of New Rd is **Nuffield College** (plan 3, A; quadrangle open 09.00–17.00, ☎ 01865 278500). It was endowed by the car-manufacturer Lord Nuffield in 1937 for postgraduate studies, particularly in the social sciences, and was the first to admit both men and women. Nuffield apparently referred to the college as 'that bloody Kremlin, where left-wingers study at my expense' (his original proposal for a business school specialising in engineering and accountancy was vetoed by the University).

The college stands on the site of the old Oxford Canal basin, part of the medieval castle precincts. It was not begun until 1949, by which time Nuffield had succeeded in persuading the architect, Austen Harrison, former Government architect in Palestine, to replace his original modernistic design with 'something on the lines of Cotswold domestic architecture'. The main entrance in New Rd leads into the spacious, quiet quadrangle, on two levels, formally laid out with a rectangular canal in the middle flanked by residential blocks with steep-pitched tiled roofs, gables and mullioned windows paying tribute to the local vernacular tradition; the small Chapel (no adm.) has windows by John Piper. Externally the main feature is the rather ungainly tower, housing the library, with its copper-clad spire.

Across the Nuffield College car park, and facing the old County Hall, is the Doric-porticoed Canal House (1828), now the residence of the Master of St. Peter's College (see below). The north side of the castle precinct is enclosed by **Bulwarks Lane**, with the buildings of Nuffield and St. Peter's Colleges on either side.

New Rd leads east to the busy **Bonn Square** (plan 3, B), the north side of which is overlooked by the pleasing Classical façade of the **New Road Baptist Church** (1819) and the old churchyard of St. Peter-le-Bailey. On the southern side is the gratuitously ugly **Westgate Centre** (1970–72), incorporating a covered shopping mall and the main Public Library. It forms part of a 'comprehensive redevelopment' scheme planned in the 1960s by the City Council which involved the virtual obliteration of St. Ebbe's, an area of working-class housing which had grown up on and near the sites of the medieval Franciscan and Dominican friaries on the marshy ground to the south of the city. This district has now been replaced by roads, car parks and shops, with some housing close to the river. Both architecturally and environmentally the results are abysmal, and plans for reconstruction are currently (2004) under discussion.

St. Ebbe's St leads south from Bonn Square to **St. Ebbe's church** (usually locked), noted for its Evangelical churchmanship; it was largely rebuilt by G.E. Street in 1862–68, but a much restored Norman doorway can be seen in the west wall. Opposite its east end, Pembroke St leads east to the recently-relaunched **Modern Art Oxford** (formerly the Museum of Modern Art; open Tues–Sat 10.00–17.00, Sun 12.00–17.00, ☎ 01865 722733, ✉ www.moma. org.uk). Housed in a former brewery, this is devoted to changing loan exhibitions, often of an innovative avant-garde character; there is a small bookshop and a good café in the basement.

The bus-infested Queen St, one of Oxford's main shopping streets, leads back from Bonn Square to Carfax, and the quieter **New Inn Hall St** leads north to **St. Peter's College** (plan 3, B; usually closed to the public, ☎ 01865 278900). It was founded as a Private Hall in 1928 at the inspiration of F.J. Chavasse, Bishop of Liverpool, to provide places for men of limited means and those wishing to be ordained in the Church of England; the project was actually carried out by his son C.M. Chavasse (later Bishop of Rochester), who was the first Master, and full collegiate status was attained in 1961.

The college stands on the site of a medieval academic hall called Trellick's Inn (afterwards New Inn Hall) and incorporates a number of earlier buildings, including the former Central Girls' School (Leonard Stokes, 1901) and the church of **St. Peter-le-Bailey** (Basil Champneys, 1874), both of which look out onto the street; the church now serves as the college chapel. The college is entered through a late Georgian house built for the Oxford Canal company in 1797, beyond which is a varied assortment of mostly unremarkable 20C buildings.

Opposite St. Peter's is the restored **gateway** of the long-vanished St. Mary's College, founded for Augustinian canons in 1453 and dissolved in 1541; Erasmus stayed there in 1497 while preparing his Greek Testament. In 1580 the site was acquired by Brasenose College, which demolished the buildings, the chapel roof being re-used in the new college chapel of 1656–66; a new college annexe was created out of the houses on the site in the 1970s, known as **Frewin Hall** (no adm.) and incorporating the undercroft of a Norman merchant's house which disappeared long ago.

To the north of St. Peter's is the **Wesley Memorial Church** (plan 3, B; Charles Bell, 1877–78), commemorating the founder of Methodism, who preached in the first Methodist meeting-house in Oxford at 32–34 New Inn Hall St opposite (a plaque marks the building). The most impressive feature of the church is its Decorated Gothic spire. From here New Inn Hall St descends to **George Street**, on the site of the Town Ditch beyond the town wall, a fragment of which can be seen in the garden of the former Oxford High School for Boys (T.G. Jackson, 1878), a characteristically exuberant neo-Jacobean building which currently (2004) serves as the Faculty of Politics and International Relations.

From the Wesley Memorial Church the quiet **St. Michael's Street** leads east to Cornmarket St, following the line of the demolished northern town wall. On the south side is the **Oxford Union Society**, founded as a social and debating club in 1823 and acquiring its present name two years later. It has long been renowned for the quality of its debates, and numerous MPs, ministers and prime ministers first tried their oratorical powers in its hall.

The oldest and most interesting part of the motley collection of brick buildings is the **Old Library** of 1857, originally the debating chamber (adm. by application only, ☎ 01865 241353). The architect was Benjamin Woodward, the architect of the University Museum, and the high-roofed Gothic interior was decorated with Arthurian scenes by Dante Gabriel Rossetti with the help of several young artistic disciples, including the William Morris and Edward Burne-Jones, both of them recent Oxford graduates; unfortunately, owing to the inadequate preparation of the plaster, they soon deteriorated, but they have been rescued in a recent restoration and can now be seen more clearly than at any time since they were first painted, especially when the lighting is switched on. Morris's roof decoration, of 1875, also survives in good repair. The present debating hall was built in 1878 (architect Alfred Waterhouse) and debates are held there on Thursday or Friday evenings in term time.

A right turn at the end of St. Michael's St leads back along Cornmarket St to Carfax.

5 ~ THE MUSEUMS AND THE SCIENCE AREA

This walk follows a route through the area to the north of the medieval town wall and takes in some of Oxford's most important cultural and scientific institutions as well as some of the more recently-established colleges. It starts at the Ashmolean Museum, whose impressive Classical buiuldings by C.R. Cockerell (1841–45) are shared with the Taylor Institute for the study of modern languages. They dominate the busy traffic junction where Beaumont St meets St. Giles.

Ashmolean Museum

Plan 1, H; open Tues–Sat 10.00–17.00, Sun 14.00–17.00, summer Thur 10.00–19.30. Closed Christmas, Easter and during St. Giles Fair in early Sept. Disabled access to ground floor. Resyaurant open same hours as Museum. ☎ 01865 278000, 🖃 www. ashmol.co.uk.

Before entering the Ashmolean it is worth looking at the St. Giles façade of the **Taylor Institution**, where Cockerell's eclectic Classicism can be seen to especially good effect. Here the Ionic columns support statues representing the languages of France, Italy, Germany and Spain. A passageway through the building, flanked by Greek Doric columns, leads directly to the museum. The main approach is through the Ionic **portico** facing Beaumont St, but it is also possible to enter, and leave, through the west wing which now contains a good **shop** in the room where John Ruskin established a school of art in the 1870s. A staircase from here leads down to the **restaurant**, well situated in the vaulted space underneath the centre of the building.

Ground floor

To the left of the main entrance is the **Randolph Gallery (room 1)**, containing Greek, Hellenistic and Roman sculptures, and Roman copies of Greek originals, mainly from the important collection known as the **Arundel Marbles**, brought together by Thomas Howard, Earl of Arundel, in the early 17C and donated to the University by the Countess of Pomfret in 1755. The sculptures are interest-

The story of Oxford's museums

The history of Oxford's museums begins in the early 17C, with the provision of a portrait gallery within the newly built Bodleian Library. Then, in 1675, Elias Ashmole, 'the greatest virtuoso and curioso that ever was known or read of in England before his time', offered the University the famous 'cabinet of rarities' amassed by Charles I's gardener John Tradescant the Elder (d. 1638) during his plant-hunting and other travels and formerly housed in his 'Ark' in Lambeth. This heterogeneous collection was given to Ashmole by Tradescant's son and for more then two centuries it was housed in the building in Broad St now known as the Old Ashmolean (Walk 1). But, starting in the 1860s, it was dispersed, those parts deemed of scientific interest being transferred to the University and Pitt Rivers Museums (see pp 128–129) and the rest to the present Ashmolean and elsewhere.

The present Ashmolean Museum—originally called the University Galleries—was erected to house the bequests of Classical statuary, Old Master drawings and, subsequently, paintings accumulated by the University in the 18C and 19C. They were greatly expanded through the generosity of Charles Fortnum, the museum's 'second founder', and W.T. Fox-Strangways, and in 1894 a large extension was added to house the burgeoning archaeological collections of objects from ancient Greece, Egypt, the Middle East and elsewhere. In 1962 the University's collections of oriental art were transferred from the Indian Institute in Broad St and elsewhere. Today the museum ranks as one of the finest outside London, with continually expanding archaeological and art collections of the first order.

The building was erected in 1841–45 to the designs of C.R. Cockerell, the most scholarly Classical architect of his generation in England. In the 1820s he had visited and excavated the Temple of Apollo at Bassae in Greece and in his façades to Beaumont St and St. Giles he made use of the peculiar form of the Ionic order which he had found there, together with motifs borrowed from Roman and Italian Renaissance architecture. The Ashmolean occupies the centre and west wing of Cockerell's bulding; in the east wing, looking out onto St. Giles façade, is the Taylor Institution, founded for the study of modern languages with a bequest from the architect Sir Robert Taylor (d. 1788). At the time of writing plans had been prepared by the architect Rick Mather for a major extension to the museum, involving the redevelopment of the area to the north of the original building (Galleries 11–32).

ing not only for their own sake but for the light they throw on 17C artistic taste. They include a much-weathered male torso of c 460 BC, the 'Arundel Homer', copied by Rubens, and a Roman copy of a Hellenistic figure of the Muse Clio, which may have inspired Michelangelo; on either side of the archway leading from the main entrance are two spectacular candelabra from Hadrian's Villa at Tivoli, restored in Piranesi's workshop in Rome and acquired in 1775 by Sir Roger Newdigate, MP for Oxford University.

Straight ahead from the entrance is a series of galleries largely devoted to **East Asian art** and arranged around a central corridor. The oldest pieces, including early Chinese **bronzes**, are in the vestibule next to the Randolph Gallery (**rooms 11–12**). To the right is the excellent **Khoan and Michael Sullivan Gallery of**

Modern Chinese Art, opened in 2000 and designed by Van Heynigen and Haward. It houses changing exhibitions of 20C Chinese paintings, some of them scrolls which can be viewed both from gallery level and from a sunken area in which sculptures are also displayed.

Rooms **14–17** house a splendid collection of **ceramics**: *inter alia*, Tang Dynasty (AD 618–906) horses and other tomb figures, blue and white porcelain from the 14C and later, some splendid lacquerwork of the Ming dynasty (1368–1644), and *famille rose* and *famille verte* dishes and jars of the 18C (one dish, of 1775, has a view of the entrance to the Botanic Garden). At the entrance to **room 19** is a life-size 13C wooden Bodhisattva; the rest of the room is mainly devoted to Japanese decorative arts and 18C Japanese painted screens are displayed in cases around the walls.

The adjacent galleries (**rooms 21–23**) are devoted to the **Indian and South East Asian collections**, with particularly striking displays of Tibetan religious objects and Gandhara sculptures of the 1C–2C AD, showing the influence of Hellenistic art. **Room 26** is devoted to **Japanese decorative art**, including porcelain and lacquerwork for both the home market—notably the tea ceremony—and for export. Changing exhibitions of Japanese art are held in **Eric North Room** (room 25), and to the north of it is the **Gerald Reitlinger Gallery of Islamic art**, with an excellent collection of Turkish, Syrian and Iranian ceramics of the 13C and later; glassware, including an early 14C Egyptian mosque lamp; metalwork from Syria and northern Iraq; and some beautiful Turkish (Iznik) and Syrian tiles.

West of the Eric North Room is the **Byzantine Lobby**, where icons are dis-

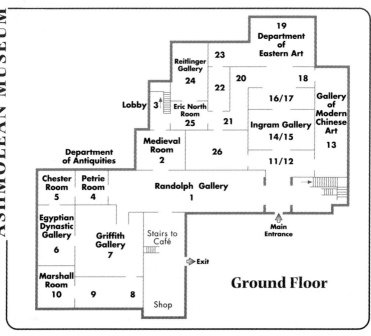

played, and from which a staircase leads to the first floor. Next to the lobby is the **Medieval Room** (room 2), containing a variety of objects displayed thematically, including English earthenware ceramics, brooches, tiles and alabaster carvings from the Middle Ages and later and a splendid 15C salt-cellar from All Souls College.

The Medieval room leads back to the Randolph Gallery, at the western end of which are the **Egyptian Galleries** (rooms 4–7). The **Petrie Room** houses Predynastic objects, mainly from the excavations of Sir Flinders Petrie (d. 1942). Next come the **Chester Room**, with scarabs, beads, seals, papyri, etc., and the **Egyptian Dynastic Gallery** which includes pottery, bronzes, jewellery, faience, glass, ivories and wooden grave goods, chronologically arranged from the First Dynasty (c 2920 BC) onwards. Many of the most impressive objects are in the **Griffith Gallery**, named after Oxford's first Professor of Egyptology. In the middle of the room is the Shrine of Taharqa from the temple at Kawa in Nubia (c 712–657 BC) adorned with bas-reliefs; other objects include mummy cases, sculpture and a fragment of domestic wall painting from Tell el Amarna (c 1345–1340 BC), and a sinister crocodile-headed deity guards the entrance to a small corner room in which more objects are displayed. Very different in character is the **Marshall Room**, containing **18C porcelain** (Chelsea, Meissen, etc.), and a particularly fine collection of Worcester dating from the second half of the 18C.

First floor

The first floor is best reached by the main staircase, with a plaster copy of the frieze from the Temple of Apollo at Bassae (the original is in the British Museum) running around the top and alluding to the archaeological interests of the architect, C.R. Cockerell. On the top landing is a 17C bust of the Earl of Arundel, collector of the Marbles in the Randolph Gallery. The small **Founders' Gallery** contains a fascinating collection of portraits of the Tradescants (by Emanuel de Critz) and of Elias Ashmole and his circle, and down a few steps to the right is the **Tradescant Room** (room 27). It contains diverse objects both from 'Tradescant's ark' and the early University collections, displayed in the manner of a Renaissance cabinet of curiosities. They include Guy Fawkes' lantern, Oliver Cromwell's death mask and the mantle of Powhatan, 'King' of Virginia and father of the more famous Pocohontas; this was brought from America before 1638, and is probably the first work of art from across the Atlantic to enter an English collection.

Beyond are the main collections of the **Department of Antiquities**, starting in the **John Evans Room** with objects from the European prehistoric period, including gold ornaments, and a large alcove for Italian and Etruscan antiquities. The Cretan collection in the **Arthur Evans Room** (room 30) is of special importance; it derives principally from the celebrated excavations of Sir Arthur Evans at Knossos, and includes Minoan seals, Linear B tablets, pottery, jewellery and fresco fragments of c 1500 BC. The **Myres Room** (room 31) contains Cypriot antiquities, including seals, jewellery and sculpture, and the **Drapers' Gallery** to the right (room 32) houses objects from the Near East including 'Luristan Bronzes' from the Zagros Mountains, items from Jericho and large Assyrian relief carvings.

The **Beazley Room** (room 33), to the left of the Myres Room, is devoted to **Ancient Greece** and contains a superb collection of pottery and vases, both black- and red-figure, arranged thematically (note especially those with scenes of music and drama, and of daily life: e.g. a shoemaker, from the 5C BC, potters in their workshop, and a helmet maker). There are also bronzes and helmets, and on the east wall is a pedimental sculpture embodying two linear measures (mid-5C BC). The reserve collection of Greek vases (open on application to the Department of Antiquities) is kept in a newly-created room over the former Sunken Court. The **Leeds Room** (room 35), west of the Beazley Room, houses objects from the **Roman Empire**, including cameos, household goods, glassware, bronzes, a fragment of fresco from the Golden House of Nero in Rome and a tombstone with portrait busts of a doctor and his wife (1C AD). There are also Anglo-Saxon objects, including, in a case on the west wall, the famous 9C 'Alfred Jewel' found in 1693 near Athelney in Somerset, where King Alfred spent the winter of 878 in hiding; it bears the inscription 'Aelfred mec heht Gewyrcan' (Alfred had me made) and may be the handle of an *aestel*, or pointer, for following lines of illuminated MSS.

Beyond the top landing of the West Staircase (note the early 16C pall from the University Church, made for memorial masses for Henry VII) is the **Heberden Coin Room** (room 37), with rich collections of Greek, Roman, Oriental, medieval English and European, and modern coins and medals, second only in importance to those of the the British Museum. A selection from all periods is always on exhibition and students are allowed to consult the main part of the collection by appointment. The adjacent **Hill Music Room** (room 42) is mainly given over to Italian and English stringed instruments of the 16C–18C, including the famous violin known as the Messiah made by Stradivarius in 1716; there is also an elaborately painted virginal made in London in 1670 and a Kirckman harpsichord dated 1772, sometimes played in recitals.

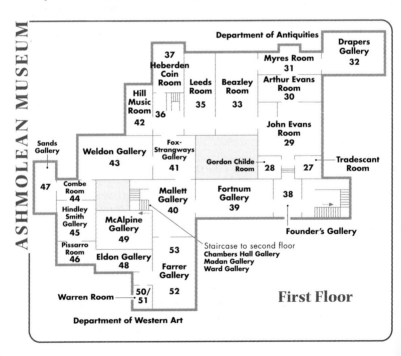

Department of Western Art

The remainder of the upper floors is occupied by a rich and diverse collection of paintings and objects displayed in an intimate manner reminiscent in some ways of a private collection. Beyond the Founder's Gallery (see above) is the **Fortnum Gallery** (room 39), containing Italian paintings of the 13C–16C, many of them of very high quality. They include (clockwise from the entrance): Ghirlandaio (attrib.), *Portrait of a Young Man*; Piero di Cosimo's bizarre *Forest Fire*; Giovanni Bellini's exquisite *St. Jerome in a Landscape*; a *Resurrection* by Tintoretto; Montagna, *Christ Carrying the Cross*; Bronzino's *Portrait of Giovanni de' Medici as a boy*, in a richly decorated contemporary frame; an enigmatic *Portrait of a Young Man in Black* (1562) by Alessandro Allori; a drawing of the *Holy Family* by or after Michelangelo; a *Virgin and Child with a view of Venice*, probably by Giorgione; Lorenzo di Credi, *Madonna and Child*; Uccello's *Hunt in a Forest*, one of the finest pictures by this master; and a *Virgin and Child* attributed to Giotto. At the far end is Titian's recently-acquired portrait of the Genoese merchant *Giacomo Doria*, dating from the early 1530s.

Renaissance medals are displayed in cases around the walls, and other cases hold works in ivory, Venetian glass and Limoges enamel (note especially a 13C casket depicting the martyrdom and burial of St. Thomas à Becket).

At the west end is the tapestry-hung **Mallett Gallery** (room 40), from which a staircase leads up to the second floor. A changing selection of the museum's superb collection of **drawings**, including works by by Raphael and Michelangelo, is permanently displayed in cases here; they were mostly acquired by the portrait-painter Sir Thomas Lawrence and were bought by the University from Lord Eldon in 1845–46. Other drawings by these and other masters can be seen on request in the **Print Room** (apply to attendant for admission).

The **Fox-Strangways Gallery**, to the right, contains 17C Dutch landscape and genre paintings, including works by Ruisdael, Koninck, van Ostade and Terborch. The **Weldon Gallery** (room 43), beyond, is mainly devoted to French, Flemish and Italian painters of the 17C; particularly notable (clockwise from the entrance) are a large-scale painting of the Roman *Gemma Tiberiana* by Rubens; Poussin's grave, tenebrous *Exposition of Moses* (1654); Van Dyck's powerful *Deposition*; Edward Pierce's splendid Bernini-esque bust of Sir Christopher Wren (c 1673); Preti, *Game of Draughts*; Lanfranco, *Christ & the Woman of Samaria*; an *Immaculate Conception* by the Spanish painter José Antolinez; a version of Van Dyck's portrait of Henrietta Maria (on loan from the Loyd Collection); Claude's *Ascanius Killing the Stag* (1682), painted in the last year of his life; Paolo de Matteis, *Choice of Hercules*, commissioned in 1712 by the English aesthete the 3rd Earl of Shaftesbury and hung in a later Rococo frame; and the terracotta maquette for Roubiliac's masterly monument to George Frederick Handel in Westminster Abbey (1762). 17C and 18C bronzes are also on display, including one of Bernini's equestrian figure of the Emperor Constantine from the Scala Regia in the Vatican.

The adjacent **Combe Room** is mostly given over to 20C paintings, including works by Steer, Sargent, Kandinsky, David Bomberg and Mark Gertler. More 20C art can be found next door in the **Sands Gallery**, opened in 2001. Particularly outstanding is the collection of works by Sickert, most of them given by the family of Ethel Sands, one of the artist's pupils; they include, on the wall immediately to the left of the entrance, his *Gallery of the Gaîté Montparnasse* (1907), versions of his *Noctes Ambrosianae* (1906) and *Brighton Pierrots* (1915); and the last version of *Ennui* (1917–18) on the opposite wall. The Sickert-inspired Camden Town Group is also well-represented, with works by Gore, Bevan and Gilman (*Interior with Mrs Mounter* c 1916–17), and there are also paintings by Matisse (*Nude on a Sofa* 1919–20), Picasso (*Blue Roofs, Paris* 1901), Braque, Ben Nicholson, Stanley Spencer, Pasmore, John Piper and Lucian Freud. Cases in the middle of the room house changing displays of 20C sculpture and in the drawers underneath are selections from the museum's collection of 20C prints and drawings; Barbara Hepworth's white marble *Talisman II* (1960) is on permanent loan.

The **Hindley Smith Gallery** (**room 45**) houses an excellent collection of French late 19C and 20C paintings. Works by Courbet, the Barbizon school artists, Boudin and the Impressionists and post-Impressionists are usually shown here, with canvases by Manet, Monet, Renoir, Toulouse-Lautrec (*La Toilette*), Van Gogh and Bonnard. There is also a particularly fine collection of landscapes by Pissarro (note especially his panoramic view of the Tuileries gardens in Paris under rain, and his view of Bedford Park, London, 1897), many of them donated by his family. Bronzes by Rodin and Degas are also on display.

The **Pissarro Room**, beyond, now houses landscape paintings, mostly British, including important early works by J.M.W. Turner (e.g. *Whalley Bridge and Abbey* to the left of the entrance, *Walton Bridge* of 1806–7 on the right-hand wall, and, to the right of the entrance, his view of the High St, Oxford, commissioned in 1810 by the local frame-maker James Wyatt)—the museum also possesses a superb collection of Turner watercolours which are placed on exhibition from time to time. Other artists represented include Gaspard Dughet (a view of Tivoli), Richard Wilson, Constable (an oil sketch of c 1829), Corot, and William Turner 'of Oxford', not to be confused with his more famous namesake. Beyond are the **Eldon Gallery** (**room 48**), where exhibitions of drawings, watercolours and prints from the museum's collection are often shown, and the **McAlpine Gallery**, used for loan exhibitions.

A vestibule at the far end of the Eldon gallery gives access to the small **Warren Room**, with English Delft ware, and then to the **Farrer Gallery** (**rooms 52–53**), devoted to the applied arts of the Renaissance. It is divided into two rooms, with silver in the first, including the Communion plate from the University Church and a particularly good collection of works by Lamerie and other Huguenot craftsmen working in early 18C London, along with watches and portrait miniatures. In the second room is the outstanding collection of bronzes and ceramics given by Charles Fortnum, with works by the Della Robbia workshop, a superb display of maiolica and bronzes by or attributed to Andrea Riccio (*Pan listening to Echo*), Giambologna and others. There are also 13C–18C rings and works in Limoges enamel.

Second floor

On the second floor, reached from the Mallett Gallery, is the **Chambers Hall Gallery** (**room 55**), devoted to 18C European paintings and sculpture, including works by Tiepolo (a luscious *Young Woman with a Macaw*), Watteau (the tiny *Repos Gracieux*), Guardi, Canaletto (*View on the Brenta*), Reynolds (*Portrait of the architect James Paine and his son*), Batoni (*Portrait of David Garrick*) and Panini; there is also a particularly attractive early 19C bust of Mme Récamier, and there are ideal heads by Canova and Nollekens.

The **Madan Gallery** (room 56) is given over to English 19C art. To the left on entering are small canvases by Bonington and Samuel Palmer, an artist especially well represented in the museum (many of his most famous pictures are kept in the Print Room). Much of the gallery is taken up by the excellent collection of Pre-Raphaelite paintings brought together by Thomas Combe, Printer to the University, and donated in 1894. Two of the leading members of the group are strongly represented, Holman Hunt by the luridly coloured *Christian Priest sheltering from Druids* and Millais by the tender *Return of the Dove from the Ark* (1851); there are also pictures by Ford Madox Brown, Arthur Hughes and Inchbold, along with late 19C artists including Leighton. Bronzes by Alfred Gilbert and other practitioners of the late 19C 'New Sculpture' are shown in glass cases, and against the long wall on the left is a massive cabinet made by Philip Webb for William Morris on his marriage in 1858 (his wife, the languid Jane, was the daughter of an Oxford stableman), painted by Burne-Jones with scenes from Chaucer's Prioress's Tale.

The final room is the **Ward Gallery**, with an excellent collection of Dutch 17C–18C paintings of flowers and still-life given in 1940, and beautifully displayed.

A right turn out of the museum leads via Beaumont St to **St John Street**, laid out with plain late Georgian houses in the 1820s and 30s. On the right is the Doric-columned circular porch of the **Sackler Library** (Robert Adam, finished 2001: no adm.); it houses the University's collections of Classical, archaeological and art historical books in a cylindrical structure inspired by French Neo-classical architecture.

To the north of the library is Pusey Place, which leads to the Ashmolean's **Cast Gallery** (open Tues–Fri 10.00–16.00, Sat 10.00–13.00). It contains over 900 casts of Greek and Roman statuary, including the Parthenon frieze, the *Apollo* from Olympia, the *Apollo Belvedere*, the *Winged Victory of Samothrace*, the *Laocoön*, the *Venus of Milo* and an excellent collection of Roman portrait busts. They are displayed in broad historical sequence, with Archaic and early Classical works (7C–5C BC) on the ground floor and Classical to Hellenistic works (5C–1C BC) in the basement below.

St. John St leads north to the rather gloomy Wellington Square, laid out in 1869–76 on the site of the old City Workhouse. The south-east side of the square is occupied by **Rewley House**, built as a girls' school but now the home of both the University's Department for Continuing Education and, since 1990, of Oxford's 36th college, catering for mature students taking part-time degree courses. The premises were converted into their present form in 1986 through a grant from the Kellogg Foundation and the college was renamed **Kellogg College** in 1994; plans were being prepared at the time of writing for the removal of the college to a new site in Banbury Rd.

A right turn from St. John St leads into Pusey St, flanked on the north side by **Regents Park College**, established as a training centre for Baptist ministers in London in the 19C; it moved to its present neo-Georgian premises in 1938, and since 1957 has been a Permanent Private Hall of the University, housing undergraduates and graduate students as well as Baptist ordinands. Opposite at the far end of the street is the impressively buttressed north flank of Pusey House chapel.

Pusey House was founded as a 'house of sacred learning' in 1884 to preserve the extensive library of the Anglo-Catholic divine Edward Bouverie Pusey (d. 1882) and to promote the study of theology in the University; since 1981 the premises have been shared with **St. Cross College**, founded for graduate students in 1965. The buildings, by Temple Moore, date from 1912–26 and are arranged around a courtyard, on the north side of which is the beautiful **Chapel** of the Resurrection (1912–14), the last major monument of the Gothic Revival in Oxford (open daily 07.30–dusk, ☎ 01865 278415; turn right on entering main doorway from St. Giles). The nave is separated from the chancel by a stone rood screen and there is an elaborate gilded ciborium by Ninian Comper over the high altar (1935–36).

Immediately to the south of Pusey House in St. Giles is **Blackfriars**, established in 1929 as Oxford's Dominican priory; the spacious Perpendicular-style chapel, by E. Doran Webb, is welcoming and serene.

St. Giles is lined with handsome buildings. On the west side, north of Pusey Lane, is the *Eagle and Child* inn (colloquially the 'Bird and Baby'), haunt in the mid-20C of the much-publicised 'Inklings', a group centred around the literary scholar and Christian apologist C.S. Lewis and the philologist and fantasy writer J.R.R. Tolkien (the interior has been reconstructed in recent years). At No. 38, in an early 19C building, is **St. Benet's Hall**, established in 1897 for Benedictine monks, and since 1918 a Permanent Private Hall.

The opposite side of the street is taken up by the buildings of St. John's College (see Walk 4). A footpath next to the *Lamb and Flag* inn leads to Museum Road, with the college's Sir Thomas White building on the south side and Keble College and the University Museum (see below) at the end. North of the *Lamb and Flag* is the impressive pedimented façade of **St. Giles House**, built in 1702 for Thomas Rowney, MP for Oxford, possibly by the local mason Bartholomew Peisley; having served for a long time as the official lodgings for the Assize judges on their visits to Oxford, the house was taken over after 1965 by St. John's, which uses it for seminars, hospitality and accommodation. Further north is **Queen Elizabeth House**, established in 1954 for the study of Commonwealth affairs and incorporating among its buildings the much-restored 17C Black Hall whose gable-end faces the street; at the time of writing plans were afoot to turn the buildings into a graduate centre for St. John's College.

The north end of St. Giles is blocked by **St. Giles church** (open weekdays 12.00–14.00), dating mainly from the 13C. The light, spacious interior contains monuments to many generations of City worthies, including the Peisley family of master-masons; their 18C successors, the Townesends, are buried in the churchyard. Immediately to the north, in Banbury Rd, is the gabled 17C *Old Parsonage Hotel*, which offers excellent teas. Opposite are the towering 'brutalist' buildings of the Department of Engineering Science and the **Nuclear Physics Laboratory** with its fan-shaped concrete tower (Philip Dowson of Arup Associates, 1970). From here Keble Road runs east alongside Keble College, which can be entered by turning right into Parks Rd.

Keble College

Plan 1, F; open 14.00–17.00 or dusk, ☎ 01865 272727 ▣ www.keble.ox.ac.uk.

History

The college was founded in 1870 as a memorial to the Rev. John Keble (1792–1866), one of the leaders of the Oxford Movement, to provide 'persons desirous of academical education and willing to live economically, with a college wherein sober living and high culture of the mind may be combined with Christian training based upon the principles of the Church of England'. Money was raised by public subscription, the Chapel, Hall and Library being given entirely by the Gibbs family of Tyntesfield (Somerset), enthusiastic Tractarians and merchant bankers who had profited by the use of guano from South America as agricultural fertiliser.

Initially, the college was governed by a council and Warden who appointed tutors; fellows were first elected in 1930, and the college became fully independent and of equal status with the older colleges in 1952, when religious tests were finally abandoned. Past members include many church leaders, bishops and archbishops, but the college has become much more secular in character, with the former Pakistani cricketer Imran Khan and Andreas Whitham-Smith, founder of *The Independent* newspaper among the most recent old members. It is now numerically one of the largest colleges in the university.

The buildings (1868–82) were designed by William Butterfield, a zealous High Churchman, and they represent one of the greatest achievements of the Gothic Revival in England. They are in his unmistakable style, asymmetrical, with red-brick walls startlingly diversified by colourful patterning and stone dressings, and ranks of chimneys punching the skyline. Equally original—for Oxford—was the arrangement of rooms opening off corridors rather than staircases as was traditional in the older colleges. Few additions were made until the 1970s, but since then the college has commissioned some good new buildings in the modern style of architecture to cater for the growing numbers of students.

The tunnel-like entrance lodge leads into **Liddon Quadrangle**, with the Hall and Library on the south side (left), residential blocks to the east and west and the towering Chapel (1873–76) facing the Hall across a sunken courtyard. The **Chapel** is entered from a passage at the west end. Its soaring vaulted interior, loosely inspired by the upper chapel in the basilica of St. Francis at Assisi, throbs with colour and decoration: polychrome brick and tiles, carved stone and marble, a floor of encaustic tiles laid in patterns of increasing elaboration as they approach the altar, and, above the blind arcading, mosaic panels of scenes from the Old Testament (nave) and the New (chancel). Over the altar is a representation of Christ in Judgment. The mosaics and stained glass are by Alexander Gibbs, who closely followed Butterfield's instructions; he was even sent to Venice to study mosaic technique. The nave seats face east, a departure from the usual college chapel arrangement of stalls.

In 1892 a small side chapel by J.T. Micklethwaite was added on the right, under the organ, to house Holman Hunt's *The Light of the World* (1853), perhaps the most famous of all Pre-Raphaelite paintings (there is a larger, later, version in St. Paul's Cathedral); it was bought by the publisher Thomas Combe and presented to the college by his widow, but Butterfield would not allow it to be hung in the main body of the chapel, which he said was 'a place of Worship, not a gallery'. To illuminate the picture, press the switch on the right-hand wall.

The Hall and Library block is relatively plain in comparison with the Chapel. Both are reached by a dramatic stone staircase under an oriel window in the centre and both can be glimpsed through glazed doors from the top landing. The **Library** retains its furnishings by Butterfield and possesses a valuable collection of illuminated MSS and early printed books. On the other side of the landing is the **Hall**, one of the largest in Oxford, containing portraits of Keble and other divines associated with the college, and a huge painting, *A Tale from Boccaccio*, by G.F. Watts (1844), on indefinite loan from the Tate Gallery, over the entrance.

To the south of Liddon Quad is the smaller, open-ended **Pusey Quad**, with the detached Warden's Lodging at the southern end and a picturesque group with a clock-tower to the west (right). A passage leads from here into a third quad, bounded on two sides by Butterfield's buildings and to the west and south by the equally startling—and in their very different way equally accomplished— **Hayward and de Breyne Buildings** by Ahrends, Burton and Koralek (1970–77); they face inwards, with sinuous glass walls echoing the line of Blackhall Rd to the west and yellow brick walls with slit windows on the outer side, recalling the fortifications of some medieval town. To the north, and accessible from Liddon Quad, is the garden, flanked on the north side by Rick Mather's brick-clad **Arco Building** (1995) and on the western side by the same architect's recently-completed **Sloane Robinson Building** (2002), containing an auditorium.

Almost opposite Keble in Parks Rd is the University Museum, another spectacular example of Victorian Gothic architecture.

The University and Pitt Rivers Museums

The **University Museum of Natural History** (plan 1, F; open daily except some days at Christmas and Easter, 12.00–17.00, ☎ 01865 272950, ✉ www.oum.ox.ac.uk) was built in 1855–60 as a centre for scientific teaching and research in the university, the object being to assemble 'all the materials explanatory of the organic beings placed upon the globe'; lecture rooms and laboratories were also provided. The building, by Benjamin Woodward of the Dublin firm of Deane and Woodward, adapted the language of the Gothic Revival to these secular purposes in a strikingly original and memorable way, influenced to some extent by the ideas of John Ruskin, a close friend of Henry Acland (later Regius Professor of Medicine), who was the chief promoter.

The **façade**, of Bath stone, has a steeply pitched roof and central tower, like a medieval Flemish or North Italian town hall, and around some of the windows there are carvings of plants and beasts by the O'Shea brothers, brought over from Ireland by the architect; lack of funds prevented the completion of the decorative scheme and matters were not helped by the attitude of the O'Sheas, who insisted on carving caricatures of the dons on some of the capitals inside the inner portal (they were obliterated, but their lively carvings of birds and cats still survive). The small octagonal building to the right is based on the Abbot's Kitchen at Glastonbury (Somerset); it was originally the chemistry laboratory.

The **interior** consists of a square courtyard surrounded by arcaded passages and covered by an iron and glass roof, the pointed-arched girders supported on clustered cast-iron columns with foliated capitals of wrought iron (by Francis Skidmore of Coventry): an aesthetic *tour de force*, though not altogether efficient from a practical point of view.

The central space is divided into a 'nave' with double aisles on either side. The zoological specimens occupy the central area and the aisles to the left; they include local dinosaur finds, and casts of a 40ft *Tyrannosaurus rex* and an iguanodon, their bones forming a counterpoint to those of the Gothic structure above. There is also a painting of the last dodo. To the right are mineralogical and geological exhibits.

The **galleries** upstairs contain excellent displays of birds, insects and building stones; there is also an observation beehive and a glass case full of cockroaches. The columns supporting the arches are each of a different stone from the British Isles, thus constituting a practical geology lesson. A plaque and display outside the Lecture Room commemorate

University Museum

the famous debate held in the Museum in 1859 between Thomas Huxley and Samuel Wilberforce, Bishop of Oxford, on the subject of evolution, in which the scientist is generally reckoned to have got the better of the argument.

In the east wall of the University Museum is the entrance to the fascinating **Pitt-Rivers Museum** (open Mon–Sat 13.00–16.30, Sun 14.00–16.30 except some days at Christmas and Easter, ☎ 01865 270927, ✉ www.prm.ox.ac.uk). It was built in 1885, to the designs of T.N. Deane, to house the ethnographic collections of General A.H. Lane-Fox Pitt-Rivers (d. 1900) and began with 15,000 objects displayed in an iron-roofed galleried hall which survives largely intact. The collection has since been expanded to include items collected by others, including such famous travellers as Mary Kingsley and Lawrence of Arabia; there are now about a million objects, constituting one of the finest anthropological collections anywhere, including Benin bronzes, a totem pole from British Columbia and items from Asia, Africa, the Americas, the Pacific islands and many other parts of the world. Following the general's instructions, the objects are arranged not by culture or geographical area but by type, so that the bemused visitor can study, for instance, masks, combs and weapons from diverse cultures crammed together in the same Victorian glass cases, often with their original labels. Temporary exhibitions are held in a modern gallery close to the entrance.

The buildings to the right of the University Museum's forecourt house the **Radcliffe Science Library** (T.G. Jackson, 1901 and Sir Hubert Worthington, 1934), the more recent reading room of which lies underneath the museum forecourt. To the east, along and behind South Parks Rd, is the University's **Science Area**. This is made up of a haphazard collection of late 19C and 20C buildings, most of them dating from the post-Second World War years and few of them of much architectural interest. Flowering trees planted along all the fronts and roadways do much to alleviate the general drabness.

The Ionic portico on the south side of South Parks Rd, opposite the Radcliffe Science Library, gives access to **Rhodes House** (usually open weekdays 14.00–18.00, ☎ 01865 270901), a lavish structure built in 1926–29 as both the headquarters of the Rhodes Trust and as a centre for Commonwealth, American and African studies. The architect, Herbert Baker, worked extensively for Cecil Rhodes in South Africa and the building, a mixture of Classical and neo-vernacular architecture, incorporates visual references to Africa, notably the bronze bird on the copper-domed rotunda copied from the carved stone birds found in the ruins of Zimbabwe.

In the impressive domed Vestibule—a miniature Pantheon—are the names of Rhodes Scholars of all nationalities who fell in the First and Second World Wars. Straight ahead is the lofty Hall, with an open timber roof and portraits of former Rhodes Scholars including Bill Clinton, former President of the USA. In the corridor outside is a beautiful tapestry by Burne-Jones of *The Romance of the Rose*, bequeathed by Baker. Everywhere, and especially in the Library upstairs (no adm.) the craftsmanship is of superb quality, reflecting Baker's early exposure to the ideals of the Arts and Crafts movement. There is also an attractive garden to the south and west, entered from Parks Rd, from which the building rises like an idealised Cotswold manor house.

An inconspicuous passage to the east of Rhodes House leads from South Parks Rd to the **Rothermere Institute for American Studies**, designed by the American firm of Kohn, Pedersen and Fox, and opened in 2001. Architecturally this is a highly successful essay in the style of International Modernism, and the south-facing reading rooms (no adm.) are light, spacious and comfortable. Next to it is the new glass-fronted **Chemistry Research Laboratory** (Robert Matthew Johnson Marshall partnership, 2004).

From the corner of Mansfield Rd enthusiasts for late 20C architecture can continue along South Parks Road to the intimidating, and now rather shabby, concrete building at the east end which houses the **Departments of Zoology and Psychology** (Leslie Martin, 1965–70); proposals to extend this formidable pile westward towards Parks Rd fortunately never came to pass. From here, footpaths lead north into the Parks and east to Mesopotamia (see Walk 6).

At the bend of South Parks Rd, opposite the Zoology and Psychology building, is **Linacre College** (☎ 01865 271650). It is housed in Cherwell Edge, a gabled red-brick 'Queen Anne' house of 1886–87 which later became a Roman Catholic convent and was extended by Basil Champneys in 1908–09. The college started life in 1926 as a society for graduates, mostly of other universities, wishing to study at Oxford, and was named after the Renaissance scholar and physician Thomas Linacre (d. 1524). It subsequently moved to the building in St. Aldate's now occupied by the Faculty of Music and became a full college in 1965. It took over the present premises in 1977, since when there have been several extensions in a manner broadly sympathetic to, and in some cases almost indistinguishable from, the older buildings; one of them, the Abraham Wing (1994), containing the main entrance, has won awards for its success in saving energy.

Mansfield Road leads south from South Parks Rd past the Institute of Virology and the architecturally rather more satisfying Pharmacology Laboratories (Architects' Design Partnership, 1985 and 1990) to **Mansfield College** (☎ 01865 270999). Founded in Birmingham in 1838 as a theological college for the Congregational (now United Reformed) Church, Mansfield College moved to Oxford in 1886 and the buildings were constructed in 1887–89; it achieved full collegiate status in 1995. It is now a normal undergraduate and graduate college, and the theological element is much diminished.

The buildings, set around spacious lawns, are the finest example in Oxford of the work of that much-employed architect Basil Champneys. They are in the late-Gothic style, echoing the older buildings of the university, and they exhibit some good craftsmanship, notably in the **Chapel** (for adm. ask at Porter's Lodge), flanking Mansfield Rd, with stained-glass windows portraying famous dissenters like Cromwell, Milton, Hampden and William Penn; in the timber-roofed Hall, and above all in the Library (no adm.), which has fine woodwork and a ceiling of painted panels in the Arts and Crafts manner.

Further on past Savile Rd is **Harris Manchester College** (Chapel open Mon–Fri 09.30–17.30, ask at Porter's Lodge for adm.; ☎ 01865 271006). Also founded as a Nonconformist training college, this time for Unitarians, the college began life in Manchester in 1786 and moved several times before settling in Oxford as Manchester College in 1889. It now offers degree courses in a number of subjects, mainly to mature students, and became a full college of the university in 1996, taking on the additional name of its main recent donor, a carpet manufacturer.

The rather dour Gothic buildings of 1891–93 are by the Manchester architect Thomas Worthington, and have not grown more lovable with age. But in the **Chapel**, to the left of the entrance, is one of the finest examples of late 19C art in Oxford: a complete set of windows by Burne-Jones, made by the Morris firm in 1895–99, and exhibiting all the felicities of that famous and fruitful creative partnership—note in particular those on the right, illustrating the *Days of Creation*. A large brick-clad neo-Georgian extension (Peter Yiangou Associates, architects) has recently been squeezed into the space between the college and Wadham College, with a pompous façade to Savile Road. The college also occupies some of the attractive stuccoed 17C and 18C houses in Holywell St, to the south.

Opposite Harris Manchester College, **Jowett Walk** runs east past a striking block of rooms for Balliol College by Richard MacCormac (phase 1 completed 1996: phase 2 under construction at the time of writing). At the end is St. Cross Road, which leads past a former school-house which served as the first home of St. Cross College (see p 126) to **St. Cross church** (usually locked), a rustic-looking building with a 12C chancel arch, 13C nave arcade and a west tower of c 1464; there were extensive restorations in the 19C. A holy well, which survives to the north of the church, has given its name to the parish, and several notable people are buried in the extensive cemetery, including Kenneth Grahame (d. 1932), the author of *The Wind in the Willows*, the aesthete Walter Pater (d. 1894), the composer Sir John Stainer (best known for *The Crucifixion*) and the theatre critic Kenneth Tynan (d. 1980).

Next to the church in Manor Rd stands **Holywell Manor** (no adm.), recorded in the 13C, but dating in its present form from the early and mid-16C. In 1930 the tenancy was granted by Merton College, lords of the manor since the 13C, to Balliol, which extended the building and has used it as a self-contained hostel for graduate students.One of the rooms was decorated by Gilbert Spencer, brother of the more famous Stanley, in the 1930s, and an attractive extension by the Architects' Design Partnership was opened in 1993.

Opposite is the uncompromisingly plain, but impressive, **St. Cross Building**

(Leslie Martin and Colin Wilson, 1961–64). Clad in yellow brick, this massive cubic structure houses the English and Law faculties and their respective libraries—reached by a monumental west-facing staircase—and the Institute of Economics and Statistics. Further on in Manor Road is the **Social Studies Faculty Centre** (Norman Foster and partners, completed 2000: being extended 2003), the first and to date the only Oxford building by this well-known firm, though not one of their most inspired creations. Beyond is the inconspicuous entrance to St. Catherine's College.

St. Catherine's College

Plan 2, H; open in daylight hours, ☎ 01865 271700, ⊠ www.stcatz.ox.ac.uk.

History

Starting life in 1868 as a society for non-collegiate students, both under-graduate and graduate, St. Catherine's only became a college in 1963, having been housed between 1888 and 1936 in the present Ruskin School of Drawing, next to the Examination Schools in the High St, and subsequently in the building now used by the Faculty of Music in St. Aldate's. The present buildings went up in 1960–64 on flat meadowland near the Cherwell to the designs of Arne Jacobsen, a Danish architect deeply influenced by the masters of the 'International Modern' style, especially Mies van der Rohe. Jacobsen also laid out the gardens and designed much of the furniture, including even the cutlery used at High Table, and the college represents one of the most complete and ambitious expressions of the ideals of the Modern Movement in either Oxford or Cambridge. St. Catherine's is now one of the largest colleges in Oxford and has a higher proportion of scientists among its fellows than any other Oxford college.

The college is approached from a passageway which leads to a water garden, enlivened by a sculpture by Barbara Hepworth; to the left is the Master's Lodgings, a Corbusian villa, and to the southeast the Music Room, an interesting double hexagon in Jacobsen's ubiquitous yellow brick. The plan of the main buildings is strictly geometrical throughout. There are two long parallel residential blocks running north and south, built of specially made yellow bricks and precast concrete beams, with large windows, affording the occupants much light but little privacy.

The porter's lodge gives access to the airy **courtyard**, enclosed by the residential blocks—not a quad in the traditional Oxford sense. On the left is the vast **Hall** (usually locked), the largest in Oxford, its bareness alleviated by colourful tapestries by Tom Phillips, and to the right are blocks for lecture rooms and the **Library** (no adm.), partly clad in bronze; there is no chapel. A vertical note is struck amid this obsessive horizontality by the jejune campanile, one of several unsuccessful attempts at tower-building in 20C Oxford. The rigour of the architecture is greatly mitigated by the planting, both in the central circular lawn, with its two carefully placed cedar trees and in the separate enclosed gardens between the buildings formed within rows of parallel walls and yew hedges.

A new block at the end of Manor Road by Hodder Architects (completed 1995) subtly reinterprets Jacobsen's idiom and at the time of writing this was being extended eastwards to create a new quadrangle and entrance to the college.

Famous members

Eric Williams, historian and first Prime Minister of Trinidad and Tobago, 1911–81
Alan (Lord) Bullock, historian, the first Master, 1914–2004
J. Paul Getty, 1892–1976

John Birt, former director of the BBC, b. 1944
Peter Mandelson, Labour politician, b. 1953
Jeanette Winterson, novelist, b. 1959

From St. Catherine's the best way back into central Oxford is along St. Cross Road to **Holywell Street**. Just south of the junction, in Longwall St, is the red-brick former **garage** of 1910 (no. 21) where the first Bullnose Morris car was produced; this has since been turned into student rooms by New College. Holywell St follows the line of the town wall and is lined on the north side (right) by attractive stone and timber houses (for the western end of the street, see Walk 1).

6 ~ JERICHO AND NORTH OXFORD

This walk explores Victorian Oxford, including the once working-class but now up-market neighbourhood of Jericho and the prosperous middle-class suburb of North Oxford, first laid out in the 1860s. It starts in the churchyard of St. Giles (see Walk 5), at the bifurcation of Banbury and Woodstock Rds.

A short distance up **Woodstock Road** on the left is the impressive but rather chilly **St. Aloysius** Roman Catholic Church (J.A. Hansom & Son, 1873–75), French Gothic in style and since 1993 the third English Oratory.

Immediately to the north is the restrained Arts and Crafts-inspired entrance to **Somerville College** (plan 1, E), built to the designs of Percy Morley-Horder in 1932–33 (☎ 01865 270600). The college was founded in 1879 in the early 19C Walton House as a hall for women students, and is named after Mary Somerville, a distinguished mathematician (d. 1872). Unlike Lady Margaret Hall (see below), Somerville has always been deliberately non-denominational (the chapel was not built until 1935). It became a fully independent self-governing body in 1926, soon after women were admitted as members of the university, and the roll of its past members is impressive, including the first female Prime Ministers of Britain (Margaret Thatcher) and India (Indira Gandhi), as well as the writers Dorothy Sayers and Iris Murdoch, the politician Shirley Williams and the broadcaster Esther Rantzen. The first male students were admitted in 1994.

The buildings, which grew up around Walton House and its spacious garden, are something of a mixed bag, with contributions by the ubiquitous T.G. Jackson (1881) and Basil Champneys (the Library, 1903), a neo-Georgian Hall of 1912–13 (architect Edmund Fisher), examples of 1960s brutalism by Philip Dowson of Arup Associates, and the more recent Dorothy Hodgkin Building (Oxford Architects Partnership, 1991), cleverly fitted in behind a row of shops in Woodstock Rd.

Returning to St. Giles churchyard, the trendy **Little Clarendon Street**, lined with restaurants and bars, leads west towards Jericho. The north side of the street (right) is dominated by the Vaughan/Fry Building of Somerville College (Philip Dowson, 1962–66), resting on a Corbusian arcade with shops, and on the opposite side are the grim **University Offices** (Sir Leslie Martin, 1969–73). From the end of the street Walton St leads north past Somerville's aggressively modernist Wolfson Building (Dowson, 1964–67) to the dignified Classical premises of the **Oxford University Press** (Daniel Robertson, 1826–30). One of the leading publishing houses in the world, the OUP was housed for a time in the Sheldonian Theatre and then in the Clarendon Building (see Walk 1). It is now a worldwide business and a major employer in Oxford, although its printing house, heir to a 500-year-long tradition, closed in 1990; new offices for the Press were then created on the site. A small museum contains some of the old printing equipment and other memorabilia (open by appointment in office hours, ☎ 01865 267527). Opposite is the decaying Grecian portico of **St. Paul's church** (H.J. Underwood, 1836), built for workers at the press and now occupied by *Freud's* café and wine bar.

Jericho, to the north of the University Press, was laid out with terraces of red-brick working-class housing—many of them now occupied by professional people—on the low-lying ground by the Oxford Canal in the mid-19C; it narrowly escaped demolition and redevelopment during the 1970s. Its major architectural monument is **St. Barnabas church**, reached by turning left from the University Press into Great Clarendon St and then right into St. Barnabas St. The church was built to the designs of Arthur Blomfield in 1869; a temple of Anglo-Catholicism, it was financed by Thomas Combe, partner in the OUP and a leading patron of the Pre-Raphaelites (the bulk of his collection can be seen in the Ashmolean Museum: see Walk 5). Unusually, the Italian Romanesque style was chosen, and the tall campanile and colourful, numinous interior (usually locked, but visible through a glass screen) bring a taste of the Mediterranean to the bricky streets around. The church stands next to the Oxford Canal, which can be reached by a footbridge at the end of Canal St.

From St Barnabas, a short walk along Cardigan St and Jericho St leads to **Walton Street**, the 'high street' of Jericho, now lined with bars and restaurants (and the *Phoenix*, Oxford's best cinema). From the northern end of the street Port Meadow (see p 142) can be reached by turning left along Walton Well Rd. But this walk follows Observatory St, nearly opposite the cinema, to Woodstock Rd and the former Radcliffe Observatory, now part of Green College (turn right at the end of Observatory St).

Green College (plan 1, C/E; ☎ 01865 274770) was established in 1979 for fellows and graduate students in clinical medicine and the social sciences and is named after its principal benefactors, Dr and Mrs Cecil Green of Dallas, Texas. It is entered from Woodstock Rd through an unpretentious set of buildings in the neo-Georgian manner, somewhat reminiscent of an 18C stable block, designed by the University Surveyor, Jack Lankester, in 1978–79. They lead into an open courtyard from which the curved north elevation of the Radcliffe Observatory can be glimpsed across the gardens.

One of the first monuments of English Neo-classicism, the **Radcliffe Observatory** (no adm.) was built in 1772–94 with funds supplied by the trustees of Dr Radcliffe's bequest (see Radcliffe Camera, Walk 1). The original architect was Henry Keene, but he was superseded after his death in 1776 by James Wyatt and it was Wyatt who designed the upper floors, including the octagonal tower for the movable telescopes (the more important 'fixed instruments' were in the wings at ground-floor level). The tower was based on the Hellenistic Tower of the Winds in Athens and is embellished at the top with exquisite reliefs of the Winds (by John Bacon, 1792–94) and surmounted by lead figures of Atlas and Hercules supporting a copper-covered globe, also by Bacon; above the first floor windows are panels of the signs of the Zodiac made in the artificial Coade stone whose precise method of manufacture long remained a closely-guarded secret.

The south front of the Observatory, from which these details can be clearly seen, is reached by turning right out of Green College and then right again into a drive which runs along the north side of the **Radcliffe**

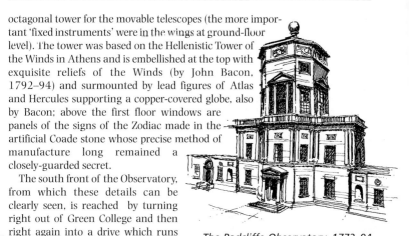

The Radcliffe Observatory, 1772–94

Infirmary. The original buildings of the Infirmary face east onto Woodstock Rd and were built to the restrained but dignified designs of Stiff Leadbetter in 1761–70, also using funds bequeathed by Dr John Radcliffe. Having greatly expanded in the 20C, the infirmary now contains some of the specialist units of the John Radcliffe Hospital, one of Britain's leading teaching hospitals, whose headquarters are in Headington. At the time of writing plans were being prepared to concentrate the whole hospital to Headington, after which the infirmary buildings will be taken over by the University.

Opposite Green College is **St. Anne's College** (☎ 01865 274800), which traces its origins to the Association for the Education of Women in Oxford, founded in 1878 and later renamed the Society of Oxford Home Students. The first permanent buildings went up in the 1930s and the society attained full collegiate status in 1952. Since then there has been extensive building, but the college still retains something of the informal character imparted by the Victorian gardens within which it has been built. It is now co-educational.

It is entered through a rather mannered gatehouse, designed in 1966 by Howell, Killick, Partridge and Amis; to the right, flanking Woodstock Rd, is the light and spacious **Hall** (Gerald Banks, 1958–60), one of Oxford's first modernist buildings, lit by a lantern in the roof. The HKPA partnership was responsible for the two idiosyncratic concrete residential blocks of 1964–68 on the eastern part of the site (four more were planned but never built), and to the north (left) is a block by Giles Gilbert Scott (1938, subsequently extended), housing the Library and common rooms; to the north a large new residential block was being built in 2004 to the designs of Kohn Pederson and Fox. The south side of the main quad is occupied by the well-detailed Clare Palley Building (Alex French Associates, 1992).

Across Bevington Rd, a little further north, are the rugged Victorian Gothic buildings of **St. Antony's College** (plan 1, C; not normally open to the public; ☎ 01865 284700), a graduate college specialising in international studies. It was founded in 1950 with a benefaction from the French shipping magnate Antonin Besse, a generous donor to Oxford, and achieved full collegiate status in 1965.

The college was first housed in the former Anglican convent of the Holy Trinity (Charles Buckeridge, 1866–68) and the recently remodelled Library still occupies the vaulted Chapel, built to the designs of J.L. Pearson in 1891–94. But with the construction of the sinister-looking but strangely impressive Hall and common rooms (Howell, Killick, Partridge and Amis, 1968–70), the centre of gravity shifted to the north. Further east, alongside Winchester Rd, is the less assertive **Nissan Institute for Japanese Studies** (Architects Design Partnership, completed 1993).

To the north of St. Antony's, facing Woodstock Rd, is the church of **St. Philip and St. James** (1860–66), one of the masterpieces of G.E. Street, Oxford's diocesan architect. The spire, based, like the church itself, on French Gothic prototypes, is one of the landmarks of North Oxford, and the powerful interior is rich in carved stone and stained glass (mostly by Clayton and Bell); since 1988 it has been denuded of many of its original furnishings and is now used as the headquarters of the Oxford Centre for Mission Studies, to which visitors should apply for admission (☎ 01865 556071).

Church Walk, a pathway along the south side of St. Philip and St. James churchyard leads east to the village-like **North Parade**, where more pubs and restaurants can be found; confusingly, it is a mile or so south of South Parade in Summertown, a mile or so to the north (the apocryphal story is that the Royalist troops defending Oxford in the Civil War paraded in North Parade, beyond the northern city limits, and their Parliamentarian foes in South Parade).

At the end of North Parade is **Banbury Road**, which cuts through the North Oxford suburb laid out by St. John's College in the second half of the 19C; despite some depredations, this still remains one of the finest examples of Victorian middle-class suburban development in England. Contrary to popular myth, most of the houses were first occupied not by dons but by successful merchants and professional men and their families. But after fellows of colleges were allowed to marry in 1877 the dons came in droves, and today 'North Oxford' still conveys distinct overtones of articulate *bien-pensant* intellectualism. Most of the houses in Banbury Rd are now occupied by university departments, language schools and hotels, but many of those in the streets on either side are still in private occupation.

A left turn from North Parade into Banbury Rd leads to St. Margaret's Rd and the entrance to **St. Hugh's College** (plan 1, A; ☎ 01865 274900), one of the former women's colleges. It was founded in 1886 by Elizabeth Wordsworth, Principal of Lady Margaret Hall and daughter of the Bishop of Lincoln, after whose predecessor, St. Hugh of Lincoln, it was named. It moved to its present site in 1916 and received a Royal Charter in 1926. The core of the college is a complex of neo-Georgian brick buildings by Buckland and Haywood of Birmingham (1914–16), entered through a domestic-looking block surmounted by a cupola. To the south are the extensive **gardens**, first laid out behind the large Victorian houses on the site and later beautified by successive fellows of the college, notably Annie M.A.H. Rogers (d. 1937) a pioneer of women's education and a famous Oxford 'character'. Old members include Barbara Castle, Labour politician, and the Burmese dissident Aung San Suu Kyi.

Later extensions include the jagged Wolfson Building of 1968 by David Roberts, an architect more represented in Cambridge than Oxford, and the impressive terracotta-clad Maplethorpe Building (David Morley 1999), reached from the college's south entrance in Canterbury Rd.

From St. Hugh's, *aficionados* of late 20C architecture can make a half-mile detour along Banbury Rd and Linton Rd to **Wolfson College** (open daylight hours, ☎ 01865 273100), one of the more architecturally ambitious new colleges in Oxford. Beginning life in 1965 as Iffley College, a society for graduates reading for advanced degrees, especially (but not exclusively) in the sciences, it changed its name in 1966, when benefactions from the Wolfson and Ford Foundations made large-scale development possible. The present buildings were erected in 1969–74 to the designs of Powell and Moya, already well known for their extensions to some of the older colleges in both Oxford and Cambridge.

The beauty of the college lies chiefly in its setting among lawns and trees beside the Cherwell; it has its own small marina or 'punt harbour', and a foot-bridge over the river leads to water-meadows and a pleasant riverside path. The low buildings are a trifle monotonous in comparison with the earlier work of this partnership, but they are cleverly planned and well grouped, especially when seen from the river.

A short walk along Chadlington Rd and Bardwell Rd leads back from Wolfson College to Banbury Rd; in the spring and summer punts can be hired at the **Cherwell Boathouse** at the southern end of Chadlington Rd, where there is also an excellent restaurant. On the east side of Banbury Rd, facing the grounds of St. Hugh's, is **Park Town**, laid out by Samuel Lipscomb Seckham in 1853–55 on land belonging to New College; this enticing but expensive arcadia is perfectly preserved, with Classical terraces and semi-detached Italianate villas set among dense plantations of trees and shrubs.

Further south is the **Norham Manor Estate**; this was laid out by the St. John's College surveyor William Wilkinson, starting in 1860, and is bounded by Norham Rd, Fyfield Rd, Norham Gardens and Banbury Rd. The houses, designed by able local architects, represent a largely successful attempt to adapt the idiom of the High Victorian Gothic Revival to domestic use. Some of the most impressive face Banbury Rd, among them nos 60 and 62, just south of Norham Rd; note especially the lively carvings over the door of no. 62, built in 1864–65 for the vicar of St. Mary Magdalen's church (architect E.G. Bruton).

Norham Rd, lined with substantial Victorian houses, leads east from Banbury Rd past the **Maison Française**, built in 1962–63 to further Anglo-French cultural studies; the Neo-classical nude in the forecourt is by Aristide Maillol. From the end a right turn into Fyfield Rd leads to Lady Margaret Hall, the most attractive of Oxford's former women's colleges.

Lady Margaret Hall

Plan 2, A; open 10–dusk, ☎ 01865 274300, ✉ www.lmh.ox.ac.uk.

History

The college, familiarly known as LMH, was founded in 1878 and owed much to the championship of Dr E.S. Talbot, Warden of Keble College, who at a great age dedicated the chapel in 1933, seven years after the college was incorporated by Royal Charter. It is named after Lady Margaret Beaufort (d.

1509), founder of St. John's and Christ's Colleges at Cambridge, and of professorships in Divinity at both universities, and has several distinguished old members, including the writer Lady Antonia Fraser, the playwright Carol Churchill and Benazir Bhutto, former Prime Minister of Pakistan. It was the first of Oxford's women's colleges to go co-educational, in 1979.

The college is entered through a massive, powerful red-brick neo-Georgian block by Raymond Erith (1963–66), courageously, if rather intimidatingly, turning its back on the modernism fashionable in other colleges of that era; on the right of the forecourt is the brick villa, extended by Basil Champneys in 1881, which housed the first students. The gateway leads into **Wolfson Quad**, with the suavely Classical Talbot Building (Reginald Blomfield, 1910) straight ahead, surmounted by a cupola. On the right is Blomfield's Wordsworth Building (1896) and a neo-Georgian block of 1925, and Erith's eccentrically proportioned **Library** is to the left. The masterly south and east elevations of Blomfield's buildings can be seen from the spacious and peaceful gardens, reached through the south range of Wolfson Quad.

The **gardens** stretch east to the River Cherwell and are overlooked on the north side by the neo-Georgian Deneke Building, by Giles Gilbert Scott (1931–33), from the northwest wing of which a passage leads to Scott's spacious neo-Byzantine **Chapel**, one of the best buildings of its date (1931–32) in Oxford (also accessible from the north side of Wolfson Quad). The beautiful domed interior contains a 14C painting of the *Flagellation of Christ* attributed to Taddeo Gaddi, a triptych by Burne-Jones (1863), and handsome woodwork.

The tree-lined, gently curving Norham Gardens leads back from Lady Margaret Hall past a motley array of spiky Gothic villas to Banbury Rd; the ponderous late 19C group at the junction of the two streets is **Wycliffe Hall**, an Evangelical Church of England theological college.

On the left, at the southern end of Norham Gardens, is the entrance to the **University Parks** (also accessible from a gateway facing Fyfield Rd). The Parks were laid out after 1853 on land acquired from Merton College; during the Civil War Charles I's artillery was encamped here. In the middle is the University Cricket Ground, with its pretty pavilion by T.G. Jackson of 1880–81, and from here there is a good view across the grass to Keble College (see Walk 5). To the east is the River Cherwell, much used by punters in the summer; it can be crossed by an elegant, concrete bridge, beyond which a path crosses the meadows to Marston (see p 143). Another walk leads from the southeast corner of the Parks between two of the streams into which the river divides (therefore known as Mesopotamia) to emerge (about 1 mile) into Marston Rd (see p 100).

The southwestern exit from the Parks leads into Parks Rd, and from here it is a short distance south to Broad St and the city centre, or west along Keble Rd to the starting-point of the walk.

THE IMMEDIATE VICINITY OF OXFORD

Because of its unusual layout, with largely unspoiled countryside extending almost into the centre of the city, there are several good walks for those who want to explore the rural surroundings of Oxford without leaving the city boundaries. Four of these walks are listed here; the places are also accessible by car or, in some cases, by bus.

1 ~ To Iffley along the river

An excellent walk leads along the towpath of the River Thames from Folly Bridge (see Walk 2) to Iffley Lock and Iffley Church. The path starts on the far side of the bridge and follows the river bank for about two miles (it is often muddy after rainfall). On the opposite bank, past Christ Church Meadow, are the college **boathouses**, built at different dates in the 20C to replace the elaborately decorated college barges, a few of which still survive in varying states of decrepitude in willow-fringed backwaters; the exploits of the oarsmen and women, and of their bicycle-riding coaches, provide visual incident during term time. Just before Iffley Lock is the *Isis Tavern*, where food and drink can be had at most times of day; the garden in front overlooks the river.

Iffley Lock is one of the three oldest locks on the Thames, dating from 1632 and rebuilt in 1923; the others were at Sandford and the Swift Ditch, near Abingdon. Over the river, which can be crossed by the lock, is the **church**, dating from c 1170–80 and one of the finest Norman parish churches in England (usually open in daylight hours). It is an aisleless building with a tower and vaulted chancel, extended eastwards in the Early English style during the 13C. The rounded west and south doorways are adorned with carvings of extraordinary and almost savage inventiveness and there is more rich carving on the upper parts of the west front, well restored in the 19C. The original late 12C stone font survives just inside the church and to the right on entering is an excellent stained-glass window by John Piper depicting creatures welcoming the Nativity of Christ; it was donated by his widow Myfanwy and installed in 1995. The tower arches are elaborately carved with chevron mouldings.

In the churchyard is a medieval cross, restored in 1857, and an extremely ancient yew tree; beyond the church path is the medieval **Rectory**, part of which has been converted into holiday accommodation by the Landmark Trust.

The village of **Iffley** still retains its rural character and tranquillity despite nearby urban development; in the main street (Church Way) is the thatched old school, now the church hall, and a little further on on the left is the former Dame School inscribed: 'Mrs Sarah Nowell's School 1822'. Beyond are two pubs, and from the end of Church Way, at Iffley Turn, the centre of Oxford can be regained quickly by bus.

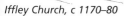

Iffley Church, c 1170–80

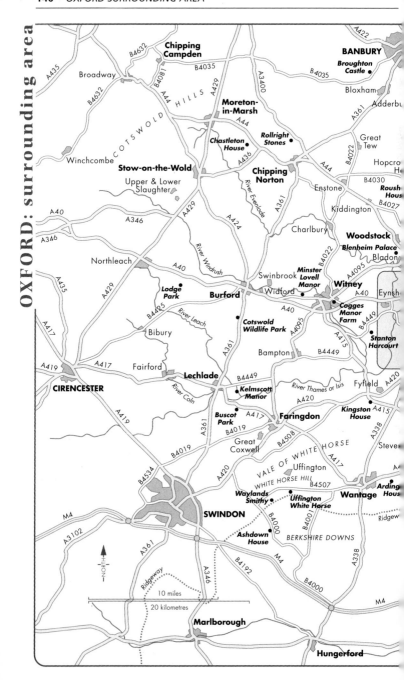

OXFORD: surrounding area

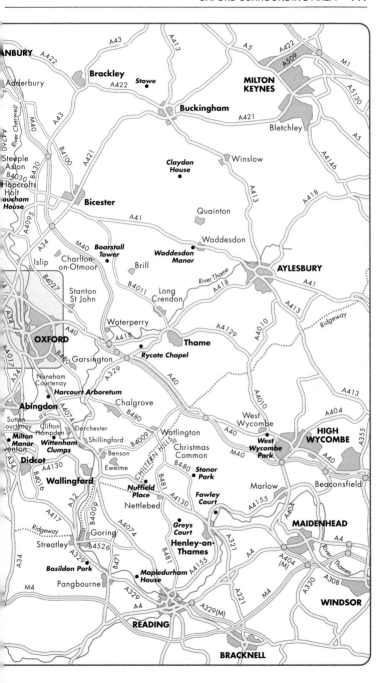

2 ~ Port Meadow, Binsey and Godstow

This interesting and varied walk starts at the beginning of the **Oxford Canal** towpath in Hythe Bridge St (see Walk 4). The canal, which leads to Coventry and the industrial Midlands, was opened in 1790 and is lined with houseboats at its southern end. On the left are the scanty remains of **Rewley Abbey**, founded for Cistercian monks in 1281; all that survives is a 15C doorway in a low wall on the far (west) side of one of the branches of the river which runs alongside the path. Further on, past an attractive iron canal bridge, the church of St. Barnabas, Jericho (see Walk 6), can be seen on the opposite side of the canal.

Soon afterwards there is a road bridge next to a former ironworks; a left turn here leads over a railway bridge to **Port Meadow**. This empty expanse of common land, frequently flooded, belongs to the Freemen of Oxford, who from at least the 11C have enjoyed the right of free pasture here; once a year their horses and other grazing animals are rounded up by a posse led by the Sheriff, who is also Curator of the Meadow, and a nominal fine imposed on the owners.

A bridge leads from Port Meadow across the main navigable branch of the River Thames and from the river towpath another path diverges left to the *Perch Inn*, where there is food, drink and a large garden. It forms part of the pretty hamlet of **Binsey**, from which a lane leads a half-mile north to Binsey **church** (open daylight hours: also accessible by road from Botley Rd and Binsey Lane), a small and very attractive 12C–13C building approached by an avenue of trees with fragments of late medieval stained glass in the east window. In the churchyard is a holy well associated with the legend of St. Frideswide; it is also the Treacle Well in Lewis Carroll's *Alice in Wonderland*.

Back on the towpath near the Perch Inn were the poplar trees whose loss in 1879 was evoked in Gerard Manley Hopkins's poem *Binsey Poplars:*

My aspens dear, whose airy cages quelled,
Quelled or quenched in leaves the leaping sun,
All felled, felled, are all felled.

The trees planted in their place have also just succumbed to the axe. The riverside path leads north to the remains of **Godstow Abbey**, a Benedictine nunnery founded in 1133 where Fair Rosamund, mistress of Henry II, was educated and where she was buried after her death at Woodstock (possibly at the hands of the jealous Queen). All that survives is a walled enclosure, dating from the 15C and later, which now serves as a shelter for cattle from a nearby farm. On the opposite side of the road bridge is the very popular riverside *Trout Inn*, where peacocks roam the garden and where meals can be obtained. From here the road leads east to the village of Wolvercote, the end of a bus route from the centre of Oxford.

3 ~ Osney and North Hinksey

Botley Rd leads west from the railway station to Osney Town, an area of 19C artisan housing. Soon after the station the road crosses the navigable part of the River Thames and a little to the south, near Osney lock and hidden among commercial premises, are the negligible remains of the once-magnificent **Osney Abbey**, founded in 1129. A left turn from Botley Rd into the busy Ferry Hinksey Rd, just after **St. Frideswide's church**, leads to a footpath called Willow Walk, at the end of which is the attractive and unspoiled village of **North Hinksey**, with its small, largely 12C church (turn left at the end of the path). In the village street to the south of the church is the *Fishes Inn*, where good food is available. It was at North Hinksey in 1874 that John Ruskin, then Slade Professor of Fine Art at Oxford University, brought teams of undergraduates (including Oscar Wilde) to mend the road so as to remind them of 'the pleasures of useful muscular work'; a plaque on a stone-built thatched cottage opposite the Fishes commemorates this somewhat quixotic episode.

A footpath next to the Fishes leads back to Ferry Hinksey Rd and Botley Rd, from which it is possible to return to Oxford by a different route by turning right and following the river towpath east to Folly Bridge (see Walk 2). Alternatively, frequent buses run to the centre of Oxford from Botley, reached by continuing north from the village street of North Hinksey.

4 ~ To Old Marston along the Cherwell

A pleasant footpath leads north alongside the Cherwell from the far side of the bridge in the **University Parks** (see Walk 5). On the western side of the river is **Wolfson College** (see Walk 5), which can be reached by a footbridge. Shortly after a road bridge is the *Victoria Arms* (the Vicky Arms), a favoured rendezvous for punters from the Cherwell Boathouse; bar meals are available here. A path leads east from here to the village of **Old Marston**, with some attractive houses of stone and thatch and a medieval church. From here there are buses back to the centre of Oxford.

5 ~ Other short excursions

The following excursions explore the area immediately beyond the Oxford bypass road. They can all be done on foot by those with both time and energy, but are more easily undertaken by car or bus.

Due east of the city, on the high ground beyond Headington, is **Shotover Country Park** (about 3 miles from Carfax), a large area of open common and woodland, commanding good views and excellent for picnics, walks and children letting off steam. It can be most easily reached by car by following Old Rd—the former main road to London—past the Churchill Hospital, or by bus by taking the Park and Ride to Thornhill Park and Ride and walking up a steep but not very long footpath.

Further south, at the far end of Iffley Rd, is the former hamlet of **Littlemore** (bus from the city centre), where the theologian John Henry Newman, vicar of the University Church of St. Mary, built the church of St. Mary and St. Nicholas in 1835–36 (architect H.J. Underwood). Originally a plain, unaisled building in the Early English style, it was enlarged in 1848 by the addition of a chancel and tower; some of the windows are by Thomas Willement. Newman gave up the living of St. Mary's (which included Littlemore) in 1843 and it was in Littlemore church that he preached his last sermon as an Anglican, on 'The Parting of Friends', to a tearful congregation. He had already converted an old stable building a short distance away in Cowley Rd into an informal religious community in which he resided and here, in 1845, he was received into the Roman Catholic church; the building, now known as **The College**, still exists, and Newman's bedroom, library and oratory can be visited (entrance in College Lane: open daily exc. Sunday 10.30–12.00, 14.00–17.00, ☎ 01865 779743). Soon afterwards, Newman left Oxford and did not return until 1878 after being made an honorary fellow of Trinity College.

To the west, and due south of Oxford, is **Templeton College**, a former management college which is now an integral part of Oxford University, providing post-experience executive courses (☎ 01865 422500: not normally open to the public). It stands in a parkland setting close to the village of Kennington (bus 35 from St. Aldate's) and was begun to the designs of Ahrends Burton and Koralek—architects of the Hayward & De Breyne building at Keble College—in 1968–69; it was doubled in size by the same firm in 1984–87. In their layout the buildings—among the best of their date in Oxford—remain faithful to the collegiate quadrangular ideal, the architects having paid particular attention to landscaping and the maintenance of a human scale within a modernist context.

To the southwest of Oxford is **Boar's Hill**, a prosperous semi-rural residential enclave accessible either by car or by a long but attractive walk on footpaths leading from Hinksey Park on Abingdon Rd through the surprisingly unspoiled village of South Hinksey and Chilswell Farm. For the lover of English romantic poetry this area is steeped in memories of Matthew Arnold's *The Scholar Gipsy* and *Thyrsis* and at the summit of Boar's Hill the archaeologist Sir Arthur Evans (1851–1941) constructed the **Jarn Mound** in the heart of:

> the high wood ... where the elm-tree crowns
> The hill behind whose ridge the sunset flames.
> The signal-elm, that looks on Ilsley Downs,
> The Vale, the three lone weirs, the youthful Thames.

The 'signal elm' has vanished and the view has been largely obscured by trees, but the mound and its surrounding wild garden and wood have been preserved and maintained by the Oxford Preservation Trust and are accessible to visitors.

North of Boars Hill and west of Oxford, is the attractive grey stone village of **Cumnor** (bus from the city centre). The large medieval church contains a late-16C life-sized statue of Queen Elizabeth I, whose favourite, the Earl of Leicester, was lord of the manor here; it was at the long-vanished Cumnor Place that his wife Amy Robsart met her death, allegedly by being pushed downstairs. Not far to the west, past the village pond, is the handsome *Bear and Ragged Staff* inn, a 16C or 17C building in which good food is served.

Further north is the quieter and even more unspoiled village of **Wytham** (pronounced White'm), accessible only by car or on foot from Godstow (see above). The attractive, mostly thatched, cottages are owned by Oxford University, as is the largely 16C manor house, Wytham Abbey, now turned into flats. In the car-park of the *White Hart* inn, where good food is served, is a square dovecot. **Wytham Woods**, to the north and west, are used by Oxford University for scientific research and are only accessible by special permit.

DAYS OUT FROM OXFORD

1 ~ The Thames Valley, the Chilterns and Henley-on-Thames

This route runs parallel to the River Thames as far as Wallingford and then cuts across the Chiltern Hills to Henley-on-Thames, one of the most attractive riverside towns and home of the annual Royal Regatta. It is easiest accomplished by car, but most of the places are also accessible by bus from Oxford.

Five miles along the A4074 road to Henley is **Nuneham Courtenay**, a neat estate village with brick cottages arranged on either side of the main road. Lord Harcourt moved to Nuneham from the family seat at Stanton Harcourt (see p 155) in 1756 and built himself a new Palladian house which was subsequently much enlarged (no adm.). He also laid out the grounds, re-erecting the old conduit-house from Carfax as an eye-catcher and demolished the village near the house; the inhabitants were rehoused in 1761–62 in the new roadside cottages, but one cottager was allowed to remain in her old home, to be immortalised by Oliver Goldsmith in his poem *The Deserted Village*.

Immediately to the south of the village is the **Harcourt Arboretum** (open May–Oct daily 10.00–17.00, Nov–Apr Mon–Fri 10.00–16.30, exc. 22 Dec–3 Jan, Good Friday–Easter Mon). It was first laid out in 1835, with many exotic trees, including sequoias (Californian redwoods) which had never been grown in England before, and Japanese maples. It is now managed by Oxford University as an extension of the Botanic Garden.

Dorchester

Three miles further on (take a right turn from the A4074) is the village of Dorchester (8 miles: buses from St. Aldate's), with its medieval abbey church.

History

In Roman times, as its name suggests, Dorchester was a military station; later it developed into an important Saxon settlement and, after the conversion of the West Saxons to Christianity by St. Birinus in the mid-7C, it was the missionary centre of southern England and the seat of the bishops of Wessex and later of Mercia. Following the Norman Conquest the see was transferred to Lincoln (1072) and Dorchester's importance declined.

Augustinian canons founded a priory here in 1140, replacing the Saxon cathedral, of which no trace remains, and the abbey church was completed c 1180. Much of the masonry of the 12C cruciform building survives, but a major rebuilding began in the late 13C, following the translation of the relics of St. Birinus in 1225. Over the next 50 years or so an aisle was added on the south side of the nave and the chancel rebuilt in a very lavish Decorated style. The west tower dates from the early 17C, after the church had become a parish church, and the building was restored by William Butterfield and Gilbert Scott in the mid-19C.

Dorchester Abbey

The entrance (usually open daylight hours) leads into the early 14C **south aisle**, built for the parishioners and flooded with light from the tall Decorated windows. Immediately in front is the lead font of c 1170, one of the finest of its kind in the country, and over the altar at the east end there is a restored 14C wall painting of the Crucifixion. An arcade of steeply pointed arches divides the aisle from the **nave**; on the corbel of one of the pillars are carvings of monks falling asleep— perhaps a warning against temptation.

The **chancel** is dominated by the great east window of c 1340, its flowing late Decorated tracery filling the whole wall; some 14C glass remains, including a panel in the third tier, on the right-hand side, showing St. Birinus preaching to Cynegils, King of Wessex. Equally unusual is the north sanctuary window, with the stone tracery designed in the form of a Tree of Jesse, the standing figures representing the ancestors of Christ, the angel Gabriel and the Three Wise Men, and more 14C stained glass. Below the south sanctuary window are the piscina and sedilia, with carved canopies of exceptional richness, enclosing small circular stained-glass windows—a most unusual feature.

There are some interesting monuments in the **south choir aisle**, especially a vigorous effigy of a knight of 'a most determined countenance' (c 1280), popularly believed to be a crusader on the point of leaping up to confront the infidel; there is also a reconstruction of the shrine of St. Birinus (1964).

Of the monastic buildings the only survivor is the Old School House just west of the abbey, which may have been the guest house. It was converted into a school c 1654, and now houses the small **Abbey Museum** (usually open Easter–Sept Tues–Sat 11.00–17.00, Sun & bank hols 14.00–17.00, ☎ 01865 340056). A garden has been created on the site of the monastic cloisters, north of the church.

There are some attractive old houses along the main street of the village, many of them built of timber and some of them thatched (there is even a thatched top to a boundary wall of mud on the west side). There are also some old coaching inns, notably the *George* (good food), opposite the Abbey gateway. From the south end of the village a footpath leads beside the **Dyke Hills**, an Iron Age earth fortification, to Day's Lock and then to the Sinodun Hills, popularly known as the **Wittenham Clumps**, from the venerable beech plantations which cluster inside the ancient (pre-Roman) earthworks at the summit; the long views from the hilltop are well worth the climb.

At Benson, a few miles along the A4074 from Dorchester, a side road diverges to **Ewelme** (also accessible by infrequent buses) a pretty village with watercress beds and a superb 15C **church** placed on the hillside next to an almshouse and school of the same date. It was built c 1432 by William de la Pole, Duke of Suffolk, who inherited the estate by marrying the heiress, Alice Chaucer, granddaughter of the poet. It is built of flint in the Perpendicular style, probably by East Anglian masons, and both inside and outside it has a distinctly East Anglian character. Several of the original fittings survive, including the font with its intricately carved cover, the chancel screens and some of the stained glass, and so too does the superb tomb of Alice, Duchess of Suffolk (d. 1475), with its recumbent alabaster effigy and figures of angels holding shields around the tomb-chest; underneath is a macabre carving of a cadaver designed to serve as a *memento mori*.

The **almshouses**, to the west of the tower, were founded in 1437 for 13 poor men and are arranged around an enclosed cloister. Next to them is the brick-built **school**, of the same date; it is still the village primary school, making it one of the oldest school buildings in the country.

The Thames Valley

South of Benson, on the banks of the Thames, is **Wallingford** (12 miles: X39 buses from St. Aldate's), reached by turning right at the junction of the A4074 and A4130 and crossing the medieval bridge.

History

Wallingford dates back to the Anglo-Saxon period and in the 11C and 12C it was one of the most important towns on the River Thames, with a castle and no fewer than 10 churches; it received its first charter, from Henry II, in 1155, two years after the signing of the Treaty of Wallingford, which ended the civil war between Stephen and his cousin Matilda. It subsequently declined in importance, becoming a quiet market town which enjoyed a modest prosperity in the 18C before being bypassed by the main line of the Great Western Railway and settling down to a humdrum provincial existence which ensured the preservation of many of the older buildings.

The centre of Wallingford is the **Market Place**, with its small colonnaded Town Hall of 1670 and Victorian Corn Exchange, now a theatre and cinema; to the north is the much-restored St. Mary's Church, one of three medieval churches still surviving. To the west, in an open space called Kine Croft, are the earthen **ramparts** of the Anglo-Saxon town, and on the north side of Kine Croft is an old house of flint housing the **Wallingford Museum** (open Mar–Nov, Tues–Fri & bank hol. Mon 14.00–17.00, Sat 10.30–17.00, Sun June–Aug 14.00–17.00, ☎ 01491 835065).

Despite inevitable modifications, the town still retains the grid plan of streets laid down in the 11C. Castle St leads north from the central cross-roads past the Lamb Arcade (a former inn, now shops), and from it a footpath leads to the right to the site of the Norman **castle**, of which only the formidable earthworks and a few fragments of flint walls remain in landscaped grounds (open 10.00–17.00 Mon–Fri, 10.00–18.00 Sat–Sun). It was built by William the Conqueror in 1067 and was used as a stronghold by Queen Matilda in the 12C, but the buildings were all destroyed by Cromwell after the Civil War, when it was an important royalist stronghold.

There are some excellent Georgian brick houses as well as some earlier timber buildings in **High Street**, which leads to the **Bridge**, first mentioned in 1141 and still retaining most of its 19 arches dating from the 13C (it was modernised in 1809). The eminent jurist Sir William Blackstone (see also All Souls College, Oxford) lived at the riverside house called Castle Priory in Thames St and is buried in the nearby **St. Peter's Church** (key usually available locally), a Georgian building with a pretty Gothick spire by Sir Robert Taylor (1777).

A detour from Wallingford along the A329 follows the river due south through the **Goring Gap**, where it breaks through the line of the chalk hills; the ancient **Icknield Way**, or Ridgeway crosses the Thames here, continuing west from the

Oxfordshire Chilterns to the Berkshire Downs. Two miles south of the village of Streatley is **Basildon Park**, a Palladian villa of 1776 (by John Carr of York) set amid landscaped grounds. It was rescued from dereliction after the Second World War by the 2nd Lord Iliffe, heir to a newspaper fortune, and was restored with great sensitivity, using features brought from other Carr houses. Lord Iliffe also introduced a notable collection of 18C furniture and pictures, including works by Batoni and Pitoni, which can still be seen in the house (National Trust; open Apr–Oct Wed–Sun & bank hol. Mon 13.00–18.00, garden opens 11.30, ☎ 0118 984 3040, ✉ www.nationaltrust.org.uk).

Pangbourne, a prosperous village a couple of miles down river, was the home from 1924 until his death in 1932 of Kenneth Grahame, author of *The Wind in the Willows*. A pretty white-painted toll bridge crossed the river to Whitchurch, on the opposite (Oxfordshire) bank and from here tortuous lanes lead to the remarkably unspoiled Thames-side village of **Mapledurham**, with a row of modest brick almshouses of 1629 and a medieval church much restored by William Butterfield in 1863. It contains monuments to the early owners of **Mapledurham House** (open Easter–Sept, Sat, Sun & bank hol. Mon 14.00–17.00, ☎ 0118 972 3350, ✉ www.mapledurham.co.uk), a large and impressive red-brick building begun c 1588 by Sir Michael Blount, Lieutenant of the Tower of London and remodelled in the 1820s; the interior contains plaster-work of 1612, as well as a good collection of furniture and family portraits (also a portrait of the poet Alexander Pope, who vainly hoped to marry one of the Blount sisters) and a well-preserved Catholic Chapel of 1797, in which Mass is still regularly celebrated. Teas are available in the timber-framed late-medieval manor house, and there is also a working **watermill** first built in the 15C, with its 19C machinery largely intact (open same days as house 13.00–17.00); corn is still regularly ground here, and the flour is on sale.

The Chilterns

From Wallingford, the A4130 crosses the **Chiltern Hills** to Henley. This is a landscape of grassy slopes dotted with hawthorns and yews, hedges festooned with traveller's joy, deep dry valleys and thick beechwoods. A maze of lanes lead to small settlements of flint and brick, often suffixed 'End' or 'Green'; many of the villages are indeed set around greens, and the whole area is criss-crossed with easily followed and well-marked footpaths.

A little to the left of the main road at the top of the escarpment is **Nuffield Place** (open May–Sept, 2nd and 4th Sundays in month 14.00–17.00, ☎ 01491 825556), a brick-built house of 1914 which was the home of the car manufac-turer William Morris, Lord Nuffield, from 1933 until his death in 1963; since then both the house and the garden have survived with few changes. A little fur-ther on is **Nettlebed**, a former coaching and brick-making village with a restored conical brick kiln, and from here the B481 leads south to the village of Rotherfield Greys and its manor-house, **Greys Court**, (National Trust; open Apr–Sept, Mon, Wed, Fri, exc. Good Friday, 14.00–17.30; gardens daily exc. Thur, Sun, 14.00–17.30; ☎ 01491 628529; ✉ www.national trust.org.uk). In its 14C heyday this was an important fortified manor house, but it later fell into disrepair and the present, smaller, house dates largely from 17C and 18C. Some of the medieval fortifications survive, as does a 16C red-brick block known as the

'Cromwellian Stables' and also the largest surviving donkey-wheel in England, by which water was drawn until 1914 from a deep well. There are beautiful gardens, including a recently constructed maze.

From Nettlebed the road leads through woods and then exhilaratingly downhill to Henley (23 miles: buses from St. Aldate's).

Henley-on-Thames

History

Henley grew up as an important Thames-side market town during the Middle Ages. The wealth of handsome Georgian houses and inns are reminders of its importance as a coaching stop between London and Oxford in the 18C and until relatively recently it was also an important centre of river transport. Today the river, now used for sport and pleasure, still plays a major role in the life of the town. The first boat race between Oxford and Cambridge was rowed here in 1829 and in 1839 the first rowing regatta was held with the object of 'producing the most beneficial results to the town'. It succeeded: Henley Royal Regatta (first week in July) is one of the premier events in both the rowing and the social calendars. During regatta week the whole place is *en fête*, bronzed oarsmen and their girlfriends mingling with ruddy-faced members of the famous Leander Rowing Club in their boaters or caps and blazers. There are numerous facilities for boat hire and for river trips, which provide good views of the houses and gardens along the waterside, and of the beautiful country beyond.

A handsome **bridge** of 1786, decorated with masks of Thames and Isis (by Horace Walpole's friend Mrs Damer) leads directly into the wide main street (Hart St) from the London direction; on either side are 18C inns, the *Angel on the Bridge* (left), white and stuccoed, the larger *Red Lion* (right), mellow red brick. Immediately beyond is the large parish **church** with its handsome early 16C west tower; the spacious interior was much restored in the 19C. Facing the churchyard are two groups of almshouses, founded in the 16C and 17C but both rebuilt in the 19C, and the 15C timber-framed **Chantry House**, possibly built to house chantry priests serving the parish church.

Hart Street is lined with inns and with Georgian-fronted houses; at its top (west) end it opens out into the former Market Place, presided over by the pretty Queen Anne-style **Town Hall** (H.T. Hare, 1900). There are more attractive Georgian houses, and some older timber buildings, in **Northfield End** and **New Street**, to the north, and at the east end of New St is the brewery of Messrs Brakspear, which traces its origins back to the 18C (but was threatened with closure at the time of writing).

South from Henley Bridge a riverside path runs south to Mill Meadows and the **River and Rowing Museum** (open Mon–Sat 10.00–17.00, Sun 11.00–17.00; café; ☎ 01491 415600, 🖳 www.rrm.co.uk), opened in 1998. Designed by David Chipperfield, this impressive new timber-clad building houses excellent displays relating to the history of Henley and district, the River Thames from its source to the estuary and the sport of rowing.

On the far (Berkshire) side of Henley Bridge the riverside footpath on the leads north to **Temple Island**, the beginning of the regatta course; the Classical temple on the island (James Wyatt, 1771) was built by Sambrooke Freeman of

Fawley Court, a red-brick house of 1684 on the opposite bank, reached from the A4155 Henley–Marlow road (The Marian Fathers; open Mar Oct Wed, Thu, Sun 14.00–17.00 exc. Easter and Whitsun weeks, ☎ 01491 574917, ✉ www.marians-uk.org/fawleycourt.html). Its much-remodelled interior contains a fascinating collection of Polish memorabilia introduced by the present occupants and in the grounds is one of the earliest Gothic follies in England, built c 1730 by John Freeman to house some of the Arundel Marbles (see p 118).

An alternative route back to Oxford for those with access to a car diverges to the right of the A4130 road along the B480 (signposted to Watlington) at the far end of the Fair Mile, northwest of the town. Five miles north of Henley on the B480 and set amid a deer park within a particularly beautiful part of the Chilterns, is **Stonor Park** (open Apr–Sept, Sun & bank hols, also Wed May–Sept and Thur July–Aug, 14.00–17.30, ☎ 01491 638587, ✉ www.stonor.com), for at least 800 years the seat of the Stonor family. Though predominantly Georgian in its external appearance, this is in origin a medieval house, remnants of which can still be seen embedded within the 18C red-brick walls. The Stonor family has never swerved from Roman Catholicism and the house was a refuge for priests, including Edmund Campion, during the times of persecution in the later 16C. It is still the Stonor family home and the interior is a fascinating amalgam of work of many different dates, from the Georgian and early 19C Gothic of the Entrance Hall to the genuinely medieval arcade of the hall of the 13C house, seen at the very end. Numerous family portraits and tapestries are on display and there are French and Italian pictures and objets d'art collected by Francis Stonor (d. 1968). The Library contains a large and important collection of Roman Catholic books, and an attic room is devoted to the memory of the martyred Edmund Campion.

The **chapel**, to the right of the entrance front, is one of only three in England where the Roman mass has been continuously celebrated without a break since medieval times and is still regularly used by local Roman Catholics. The brick tower dates from 1416–17, but the interior is entirely of the late 18C.

From here the B480 returns to Oxford, passing over the Chiltern escarpment near **Christmas Common**, where there are excellent walks and views. A few miles after the small market town of Watlington is **Chalgrove**, site of an important engagement in the Civil War, in which John Hampden was killed; the church here has a good set of 14C wall paintings. Just before the outskirts of Oxford is **Garsington**, with its early 17C manor house (no adm., but visible through gates), the home of Lady Ottoline Morrell, who laid out the formal gardens and entertained many of the leading early 20C literati, including D.H. Lawrence, in the house; an opera festival is held here each June.

2 ~ Abingdon, the Berkshire Downs and the Vale of the White Horse

This route explores the country to the south and southwest of Oxford, until 1974 part of Berkshire. It starts in Abingdon, which lies on the River Thames 6 miles south of Oxford (reached via A34; buses from St. Aldate's).

Abingdon

History

The town owes its existence to its abbey, founded in the late 7C and one of the most important in medieval England. Having twice been destroyed by the Danes, it was re-established in the 10C and was rebuilt in the 12C. Royal visitors included Edward the Confessor, Queen Matilda—who took refuge here after escaping from Oxford Castle in the snow in 1142—and Henry VIII, who spent three months here to avoid an outbreak of the plague. Notwithstanding this, Abingdon was one of the first of the larger abbeys to be dissolved at his command in 1538.

There was no love lost between abbey and town, the former owning all the markets and fairs and imposing numerous tiresome restrictions. Furthermore, the town had a fine church of its own and when the abbey was dissolved the townsfolk did not lift a finger to save it; consequently there is not much left of the abbey buildings. Abingdon later flourished as the county town of Berkshire—an honour hotly disputed with Reading—and as a centre for malting and brewing. It also had, and still retains, an unusual number of charitable foundations.It has grown a lot in the second half of the 20C, but its historic centre survives and retains a character totally distinct from that of Oxford.

The centre of Abingdon is the triangular **Market Place** which grew up outside the gates of the Abbey in the Middle Ages. On the east side is the 15C **Abbey Gatehouse**, with a figure of the Virgin Mary, patron saint of the Abbey over the central arch (the head is a 19C replacement), and beyond are the fragmentary remains of the monastic buildings. **St. Nicholas' Church**, which adjoins the gatehouse, was built in the 12C for travellers, but has been much altered subsequently, notably in the 15C, when new large windows were inserted and a tower built; the river Stert, which ran and still runs under the nave, was the abbey boundary.

On the south side of the gatehouse was the medieval St. John's Hospital, founded in the 12C but adapted for civic purposes after the Reformation. The buildings immediately adjoining the gateway became the **Guildhall**, Classicised in the 18C, with an impressive Council Chamber of 1731–32 (adm. only by arrangement). To the south, facing Bridge St, is an open courtyard (Roysse Court) on the east side of which is the **Roysse Room**, originally the Common Hall of the Hospital but refounded in 1563 by John Roysse as a grammar school for 63 scholars. The school moved to its present site, away from the town centre, in 1870 and the old schoolroom, remodelled in 1911, has since been used for public functions.

The south side of the Market Place is taken up by the splendid **County Hall**, built in 1678–82 by Sir Christopher Wren's master mason Christopher Kempster and showing Wren's Classical predilections in the majestic giant Composite order which encompasses the building. The arcaded ground floor is open and formerly sheltered the market stalls; the upper floor, once used for the Berkshire assize courts, has very large arched windows, and the hipped and balustraded roof is topped by a cupola. The upper floor is now a **museum**, devoted to local history and contemporary crafts (open daily 10.30–16.00, ☎ 01235 523703); by an ancient custom, buns are thrown by visiting monarchs from the windows to the clamouring populace.

Bridge St leads from the Market Place to **Abingdon Bridge**, built by one of the town's guilds in 1416–17; from it there are good views of the town and river, and on the opposite side is a large expanse of open meadow and footpaths. On the west side of Bridge St, close to the river, is the grim **Old Gaol**, built in 1805–11 for prisoners who had formerly been accommodated in the Abbey gatehouse; it is now an arts and leisure centre.

Opposite, in Thames St, is the former Abbey mill (the mill stream was dug in the 10C), and on the north side of the street is the inconspicuous entrance to what remains of the old **Abbey Buildings** (open Apr–Sept Tues–Sun 14.00–16.00, closed Oct–Mar exc. by appointment, ☎ 01235 525339). These comprise: part of the former granary, later turned into cottages; the Checker (Exchequer), a two-storeyed 13C stone building with a remarkable 13C chimneystack, the finest of its date and type in England, and a handsome rib-vaulted chamber on the ground floor; the timber-roofed Checker Hall, turned into a theatre in 1953 after centuries of domestic use; and the impressive Long Gallery, dating from c 1500 and originally subdivided into rooms for the exchequer clerks, the 'gallery' being the passageway running along the north side, lit by unglazed windows. The site of the Abbey church is to the north, in an area now known as the **Abbey Gardens**: the 'ruins' were placed here as a garden ornament in the 19C, making use of fragments of stone dug up in the vicinity.

The most attractive street in Abingdon is **East St. Helen's Street**, which runs southwest from the County Hall; the houses range in date from the 15C to the 18C and are constructed of stone, timber—always plastered over—and red brick. At the end is the handsome 13C tower and spire of **St. Helen's Church** (open Easter–Sept Mon–Sat 10.00–16.00, ☎ 01235 520144). The church itself dates mainly from the 15C and is unusual in that it is wider than it is long, with five parallel aisles, the result of successive expansions to accommodate the town's flourishing religious guilds.

The entrance leads into the North, or Jesus, Aisle with dingy monuments to local worthies on the walls and the restored tomb of John Roysse, the founder of Abingdon School, opposite the entrance. Next comes the 14C Lady Aisle (for the Guild of Our Lady), with a unique set of **paintings** on the wooden ceiling of the chancel, mostly of Old Testament kings and prophets, dating from c 1390. The central aisle was added c 1420, as was that to the south (the St. Katherine Aisle), for the Fraternity of the Holy Cross, and finally the South or Reade Aisle was built in 1539. There is a good pulpit of 1636 and a carved mayoral pew of 1706, with its sword rest of the same date.

A remarkable collection of almshouses surrounds the churchyard, all of them now administered by the Christ's Hospital charity, founded in 1553, and all still fulfilling their original purpose: to provide accommodation for the elderly. On the north side, next to the church, are **Twitty's Almshouses** (1707), urbane red brick with a wooden cornice and pediment. Beyond, on the west side, is **Long Alley**, built by the Fraternity of the Holy Cross in 1446 but much altered in the 16C, when the unusual wooden cloister walk appears to have been added. The porches date from 1605 and contain paintings of that date in the pediments; the panelled Hall (open on application to the Matron) is hung with portraits of benefactors, including a conjectural one of the two builders of Abingdon Bridge. The **Brick Alley almshouses**, on the south side of the churchyard near the river, were built in 1718 by two local craftsmen, Samuel Westbrook and Charles Etty. Beyond is an attractive riverside walk.

Ock St leads west from the centre of Abingdon to the A34 roundabout, and the next exit to the south leads via the A4130 past the intimidating mass of Didcot power station to the **Didcot Railway Centre** (open weekends all year, also school holidays and daily June–Aug, 10.00–17.00, ☎ 01235 817200, ✉ www.didcotrailwaycentre.org.uk), dedicated to the history of the Great Western Railway ('God's Wonderful Railway' to enthusiasts). It is entered from Didcot Parkway station, an important railway junction, which is reached by frequent trains from Oxford; on 'steam days' (mainly summer Sundays) there are free rides for visitors behind GWR locomotives.

Those who are not interested in railways can take a minor road north from the A34/A4130 roundabout into the village street of Milton, at the far end of which is **Milton Manor** (open Easter and May bank hol. weekends and daily in last two weeks of July & Aug, tours on the hour 14.00–16.00, ☎ 01235 831287.)

Paul Calton, the descendant of a London goldsmith, almost certainly built the core of the neat red-brick house soon after buying the estate in 1659, but in 1764 it was acquired by Bryant Barrett, lace-maker to George III, and a year later he employed Stephen Wright, master mason in the King's Works, to add wings, one of them containing a Roman Catholic chapel which survives intact with its 18C Gothic decoration, and a Gothic Library below. Since then, the house has remained substantially unaltered.

A lane on the other side of the A34/A4130 roundabout leads to **Steventon**, a large village with a remarkable collection of well-preserved timber-framed houses dating from the 14C to the 17C, some of them of cruck construction. Many of the best houses are beside the Causeway, a raised tree-lined roadway leading to the church from the village green. It was made by Westminster Abbey, lords of the manor in the Middle Ages; their property was administered from the house near the church, now known as Priory Cottages, which still retains its medieval open hall.

To the west of Steventon a string of attractive villages nestles beneath the slope of the Berkshire Downs, south of the A417 Streatley–Wantage road (turn right from the A4130 at Rowstock roundabout). At **East Hendred** is Champs Chapel, a small 15C chantry chapel with attached priest's house, containing a local history museum (open Apr–Sept Sun 14.30–16.30, Oct–Mar first Sun in month 14.30–15.30, ☎ 01235 833312). Further west at Ardington is **Ardington House**, a plain but well-proportioned brick building of 1719–21 with a beautifully carved wooden staircase, of unusual design inside (occasionally open spring & summer afternoons, ☎ 01235 833244). The village of Ardington, like its neighbour **Lockinge**, forms part of a still-flourishing estate formed in the 19C by the Loyd family (later Lords Wantage); both villages are well maintained and free from obtrusive development.

The Berkshire Downs

Wantage (15 miles; buses from St. Aldate's) is a small market town, recently much enlarged to the north. It was allegedly the birthplace in AD 849 of King Alfred, and his statue (1877) proudly presides over the market place. In an attractive brick-fronted former cloth-merchant's house to the south of the churchyard is the **Vale and Downland Museum**, with a permanent display explaining the history of the surrounding area, and changing exhibitions (open

Mon–Sat 10.00–16.30, Sun 14.30–17.00; ☎ 01235 771447, ✉ www.wantage.com/museum).

From Wantage the B4507 road winds west just below the Berkshire Downs, parallel to the ancient **Ridgeway** track which pursues its path along the hilltop from Goring to Avebury (Wiltshire), allowing exhilarating walks; 'Ridgeway Explorer' buses from Wantage and elsewhere on the route make it possible for those without cars to walk along the path on summer weekends (☎ 01635 820028). Its course is punctuated by prehistoric burial mounds and hill forts, of which the most extensive is **Uffington Castle** (about 6 miles west of Wantage: car parking nearby); close to it on the bare downland is the ancient figure of a **White Horse** cut into the chalk hillside, giving its name to the Vale of White Horse, over which there are extensive views. A mile west along the Ridgeway from White Horse Hill is **Wayland's Smithy** (also accessible by road from Ashbury), a well-preserved prehistoric long barrow surrounded by trees.

Just off the B4000 road from Ashbury to Lambourn, a village largely devoted to racing stables, is **Ashdown House** (National Trust: open Apr–Oct Wed and Sat 14.15–17.15, guided tours on the hour, ☎ 01491 528051, ✉ www.nationaltrust.org.uk). Built of locally quarried chalk ('clunch') in the 1660s as a hunting lodge by the 1st Earl of Craven, it is a tall, square dolls' house-like building probably designed by William Winde. The interior, only part of which is shown, is mainly notable for a fine collection of 17C **portraits** of Lord Craven, his family, and various members of the Stuart Court, notably Charles I's sister Elizabeth, Queen of Bohemia (the 'Winter Queen'), who was protected by Lord Craven after being sent into exile by the Thirty Years' War. The tour concludes on the roof, designed as a 'stand' for viewing the chase.

The B4000 leads north from Ashbury to the A420 Oxford-Swindon road at Shrivenham. A little to the east, a side road leads to **Great Coxwell**, famous for its a magnificent early 13C **tithe barn** (open daily 'at reasonable hours') built for the monks of Beaulieu Abbey (Hampshire) and said by William Morris (cf. Kelmscott, below) to be 'as noble as a cathedral'. It is built of rubble stone, and the Cotswold stone-tiled roof is supported on oak timbers hardly altered over the last 700 years.

Further on is **Faringdon** (17 miles; buses from Oxford), a small town grouped around a **Market Place** lined with Georgian-fronted houses and inns, with the colonnaded 17C Town Hall at one end and the large handsome church at the other. The **church** (often locked: for access ask at Tourist Information Centre in Market Place) has round-arched nave arcades of c 1200 and a 13C chancel; there is much rich carving inside, and a good collection of monuments, including some 14C–16C brasses.

On a hilltop to the south of the town (and clearly visible from the A420 bypass) is **Lord Berners' Folly**, a battlemented brick tower 104ft high, mysteriously rising from a grove of trees (open Easter–Sept, first Sun in month 11.00–17.00). Built in 1935 by the very eccentric nobleman whose name it bears, to the designs of his architect friend the 7th Duke of Wellington, it is perhaps the last building of its kind in England.

From Faringdon the busy road A420 skirts the edge of the Vale of White Horse, with the line of the Berkshire Downs on the southern skyline. On the edge of Kingston Bagpuize (10 miles from Oxford) is **Kingston House** (open some weekends March–Sept 14.30–16.30, ☎ 01865 821659), an impressive red-brick building dating in its present form from the early years of the 18C. The builder was probably Edmund Fettiplace (d. 1710), a member of an important local family whose tomb can be seen in the adjacent church, and the external detailing recalls some of the contemporary work in Oxford. The interior retains many of its original features, including a cantilevered wooden staircase and some impressive stone chimneypieces. Much of the original formal **garden** layout also survives, including some iron gates and a gazebo approached by a raised walkway.

Further along the A420 is **Fyfield**, an attractive village bypassed by the road; the *White Hart Inn* (good bar meals) has an open 15C hall built for the priests of a chantry established in 1442.

3 ~ Burford, the Cotswolds and the upper Thames

Upstream of Oxford the 'stripling' River Thames flows through quiet countryside, lined with willows and being companionably joined by its many Cotswold tributaries. This route follows the route of one of these rivers, the Windrush, west into the Gloucestershire Cotswolds and returns on the Berkshire side of the Thames.

The main A40 road leaves Oxford at the northern bypass; an alternative route follows the Botley Rd west, and crosses the Thames at Swinford toll bridge, joining the A40 to the north of **Eynsham**, a former market town whose medieval abbey disappeared virtually without trace after the Dissolution. A couple of miles south is the village of **Stanton Harcourt**, where the impressive cruciform church, remodelled c 1250 and again in the 15C, contains an impressive set of tombs of the Harcourt family after whom the village is named. They came from Normandy with William the Conqueror and parts of their **Manor House** survive (no adm. at time of writing), including the cavernous late medieval Kitchen and the former domestic Chapel, built in the 1460s and now called Pope's Tower after the poet Alexander Pope, who completed his verse translation of Homer's *Iliad* in the top room in 1718.

Fourteen miles west of Oxford by the A40, off the B4022 just to the east of Witney, is the excellent **Cogges Manor Farm Museum** (open mid-March–Nov Tues–Fri & bank hol. Mon 10.30–17.30, Sat, Sun 12.00–17.30, ☎ 01993 772802, ✉ www.westoxon.gov.uk/culture/cogges.cfm; buses from Oxford to Witney pass nearby).

The **farmhouse** incorporates the hall of a stone manor house built by the de Grey family (see Greys Court) in the 13C, but the most impressive part of the building is the east wing of c 1680, built on the site of the medieval solar by Francis Blake, a London woollen-draper who also paid for the clock turret on Witney's Butter Cross. The estate was sold to the Harcourt family in 1725 and the house then became a farmhouse until being taken over by Oxfordshire County Council in 1974; it is now shown as it was in the late 19C and early 20C, and some of the late 17C painted decoration is visible in an upstairs room.

Visitors are also encouraged to explore the extensive stone-built **barns** and farm buildings, the oldest of which date from the 17C, and to admire the farm animals and vehicles; there is a permanent display of blanket-making and demonstrations of cooking and rural crafts are held from time to time.

Cogges is an older settlement than nearby Witney and a **historical trail** leads from the Manor Farm to the site of the medieval village, mentioned in Domesday Book, the moated enclosures of the 'castle' which antedated the present house, and the **church**, which served both the medieval parishioners and the monks of a small alien priory dissolved in 1414; the north chapel is a good example of late Decorated work (c 1340) and contains the effigy of a female member of the de Grey family.

Witney

Witney (buses from Gloucester Green and George St) is a small but expanding town of considerable interest. It owes its origins to the Bishops of Winchester, who developed the town in the 13C, but it acquired a new prosperity in the 18C founded on the manufacture of blankets, which are still made here in the well-designed buildings in Mill St, beside the River Windrush, whose waters once powered the looms. This prosperity is reflected in the sturdy, predominantly Georgian domestic architecture of the town.

In the long High St, south of the river, is the former **Blanket Hall**, built in 1721 for the weighing and measuring of blankets; its pediment carries a clock, and its roof a cupola and bell turret. Nearby, in Gloucester Court Mews, is the **Witney and District Museum** (open Apr–Sep Wed–Sat 10.00–16.00, Sun 14.00–16.00, ☎ 01993 775915), with displays relating to the history of the area. The centre of the town is **Market Square**, with a small 18C Town Hall (one room over an open ground floor), two Georgian hotels, a Victorian Corn Exchange, and the rustic-looking **Butter Cross** of timber and Cotswold stone (c 1600) topped by a cupola and clock turret (1683).

To the south of Market Square the road is divided into two by a long green, running up to the **church**, which has an impressive early 13C central tower and spire, similar to that of Christ Church Cathedral in Oxford. The church dates largely from the 13C, though there were later additions, notably a number of richly decorated chantry chapels and windows of the 14C; there was a very thorough restoration in the 1860s. On the left of the church is a group of almshouses, originally built for the widows of blanket makers in 1724, but rebuilt in the Gothic style in 1868, and to the west is the Henry Box School of 1660, still in use.

Some of the houses along the green are much older than they look; two were used by Oxford colleges as retreats from outbreaks of the plague. The site of the Bishops of Winchester's 12C **palace**, in the grounds of Mount House, east of the church, was uncovered in 1984, and it is possible to see the foundations Mon–Fri 10.00–17.00 and on Saturday and Sunday afternoons from Easter to September, from 14.00–16.00.

The Windrush Valley

The valley of the river Windrush west of Witney is punctuated by a series of attractive villages. The main A40 road runs along the ridge well above the river, and the valley, reached by narrow lanes, is for the most part peaceful and unspoilt. At **Minster Lovell** (about 4 miles west of Witney on B4047) the village street, lined with houses of local limestone, some of them thatched, leads to a narrow lane which gives access to the attractive Perpendicular **church**. It is a cruciform structure, with a central tower, and was probably built c 1430 by William, Lord

Lovell, whose family had been lords of the manor since the 12C. Some of the original 15C glass survives and there is also a fine alabaster tomb with the effigy of a knight, either William, Lord Lovell (d. 1455) or his son John (d. 1465).

The ruins of the Lovells' **Manor House** lie immediately beyond the church, on the banks of the Windrush (English Heritage, open 'at any reasonable time'). The house was built, like the church, by Lord Lovell and in its 15C heyday it was one of the most important houses in Oxfordshire. Set round three sides of a courtyard, facing the river, its central block comprised a hall, chapel and solar (great chamber); lodgings for members of the household and guests occupied the west range and on the east side there were kitchens, domestic offices and stables.

The crenellated tower at the south end of the west range was probably added by Francis, Lord Lovell, c 1477–85; he was one of the favourites of Richard III, prompting the rhyme: 'The Cat, the Rat and Lovell the Dog/Rule all England under the Hog [the emblem of Richard III]'. His estates were taken over by the Crown after the Battle of Bosworth and the house fell into ruin in the mid 18C.

The church at **Swinbrook**, about 2 miles west of Minster Lovell, contains a spectacular set of monuments to five generations of the Fettiplace family, who lived at the nearby great house, demolished in 1805. They are on the north chancel wall, and take the form of two sets of three life-size figures (early and late 17C) elegantly reclining one above the other as if they are in bunk beds. In the churchyard (just west of the porch) are the graves of the writer Nancy Mitford (d. 1973) and her sister Unity (d. 1948), both of whom spent much of their childhood at Swinbrook.

From here, a short walk across fields (or a rather longer drive by car) leads to **Widford**, a small hamlet by the Windrush with an isolated, mainly 13C, church built on the site of a Roman villa; the rustic interior retains its old box pews, and fragments of a 14C wall painting are visible in the chancel.

Near Burford the country begins to take its character from the Cotswold Hills, of whose beautiful grey or golden limestone the small towns and villages are built.

Burford

Burford (23 miles; just north of A40; buses from Gloucester Green) is a small town understandably very popular with visitors, both for its beauty and for its position on the edge of the Cotswolds.

History

In the later Middle Ages it was one of the principal centres of the lucrative wool and cloth trade, and was described in the 16C as 'a very great market town replenished with much people'. Until the late 18C, when the present main road was built and bypassed the town, it lay on the road from Gloucester to London and drew wealth from its many inns, even after the local wool trade declined in the 17C. The town stagnated in the 19C, but from an aesthetic point of view this was a blessing in disguise, since it ensured the survival of a remarkable collection of old houses, some timber-framed, some of the beautiful local stone, dating from the 15C to the 18C. Prosperity returned in the 20C, but there was a price to pay in the form of a never-ending stream of traffic, especially at summer weekends; those who can do so are well advised to visit Burford at less busy times.

The heart of Burford is the long **High Street**, partly tree-lined, which runs downhill from the A40 to the River Windrush. Halfway down, at the corner of Sheep St, is the **Tolsey Museum** (open Apr–Oct Tues–Fri 14.00–17.00, Sat, Sun & bank hol. Mon 11.00–17.00, ☎ 01367 822178), occupying the 16C former town hall; the collection includes the charters, seals and maces of the Town Council, along with exhibits illustrating the history of the town. Opposite, on the east side, are some of the oldest houses in the town, with timber façades dating from the late 15C, and further down on the same side is a magnificent early 18C house embellished with giant Corinthian pilasters, built for a lawyer but since 1849 the **Methodist Church**.

To the west of the High St at the bottom of the hill is **Burford Priory** (no adm.), built by Sir Lawrence Tanfield on the site of a medieval hospital at the end of the 16C, enlarged by William Lenthall, Speaker of the Long Parliament, in the 17C, but half demolished in 1809.

Church Lane leads east from the foot of the High St, past the former Grammar School, founded in 1571, and the rebuilt 15C almshouses to the parish **church**, one of the finest in Oxfordshire. It began life as a Norman building, parts of which survived rebuilding and expansion in both the 13C and 15C; today the predominant impression is of the latter period, when the prosperity of the town was at its height. The church played a part in English history in May 1649, when Oliver Cromwell imprisoned 340 rebel Levellers inside the building, three of whom were later shot in the churchyard, which now houses a splendid collection of late 17C and early 18C 'bale' tombs of wool merchants, copiously adorned with carvings of cherubs, skulls and flowers.

Externally, the most notable features are the tower with its 15C spire, and the array of large Perpendicular windows, typical of Cotswold 'wool churches'. The church is entered through a magnificently carved 15C porch, to the left (west) of which is the unusually placed **Lady Chapel**, a 15C reconstruction of an earlier detached chapel built by the Merchant Guild; it contains a series of monuments to the Sylvester family, who lived in a large stone house of 1558, now called Falkland Hall, at the foot of the High St. The **nave**, aisles and clerestory also date from the 15C, but the crossing and lower stages of the tower are 12C work, as is the west wall which still retains its richly carved Norman doorway. Against the northwest crossing pier is a wooden 15C chantry chapel which survived the Reformation to become the family pew of the owners of Burford Priory.

The **chancel** dates from the 13C, but the north and south chapels were added in the 15C; the north chapel is largely taken up by a splendid Classical **monument** to Sir Lawrence Tanfield of Burford Priory (d. 1625) and his wife (note the grisly skeleton underneath). Less pretentious is the monument on the southwest crossing pier to Christopher Kempster (d. 1715), a local mason and quarry-owner who worked with Sir Christopher Wren on many of his buildings, including Tom Tower at Christ Church, Oxford, and Abingdon County Hall.

Into the Cotswolds

To the southwest of Burford at Broadwell on the A361 Lechlade road is the **Cotswold Wild Life Park**, with a collection of animals, birds, insects and reptiles from all over the world in the attractive grounds of the 1804 manor house (open daily exc. Christmas 10.00–18.00, ☎ 01993 823006, ✉ www.cotswold wildlifepark.co.uk). West of Burford the A40 road leads into the heart of the

Gloucestershire Cotswolds, with their many scenic and architectural attractions (see *Blue Guide England*). Shortly after the entrance gates to Sherborne Park, a few miles west of Burford, a narrow lane leads south (left) to **Lodge Park** (National Trust: open Apr–Oct Mon, Fri, 11.00–16.00, Sun 11.00–15.00, ☎ 01451 844130, ✉ www.nationaltrust.org.uk), built in 1634 by John Dutton, owner of the Sherborne Estate, as a grandstand for viewing deer-coursing; it is an accomplished villa-like stone building in the Classical style with a grand upstairs banqueting room in which family portraits are displayed.

A little further along the A40 a side road leads to **Northleach** (buses from Oxford and Burford), an unusually well-preserved small town whose heyday was in the 15C and 16C. The splendid early 15C **church**—one of the finest in the area—has a beautiful west tower and north porch and a superb collection of wool merchants' brasses, and there is a collection of mechanical musical instruments in the former Grammar School (open daily 10.00–18.00).

The A429—the Roman Foss Way—leads southwest from here to Cirencester, the Roman *Corinium*, and a left turn at Fossbridge, a couple of miles south of Northleach, leads southeast along minor roads through a succession of pretty Coln Valley villages—Coln St. Dennis; **Bibury**, considered by William Morris (see below) to be the most beautiful village in England, and now one of the most-visited; and the more secluded Coln St. Aldwyns (good food at the *New Inn*)—to **Fairford**, a small town in the flat land to the north of the Thames. The superb Perpendicular Gothic **church**, one of the finest of its date and type in England, was begun in the 1490s by John Tame, a local clothier, and retains an almost complete set of stained glass windows which rank among the most important examples of late-medieval art in England.

The upper Thames

The A417 road leads east from Fairford to **Lechlade** (23 miles from Oxford), a small town with another late 15C church standing at the confluence of four rivers: the Coln, the Leach, the Cole and the Thames. At St. John's Lock is a Victorian statue of Old Father Thames; originally made for the Crystal Palace, it was subsequently moved to the source of the Thames near Cirencester, but moved again, for greater safety, to its present site.

A little to the east of Lechlade, a side road leads back over the Oxfordshire border to the grey stone **Kelmscott Manor**, dating from the late 16C and C17 and famed for its association with William Morris, the guiding spirit of the Arts and Crafts movement (open Apr–Sept Wed 11.00–13.00, 14.00–17.00, and 3rd Sat of month 14.00–17.00, Thur, Fri by appointment, ☎ 01367 252486, ✉ www. kelmscottmanor.co.uk). Built as a farmhouse in the local vernacular style, its visual qualities, combined with its remoteness, encouraged Morris to lease it as a summer residence from 1871 until his death in 1896; he called it 'heaven on earth' and introduced it into his utopian romance *News from Nowhere*, though Dante Gabriel Rossetti, who virtually took up residence there, called it 'the doziest dump of old grey beehives'; he nevertheless found solace with Morris's wife Jane, the subject of innumerable soulful portraits by him, some of which can be seen in the house, along with an excellent collection of pictures, furniture and hangings once owned by Morris, and works by Burne-Jones, Philip Webb, and Ford Madox Brown. There are also examples of Morris's own famous wallpapers and chintzes, and older pictures, tapestries and items of furniture which he acquired.

Near the house is a pair of cottages built in 1902 by Jane Morris in memory of her husband; they were designed by Philip Webb, and carry a decorative plaque also designed by him, and just beyond is the excellent *Plough Inn*. Morris was buried in the churchyard, near the hedge to the right of the entrance gate, behind a small bay tree. A ridge-shaped stone designed by Webb marks the spot. Though no churchgoer, Morris would have approved of the unrestored texture of the homely **church**, the earliest parts of which date from the late 12C.

The A417 Faringdon road leads across the Thames from Lechlade past the well-preserved stone-built village of Buscot to **Buscot Park** (open Apr–Sept Wed–Fri, also Easter bank hol. weekend and some summer weekends 14.00–18.00; grounds only Apr–Sept Mon–Fri 14.00–18.00; ☎ 01367 240786, ✉ www.buscot-park.com). It was built c 1780, to the designs of an unknown architect, by Edward Loveden Townsend and was sold in 1880 to the financier Alexander Henderson (afterwards 1st Lord Faringdon), chairman of the Great Central Railway. He made a number of changes to the plain Georgian house, employed Harold Peto to lay out a magnificent garden and amassed a notable collection of pictures and furniture, which was greatly expanded by his grandson the 2nd Lord Faringdon, who succeeded him in 1934. The 2nd Lord and his architect Geddes Hyslop also restored the exterior of the house to its original late-Georgian appearance and made further alterations to the interior.

The rather austere exterior gives no inkling of the riches to be found within: gold-painted chairs and sofas designed c 1800–04 by the connoisseur Thomas Hope for the Egyptian Room in his London house; ceramics and other objets d'art from Italy, Germany, Spain, France and China; portraits by Italian Renaissance masters and by Rembrandt, Rubens and Murillo; Burne-Jones's hauntingly beautiful paintings of *The Legend of the Briar Rose* (the Sleeping Beauty), completed in 1890, which hang in the Saloon; and, in two upstairs rooms, works by Rossetti (including Jane Morris as Pandora), Watts, Leighton and Ford Madox Brown.

Nest to the house is the **East Pavilion**, built in the 1930s and decorated with mural paintings by Lord Hastings, a pupil of Diego Rivera, celebrating the socialist affiliations of the 2nd Lord Faringdon, who entertained leading members of the Labour Party here in the 1930s and 1940s. Beyond is Harold Peto's Italianate **water-garden**, linking the house with a large lake created in the 18C. To the west of the house is the former kitchen garden, attractively replanted by the present Lord Faringdon.

Three miles east of Buscot is Faringdon (see p 154) and from here it is a ¾ hour drive back to Oxford.

4 ~ Blenheim Palace and beyond

Blenheim Palace is historically one of the most interesting, and architecturally one of the most spectacular, of all English houses. It is situated on the edge of the small town of Woodstock, 8 miles from Oxford, and is easily reached by car or bus from the city centre via the A44 Evesham road. Just before Woodstock, a left turn onto the A4095 (signposted Witney) leads to **Bladon**, the Blenheim estate village, where Sir Winston and Lady Churchill are buried in the churchyard. The body of the statesman, who was born at Blenheim, was brought here after his funeral in St. Paul's Cathedral in 1965, the train carrying his coffin watched by silent crowds. At the southern entrance to Woodstock on the A44 is the Hensington Gate, proclaiming the entrance to Blenheim Palace with a Baroque flourish.

Blenheim Palace

Open daily mid-Mar–Oct 10.30–16.45; gardens and park open daily all year 09.00–16.00 winter, 09.00–18.00 summer, ☎ 01993 811325, ▨ www. blenheimpalace.com. Buses from Magdalen St every half hour).

Palace for a Duke

Blenheim stands within a former royal hunting park in the Forest of Wychwood, originally much larger than it is now. Henry II enjoyed secret rendezvous with the 'Fair Rosamund' here and Elizabeth I was imprisoned for a time by her sister Mary Tudor in the royal lodge, which was beseiged and badly damaged in the Civil War.

In 1705 the estate was given by by Queen Anne to John Churchill, 1st Duke of Marlborough, allied commander against the forces of Louis XIV at the crucial battle of Blindheim or Blenheim (pronounced Blen'm) on the banks of the Danube, and Parliament promised sufficient funds—or so it was thought—for the building of a great palace which would vie with those of Louis XIV's France. He chose as his architect Sir John Vanbrugh, who employed as his assistant Nicholas Hawksmoor, protégé of Sir Christopher Wren.

The project soon ran into difficulties. The Whig-dominated government which had approved the building of the palace fell in 1710 and a year later Marlborough's Duchess was displaced from the favour of the Queen and dismissed from her royal appointments, as was her husband. Work came to a halt after public funding dried up in 1712, but it resumed four years later at the Duke's own expense. By then, however, Vanbrugh had alienated the Duchess and was dismissed. The palace was finally finished under Hawksmoor's supervision and, through the Duchess's vindictiveness, Vanbrugh was forbidden even to enter the grounds. The final cost was £300,000, three times the original estimate.

The estate was eventually inherited by Marlborough's grandson Lord Spencer, who became 3rd Duke and brought a magnificent collection of books to Blenheim, which was dispersed by his profligate descendants in the 19C. The most important later contributions were made by the 4th Duke, who employed Capability Brown to create the present superb landscape setting in the 1760s, and by the 9th—cousin of Sir Winston Churchill—who married the immensely wealthy American heiress Consuelo Vanderbilt; he restored and refurnished the state rooms and in 1908–30 brought in the Frenchman Achille Duchêne to make formal gardens east and west of the palace, thus re-creating something of the original character lost by Brown's landscaping.

The Palace

Blenheim Palace is built of an ochre-coloured limestone from Burford. It faces north over the valley of the River Glyme, a paltry stream which was dammed by Brown to form the present lake. Visitors enter through an intimidating **gateway** leading into the east (Kitchen) courtyard, one of two service courts planned by Vanbrugh on either side of the house.

Another gateway on the far side of the courtyard gives access to the open **Entrance Court**, a Baroque stage set presided over by the vast bulk of the house. It consists of a main block with a Corinthian portico and pedimented attic, flanked by curved walls which terminate in massive towers topped by what Hawksmoor called 'eminencys', adding a note of almost Gothic fantasy to what is otherwise a building of Roman austerity and seriousness, befitting the military hero for whom it was created. Colonnades stretch forward from the towers to the service courtyards, each of which has an extraordinary turret—almost certainly designed by Hawksmoor—over the entrance, with sculptural enrichments by Grinling Gibbons (e.g. English lions savaging French cockerels) designed to drive home the chauvinistic message.

Inside the palace, groups of visitors are conducted by guides through a series of immensely impressive rooms, starting in the dignified, stone-clad **Great Hall** lit from above by windows in the attic; the ceiling painting by Sir James Thornhill depicts Marlborough showing Britannia the battle plan of Blenheim. Note also the Grinling Gibbons stone carvings, the elaborate brass locks of the entrance door and, at the far end, the bronze copies (commissioned by the 1st Duke) of two of the most famous statues of Classical antiquity: the Dancing Faun and the Medici Venus.

A suite of rooms to the right, once occupied by Marlborough's domestic chaplain, contains the bedroom in which Sir Winston Churchill was born. They now house an **exhibition** of photographs and other Churchill memorabilia, including some of his own paintings.

The rooms on the garden front originally comprised two 'apartments', each made up of an anteroom, drawing room and bedroom, on either side of the central Saloon. Substantial redecoration occurred in the late 18C and again a century later, but the first three rooms still retain their original ceilings by Hawksmoor; much of the furniture is French, acquired in the 19C. There is also a superb collection of family portraits, including, in the **Red Drawing Room**, Reynolds's portrait of the 4th Duke and his family—perhaps the finest of all his group portraits—and, opposite it, Sargent's equally magnificent portrait of the 9th Duke with his wife, and children; there are also portraits by Van Dyck and 17C bronzes. Next door, in the **Green Writing Room**, are two of the famous 'Blenheim Tapestries' woven in Brussels and commemorating the victories of the 1st Duke.

The walls and ceiling **Saloon** or state dining room, at the centre of the garden front, are painted in *trompe l'oeil* fashion by Louis Laguerre (who has included himself among the characters portrayed) and the marble doorcases were designed by Gibbons. The three **state rooms**, redecorated in a luxurious French Rococo manner at the end of the 19C, are hung with 'Blenheim tapestries' and filled with excellent French furniture; in the centre of the first room is a copy of the note written by Marlborough to his wife, on the back of a tavern bill, asking her to let the Queen know that the battle at Blenheim had been won. The tour ends in the **Library**, designed by Hawksmoor and occupying the whole of the west wing; the magnificent plaster ceiling is by Isaac Mansfield (see Senate House, Cambridge). Originally intended as a picture gallery, the room was adapted to house the 3rd Duke's books, which were, alas, sold in 1872 (the present books were mostly brought in by the 9th Duke). In the entrance bay is a

BLENHEIM PALACE

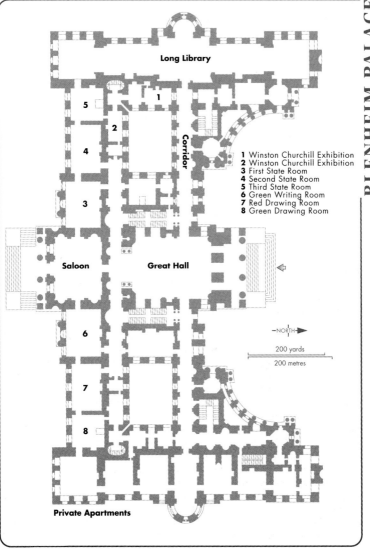

Long Library

5

2

4

Corridor

3

1 Winston Churchill Exhibition
2 Winston Churchill Exhibition
3 First State Room
4 Second State Room
5 Third State Room
6 Green Writing Room
7 Red Drawing Room
8 Green Drawing Room

Saloon

Great Hall

← NORTH →

200 yards

200 metres

6

7

8

Private Apartments

statue of Queen Anne, by Rysbrack, who also carved the bust of the 1st Duke in the central bay; at the far end is a 'Father' Willis organ introduced by the 8th Duke in 1891, on which a resident organist entertained the house-party guests.

From the end of the library, visitors are directed to the **Chapel**, completed in 1732, where the grandiose monument to Marlborough and his Duchess, by Rysbrack and William Kent, adorns one of the walls.

Gardens and park

To the west of the house are the superb **water terrace gardens** laid out in a formal manner by Achille Duchêne in 1925–30; in one of the two pools in the lower garden is a model, given to the 1st Duke, of Bernini's fountain in the Piazza Navona in Rome. From here paths lead through woodland, above the lake, to the **Temple of Diana** (by Chambers) and the Rose Garden.

To the south of the palace there was originally a parterre laid out by Vanbrugh and Henry Wise, but this was swept away by Capability Brown in favour of a bare lawn; it is overlooked by Vanbrugh's majestic **garden front**, with its marble bust of Louis XIV, captured by the 1st Duke at the siege of Tournai in 1709, crowning the centre like a trophy. Beyond is the **Italian garden**, laid out by Duchêne, starting in 1908; the fountain in the centre is by the American sculptor Ralph Waldo Storey.

Capability Brown comes into his own in the **park**, one of the most extensive and beautiful of all his landscapes. To the north of the palace is the lake, crossed by Vanbrugh's colossal **bridge** built when the River Glyme was no more than an insignificant stream; it was originally designed to be surmounted by towers and arcading and thus to be considerably larger even than it is now. The old royal manor house, in which Vanbrugh had hoped to take up residence, stood close to its north end, near the 'bower' where Henry II and Rosamund are supposed to have had their amorous encounters.

At the top of the hill beyond stands the **Column of Victory**, built under the supervision of Lord Herbert (later 9th Earl of Pembroke) in 1727–30, after designs by Hawksmoor; it is surmounted by a lead statue of the 1st Duke. From here, footpaths lead around the lake and through the park, the easternmost following the head of the lake, with excellent distant views of the palace and then going uphill to the **triumphal arch** (by Hawksmoor, 1723) which leads into Woodstock.

Woodstock

Originally called New Woodstock to distinguish it from an older settlement further north, the town was founded by Henry II in 1164 as part of his royal manor. It was for a long time a centre of the gloving industry, and gloves are still made here.

The Classical **Town Hall** (William Chambers, 1766) looks out onto the triangular market place; the arcaded ground floor was enclosed in 1898. On the south side is the large and famous *Bear Hotel*, with a good restaurant. Further west, towards the entrance to Blenheim Palace, is the mainly Victorian **church**, until the 18C a chapel of ease to Bladon parish church. Opposite is Fletcher's House, the home of the recently rearranged **Oxfordshire Museum** (open Tues–Sat 10.00–17.00, Sun 14.00–17.00, ☎ 01993 811456), with displays relating to the history of the county from prehistoric times to the 20C.

The northern Cotswolds

The A44 road leads north from Woodstock through limestone country: rather treeless uplands, with shallow valleys watered by clear smooth-flowing rivers, fields divided by drystone walls, or low hedges thickly entangled with traveller's joy, the sheen of whose silver-plumed seed-heads brightens the autumn and winter landscape. Twenty miles from Oxford is **Chipping Norton** (buses from Gloucester

Green), a busy stone-built market town whose large and splendid **church**, mostly of c 1485, is evidence of its prosperity in the great days of the Cotswold wool trade. On the western outskirts is the Bliss Tweed Mill (now apartments); this was built in the 1870s to resemble a country mansion and its tall chimney, designed in the form of a Tuscan column and rising from a domed tower, is a striking landmark.

To the north of Chipping Norton, in high country on the Warwickshire border, are the mysterious **Rollright Stones** (follow A44 to junction with A436, then turn right along minor road). They comprise a prehistoric stone circle 100ft in diameter, with a larger outlier called the King's Stone, 8ft high.

Just after the A44/A436 junction, a clearly-signposted lane leads left to **Chastleton House** (open Apr–Sept, Wed–Sat 13.00–16.00, Oct Wed–Sat 13.00–15.00, adm. by timed tickets; advance booking advisable Saturdays and holidays, ☎ 01608 674355 or 01494 755585, ✉ www.nationaltrust.org.uk), one of the best-preserved and most romantic Jacobean houses in England. It was built in 1607–12 by a lawyer, Walter Jones, descendent of a Witney wool merchant. He bought the estate in 1603 and the house still retains most of its original interior decoration and some of its 17C furnishings. Having descended in the family, with steadily diminishing resources to maintain it, it was acquired by the National Trust in 1991.

The **house** is built of an attractive local limestone and is laid out around a small internal courtyard, with crenellated towers containing staircases on either side of the gabled main building. Inside there is excellent early 17C woodwork and plasterwork, as well as tapestries and needlework of the same period, and family portraits. The Bible taken by Charles I to the scaffold is preserved in the Library and there is also a secret hiding-place used by the Royalist grandson of the builder when Cromwellian troops visited the house in 1651; above, on the top floor, is a superb barrel-vaulted Long Gallery. The walled **topiary garden** to the right of the entrance probably also dates from the 17C and has been little altered by subsequent changes in taste.

Those wishing to explore more of this part of the Cotswolds should continue along the A44 to **Moreton-in-Marsh** (trains from Oxford), a small roadside town over the Gloucestershire border. A few miles to the northwest a right turn along the B4081 leads to **Chipping Campden**, one of the most beautiful small towns in this part of England (see *Blue Guide England*), its handsome houses of honey-coloured local stone and its splendid 15C parish church and nearby 17C almshouses bearing witness to the prosperity of the Cotswold cloth industry. A left turn along the A429—the Roman Foss Way—at Moreton-in-Marsh leads to **Stow-on-the-Wold**, another market town situated, as its name suggests, on the top of a hill, from which a detour can be made to **Lower and Upper Slaughter**, two of the best-known villages in the Gloucestershire Cotswolds. Just south of Stow, the A424 diverges from the Foss Way and crosses the bare hills to Burford (see p 157), from which it is a drive of about ¾ hours back to Oxford.

5 ~ Rousham, Banbury and north Oxfordshire

The A4280 road leads north from Oxford into hilly countryside dotted with attractive stone-built villages, less famous than those of the Cotswolds further to the west but interspersed with impressive country houses in their parkland setting.

Rousham House and Gardens

Twelve miles north of Oxford, on a signposted side road, is **Rousham House and Gardens** (garden open daily throughout the year 10.00–16.30, house Apr–Sept Wed, Sun & bank hols 14.00–16.30; ☎ 01869 347110, ◪ www. rousham.org. Accessible by bus from Magdalen St, or by train to Heyford station). The house was built in 1635 by Sir Robert Dormer, but Rousham is best known today for its 18C garden, the most complete surviving example of the work of William Kent, 'the father of English landscape gardening'. He was employed in 1738–40 by General James Dormer, a friend of Alexander Pope, to remodel the house and to modify and perfect the landscaping already begun by Charles Bridgeman. When the General died in 1743, Rousham passed into the possession of his cousin, Sir Charles Cottrell, and it has since remained in the family.

Visitors buy their tickets to the **gardens** in the stable block and proceed to the opposite side of the house, where a lawn or bowling green stretches to a point at which the ground falls away to the River Cherwell. The heart of Kent's garden—a miniature wooded Arcadia full of poetic Classical references and visual surprises—lies to the left, out of sight of the house. It is punctuated by carefully placed Classical statuary and architectural features, notably the monumental rusticated arcade known as **Praeneste** (the Latin name for Palestrina, the hilltop town to the south of Rome), overlooking the river, and two rusticated cascades in a tree-lined glade known as **Venus' Vale**, presided over by a lead copy of the Medici Venus and statues of other Classical deities (by Van Nost). From this point a serpentine path leads past a distinctly uninviting 'cold bath' to the **Temple of Echo**. The return route meanders along the valley floor to a natural amphitheatre and a stone pyramid, from which a short ascent leads to the beautifully planted and maintained **walled gardens**, containing a dovecot dating from 1685 with its original potence (revolving ladder).

The 17C **house** was built on an H plan, but Kent extended it and gave it a more medieval appearance by adding battlements and reglazing the windows. Inside, his main contribution was the creation of the Painted Parlour, exquisitely decorated in the neo-Palladian manner and still containing General Dormer's collection of Italian bronzes. Kent also created the Great Parlour, built to house the General's books but remodelled in 1764 as a 'great room', with excellent Rococo plasterwork by Thomas Roberts of Oxford. The other rooms date from the 17C and the mid-19C, and a good display of family portraits hangs on the walls.

North of Rousham the A4280 passes through gently undulating country, the fields large and dotted with clumps of woodland. As the road nears Banbury the building stone is tinged with iron oxide, giving it a rich brown or ochre colour; Deddington and Adderbury are large villages of prosperous-looking brown houses built of this stone. The church at **Adderbury** is one of the largest and finest in the Oxford area; begun in the 13C, it has a splendid west tower and spire of the 14C and a magnificent chancel built in 1408–19 by the mason Richard Winchcombe—the first master mason for the Divinity School in Oxford—out of funds provided by William of Wykeham, the founder of New College.

Banbury

Two miles further on is Banbury (also accessible by the M40 motorway or by frequent trains from Oxford), the 'capital' of north Oxfordshire and an important market town which has undergone many vicissitudes since its foundation in the early Middle Ages. Its most famous structure, the **Cross**, celebrated in nursery rhyme, and standing at the junction of High St and Horse Fair at the entrance to the town, is a replacement of the original (by J. Gibbs, 1859), and may not even be on the same site. The medieval castle vanished without trace after the Civil War and the **church**, just to the north of the Cross, was demolished at the end of the 18C, to be replaced by the present massive Classical building by S.P. Cockerell (1797). Manufacturing industry arrived with the advent of the Oxford Canal and the railway in the 19C and the town has grown greatly in recent years. But many old buildings remain, especially in and around the **Market Place**, including some large timber-framed inns, notably the *Reindeer*, which contains well-preserved 17C panelling and in which good food can be had.

On the site of an old wharf by the Oxford Canal, and accessible over the river from the market place through the adjacent Castle Quay shopping centre, is the excellent **Banbury Museum** (open Mon–Sat 09.30–17.00, Sun and bank hols 10.30–16.30, ☎ 01295 259855, ✉ www.banburytown.co.uk/museum), in which the history of the town and region is expertly told through a permanent display in a well-designed new building. There is a good restaurant overlooking the canal, where the legendary Banbury Cakes figure on the menu, and guided tours are given of the adjacent **Tooley's Boatyard** (Thur and Sat afternoons: for information ☎ 01295 272917), incorporating what is claimed to be England's oldest working dry dock, long famous for the building and restoration of canal boats.

Two miles southwest of Banbury on the B4035 Shipston-on-Stour road is **Broughton Castle**, a semi-fortified house built of the characteristic brown local stone and beautifully situated in a moat (open mid-May–mid-Sept Wed and Sun, also bank hol. Sun/Mon and Thur in July/Aug 14.00–17.00, ☎ 01295 276070 or 722547, ✉ www.broughtoncastle.demon.co.uk). It dates back at least to the early 14C, when it belonged to Sir John de Broughton (d. 1315), who is buried in the adjacent **church**, an impressive 14C building with a broach spire. The manor was purchased in 1377 by William of Wykeham, Bishop of Winchester (see New College, Oxford), and in 1406 his heir Sir Thomas Wykeham built the gatehouse which still commands the entrance to the courtyard. The estate later passed by marriage to the Fiennes family, Lords Saye and Sele, and the house was completely remodelled and enlarged in 1551–54, giving it an unmistakably 16C appearance.

The **interior** contains work of the 14C, the 16C—some superb panelling and plaster ceilings—and also of the 18C and 19C. Artistically the finest piece of wok is a splendid chimneypiece of the 1550s in an upstairs bedroom in the sophisticated Mannerist style of the Palace of Fontainebleau in France, with a scene from Ovid's *Metamorphoses* in the overmantel. Broughton was an important centre of the opposition to Charles I in the 1630s, when the Lord Saye of the time—known as 'Old Subtlety'—acted, in the Royalist historian Clarendon's biased words, as 'the pilot that steered all those vessels freighted with sedition to destroy the government', and visitors are shown an attic room in which he and his friends are said to have plotted.

There is an attractive walled **knot garden** south of the house, created in the 20C to complement the ancient setting. From here there are good views of the south front of the house, with the two prominent gabled projections housing the 16C staircases and the crenellated medieval chamber block.

From the nearby village of Tadmarton a minor road leads to **Bloxham**, a large ironstone village with another of the splendid late medieval churches which attest to the prosperity of north Oxfordshire in the 14C and 15C; it has a particularly graceful 14C spire and inside there is a very fine 15C south chapel, possibly by Richard Winchcombe, the master mason who worked at Adderbury church (above), a 15C rood screen with some of its original painting and glass by the Morris firm in the east window (1869). From here the A4280 Banbury–Oxford road is easily reached.

An alternative, and longer, route back to Oxford leads through quiet and attractive upland country along the A361 and B4022 to **Great Tew**, one of the most beautiful villages in Oxfordshire. Much of its charm derives from a careful landscaping scheme carried out in the early 19C, in which the existing thatched stone cottages were retained and beautified and trees planted in profusion to enhance their picturesque qualities. The man responsible for the landscaping was the prolific writer and gardener John Claudius Loudon, who set up an experimental farm here in 1809–11. There is an excellent monument by Chantrey to Mary Anne Boulton (d. 1829) in the medieval church above the village, and good food can be had in the *Falkland Arms* inn. From here a few minutes' drive by car leads to the A44 at Enstone, from which Oxford can be reached in about ¾ hour.

6 ~ Waddesdon, Claydon and Stowe

The landscape to the northeast and east of Oxford is pleasantly rural, mostly low-lying but diversified by isolated hills, outliers of the Chilterns, which, rising from the plain, give the impression of greater height than they actually have. Once over the Buckinghamshire county boundary, only a few miles from Oxford, stone gives way to timber and brick as building materials, sometimes supplemented with earth or 'witchert' walls. But the main interest for the visitor lies in the presence of some of the finest country houses in the south of England, unfortunately not easily visited by those without a car.

Leaving Oxford from the north, the busy A34 road runs along the north side of **Otmoor**, an area of flat and empty wetland fringed by small villages, still quiet and lonely in spite of their proximity to Oxford and the M40 motorway; the mysterious centre of the moor is the habitat of many rare species of insects, plants and butterflies.

Waddesdon Manor

Just before Bicester the A41 Aylesbury road diverges south and a few miles along it is the unmistakably Victorian estate village of Waddesdon, with Waddesdon Manor perched patriarchally on the hill above (owned by the National Trust/Lord Rothschild; open Apr–Oct Wed–Sun, also bank hol. Mon 11.00–16.00, last recommended adm. 14.30; gardens Mar–mid-Dec Wed–Sun 10.00–17.00; admission to house by timed ticket; for advance reservations ☎ 01296 653226, ✉ waddesdon.org.uk).

Visitors are ushered at the allotted time into a vestibule, where guides explain the history of the house and family. Thereafter it is possible to wander freely through the **ground floor** rooms and enjoy the works of art at one's own pace.

Home of the Rothschilds

One of the most sumptuous of all English country houses, Waddesdon Manor was built in 1877–83, on a virgin site purchased from the Duke of Marlborough, by Baron Ferdinand de Rothschild, head of the Austrian branch of the famous banking family which had already established itself in mid-Buckinghamshire. It was designed by a French architect, Hippolyte Gabriel Destailleur, in an eclectic French Renaissance style, incorporating features inspired by Blois, Chambord, and other chateaux: visually a somewhat indigestible mixture, though undoubtedly grand. Its main claim to fame, though, is the priceless collection of furniture, porcelain and works of art amassed by Baron Ferdinand and his successors: probably the finest collection of its kind in England outside the Wallace Collection in London. The setting is also superb, with formal and landscaped grounds dotted with statuary to create a 19C version of a Watteau-esque arcadia.

There are important pictures by English, French and Dutch artists, including some of Gainsborough's and Reynolds's finest full-length portraits, as well as works by de Hooch, Ruisdael, Terborch, Dou, Cuyp and Watteau. There is also 18C French furniture of the highest quality, much of it by famous craftsmen and some of it made for the royal family, and an excellent collection of Sèvres and Meissen porcelain. These and other items are arranged in rooms of exquisite beauty, several of them incorporating 18C chimneypieces and *boiseries* rescued from abandoned French houses.

Upstairs on the **first floor** there is more Sèvres porcelain, including a 300-piece service given by Louis XV to the Austrian ambassador in 1766, a room containing a series of melodramatic but captivating paintings of the Sleeping Beauty legend commissioned from the Russian artist Leon Bakst by James de Rothschild in 1913. The bedroom suites contain more superb 18C French furniture, English and French 18C pictures (including Reynolds's *Garrick between Comedy and Tragedy*, one of his wittiest and most engaging works), and 18C Rococo woodwork.

To the left of the main body of the house is the **Bachelors' Wing** (open Wed–Fri 11.00–16.00), mainly decorated in a 16C style, with genuine French 16C panelling and a chimneypiece of the same date in the Billiard Room. The wing originally housed late medieval and Renaissance items given to the British Museum in 1898, but in their place there are now items of the same period collected by later Rothschilds, most of them from northern Europe, including armour, jewellery, silver, glass, Limoges enamels and illuminated manuscripts. Visitors are also encouraged to explore the **cellars**, where rare vintages from the Rothschild vineyards in France are tantalisingly stacked away (there is also a good **restaurant** and a shop where wine can be purchased).

The **gardens**, by the French designer Laine, are very extensive: formal to the south of the house, more 'natural' to the west, where there are examples of rare trees and shrubs. There is also an **aviary**, extravagantly Rococo in its architectural character and filled with exotic birds. Examples of statuary from various sources are dotted among the trees, including a *Shepherd Boy and Dog* by the 19C Danish sculptor Thorvaldsen.

From the village of Waddesdon quiet lanes run north through a peaceful agricultural landscape. On a remnant of the long-vanished Great Central main railway line is the **Buckinghamshire Railway Centre** (open daily March–Oct 10.30–17.30, ☎ 01296 655720, 🖾 www.bucksrailcentre.org.uk), containing many steam locomotives and related railway memorabilia. It is entered through the re-erected former LMS railway station in Oxford, demolished in order to build the Saïd Business School (see p 115); the building was originally erected in 1851 by the contractor for the Great Exhibition in Hyde Park, London, using the same iron castings. The village of **Quainton**, on the hill to the north, has a windmill, a church with excellent 17C and 18C monuments to the Dormer family and a row of almshouses dated 1687.

Claydon House

Two miles north of Quainton, and approached from the village of Middle Claydon, or directly from Oxford via Bicester (A34 and A41) is Claydon House (open Apr–Oct Sat–Wed 13.00–16.30, ☎ 01296 730349, 🖾 www.nationaltrust.org.uk). This is a magnificent fragment of a much larger building constructed by Ralph, Lord Verney, between 1759 and 1771. The Verneys had owned land in Middle Claydon since the 15C and the south or family wing (not open) survives from a house built of 1620. The design of the present house was worked out by Lord Verney with the help of a London carpenter and builder, Luke Lightfoot, but in 1768, infuriated by Lightfoot's dilatory habits, he turned to the neo-Palladian amateur architect Sir Thomas Robinson to modify the design. Lightfoot was dismissed, having been damned by Robinson as 'an ignorant knave, with no small spice of madness in his composition', but not before he had created some of the finest examples of Rococo work in England in the interior, much of it carved in wood (not plaster, contrary to first appearances). Soon afterwards, Lord Verney fell deeply into debt and in 1792 two-thirds of his new house, including a large domed rotunda, was demolished. But what remains is a magnificent example of mid-18C interior decoration at its most creative.

The house faces west onto tranquil parkland, landscaped in the late 18C. Next to it is the medieval **church**, which contains a superb monument of 1653 by the London sculptor Edward Marshall. Inside the **house**, Lightfoot's work is seen at its most extravagent in the vast, empty North Hall; he called it 'such a Work as the World never saw': a judgement with which most visitors will agree. The remaining ground floor rooms—the Saloon and the Library—are in a more conventional Palladian style, but the top-lit Staircase Hall was decorated after Lightfoot's dismissal in the Neo-classical manner popularised by the Adam brothers; the exquisitely beautiful staircase of inlaid wood, with its swirly iron balustrade containing representations, in iron, of husks and ears of corn is a triumph both of craftsmanship and of creative stylisation. The hand of Lightfoot in evidence again on the **first floor**, especially in the Gothic Room and the Chinese Room, one of the most engagingly frivolous examples of 18C chinoiserie in England, with bamboo furniture made in Canton c 1800. A very different mood is conjured up in the bedroom of the great Victorian nursing reformer Florence Nightingale, sister of Parthenope, Lady Verney, and a frequent visitor to the house in the second half of the 19C. Elsewhere on this floor there are 17C family portraits and mementoes of the travels of later members of the family, including a complete Javanese gamelan.

Stowe

Claydon was rebuilt by Lord Verney in competition with an even grander house, Stowe, two miles to the north-west of Buckingham (reached from Oxford via Bicester and the A421), and about half an hour north of Claydon by car. For many years the seat of the Temple and Grenville families, in whose orbit half of Buckinghamshire once revolved, the house and its even more famous gardens date mainly from the 18th century, when they belonged first to Lord Cobham, a soldier and fervant Whig, and subsequently to his nephew Lord Temple, who succeeded him in 1749, and Temple's nephew the 1st Marquess of Buckingham. The family's notorious pride reached its apogee in the early 19th century, but debt struck in 1848, the magnificent collections were sold, and in 1921 the house was sold too. It is now a well-known public school, but the grounds have passed to the National Trust, which has carried out an extensive programme of restoration.

The **house** is open to the public during Easter and summer holidays (☎ 01280 818282). One of the largest country houses in England, it is approached from the west by an unusually long, straight drive past a pair of domed pavilions designed originally by James Gibbs c 1728, and is entered from the north through a portico designed by Sir John Vanbrugh in the 1720s; from the main block curved colonnades of the 1770s stretch forward to enfold visitors. The interiors, designed by a bewildering succession of architects and craftsmen, both English and Italian, are now bereft of their once magnificent furnishings, but are well worth seeing for their purely architectural qualities: finest of all is the magnificent oval-shaped saloon,one of the grandest Neo-classical rooms in England, which leads out onto the garden front, designed by Robert Adam and the amateur architect Thomas Pitt, Earl of Camelford, in 1772–74.

The **gardens** (open March–Dec Wed–Sun 10.00–17.30: close 16.00 Nov, Dec, ☎ 01820 822850, 🖾 www.nationaltrust.org.uk) represent perhaps the greatest achievement of the English 18C landscape gardening movement. Originally designed by Charles Bridgeman, they were extended in the 1730s by William Kent and his pupil Lancelot or 'Capability' Brown and were subsequently re-modelled in the second half of the 18C, retaining some of their existing architectural features; the profusion of temples and other garden buildings may well relate to the Temple family's motto 'Templa quam dilecta', or 'How lovely are thy temples'. They are entered to the east of the house close to the superb **Temple of Concord and Victory** (c 1749), which looks out onto the Grecian Valley, in the creation of which Capability Brown was involved. To the south is the area known as the **Elysian Fields**, landscaped by Kent, and, like Kent's garden at Rousham, rich in Classical allusion. Close by is the medieval **church** (the old village disappeared beneath the gardens), and beyond the Elysian Fields is a long ornamental lake crossed by a covered **Palladian bridge** (1738), one of only three known to exist. It is also worth searching out the Gothic Temple by James Gibbs (1741-42), Kent's Temple of Venus (1732), and Vanbrugh's Rotondo (1721), while the view of the **south front** of the house from the opposite side of the lake is one of the serenely magnificent in England: an epitome of 18C ideas of natural and architectural beauty.

7 ~ West Wycombe

The quickest way to reach West Wycombe from Oxford by car is to take the M40 motorway to junction 5 at Stokenchurch and then to follow the A40—the old Oxford-London road—through the Chilterns for about 5 miles. At the bottom of a beautiful valley is the village of **West Wycombe** (23 miles: served by buses from Oxford to High Wycombe), lined with attractive timber-framed houses interspersed with 18C brick buildings, including a large 18C coaching inn, the *George and Dragon* (good food).

West Wycombe Park

To the south of the village is the 18C **West Wycombe Park**, set in an Arcadian landscape which artfully enhances the 'genius of the place' (National Trust: open June–Aug, Sun–Thur 14.00–17.15; grounds only Apr and May, Sun, Wed and bank hol. Mon 14.00–17.15; ☎ 01494 513569, ✉ www.national trust.org.uk).

History

The estate was bought in 1698 by Sir Francis Dashwood, a wealthy merchant, but both house and grounds owe their present appearance to his son, the second Sir Francis. As a young man he travelled extensively on the Continent and in 1733 he became one of the founders of the Society of Dilettanti, in which scholarship and conviviality were mixed in equal measure. He began to lay out the grounds in the 1730s, and in 1748 he began to rebuild the house, essentially to his own designs, each of the façades having a different Classical character. In 1770–82 the grounds were further beautified by Thomas Cook, a pupil of Capability Brown, and Nicholas Revett, co-author of the *Antiquities of Athens*, who also designed the west portico (also known as as the Temple of Bacchus). Since then, both house and its surroundings have remained largely unchanged and the house still retains many of the pictures and much of the furniture bought for it by Sir Francis.

The **house** is entered from the south through a two-storeyed loggia. The interior was decorated internally over a period of some 20 years, starting in the 1750s, and shows Sir Francis's growing interest in Neo-classicism, especially in the Entrance Hall, which has a floor based on Roman mosaic pavements originally covering a heating system based on a Roman hypocaust. Many of the rooms have colourfully painted ceilings by an Italian painter, Giuseppe Borgnis, and his son Giovanni, inspired by antique and Renaissance models. There are also Brussels tapestries, marble chimneypieces by Henry Cheere, good examples of mid-18C English and French furniture and some superb Rococo mirrors. There are several portraits of Sir Francis—including one of him in a turban and another dressed as a monk—and a representative collection of Old Masters, including works by Ribera and Salvator Rosa; some of these are displayed in the beautifully proportioned Music Room, with ceiling paintings based on prototypes by Raphael and the Carracci in the Villa Farnesina and Palazzo Farnese in Rome.

The **gardens** are among the finest to survive from the mid-18C; Benjamin Franklin called them 'a paradise'. A ha-ha runs to the south of the house, separating it from the agricultural landscape which forms an important part of the view, and at the end of the terrace which runs alongside it is the **Temple of the Winds**.

built in the late 1750s and based loosely on the Tower of the Winds in Athens. Lower down is the lake, used in Sir Francis's time for mock naval battles, with a cascade at the east end and Revett's **Music Temple** of 1771 on an island in the middle. There is a screen of trees beyond, separating the gardens from the main road, and to the south of the Broad Walk—a remnant of the formal layout of the the 1730s—is the **Temple of Venus**, a deity much honoured by Sir Francis.

To the north of the village is a steep hill which forms an important part of the backdrop to the gardens, and on the hillside is the deliberately gloomy flint-built Gothic entrance to the **Hell-Fire Caves** (open daily Mar–Oct, Nov–Feb Sat/Sun only, 11.00–17.30, ☎ 01494 533739), excavated by Sir Francis Dashwood in 1750–52. The ostensible aim was to provide work for the local labour force, by supplying chalk for a new road to High Wycombe, to the east. But in the course of the excavations a number of underground chambers were created, among them a domed 'Banqueting Hall' with niches for statuary, and legend has consecrated these mysterious spaces to the activities of the so-called Hell-Fire Club, made up of Dashwood and some of his disreputable friends. The caves, some of them hung with stalagmites and stalactites, are now enlivened by wax tableaux and by a recorded commentary from the late Sir Francis.

A steep climb leads from the caves to the **church**, built on the hilltop within the earthworks of an Iron Age hill fort (usually open Oct, Nov and Mar, Sun 14.00–16.00; Apr–Sept, Sat, Sun and bank hols, also Mon–Fri in June–Aug, 14.00–17.00). Though medieval in origin, it was almost entirely rebuilt by Sir Francis in 1752–62 and now ranks as one of the finest 18C parish churches in England, its superb plaster decoration and wooden fittings surviving virtually intact. The comfortable pulpit and diminutive font bear witness to Sir Francis's heterodox religious opinions, which led him to produce a simplified *Book of Common Prayer* in collaboration with his friend Benjamin Franklin. Sir Francis also added an extra storey to the medieval tower, and at the top he placed a gold-painted ball with internal seating (the notorious politician John Wilkes called it 'the best Globe Tavern I was ever in').

To the east of the church, commanding an extensive view towards High Wycombe, is the forbidding flint-built **mausoleum**, built in 1763–64 out of funds supplied by George Bubb Dodington, a member of the Hell-Fire Club. Here Sir Francis and other members of his family are buried.

Those wishing to explore the country between West Wycombe and Oxford by car should remain on the A40 and turn right onto the B4012 just after Postcombe. A mile or two further on is **Thame** (13 miles: buses from Oxford to Aylesbury), a well-preserved market town with a wide main street lined with inns, including the Georgian-fronted *Spread Eagle*, a favourite resort of the glitterati in the 1930s (see John Fothergill's *An Innkeeper's Diary*). The large cruciform **church** was built in the 13C by the medieval Bishops of Lincoln, who had a house nearby. It was enlarged in the 14C and the prominent central tower was heightened in the 15C; there is some good early 16C and 17C woodwork inside and in the centre of the chancel is a large and impressive monument to Lord Williams (d. 1559), who lived in the largely vanished house at Rycote (below). Nearby, in Church Lane, is the former Grammar School of 1569, founded by Lord Williams, where John Hampden was a pupil.

From Thame the B4011 road can be followed back over the Buckinghamshire border to **Long Crendon**, a large village with many attractive houses of brick and timber. Near the large, mainly 13C, church is the Court House, a 14C building with a timber-framed upper floor, probably first used as a wool store and later as the meeting place of the manorial court.

A few miles further on, to the north of the B4011, is **Brill** (12 miles from Oxford), a large hilltop village of very distinctive character, nearly 700ft above sea level and commanding wide views in all directions. Houses and cottages, mostly of brick, are set round a wide green and a square, and to the west, on the edge of a common, is a 17C wooden **windmill** (open Apr–Sept, Sun 14.30–17.30).

Two miles west, and approached through a farmyard, is **Boarstall Duck Decoy** (National Trust: open Apr–Aug weekends & bank hol. Mon 10.00–17.00, Wed 16.00–19.00, ☎ 01844 237488, ✉ www.nationaltrust.org.uk). The decoy is a rare survival from the end of the 17C, when the ducks were trapped, killed and sent to market. The lake on which the decoy 'pipes' are set is surrounded by a large area of woodland, with a nature trail, especially beautiful when the bluebells are out in springtime. A short distance to the south, next to the church, is **Boarstall Tower**, the formidable stone gatehouse of a moated 14C manor house (demolished in the 18C), remodelled in 1615 as a hunting lodge or 'banqueting house' (National Trust, open Apr–Oct Weds and Bank Hol. Mon 14.00–18.00). From here a minor road leads back to Oxford through Horton-cum-Studley and Stanton St. John.

An alternative route back from Thame to Oxford follows the A329 road to the lonely **Rycote Chapel** (owned by English Heritage: open Apr–Sept Fri–Sun & bank hol. Mon 14.00–18.00, ✉ www.english-heritage.org.uk), built as a private chantry chapel by Sir Richard Quartermayne in 1449, and remarkable for its profusion of 15C and 17C woodwork. The Perpendicular Gothic chapel, together with the vanished great house which stood nearby, was bought in 1539 by Lord Williams of Thame, from whom it descended to the Norreys family. They constructed the two canopied pews of 1610 and 1625 which dominate the interior, the second of them, it is said, to mark a visit by Charles I. James Bertie, Earl of Abingdon, a noted High Churchman, was responsible for adding the splendid wooden reredos and communion rails of 1682, since when the Chapel has remained virtually unchanged.

From here it is a short journey back to Oxford via the M40 at junction 7 and the A40. Gardeners might wish to make a detour from Wheatley (follow signposts) to the **Waterperry Gardens**, a combination of ornamental gardens, nursery gardens, training school in practical gardening for professionals and amateurs alike, and garden sales centre (open Apr–Oct daily 09.00–17.30, closes 18.00 at weekends, and Oct–Mar exc. Christmas/New Year hols 09.00–17.00; ☎ 01844 339226, ✉ waterperrygardens.co.uk). It is both the fulfilment and the continuation of the work of Miss Beatrix Havergal, who moved here in 1932 with £350 and six students. Her aim was to educate women in all aspects of horticulture, both decorative and utilitarian, hence the enormous variety of plants grown here: flowering trees, shrubs, herbaceous and alpine flowers, roses, fruit trees, soft fruits and exotics grown in glasshouses.

The small but very attractive **church** retains evidence of its Anglo-Saxon origins; there is also a good collection of medieval stained glass, monuments of different dates, and 17C and 18C woodwork, including a complete set of box pews.

CAMBRIDGE

Practical information

Getting to Cambridge

By air
Heathrow, Gatwick, Luton and Stansted airports are connected to Cambridge (Drummer St bus station) by *National Express/Cambridge Coach Services Jetlink* buses (☎ 08705 808080 or 01223 423900, ✉ www.nationalexpress.com). The buses from Heathrow (Terminal 4 and Central Bus Station) run at roughly hourly intervals throughout the day (exc. Christmas Day) from 05.00–22.50, the journey taking about 2¾ hours at a cost of £22 single, £28 period return. Those from Gatwick (north and south terminals) leave at two-hourly intervals from 04.50–21.50 and take 3½ hours (£26 single, £32 period return); those from Luton leave two-hourly from 06.35–22.35 and take 1½ hours (£10 single, £14 period return), and those from Stansted run hourly day and night and take 45 minutes (£6 single, £10 period return). Stansted is the nearest airport to Cambridge and is connected by direct **trains** which run approximately every hour weekdays (less frequently Sundays) and take half an hour: the single fare is £6.

By train
The quickest, but not the cheapest, way of getting to Cambridge from London is by train. The **railway station** is in Station Rd, off Hills Rd (1¼ miles from the city centre, ten minutes by frequent bus service). There are fast trains to and from London Kings Cross every half hour daily (hourly in the evenings and weekends), the journey taking 50 minutes; trains also run less frequently to and from London Liverpool St Station (approximate time 70–90 minutes). The trains are operated by WAGN, and a day return costs £14.60; for times, ☎ 08457 484950 (National Rail Enquiry service), ✉ www.nationalrail.co.uk.

Cambridge is also connected by train to Norwich and East Anglia, the north of England and Scotland, but there is no direct train to Oxford.

By bus
The cheapest way of getting from London to Cambridge by public transport is by **National Express** bus, but the buses run less frequently than those between Oxford and London. They leave Victoria Coach Station daily for Drummer St bus station, in the city centre, every half hour from 08.30 (09.00 Sat/Sun) to 23.30,

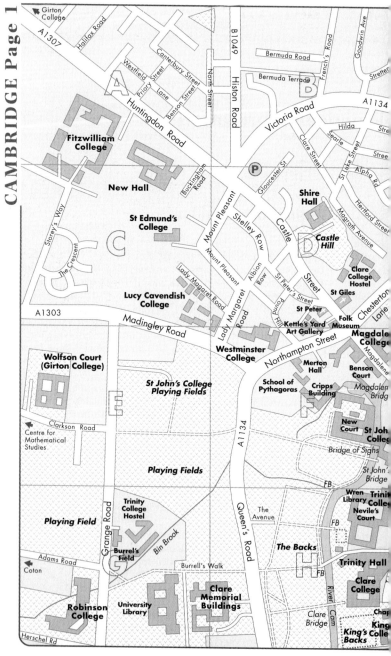

Girton College

A1307

Halifax Road

Westfield

Priory Lane

Benson Street

Canterbury Street

North Street

B1049

Bermuda Road

Goodwin Ave

Histon Road

Bermuda Terrace

Stretten

A1134

Victoria Road

Hilda

Searle

French's Road

St Luke Street

Stre

Stree

Clare Street

Alpha Rd

Huntingdon Road

Fitzwilliam College

Buckingham Road

P

Gloucester St

Shelley Row

Castle Street

Shire Hall

Magrath Avenue

Hertford Street

New Hall

St Edmund's College

Mount Pleasant

Mount Pleasant

Albion Row

St Peter's Street

Castle Hill

Clare College Hostel

St Giles

Storey's Way

The Crescent

C

Lady Margaret Road

Lady Margaret Road

Pound Hill

St Peter's Street

Chesterton Lane

Lucy Cavendish College

A1303

Madingley Road

Westminster College

Northampton Street

Kettle's Yard Art Gallery

St Peter

Folk Museum

Magdale College

Magdalene

Wolfson Court (Girton College)

St John's College Playing Fields

Merton Hall

School of Pythagoras

Cripps Building

Benson Court

Magdalen Bridge

Clarkson Road

Centre for Mathematical Studies

E

New Court

St Joh Colle

Bridge of Sighs

Playing Fields

A1134

Queen's Road

St John' Bridge

FB

Wren Library

Trinit Colle

Nevile's Court

Playing Field

Grange Road

Trinity College Hostel

Bin Brook

The Avenue

FB

Adams Road

Coton

Burrell's Field

G

Burrell's Walk

The Backs

FB

Trinity Hall

Clare College

Robinson College

University Library

Clare Memorial Buildings

River Cam

Clare Bridge

Chap

Herschel Rd

King's Coll

King's Colle Backs

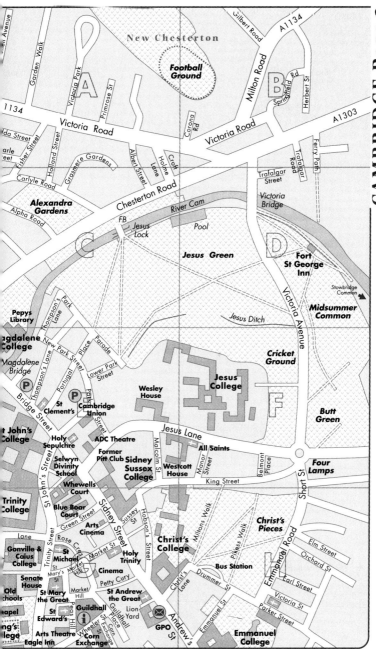

CAMBRIDGE Page 3

Herschel Road

Robinson College

University Library

Clare Memorial Buildings

King's Backs

King's Bridge

King's College

Clare Hall

St Chad's (St Catherine's College)

Grange Road

Rugby Ground

A

West Road

Queens' Garden

Queens' College

River Cam

Queen's Road

B

FB

Cripps Ct (Selwyn College)

West Gardens

Concert Hall

History Faculty

Harvey Court (Caius College)

Law Faculty

Cripps Ct

Anc

Cranmer Road

School of Divinity

Fisher Ct

Silver Street

Wie

Newham

Arts Faculties

Laundre Green

Pinehurst

Leckhampton House

Selwyn College

Museum of Classical Archaeology

Darwin College

Sidgwick Avenue

Granta Inn

Selwyn Gardens

Grange Road

Newnham College

C

Ridley Hall

Ridley Hall Road

Newnham Walk

Malting Lane

D

FB

Grange Gardens

Playing Field

Coe F

Newnham Road

A1134

Wolfson College

Playing Field

Clare Road

A603

Barton Road

Lammas Land

F

FB

P

Newham Croft

E

Hardwick Street

Derby Street

Grantchester Street

Lammas Field

Road

Merton Street

Chedworth Street

Owlstone Rd

Playing Field

Millington

Marlowe Road

Ellisley Avenue

Grantchester Meadows

South Green Road

Sports Grounds

G

River Cam

H

Playing Fie

Grantchester

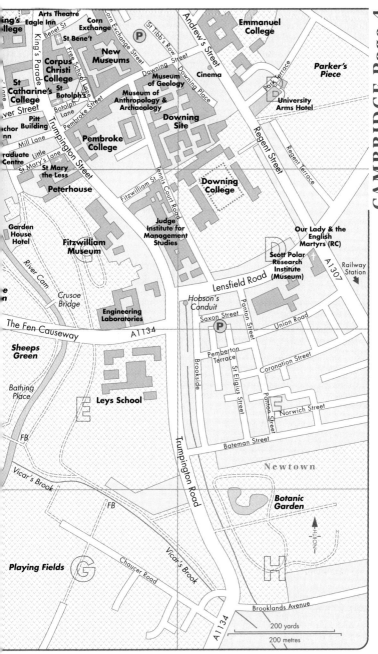

King's College

Arts Theatre
Eagle Inn
Corn Exchange
Benet St
St Bene't
Free School Lane
King's Parade
Corn Exchange Street
New Museums
St Tibb's Row
Andrew's Street
Emmanuel College
Parker's Piece

Corpus Christi College
St Catharine's College
St Botolph's
Botolph Lane
Pembroke Street
Downing Street
Museum of Geology
Cinema
Downing Place
Park Terrace

Pitt Building
Anchor Inn
Trumpington Street
Mill Lane
Museum of Anthropology & Archaeology
Downing Site
University Arms Hotel
Regent Street
Regent Terrace

Graduate Centre
St Mary's Lane
Little St Mary's Lane
Pembroke College
Fitzwilliam St
St Mary the Less
Peterhouse
Tennis Court Road
Downing College

Garden House Hotel
Fitzwilliam Museum
River Cam
Judge Institute for Management Studies
Our Lady & the English Martyrs (RC)
Scott Polar Research Institute (Museum)
A1307
Railway Station

Crusoe Bridge
Engineering Laboratories
Lensfield Road
Hobson's Conduit
Saxon Street
Panton Street
Union Road

The Fen Causeway
A1134
Sheeps Green
Bathing Place
FB
Leys School
Brookside
Pemberton Terrace
St Elgius Street
Panton Street
Coronation Street
Norwich Street
Bateman Street
Newtown

Vicar's Brook
FB
Trumpington Road
Botanic Garden
NORTH

Playing Fields
Chaucer Road
Vicar's Brook
A1134
Brooklands Avenue

200 yards
200 metres

picking up passengers at Millbank, Embankment, Aldgate, Mile End tube station, Bow, and Stratford bus station. The journey time is two hours, and buses stop at Trumpington Park-and-Ride before reaching Cambridge; ☎ 08705 808080 for information and booking seats ✉ www.nationalexpress.com. The single fare is £8.50, day return £9.

Cambridge is linked to Oxford by hourly *Stagecoach Express* X5 buses (☎ 01604 676060, ✉ www.stagecoach.express.co.uk); the journey takes about three hours.

There is also a good service of local buses; the County Council has a Passenger Information Line (☎ 01223 717740). *National Express* long distance buses serve many parts of the country (☎ 08705 808080); for nationwide bus times contact Traveline (☎ 0870 608 2608, ✉ www.traveline.org.uk).

By car

The quickest route from central and east London is along the M11. From west London it might be quicker to use the A1(M) and then the A505 and A10 roads. The journey time by either route is about 1¼ hours, longer at busy times. From Oxford the most direct route is via Milton Keynes and skirting the south of Bedford (A421, then A428), though some people prefer using the M40, M25 and M11. Either way, at least 2 hours should be allowed for the journey.

Parking The main central car parks are in Lion Yard, Park St (behind the Round Church), Gonville Place and the Grafton Centre (see map); none of these is far from the city centre. The Lion Yard car park is the busiest. There is some limited street parking, although the heart of the city is completely closed to traffic.

Those bringing their cars to Cambridge for the day are strongly recommended to use the excellent **Park and Ride** service which operates 07.00–20.00 Mon–Sat every 10 minutes from: **Madingley Rd**, close to the M11 (junction 13) and the road to Bedford and Oxford, every 10 minutes (also Sun); **Cowley Rd**, near the Science Park and A45; **Newmarket Rd**, near the junction with A45 (also Sun); **Babraham Rd**, next to the A1307; and **Trumpington**, next to the A10 and close to the M11 at junction 11. Parking is free of charge.

Passengers from Madingley Rd and Newmarket Rd are disgorged at Bridge St or Emmanuel St; for those from Cowley Rd, Babraham Rd and Trumpington the nearest stop to the city centre is Emmanuel St.

Where to stay

Accommodation of all kinds is plentiful in Cambridge, but most of the cheaper establishments are some way away from the centre of the city. It is advisable to book in advance if possible, especially in the peak summer period from mid-June to the end of August. The **Tourist Information Centre**, Wheeler St, Cambridge CB2 3QB (open Mon/Tues, Thur/Fri 09.00–18.00, Wed 09.30–18.00, Nov–Mar closes 17.30; Sat 09.00–17.00; Easter–Sep Sun and bank hols 10.30–15.30; ☎ 01223 322640, ▯ 01223 457588, ✉ www.tourism.cambridge.com) runs a useful hotel booking service (☎ 01223 457581, ▯ 01223 457589) as well as supplying information about tours (☎ 01223 457574), cultural events, etc.; its booklet *Where to Stay in and around Cambridge* lists all accommodation in the city and a selection of farmhouses, etc., in the vicinity, with prices. The following list comprises the main hotels in the city centre, listed roughly in order of price, and a selection of smaller and cheaper places outside, with preference being given to places closer to the centre. For special offers and short breaks in some of the larger hotels, ☎ 01223 457578 or visit the Cambridge Tourist Information Office website, www.tourism.cambridge.com.

Hotels

£££

Crowne Plaza, Downing St, CB2 3DT, ☎ 01223 464466, ▤ 01223 464440, ✉ www.crowneplaza.com. Do not be deceived by the seemingly Georgian façade of this huge 198-bed hotel, for the building is in fact only a few years old. It stands very close to the city centre, cheek-by-jowl with some of the university's scientific departments, and the quality of the rooms and service are of the high standards expected from the chain of which it forms a part. There is a bar and restaurant and car parking is provided.

Garden House, Granta Place, Mill Lane, CB2 1RT, ☎ 01223 259988, ▤ 01223 316605, ✉ www.moathousehotels.com. This 117-room modern hotel, part of the *Moat House* chain, has perhaps the best situation of any hotel in Cambridge, overlooking meadowland by the Cam on the south side of the city centre. There is a heated indoor swimming pool, jacuzzi, etc., and the restaurant is one of the best in Cambridge.

Gonville Hotel, Gonville Place, CB1 1LY, ☎ 01223 366611, ▤ 01223 315470, ✉ www.gonvillehotel.com. A comfortable 64-bed hotel, part of the *Best Western* chain, in a bland 1960s building, recently remodelled, on the south side of Parker's Piece, not far from the city centre. Restaurant.

Holiday Inn Cambridge, Bridge Rd, Impington, CB4 9PH, ☎ 0870 400 9015, ▤ 01223 233426, ✉ www.holiday-inn.com. Large modern hotel close to A14 road on northern edge of city.

Meadowcroft Hotel, Trumpington Rd, CB2 2EX, ☎ 01223 346120, ▤ 01223 346138, ✉ www.meadowcroft.co.uk. A small, much-praised hotel with 12 comfortable rooms decorated in a Victorian style and a large garden.

Royal Cambridge Hotel, Trumpington St, CB2 1PY, ☎ 01223 351631, ▤ 01223 352972, ✉ www.zoffanyhotels.co.uk. Taking up most of an early 19C brick terrace by a busy street at the southern edge of the historic centre of Cambridge, close to the Fitzwilliam Museum, this long-established 57-room hotel is well located and has a restaurant and car park.

University Arms, Regent St, CB2 1AD, ☎ 01223 351241, ▤ 01223 315256, ✉ www.devereonline.co.uk. A massive rather institutional-looking Victorian pile overlooking Parker's Piece just south of Emmanuel College, with a modern extension containing the main entrance to busy Regent St. The 115 recently refurbished rooms are comfortably furnished and there is a large high-ceilinged dining room.

££

Arundel House Hotel, 53 Chesterton Rd, CB4 3AN, ☎ 01223 367701, ▤ 01223 367721, ✉ www.arundelhousehotels. This 103-room hotel is situated in a row of Victorian houses on a main road overlooking the Cam to the north of

the city centre, easily reached on foot across Jesus Green. Comfortable, somewhat chintzy interior; restaurant and large conservatory where meals are also offered.
Ashley Hotel, 74 Chesterton Rd, CB4 1ER, ☎ 01223 350059, ▤ 01223 350900, ▨ www.arundelhousehotels. Managed by the Arundel House Hotel, and also in a Victorian house, this is a smaller establishment with 16 recently-refurbished rooms.
Cambridge Lodge Hotel, 139 Huntingdon Rd, CB3 0DQ, ☎ 01223 352833, ▤ 01223 855166. 15-room hotel in 20C neo-Tudor house on northeast side of Cambridge, convenient for Girton, Fitzwilliam, etc. Restaurant attached.
Lensfield Hotel, 53 Lensfield Rd, CB2 1EN, ☎ 01223 355017, ▤ 01223 312022, ▨ www.lensfieldhotel.co.uk. 30-room family-run hotel in an early 19C terrace set back from the main road on the south side of the city centre, near the Fitzwilliam Museum. Restaurant.
Regent Hotel, 41 Regent St, CB2 1AB, ☎ 01223 351470, ▤ 01223 566562, ▨ www.regenthotel.co.uk. A friendly, recently renovated hotel with 26 rooms in an attractive early 19C brick house opposite Downing College near the city centre.

Guest houses and bed and breakfast

£

Acorn Guest House, 154 Chesterton Rd, C4 1DA, ☎ 01223 353888, ▤ 01223 350527, ▨ www.acornguesthouse.co.uk. Small family-run establishment with ten rooms; parking available.
Cambridge Youth Hostel, 97 Tenison Rd, ☎ 01223 354601, ▤ 01223 312780. Cheap, basic accommodation quite conveniently located near railway station.
De Freville House, 166 Chesterton Rd, CB4 1DA, ☎ 01223 354993, ▤ 01223 321890. Well-maintained Victorian house with eight rooms on a main road about a mile northeast of city centre; parking available.
Regency Guest House, 7 Regent Terrace, CB2 1AA, ☎ 01223 329626, ▤ 01223 301567, ▨ www.regencyguesthouse.co.uk. Eight rooms, overlooking Parker's Piece.
Southampton Guest House, 7 Elizabeth Way, CB4 1DE, ☎ 01223 357780, ▤ 01223 314297, ▨ www.southamptonhouse.com. Small, comfortable five-roomed B&B on a main road about a mile northeast of city centre.
Worth House, 152 Chesterton Rd, CB4 1DA, ☎/▤ 01223 316074, ▨ www.worth-house.co.uk. Small, recently-refurbished guest house.

Self-catering and campsites

Milton Villas Home to Home Apartments, 78 Milton Rd, CB4 1LA, ☎ 01223 323555, ▤ 01223 563509, ▨ www.accommodationcambridge.co.uk. 5 apartments in Victorian houses north of city centre.

For other self-catering accommodation visit ▨ www.tourismcambridge.com, or contact the Tourist Information Centre.

The closest campsite is **Cherry Hinton Caravan Club Site**, ☎ 01223 244088, ▨ www.caravanclub.co.uk. Situated in the suburban village of Cherry Hinton, not far from the city centre (bus service), it has tent pitches as well as caravan space.

Food and drink

Cambridge has restaurants to cater for all tastes and all pockets, though there are fewer than in Oxford. The selection below is arranged in two price categories, and a selection of cheaper restaurants, pubs, etc. in or near the city centre is also given. For opening hours, etc., see the introductory remarks on Food and Drink in the Practical Information section on Oxford (p 44).

Restaurants

££

Loch Fyne Restaurant, 7 Trumpington St, ☎ 01223 362433. Opposite Fitzwilliam Museum; fish and seafood.

Midsummer House, Midsummer Common, ☎ 01223 369299. Outstandingly good though expensive French/international food in idyllically situated riverside house with conservatory, near college boathouses to northeast of city centre (reached from Victoria Avenue). Generally reckoned to be the best restaurant in Cambridge.

Michel's Brasserie, 21–24 Northampton St, ☎ 01223 353110. This attractive restaurant offers good, reasonably priced French food in an 18C building, formerly the Clergy Widows' Almshouses, close to Kettle's Yard on north side of Magdalene Bridge.

Restaurant 22, 22 Chesterton Rd, ☎ 01223 351880. Good quality restaurant in unpretentious brick house on inner ring road northeast of city centre, north of River Cam near junction with Victoria Avenue.

Venue on the Roof, Arts Theatre, Peas Hill, ☎ 01223 578927. Pre-theatre meals in restaurant on top floor of theatre.

The restaurants at the *Garden House Hotel*, the *University Arms* and the *Arundel House Hotel* are also recommended.

£
English/Eclectic

Browns, 23 Trumpington St, ☎ 01223 461655. Like its Oxford counterpart, a resort of the local *jeunesse dorée*—or aspirants to that status. Good if not outstanding food in convenient location opposite Fitzwilliam Museum.

Hobbs Pavilion, Parker's Piece, ☎ 01223 367480. Well situated next to University Arms Hotel overlooking Parker's Piece, this 1930s' sports pavilion, named after the famous Surrey and England cricketer who played here, offers standard English food during the day and a more Mediterranean-style menu in the evenings.

No 1 King's Parade, ☎ 01223 359506. International cuisine in cellars of a building at the corner of King's Parade and Bene't St, opposite King's College. Good value lunches. Wine bar.

Rainbow Vegetarian Bistro, 9A King's Parade, ☎ 01223 321551. In an alley opposite King's; self-explanatory (closes 21.00).

The Vaults, 14A Trinity St, ☎ 01223 519345. Subterranean bar-restaurant in heart of university area. Good, varied food, somewhat trendy clientele.

French

Chez Gerard, 27–28 Bridge St, ☎ 01223 448620. Reliable French-style food, part of chain, conveniently situated near Round Church.

Le Gros Franck, 57 Hills Rd, ☎ 01223 565560. Probably the best-value French food in Cambridge: café during the day, serious eating in the evenings. Near railway station.

Pierre Victoire, 90–92 Regent St, ☎ 01223 570170. Good-value food in somewhat nondescript premises. Part of a reliable chain.

Italian

Pizza Express, 7A Jesus Lane, ☎ 01223 324033. As in Oxford and elsewhere the Pizza Express chain has shown great imagination in bringing to life an old building, in this case the former Pitt Club of c 1865. Here too the good quality of the pizzas and house wine is enhanced by the ambience, with its overtones of Victorian masculinity. Another branch of this popular chain is in St. Andrew's St.

Trattoria Pasta Fresca, 66 Mill Rd, ☎ 01223 352836. Good, reasonably priced Italian restaurant some distance southeast of city centre; pasta, pizza, etc., plus vegetarian dishes in informal, relaxed surroundings.

Greek/Turkish

Efes, 78–80 King St, ☎ 01223 500005. Good value Turkish food, south of Jesus Lane. Kebabs figure prominently on the menu.

Varsity Restaurant, 35 St. Andrew's St, ☎ 01223 356060. Cambridge has a long tradition of east-Mediterranean cuisine, and this is the oldest-established restaurant in town, run by Cypriots and offering good basic no-frills food in popular restaurant opposite Emmanuel College; excellent value.

Chinese

Charlie Chan, 14 Regent St, ☎ 01223 361763. Good Cantonese restaurant in modern building close to city centre.

Kam's Chinese Restaurant, 39 Regent St, ☎ 01223 566881. One of the more recently-opened Chinese restaurants in this street; the oriental buffet offers good variety and excellent value. Overlooks Parker's Piece.

Thai

Bangkok City, 24 Green St, ☎ 01223 354382. Another Thai restaurant, this time in city centre.

Sala Thong, 35 Newnham Rd, ☎ 01223 323178. Good Thai restaurant west of River Cam near Darwin College, reachable by path across the meadow from Mill Lane.

Indian

Curry Centre is nearby at 45 Castle St, ☎ 01223 363666.

Curry Queen, 106 Mill Rd, ☎ 01223 351027. Good Indian restaurant some distance from city centre.

Golden Curry, 111–13 Mill Rd, ☎ 01223 329432 is also recommended.

Maharajah, 9 Castle St, ☎ 01223 358399. Close to city centre, beyond Kettle's Yard and Folk Museum; highly recommended.

Pubs

Anchor, Silver St. Popular pub close to river and punts.

Castle Inn, Castle St. Good basic pub, excellent beer, sandwiches, etc, convenient for Kettle's Yard.

Eagle, Benc't St. Old inn, very well refurbished with labyrinthine interior and open yard; excellent value, nourishing food and good Greene King local beer.

Fort St. George, Midsummer Common. Riverside pub a little outside city centre, near college boathouses.

Granta, Mill Pond, Newnham Rd. Beautifully situated on far side of Cam.

Among the pubs outside the city centre, the *Ancient Shepherds* at Fen Ditton, the *Three Horseshoes* at Madingley (especially good food) and the *Red Lion* and the *Blue Ball* at Grantchester can be recommended,

Cafés and tea shops

Café Trinity, 15 Trinity St. Tea/coffee shop in heart of university area, serving breakfasts and lunches too.

Clowns, 54 King St. Bohemian coffee house near Jesus College, decorated with children's art, etc. Interesting clientele.

Copper Kettle, 4 King's Parade. Large, centrally located café/tea shop populated by students, tourists and worried-looking dons. Basic décor.

Fitzbillies, 52 Trumpington St. Archetypal tea shop next to an up-market baker's shop, also serving coffee, lunches and evening meals. Chelsea buns a speciality.

The Little Tearoom, All Saint's Passage—traditional tea-shop in green oasis off Trinity St near Trinty and St. John's colleges.

Michaelhouse Café, Trinity St. Good, reasonably priced café in medieval church in heart of university area. Excellent recent conversion of a formerly under-used historic building.

The *Orchard Tea Rooms* at Grantchester, immortalised by Rupert Brooke, are in a category of their own.

Getting around Cambridge

Since distances are not very great in Cambridge it is easy to dispense entirely with wheeled transport, unless you wish to explore the environs or if your hotel is away from the city centre. However, there are frequent **buses** to all outer areas, most of them leaving from Emmanuel St (operated by Stagecoach Cambus, www.stagecoach-cambus.co.uk, ☎ 01223 423578). **Taxis** are also reliable and not over-expensive (A1 Taxis, ☎ 01223 525555; Andycabs, ☎ 01223 571144; Cabco, ☎ 01223 711111, Camtax, ☎ 01223 313131, etc.). **Cycling**, as in Oxford, is a pleasure, not least because of the flat terrain and the network of tracks through the meadowland and commons which almost encircle the city centre; cycles can be hired from Ben Hayward Cycles, 69 Trumpington St (☎ 01223 352294) and Geoff's Bike Hire, 65 Devonshire Rd, near the railway station and close to the Youth Hostel (open daily, ☎ 01223 365629); **guided cycle tours** of Cambridge are operated by this firm during the summer. **Car hire** is possible through Avis (☎ 01223 212551), Budget Rent-a-car (☎ 01223 323838) and University Autos (☎ 01223 515151).

Sightseeing

Cambridge is in some respects more visitor-friendly than Oxford. The city centre is smaller, it benefits from being almost entirely traffic free, and the countryside never feels far away. Most of the **colleges** are open during daylight hours and there are fewer intimidating notices deterring visitors than in Oxford colleges. On the other hand all the colleges close during the summer examination period (Apr–mid-June) and at Christmas and Easter. As in Oxford, they also often close unexpectedly during normal opening times. Some of the larger and more frequented colleges levy admission charges, especially during the spring and summer.

Like Oxford, Cambridge is best explored on foot. There are however, as in Oxford, **open-top bus tours** operated by the *City Sightseeing* (☎ 01223 362444) and *Guide Friday* (☎ 01708 866000); they leave from the railway station and Emmanuel St and tickets cost between £6 and £8.50. Guided **walking tours** are organised by the well-qualified Cambridge Blue Badge Guides, starting at regular intervals from the Tourist Information Centre and costing £7.25 per person (www.tourism.cambridge.com, ☎ 01223 457574). But it is not difficult to see everything that is accessible on one's own, and in one's own time.

Festivals and annual events

Cambridge has several annual events and festivities peculiar to itself, including:
Lent Bumps: college boat races held on the River Cam, alongside Jesus Green and Midsummer Common, at the end of February.
Cambridge Science Festival: mid-March (www.cambridgescience.org, ☎ 01223 766766)
Strawberry Fair, Midsummer Common, at the end of the first week in June; claims to be Britain's largest open-air community fair, much resorted to by devotees of alternative lifestyles.
May Bumps: college boat races on the Cam, held paradoxically in mid-June.
Midsummer Fair, Midsummer Common: one of the largest fun fairs in England, dating back to 1211 and held late June.
General Admissions and the conferment of honorary degrees takes place in the Senate House, usually in the second week of June (May Week).
Cambridge Film Festival: mid-July (www.cambridgefilmfestival.org.uk, ☎ 01223 514444). Held in Arts Picture House: advance releases, golden oldies, etc.
Cambridge Folk Festival: late July (www.cam-folkfest.co.uk). World-famous among aficionados.
Festival of Nine Lessons and Carols, King's College Chapel, Christmas Eve. A hallowed English institution.

NB Cambridge **academic terms** run from October to early December (Michaelmas), mid-January to mid-March (Lent) and mid-April to mid-June (Easter).

Entertainment

Cambridge is a very lively centre for the arts, not only during university terms, but also in the summer holiday season when a number of festivals are held. There are listings of events in the *Cambridge Agenda* available from the Tourist Information centre and elsewhere.

Drama

The main theatre is the **Arts Theatre**, St. Edward's Passage (☎ 01223 503333/ 504444, ✉ www.cambridgeartstheatre.com), a moderately-sized building offering a varied programme of professional and amateur productions, including opera and dance. Professional, usually modern, drama is performed in the **Cambridge Drama Centre**, Covent Garden (☎ 01223 511511, ✉ www.dramacentre.co.uk; details and tickets also from the Corn Exchange, ☎ 01223 357851), and there is also professional and amateur drama at the **Mumford Theatre**, East Rd, which is part of Anglia Polytechnic University (☎ 01223 352932). The **ADC Theatre**, Park St (☎ 01223 359547, ✉ www.adctheatre.com) plays host to the University Amateur Dramatic Club and other student groups in term time, and usually offers performances in the summer too. A **Shakespeare festival** is held each July and August, with professional performances in college gardens and elsewhere (☎ 01223 357851, ✉ www.cambridgeshakespeare.com).

Music

The **Corn Exchange**, Wheeler St (☎ 01223 357851, ✉ www.cornex.co.uk), a converted Victorian building opposite the Tourist Information Centre, contains a large auditorium in which jazz concerts and other large-scale performances are held as well as operas, musicals, ballets and concerts of classical music by leading orchestras. Other classical concerts are held in the recently refurbished **West Road Concert Hall** (☎ 01223 503333). Concerts and recitals, both amateur and professional, are held throughout the year in the **college chapels**; information is posted throughout the city, in the Tourist Information Centre, and in the free publication *Cambridge Agenda*, which also lists plays and other arts events. **Choral services** are sung in term time by the choirs of King's and St. John's Colleges; see under the colleges for times.

There is a **Summer Music Festival** in late July and August (☎ 01223 503333, ✉ www.cambridgesummermusic.com), with concerts held in college chapels and elsewhere. Concerts by leading ensembles are given in late July and early August in connection with the annual **Early Music Summer School** at Trinity Hall (☎ 01223 847330).

Cinemas

There is a large multi-screen **Warner Village Cinema** in the Grafton Centre (☎ 08702 406020); it shows the usual films on general release. The **Arts Picture House**, St. Andrew's St (☎ 01223 572929, ✉ www.picturehousecinemas. co.uk) is a smaller two-screen cinema with a more varied and highbrow repertoire, as the name suggests.

Sporting and leisure activities

Boating Punts and rowing boats can be hired from Easter to October at Quayside (off Bridge St), Garret Hostel Lane and Mill Lane; the cost is about £10–£12 per hour, and a large (returnable) deposit is expected. The most popular route is along the Backs, but it is also possible to go up river from Mill Lane to Grantchester (allow 2 hours each way); chauffeured punts are available at a price. For information contact Scudamore's in Mill Lane (☎ 01223 359750, ✉ www.scudamores.com) or Granta Punts (☎ 01223 301845, ✉ www.puntingincambridge.com).

Swimming The **Parkside Pool**, off Gonville Place, has recently been rebuilt and offers a Health Suite (sauna, spa and solarium) as well as the usual attractions (☎ 01223 446100/446104, ✉ www.cambridge.gov.uk/leisure/parkside). There is an **open air pool** at Jesus Green, open mid-May–mid Sept, ☎ 01223 302579.

For other sports, contact the City Council's sports development service (☎ 01223 457534/5, ✉ www.citysport.org.uk).

Parks and gardens

Cambridge is exceptionally well supplied with open spaces within easy walking distance of the city centre. **Jesus Green** and **Midsummer Common** are large tracts of unenclosed common land beside the River Cam to the northeast of the central area. **Parker's Piece** and **Christ's Pieces** are smaller spaces to the east, and to the south are **Coe Fen** and **Lammas Land**, on either side of the river. To the west are the world-famous **Backs**, comprising the land on either side of the river between St. John's and Queens' Colleges, most of it in collegiate ownership and therefore with some entry restrictions; the views of the colleges from the Backs are superb. The **University Botanic Garden**, between Trumpington Rd and Hills Rd to the south of the city centre, is a large and relatively unfrequented area of outstanding botanical interest and great beauty.

Shopping

At the latest count there were 879 retail establishments in Cambridge, including over 100 **clothes shops**. Many of the main stores have branches in the city centre, which is a little more tranquil than Oxford's, or in the covered shopping centre in Lion Yard. There is also a modern shopping complex at the **Grafton Centre**, to the east of the city centre and well served by buses. Food and much else can be purchased in the open-air **market** next to Great St. Mary's on a site which it has occupied since time immemorial.

Not surprisingly, Cambridge is well supplied with **bookshops**, of which the largest is *Heffer's*, Trinity St. There are also the inevitable *Borders* (12–13 Market St) and *Waterstone's* (22 Sidney St). There are also good second-hand bookshops and shops specialising in publishers' remainders (e.g., *David's* in St. Edwards Passage; *Galloway & Porter*, 30 Sidney St).

Museums and galleries

Cambridge and County Folk Museum, Castle St (☎ 01223 355159), open Mon–Sat 10.30–15.00, Sun 14.00–17.00, closed Mon from Oct–Mar. Interesting collection of domestic 'bygones' housed in former inn. Adm. charge.

Fitzwilliam Museum, Trumpington St (☎ 01223 332900, ✉ www.fitzmuseum. cam.ac.uk), open Tues–Sat and Bank hol Mon 10.00–17.00; Sun 14.15–17.00. One of the finest art museums outside London, with superb Egyptian, Greek and Roman, and oriental collections, as well as outstanding Old Master paintings and drawings. Special exhibitions.

Kettle's Yard, Castle St (☎ 01223 352124, ✉ www.kettlesyard.co.uk), open Tues–Sun and Bank Hol. Mon 11.30–17.30; house Tues–Sun 14.00–16.00. Collection of modern art amassed by former Tate Gallery curator Jim Ede and housed in converted cottages. Exhibitions of modern art in purpose-built gallery adjoining.

Museum of Archaeology & Anthropology, Downing St (☎ 01223 333516, ✉ http://cumaa.archanth.cam.ac.uk), open Tues–Sat 14.00–16.30; opens 10.30 Tues–Fri from mid-June to early Sept. Collections of local antiquities, world prehistory and anthropology from throughout the world.

Museum of Classical Archaeology, Sidgwick Avenue (☎ 01223 335153, ✉ www.classics.cam.ac.uk/ark.html), open Mon–Fri 10.00–17.00, Sat 10.00–13.00 in term time only. Excellent collection of plaster casts of Classical sculpture.

Scott Polar Research Institute and Museum, Lensfield Rd (☎ 01223 336540, ✉ www.spri.cam.ac.uk), open Mon–Sat 14.30–16.00. Important collections relating to the Arctic and Antarctic.

Sedgwick Museum of Earth Sciences, Downing St (☎ 01223 333456, ✉ www.esc.cam.ac.uk/SedgwickMuseum), open Mon–Fri 09.00–13.00, 14.00–17.00, Sat 10.00–13.00. Fossils, dinosaurs, minerals, gems and much else.

University Museum of Zoology, Downing St (☎ 01223 336650, ✉ www.zoo.cam.uk/museum), open university vacations Mon–Fri 10.00–13.00, 14.00–16.45; term time 14.00–16.45 only. Stuffed and fossilised animals including specimens donated by Charles Darwin.

Whipple Museum of the History of Science, Free School Lane (☎ 01223 330906, ✉ www.hps.cam.ac.uk/Whipple), open Mon–Fri exc. public holidays 13.30–16.30. Outstanding collection of scientific instruments.

Many buildings are closed on **Bank Holidays** (see under Oxford, p 54).

Activities for children

Though the colleges will be of limited interest to many children, except perhaps for A.A. Milne's original *Winnie-the-Pooh* manuscript in Trinity College Library, there are several museums which have much to offer children. They include the **Folk Museum**, the **Museum of Archaeology and Anthropology** (masks, totem pole, etc.) and the **Museum of Zoology**. The **Fitzwilliam Museum** takes children seriously and provides an excellent discovery trail. There are plenty of places to relax and unwind close to the city centre (see Parks and Gardens above), and there are playgrounds near Newnham Rd and on Jesus Green. Many children will also enjoy **punting** in the summer.

Outside Cambridge (see the relevant parts of the main text), there is the **Farmland Museum** at Denny Abbey, with interactive displays, the Home Farm at **Wimpole Hall** (plenty of real animals), the **Imperial War Museum** at Duxford, with its splendid collection of military aircraft, and **Linton Zoo**, ten miles south-east of Cambridge on B1052 (open all year exc. Christmas 10.00–17.15 or dusk, ☎ 01223 891308). **Anglesey Abbey** with its extensive gardens and working watermill makes another good afternoon out, and **Audley End** has a superb dolls'-house and quantities of stuffed birds. For horse-lovers a trip to **Newmarket** should prove enjoyable, especially if it includes a visit to the National Horseracing Museum and the National Stud. Readers of *The Children of Green Knowe* will also enjoy the Manor House at **Hemingford Grey** (only open by appointment: see entry in main text).

Additional information

Banks and post office

The main **banks** all have branches in the centre of Cambridge, with cash (ATM) machines. There are **bureaux de change** at Lloyds Bank, 3 Sidney St and Barclays Bank, 30 Market Hill, Natwest at the corner of Bene't St and King's Parade, and elsewhere. The main **post office**, St. Andrew's St, is open Mon–Fri 09.00–17.30, Sat 09.00–12.30 (☎ 01223 351212).

Disabled travellers

Nearly all of the college courts are accessible to the disabled, but there are steps into some halls and other areas. Wheelchair access is possible to the Fitzwilliam Museum, and there is restricted access to most of the other museums in the city and around; see the leaflet *Museums in Cambridgeshire* published by Cambridgeshire County Council, and telephone in advance in case of uncertainty. Many Cambridge buses have low floors, and it is not too difficult to negotiate the kerbs of the city centre streets. The Cambridge City Council leaflet *Services for Disabled People* (available from the Guildhall, Cambridge CB2 1BR) gives information on disabled parking, access to toilets, sports facilities, etc. The Shopmobility scheme run by Cambridge City Council (☎ 01223 457452, ✉ www.cambridge.gov.uk/shopmo) provides powered wheelchairs and scooters, and also an escort service.

Emergencies and medical services

The hospital is Addenbrooke's, Hills Rd (☎ 01223 245151). For an ambulance, dial 999.

Libraries

The Central Library is in Lion Yard (☎ 01223 365252) and contains a good reference section. It is open 09.00–19.00 Mon–Fri, 09.00–17.30 Sat. Other libraries are only open on special recommendation.

Personal security

The same remarks apply as to Oxford (see p 53). The **police station** is in Parkside (☎ 01223 358966).

The Colleges

Cambridge University has 31 colleges or 'approved societies', of which 26 are for undergraduates and graduates, and five for graduates only (some of which admit a few mature students as undergraduates). Three colleges are for women only (Newnham, New Hall and Lucy Cavendish); all the former men's colleges now admit women. There are some 17,000 students in the university (2003), of whom about a third are graduates. The university website is ✉ www.cam.ac.uk, and has links to the websites of colleges and academic departments. The names of the colleges, with the usually accepted dates of foundation, are as follows:

Peterhouse, 1284
Clare, 1338
Pembroke, 1347
Trinity Hall, 1350
Corpus Christi, 1352
King's, 1441
Queens', 1448
St. Catharine's, 1473
Jesus, 1496
Christ's, 1505
St. John's, 1511
Magdalene, 1542
Trinity, 1546
Gonville and Caius, 1557
Emmanuel, 1584
Sidney Sussex, 1596
Downing, 1800

Girton, 1869 (in Cambridge since 1873)
Newnham, 1871 (women only)
Selwyn, 1882
New Hall, 1954 (women only)
Churchill, 1960
Darwin, 1964 (graduates)
Clare Hall, 1965 (graduates)
Wolfson, 1965 (graduates)
Lucy Cavendish, 1965 (graduate women)
Fitzwilliam, 1966
Hughes Hall, 1968
St. Edmund's, 1975 (graduates)
Homerton, 1976
Robinson, 1977

Walks in Cambridge

1 ~ THE HEART OF THE UNIVERSITY

This walk starts at the northernmost end of **King's Parade**, the centre of academic Cambridge. On the western side is King's College and beyond it, overlooking a lawn, are the 18C Senate House and former University Library. The vista is closed to the north by the 19C buildings of Gonville and Caius College and to the east is the tower of the University Church of Great St. Mary's, begun in the late 15C. The broad expanse of the street is the result of the clearance of merchants' houses and of the Provost's Lodge of King's College, in the 18C and early 19C; before this the area was much less spacious.

St. Mary the Great

Great St. Mary's (plan 2, G) is not only the university church; it is also the principal parish church of Cambridge. In the past it was used, like the University Church in Oxford, for academic purposes requiring a large meeting place. The University held disputations here and it was used for degree-giving ceremonies until the Senate House was opened in 1730.

History

There has been a church on the site at least since the 12C, but the present building dates from 1478–1519 (the tower was not finished until 1608). Two kings, Richard III and Henry VII, and many eminent statesmen and ecclesiastics, contributed to the cost of the building. Henry VII also gave the timber for the roof. St. Mary's has the lofty simplicity of the late Perpendicular style in East Anglia, but virtually all the original fittings fell victim to the destructive iconoclasm unleashed by the Reformation.

Many leading reformers preached here, some of whom later died at the stake during Mary Tudor's efforts to restore the old faith. The body of the German theologian Martin Bucer was buried here, but was exhumed and burned on Market Hill and the church was cleansed of his presence in an elaborate ceremony. When Elizabeth I came to the throne his ashes were given reverent reburial (brass floor plate in the chancel, south side).

The **entrance** is through the south porch; ahead to the left is the **font** (1632), still medieval in design though with Renaissance decoration. Behind is the **tower**, which can usually be climbed for a splendid view (adm. charge); the chimes of the clock (1793) are now familiar everywhere as those of Big Ben. Under the tower arch is the **organ**, built by Bernard Schmidt ('Father Smith') for St. James's Piccadilly, London, and bought by the University in 1692.

The body of the church consists of a clerestoried **nave** and aisles, with an unaisled chancel; as in other East Anglian churches of the same period, the spandrels of the nave arcades and chancel arch are filled with intricate patterning, and the fine timber roof still survives in its Tudor magnificence. Galleries were built in 1735 to accommodate the large congregations which gathered on special occasions or to hear the university sermon (attendance at which was compulsory for undergraduates), and an enormous three-decker pulpit, designed by James Essex, and nicknamed 'Golgotha', was also installed at the west end; its woodwork was used to make vestry and side chapel screens when both it and some of the galleries were removed in 1863.

At the east end of the **north aisle** is the hearse cloth of Henry VII, used when his requiems were sung, and close to it is an early 16C carved wooden chest. The **pulpit**, on the north side of the chancel steps, can be pulled out on rails into the middle of the nave; it is one of the few movable pulpits in England. In the **chancel**, behind the high altar, is a gilded wood sculpture of *Christ in Majesty* (Alan Durst, 1960), and there is good stained glass by Hardman (1867–69). A new parish organ (by Kenneth Jones and Associates) was installed in 1991.

The Central University Buildings

Most of Central Cambridge is taken up by the buildings of the colleges and, at least as compared to Oxford, the University makes a relatively modest showing. The most prominent University buildings both date from the 18C, and both look out onto King's Parade. To the north is the **Senate House** (plan 2, G; no adm.) built in 1722–30 to the designs of James Gibbs, the architect of St. Martin in the Fields in London. It was intended to be part of a group of new University buildings, with a matching block to the south for the printing press and offices, and an east-facing library between, designed to house a recent gift of some 30,000 books by King George I. As one wit remarked:

'The King, observing with judicious eyes
The state of both his Universities
To one he sent a regiment. For why?
That learned body wanted loyalty.
To t'other he sent books, as well discerning
How much that loyal body wanted learning.'

To which the following rejoinder was made:

'The King to Oxford sent his troops of horse,
For Tories own no argument but force.
With equal care to Cambridge books he sent,
For Whigs allow no force but argument.'

But of the buildings originally planned only the Senate House materialised in Gibbs's lifetime. It has a dignified south-facing façade of stone, enlivened by giant Corinthian columns, with an engaged temple front to mark the centre. Inside there is one long galleried room, with a rich plaster ceiling by Gibbs's collaborators Artari and Bagutti, and handsome woodwork by the James Essexes, father and son. There are statues of the 6th Duke of Somerset (Rysbrack, 1756) and the younger William Pitt (Nollekens, 1812) at the east end.

The Senate House superseded Great St. Mary's as the location for University ceremonies and large gatherings. Congregations are still held here three times a term, at which degrees are conferred, but the most splendid occasion is the summer General Admissions, when honorary degrees are bestowed and a procession of richly robed University dignitaries, led by Esquire Bedells carrying maces, wends its way round and into the building.

To the south (left) of the Senate House is the lively neo-Palladian frontage of the **Old Schools** (Stephen Wright, 1754–58: no adm.), faced, like the Senate House, in white Portland stone. It was built as a University Library and replaced the medieval entrance gateway to the Schools or lecture rooms; the gateway was re-erected at Madingley Hall (see p 269), where it can still be seen. Stephen Wright was a protégé of the Duke of Newcastle, Chancellor of the University and a leading Whig, who used his influence to quash the earlier scheme supplied by James Gibbs, an architect much favoured by the Tories. Behind the 18C façade is a small courtyard (no adm.) made up of unpretentious buildings of medieval origin originally housing a Divinity School, lecture rooms, chapel and library. They were built of rubble stone between c 1350 and 1467, but there have been many alterations and little of the original structure is now visible, except on the southwest side, visible from the entrance in Trinity Lane (see p 201). The buildings are now occupied by University offices and the University Combination Room.

On the lawn in front—laid out in the 18C after the demolition of the old houses which blocked the view along King's Parade—is a 19C copy of the huge Roman stone urn known as the Warwick Vase (the original is in the Burrell Collection, Glasgow). To the south is the Chapel of King's College.

King's College

Plan 2, G/4, A. Grounds open daytime all year exc. 25 Dec–4 Jan and mid-Apr–mid-June: entrance in winter months from King's Parade or from the Backs in Queen's Rd; summer from Trinity Lane—signposted from King's Parade entrance—or the Backs.

A royal foundation

King's College was founded in 1441 as 'The King's College of our Lady and St. Nicholas in Cambridge' by Henry VI, the 'royal s2aint' of Wordsworth's famous sonnet ('Tax not the royal saint with vain expense'). It began quite modestly with provision for a Rector and 12 scholars, to be housed in a building opposite the entrance to Clare College; this was the Old Court, now part of the University Offices (see above). But by 1445 the King was planning a much more ambitious scheme, which envisaged a foundation of a Provost and 70 scholars, to be drawn from his newly established school at Eton, with a series of magnificent buildings ranged round a huge court—a plan based on that of William of Wykeham's New College, Oxford.

To clear the chosen site, south of Old Court and Clare College, the recently opened God's House had to be removed (see Christ's College), the church of St. John Zachary pulled down, houses and wharves along the river demolished and streets diverted. Of all the grand plans, only that for the chapel was even started in the King's lifetime, for in 1455 the Wars of the Roses broke out, and in 1461 he was deposed.

The chapel was completed by the first Tudor kings, but the students and fellows had to make do with the buildings in Old Court until the early 18C. Then in 1724 James Gibbs, already busy with the Senate House, made new plans for a Great Court south of the chapel, an earlier scheme by Nicholas Hawksmoor having been set aside. But history repeated itself and only one part of the project materialised: the Fellows' Building opposite the present main gates in King's Parade. Over 100 years elapsed before the court was completed by William Wilkins, in a Tudor-Gothic style which admirably complements that of the chapel.

Until the second half of the 19C only Etonians were admitted to King's and its members were also exempt from university examinations. These somewhat inhibiting privileges were removed by the 1870s, after which the college expanded rapidly and quickly established an enviable academic reputation, particularly in the arts and humanities. It was the main nursery of the Bloomsbury Group and became well-known in the 20C for its left-wing politics. In 1972 it became one of the first men's colleges in either university to admit women.

The Chapel

King's College Chapel (open during term Mon–Fri 09.30–15.30, Sat 09.30–15.15, Sun 13.15–14.15, also 17.00–17.30 Apr–Oct; vacation Mon–Sat 09.30–16.30, Sun 10.00–17.00; adm. charge; ☎ 01223 331212, ☒ www.kings.cam.ac.uk) is perhaps the greatest achievement of English Late Gothic architecture: in Wordsworth's words an 'immense/ And glorious work of fine intelligence' whose beauty is enhanced by the superb state of preservation of its internal fittings. The richness and variety of its decoration and furnishing reflect the changes in taste that took place during the 100 or so years it took to complete and also the differences in outlook between the college's saintly and ill-starred founder and his more worldly successors.

Work began in 1446, under Henry VI's master mason Robert Ely, but stopped abruptly in 1461 when the King was defeated at the Battle of Towton; one great stone, half-cut at the time, remained untouched for over two centuries and was eventually used as the foundation stone of the Gibbs Building. Some progress was

Entrance to side chapel in King's College Chapel

made between 1476 and 1483 under Henry's Yorkist successors, but it was not until Henry VII visited Cambridge with his mother Lady Margaret Beaufort in 1506 that vigorous building began again, this time directed by John Wastell. The stonework was finished by 1515, but much remained to be done inside, and it is to Henry VIII that the chapel owes the fine woodwork and almost all the windows.

The plan is simple: an unaisled rectangle 289ft long, 40ft wide and 80ft high, spanned by stone fan vaults of exquisite delicacy, designed and built by Wastell, and lit by windows so enormous that the building is in effect walled in glass; side

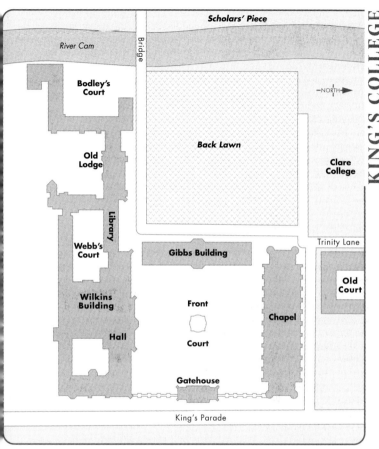

KING'S COLLEGE

chapels are placed between the huge buttresses which support the vault. At each of the four corners are tall ogee-capped turrets displaying the portcullis and rose of the Tudor dynasty—motifs that also crop up regularly inside the antechapel, along with the dragon, the Beaufort greyhound, the French fleur-de-lis and the crown. The **antechapel** takes up the whole of the western half of the building and was not completed internally until 1515: hence the rich display of heraldic ornamentation, in contrast to the relative austerity of the wall surfaces in the eastern part of the chapel, built in the time of Henry VI, who explicitly forbade 'busy moulding'.

The chapel has the rare—and, for Cambridge, unique—good fortune of possessing a complete set of pre-Reformation **stained and painted glass windows** (except the west window, a 19C Last Judgement, and the upper half of the southeast window). They were made between 1515 and 1547 by Netherlandish and English glass painters working under Henry VIII's glaziers, first Barnard Flower and later Galyon Hone, to designs believed to have been prepared by Vandenhoute of Mechelen and, from 1526, Dierick Vellert of Antwerp. Together, they comprise the most complete collection of early 16C glass in England.

Each of the windows contains four main scenes. Starting on the north side, west end and continuing clockwise around the chapel, the **lower lights** tell the story of the Virgin Mary and the life of Christ up to the Passion, which is depicted in the east window. The windows on the south side depict (east to west) the Resurrection, Pentecost, Acts of the Apostles, and finally the Assumption and Coronation of the Virgin. The **upper lights** depict Old Testament 'types' or pre-figurations of the scenes depicted below, e.g., the Temptation of Eve above the Annunciation in the third window from the left on the north side.

The **side chapels** also contain 15C and early 16C glass, most of it brought from elsewhere and installed in 1920 and 1991; notable examples are in the northwest side chapel and in the glass screens between the antechapel and other adjacent side chapels. The chapel immediately to the left of the north porch contains a *Crucifixion* by Craigie Aitchison (1994). Another chapel on the south side has a brass to Robert Hacumblen (d. 1528), Provost at the time of the chapel's completion, and a large monument to John Churchill (d. 1703), son of the first Duke of Marlborough.

The antechapel is divided from the choir by the **screen**, an outstanding example of Renaissance woodwork dating from c 1533–36. Richly carved throughout with Classical pilasters, armorial motifs, 'grotesques' and arabesques by a team of craftsmen probably led by a Spanish sculptor, it bears the initial of Henry VIII (the donor) intertwined with that of his queen, Anne Boleyn, whose family crest of a falcon appears alongside the Tudor rose. The organ case dates from 1686–88, but incorporates parts of an earlier case dating from the time of Henry VIII; the organ itself has pipework by the celebrated late 17C builder Renatus Harris.

On the east side of the screen is the early 16C bronze **lectern**, engraved on one side with roses and on the other with the four Evangelists and their beasts and topped by a small statue of Henry VI. The wooden **stalls** are contemporary with the screen, and by the same craftsmen; the upper seats are surmounted by round arches resting on delicate balusters of Renaissance inspiration; the canopies of the stalls on the north and south sides of the chancel date from 1675–78, but repeat the original design. Behind are exquisitely carved heraldic panels (1633) showing the coats of arms, with supporters, of the English monarchs from Henry VI to Charles I; on the north side (left) are the arms of Eton College and Oxford University and on the south those of King's College and Cambridge.

The **altarpiece** is Rubens's exuberant *Adoration of the Magi* (1634), painted for a nunnery in Louvain (Leuven) in Belgium and given to King's in 1961. Its installation in 1968 necessitated the removal of the early 20C panelling and the steps on which the altar then stood, and it could be argued that, for all its superb dramatic and painterly qualities, the picture does not harmonise well with its surroundings. Some might take issue also with the modernistic light fittings introduced at the same time. To the right of the chancel is the War Memorial **Chapel** in which the names of King's men who died in the two World Wars (including Rupert Brooke) are inscribed.

A doorway on the north side of the chancel leads into the north chapels, in which an excellent **exhibition** is mounted. As well as 15C service books, and other treasures, there are drawings and models which admirably explain the construction of the building and its incomparable fan vault.

The choir of King's College is one of the most famous in the world, though rivalled in quality by the other collegiate choral foundations in Cambridge and

Oxford. **Choral services**, which members of the public are welcome to attend, are held in term-time (Mon–Sat 17.30, Sun 10.30 and 15.30 exc. first Sun in month when evensong is sung at 18.00; Monday services are sung by a mixed student choir. Adm. through main gate in King's Parade).

The south side of the chapel looks out onto the broad expanse of **Great Court**, in the centre of which is a statue of Henry VI. To the right (west) is the noble Classical façade of the Fellows' or **Gibbs Building** (1724–49): an effective foil to the Gothic pinnacles of the chapel, with its massive central gateway, surmounted by a lunette or 'Diocletian' window, leading to the Backs. The neo-Tudor south range of the Court, including the **Hall** (no adm.) is by William Wilkins (1824–28), and Wilkins was also responsible for the attractive screen and **gate-house** which separate the college from King's Parade, on the far side of which is a domed Victorian postbox, a much-loved feature of the local scene.

Between the chapel and the river is a sweeping lawn and across the bridge (by Wilkins 1819) is the King's section of the Backs, in spring carpeted with crocuses and daffodils. On the south side of the lawn are the former **Provost's Lodge**, by Wilkins, and the neo-Tudor **River Court** (G.F. Bodley, 1893), and to the north is the 17C south range of Clare College.

Famous members

Christopher Tye, composer, c 1500–73
Francis Walsingham, statesman, c 1530–90
John Harrington, inventor of the water closet, 1561–1612
Edmund Waller, poet, 1606–87
George Monk (Duke of Albemarle), soldier and statesman, 1608–70
Charles 'Turnip' Townshend, statesman and agriculturalist, 1674–1738
Robert Walpole, statesman and Prime Minister, 1676–1745, and

his son **Horace**, aesthete and man of letters, 1717–97
M.R. James, scholar and writer of ghost stories, 1862–1936
Roger Fry, art critic, 1866–1934
E.M. Forster, novelist, 1879–1970
John Maynard Keynes, economist, 1883–1946
A.V. Hill, physiologist, Nobel prizewinner, 1886–1977
Rupert Brooke, poet, 1887–1915
P.M.S. Blackett, physicist, Nobel prizewinner, 1897–1974
Alan Turing, computer scientist, 1912–54

Leaving King's College by the west entrance on the far side of the Cam, a right turn along the pathway parallel to Queen's Rd gives a superb view across the Backs towards King's College Chapel, with the Gibbs Building to its right and Clare College on the left. At the end of the path is the west entrance to Clare College.

Clare College

Plan 1, H; open 10.00–17.00 except two weeks in mid-June: adm. charge late Mar–Sept; ☎ 01223 333200, ✉ www.clare.cam.ac.uk: adm. also from Trinity Lane.

History

Founded as University Hall in 1326 by Richard de Badew, Chancellor of the University, Clare College is the second oldest in Cambridge (King's Hall and Michaelhouse were slightly older, but both were absorbed into Trinity College in the 16C). It was refounded in 1338 by three-times-widowed Elizabeth de Clare, grand-daughter of Edward I, and the name was then changed to Clare Hall; it became Clare College only in 1856.

The largely uniform appearance is due to a complete rebuilding in Ketton and Weldon stone which started in 1638 and continued spasmodically over the next 80 years under the direction first of John Westley and then of Robert Grumbold, Cambridge's leading master mason of the late 17C. A long interruption was caused by the Civil War, when the Parliamentarians seized the building materials to refortify Cambridge Castle; Oliver Cromwell eventually, if belatedly, compensated the college for the loss. The buildings were originally a stylistic hybrid, but many of the more Gothic elements, like the battlements and pointed windows, were removed in the 18C. The man responsible for Classicising the elevations was James Essex and he also completed the Chapel begun to the designs of Sir James Burrough in 1763.

Clare was a small but socially exclusive society in the 18C, when it was popular for the sons of the Whig aristocracy and leading American colonists, and it did not grow significantly until the 20C. Since there was no room to expand on the old site the college had to leap the river and in 1923–34 the massive Memorial Buildings went up to the designs of Giles Gilbert Scott to the west of Queen's Rd (see p 265). In 1957–58 another hostel was built on the slopes of Castle Hill (see p 254) and it is in these two places that the bulk of the students now live.

Main gateway

The wrought-iron west gateway (Thomas Warren, 1714) leads to **Clare Bridge**, the oldest in Cambridge; it was built in 1638 by the master mason Thomas Grumbold, whose son Robert was responsible for completing the college's buildings. On the left is the **Fellows' Garden**, one of the most beautiful in Cambridge. From the bridge there is a good view of the college's **west range**, the foundations of which were laid in 1640, though work did not begin in earnest until 1669; the upper two floors are emphasised by giant Ionic pilasters in keeping with the growing Classicism of the post-Restoration period.

The buildings are arranged around a single court, which has changed little since the 17C. To the left, in the north range, is the **Hall** (often locked), dating from 1688, but with a late 19C ceiling and woodwork above the dais; over the doorway of the Small Hall, to the left of the entrance passage, is a 15C stone panel carved with the college arms, the sole surviving feature of the medieval buildings. Beyond the Hall, in the northeast corner of the Court, is the entrance to the **Chapel**, which replaced its 16C predecessor in 1763–69. The beautiful antechapel takes the unusual form of an octagonal vestibule lit from above by a domed lantern, embellished with attractive plasterwork. There is more good plasterwork, of a more restrained Neo-classical kind, on the barrel-vaulted ceiling of the chapel itself; note also the fine 18C woodwork and the altarpiece of the *Annunciation*, by Giovanni Cipriani, set in an impressive wooden reredos. On the north side (left), immediately on entering the chapel, is a modern stained-glass window commemorating two fellows: Hugh Latimer, one of the 'Oxford Martyrs' burnt at the stake in the reign of Mary Tudor, and Nicholas Ferrar, founder in 1625 of the Little Gidding religious community (see p 295), whose small church appears in the picture. Ferrar's earlier support of pioneering ventures in Virginia anticipated the American connection with the college in the 18C, strengthened in more recent times by Paul Mellon, an old member who established an exchange scheme with Yale University.

The main **gateway** on the far (east) side of the Court is surmounted by a busily detailed Mannerist 'frontispiece' of 1638–41, and there is a similar, though somewhat more restrained, frontispiece on the far side, facing Trinity Lane. Over the passage through the gateway is one of the last fan vaults to be erected in Cambridge.

Famous members

Hugh Latimer, divine, 1485?–1555

Nicholas Ferrar, divine, 1592–1637

Thomas Pelham-Holles, Duke of Newcastle, statesman, Prime Minister and Chancellor of Cambridge University, 1693–1768

Lord Hervey, author of the *Memoirs of the Reign of George II*, 1696–1743

Lord Cornwallis, English Commander-in-Chief in the American War of Independence, afterwards Governor-General of India, 1738–1805

Rowan Williams, Archbishop of Canterbury at the time of writing

---

Opposite the entrance to Clare is the former **Old Court of King's College**, begun in 1441 and sold to the University in 1829 when the New Court of King's was built. It is entered through a handsome gate tower, the lower parts of which date from the 15C and the rest from the 19C (J.L. Pearson, 1887–90); from under the gate tower the 14C and 15C west range of the Old Schools can be seen straight ahead, with the library of Gonville and Caius College (formerly part of the University Library) to the left. Immediately to the north of Clare College is Trinity Hall.

Trinity Hall

Plan 1, H; open daylight hours exc. end Apr–mid-June, ☎ 01223 332500, ✉ www.trinhall.cam.ac.uk.

History

The only old Cambridge college to be called a hall (its original title was 'The College of the Scholars of the Holy Trinity of Norwich'), Trinity Hall was founded in 1350 by the Bishop of Norwich, William Bateman, who also refounded Gonville Hall (see Gonville and Caius College, p 203) in the following year. As well as being an eminent churchman, Bateman was a leading authority on canon and civil law and his college was founded to provide men trained in law who could replenish the ranks of the profession decimated by the Black Death.

Until well into the 19C Trinity Hall remained a college of lawyers; most of its fellows had large legal practices in London, and the consequent coming and going may have influenced the college in the 17C to make financial provision for the improvement of the roads leading into Cambridge. The milestones bore the college insignia and one can still be seen in Trumpington Rd (west side) almost opposite Brooklands Avenue. The strong traditional connection with the law still remains and the college also has a formidable reputation on the river, dating from the 1880s and 1890s. The college has an engagingly intimate character, well captured by Henry James when he wrote: 'If I were called upon to mention the prettiest corner of the world, I should draw a thoughtful sigh and point the way to the gardens of Trinity Hall'.

The college is entered through an inconspicuous doorway in Trinity Lane. The entrance leads into the **principal court**, 'comfortable and a little phlegmatic' in Pevsner's words. The buildings date from the mid- to late 14C and are thus among the oldest in Cambridge, but they were refaced in stone and Classicised in 1741–45 by Sir James Burrough and James Essex the elder; the north or outer face has remained relatively unaltered and can be seen from North Court, entered through a passage in the north (right-hand) range. The east or entrance side was again rebuilt, by Salvin, after a fire in 1852.

On the south side (left) is the domestic-looking **Chapel**, the smallest in Cambridge and described (or dismissed) in the 18C as 'a neat and elegant small room, more like the chapel of a nobleman's family than of a society'. It was licensed for worship between 1352 and 1366 but was completely remodelled in 1729–30 by the Master, Sir Nathaniel Loyd. The piscina is the only visible relic of the old building, tidied away behind a hinged panel on the south side. Over the altar is a large Mannerist painting of the *Visitation* by Tomaso Manzuoli (1560), and there is a 18C screen dividing the main body of the building from the diminutive antechapel. The splendid 18C plaster ceiling is decorated with heraldic emblems. The **Hall** (usually locked), in the west range, was remodelled in 1743–45, when the original timber roof was obscured by the present flat plaster ceiling; further alterations took place in 1892.

An archway in the west range gives access to the gardens by the river. Immediately to the right is the **Old Library**, an attractive red-brick building of c 1584 with a typically East Anglian stepped gable on the west side facing towards the Cam; the interior (no adm.) remains practically unaltered, and still retains the old arrangement of sloped reading desks, benches and chained books also to be found at Merton College, Oxford. To the left is the **Master's Lodge** (Salvin, 1852; rebuilt 1890), and beyond, to the right of the garden, are the neo-Tudor **Latham** and **Thornton Buildings** (Grayson and Ould, 1890–1910); the gatehouse between these two buildings incorporates a 14C arch removed from the site of the original entrance court, which stood on the site of the present 19C South Court. At the far end, next to Garret Hostel Bridge, is the well-detailed **Jerwood Library** (Freeland, Rees and Roberts 1999), its brick, gabled exterior blending in well with the college's older buildings without imitating them.

Famous members

Sir John Paston, of the Paston Letters, 1442–79 (also Peterhouse)

Stephen Gardiner, Bishop of Winchester, famed for the persecution of Protestants under Mary Tudor, 1483–1555

Lord Howard of Effingham, admiral and commander of the English fleet against the Spanish Armada, 1536–1624

Robert Herrick, poet, 1591–1674

Lord Chesterfield, statesman, wit, letter-writer, 1694–1773

Richard Fitzwilliam, founder of the Fitzwilliam Museum, 1745–1816

Bulwer Lytton, novelist and statesman, 1803–73

F.D. Maurice, theologian and social reformer, 1805–72

Leslie Stephen, man of letters and father of Virginia Woolf and Vanessa Bell, 1832–1904

J.B. Priestley, writer, 1894–1984

Lord Howe, politician, b. 1926

Nicholas Hyntner, currently (2004) director of the National Theatre, b. 1956

Garret Hostel Lane runs along the north side of Trinity Hall and crosses the Cam by a concrete footbridge (1960) from which there is a good view of the new Jerwood Library; the bridge gives access to a path leading across the Backs to the University Library (see Walk 4). From the front of Trinity Hall, **Senate House Passage** leads back past the 16C Gate of Honour of Gonville and Caius College (left: see below) to the starting point of the walk.

From here a left turn into Trinity St gives access to Gonville and Caius College.

Gonville and Caius College

Plan 2, G; usually open Oct–Maundy Thur daylight hours; Good Fri–early May and mid-June–Sept 09.00–14.00; closed mid-May–mid-June and all bank hols; ☎ 01223 332400, ✉ www.cai.cam.ac.uk.

History

Usually known as Caius (pronounced 'Keys'), the college was founded in 1348 as Gonville Hall by Edmund Gonville, a Norfolk clergyman, on part of the site of the present Corpus Christi College. Gonville died in 1351, entrusting his college to William Bateman, Bishop of Norwich, and Bateman moved it in 1353 to its present position next to Trinity Hall, which he himself had just founded. The college was dedicated to the Annunciation of the Virgin Mary, and the Annunciation is still shown on the college seal.

In 1557–58 the college, which was not prospering, was refounded by another Norwich man, John Keys or Caius, who became Master in 1559. He had been a student at Gonville Hall in 1529 and was afterwards a Fellow, before going to Italy in 1539. He taught philosophy in Padua, where he also studied medicine, and on returning to England he achieved great renown as a physician. Although imbued with the New Learning, Caius had a great respect for tradition, and he retained not only Gonville's old buildings, but also his Latinised name in the title of the new foundation.

In 1565, at 04.00 on 5 May (sunrise by the old calendar, and judged to be an auspicious hour) the foundation stone of his new Caius Court was laid. He ordained that for health reasons it should be of three sides only, to admit sunlight and fresh air (a pattern followed by a number of later Cambridge colleges); he also laid down strict rules on cleanliness and behaviour. Like many of his contemporaries, he enjoyed 'conceits', and he incorporated a number of symbolic 'devices' in the new buildings. Most of these have now disappeared, but the 'academic path' he designed for his students still remains. It led from the Gate of Humility (originally at the Trinity St entrance, now in the Master's garden) to the Gate of Virtue on the east side of Caius Court, and finally to the Gate of Honour (south side of Caius Court), which took the successful scholar to the Schools. The gates are among the earliest buildings in Cambridge to show the influence of Renaissance architecture. Caius died in 1573, after some years of increasingly unhappy relations with his own fellows and with other college Masters, which culminated in 1572 with the destruction of the Catholic vestments and the vessels he had carefully preserved.

The medical tradition of the college, established even before the time of Caius himself, still survives. Until the 19C there were also strong traditional links with the county of the founders; before 1852 almost all Masters came from the diocese of Norwich.

When approached from King's Parade, the college makes its presence felt by the highly embellished Victorian **gate tower** built to the French Renaissance designs of Alfred Waterhouse in 1868–70. The entrance, however, is through a more modest doorway in Trinity St. It leads into **Tree Court**, rebuilt in 1868–70 by Waterhouse but dating originally from the early 17C when funds were supplied by Thomas Legge, Dr Caius's successor as Master, and the medical fellow Stephen Perse, founder of Cambridge's first grammar school, the Perse School. Waterhouse's lively, if somewhat overbearing, architecture, is rich in towers, pinnacles, turrets and other ornamental flourishes, and there are niches on the outer side carrying busts of benefactors and famous members of the college.

On the west side, facing the entrance, is the **Gate of Virtue** (1567–69): a gate tower of the traditional medieval type, but adorned with Classical pilasters in anticipation of the 'Towers of the Orders' which became a fad in early 17C Oxford. It leads into **Caius Court**, unpretentious and domestic-looking, except for the curious, diminutive **Gate of Honour** (left), which leads to the Senate House. Its richly ornamental character recalls the temporary ceremonial archways put up to honour 16C rulers, and its diminutive doorway (still Gothic in form) evokes Biblical homilies about the narrowness of the gate which leads to eternal life. The Court is faced with ashlar stone from Ramsey Abbey, demolished after the Dissolution of the Monasteries.

On the north side of Caius Court (right on entering) is the **Chapel**, which formed part of the original Gonville Hall. Completed by 1393, it was greatly altered in 1637, when the east end was extended, and the wood-panelled ceiling with its cherubs and rays of light installed; the cherubs were removed by the arch-iconoclast William Dowsing in 1643 but were reinstated after the Restoration. In 1718–26 the exterior was faced in stone by John James, assistant surveyor to St. Paul's Cathedral in London, and he was also responsible for most of the internal woodwork. There were further external alterations in the 19C; the apse at the east end was added by Waterhouse in 1870, with mosaics by Antonio

Salviati. There are some fine 16C and 17C monuments: to Dr Caius (1573–75; north wall, nearest the altar)—a tomb chest under a canopy supported by Corinthian columns, carved by Theodore Haveus of Cleves in Germany, 'a skilful artificer and eminent architect'; to Dr Perse (d. 1615; north wall), possibly by Maximilian Colt; and to Dr Legge (d. 1607; south wall). On the south wall, behind a hinged panel above the stalls, is the old piscina of the 14C chapel.

To the north of the Chapel is the medieval **Gonville Court**, Classicised and refaced in 1753–54 by the then Master, Sir James Burrough. On the west (left) side is the neo-Elizabethan **Hall** (Anthony Salvin, 1853: no adm.), with a handsome hammerbeam roof and a gallery with the Royal Arms (of c 1603) above. Behind the dais, in a curtained glass case, is the flag flown at the South Pole in 1912 by Captain Scott's last expedition, of which Edward Wilson (an old member of Caius) was medical officer and a member of the small party which perished with Scott on their return journey to base. The Hall can be seen from Trinity Lane.

The south side of the college abuts onto Senate House Passage. Next to the Senate House, and opposite the Gate of Honour, is the former University Library (C.R. Cockerell, 1837–42), built to supplement the existing 18C library in the Old Schools (see above) and since 1996 housing the college **Library**. In Cockerell's original plans the building was intended to form just one side of a magnificent new court whose construction would have entailed the complete demolition of the Old Schools. But parsimony prevailed and the architect's grand designs remained unfulfilled, like those of Nicholas Hawksmoor, James Gibbs and Robert Adam before him. Even so, the library, described by Cockerell as 'a fragment of a great quadrangle: a vast vaulted fire-proof enduring plain building', is one of the finest works of Classical architecture in Cambridge, its spacious barrel-vaulted interior (no adm.) bearing comparison with Sir Christopher Wren's better-known library at Trinity College.

At the west end of Senate House Passage, facing the former Library, is the **lecture room** for Gonville and Caius College designed by Alfred Waterhouse, with the date 1883 on the gable-end to the street; the building was expertly converted into the Bateman Auditorium in 1996. In 1901–04 the college expanded across Trinity St with the building of **St. Michael's Court** (Sir Aston Webb: south range by Murray Easton, 1934), and in 1960–62 the college's patronage of adventurous architecture resumed with the building of Harvey Court on the far side of the Cam in West Rd (see p 262).

Famous members

Thomas Gresham, founder of the Royal Exchange, 1519–79

William Harvey, discoverer of the circulation of the blood, 1578–1657

Jeremy Taylor, theologian, 1613–67

William Wilkins, architect, 1778–1839

John Venn, logician and inventor of the Venn diagram, 1834–1923

Sir David Salomons, electrical engineer and founder of the RAC, 1851–1925

Charles Wood, composer, 1866–1926

Edward Wilson, Antarctic explorer, 1872–1912

Harold Abrahams, Olympic athlete (*Chariots of Fire*), 1899–1978

Francis Crick, discoverer of DNA, b. 1916, and ten other Nobel prizewinners

Facing the entrance to the college is **St. Michael's church**, built in the early 14C by Hervey de Stanton (d.1327), the founder of Michaelhouse, one of the colleges incorporated by Henry VIII into his new foundation of Trinity (see below). It orig inally served both as the college chapel for Michaelhouse and as a parish church, hence the unusual arrangement of a nave (for the parish) that is slightly shorter than the chancel. The nave now houses a good café; it is lit at the west end by a large Decorated window. Hervey de Stanton was buried in the chancel, where services are still held. There is a good set of medieval stalls, possibly made for the chapel of King's Hall, another of the constituent parts of Trinity, and on the right is a set of sedilia and an elaborate ogee-arched doorway—an excellent example of Decorated Gothic—leading to a small chapel with ogee-shaped niches on either side of the east window.

From here, a left turn into **Trinity Lane** leads past a picturesque row of gables and chimneys belonging to the south range of the Trinity College's Great Court (right). At the right-angled bend at the end is **Nevile's Gate**, a re-erected stone tri umphal arch of c 1610 which formerly stood in Nevile's Court (see below); oppo site is the red-brick Hall of Gonville and Caius College. Back in **Trinity St** there are several old houses, including the former Turk's Head Inn (No. 14), a gabled tim ber-framed building of c 1600; further north, facing the entrance to Trinity College, is *Heffer's Bookshop*, the largest and most comprehensive in Cambridge.

Trinity College

Plan 2, G; open daily 10.00–17.00 exc. third week in June and first week in Oct Adm. charge mid-Mar–Oct; ☎ 01223 338400, ✉ ww.trin.cam.ac.uk.

The College

The college is separated from Trinity St by an attractive cobbled forecourt, to the right of which is a small lawn with an apple tree directly descended from one at Woolsthorpe Manor (Lincs), home of Sir Isaac Newton, perhaps the college's most famous alumnus. The tree at Woolsthorpe was the one which, according to legend, first set Newton thinking about 'the notion of gravitation', and the room where he lived and wrote his *Principia Mathematica* are to the right of the gate house (staircase E, no adm.).

The massive turreted brick **Great Gate** was begun c 1490 as part of King's Hall, but the upper stages were not added until 1528–35; the name of Edward II is carved over the entrance, but the crude statue above is of Henry VIII. In his hand is not a sceptre but a chair-leg—an undergraduate joke which has now become a hallowed tradition. The statue was put up by the Master, Thomas Nevile c 1615, as were the equally ham-handed statues of James I, Queen Anne of Denmark and Charles I on the inner side (that of James I has been replaced).

Great Court was created between 1597 and 1615 and would still be recognis able to Dr Nevile were he to return. Its irregularities can mostly be explained by Nevile's decision to retain some of the existing buildings. The oldest of these is **King Edward's Tower** (1428–32), on the north side (right on entering), formerly part of King's Hall but originally standing some distance to the south. Nevile moved it to its present position next to the Chapel and installed the statue of Edward III (wearing Elizabethan armour and impaling three crowns on his sword) and a clock replaced in 1726 and given a new mechanism in 1910; it strikes the hour twice.

Cambridge's largest college

The largest of Cambridge's colleges, Trinity was founded by Henry VIII at the end of 1546, a month before he died, and was well endowed with property, much of it derived from the newly suppressed monasteries. The buildings spread over the sites of two older colleges, King's Hall and Michaelhouse, and two hostels, including the Physwick Hostel of Gonville Hall. King's Hall already had a long royal connection, having been established by Edward III in 1337 as a training-ground for public servants, and it continued, with some fluctuations of fortune, to enjoy the patronage of later monarchs. Initially, it drew most of its scholars from the choristers of the Chapel Royal, hence their designation as 'King's Childer'.

Michaelhouse was a more modest establishment. It was founded in 1324 by Edward II's Chief Justice and Chancellor of the Exchequer Hervey de Stanton, but it never enjoyed the same wealth and prestige as its neighbour and, with the exception of the chapel, St. Michael's church (see above), none of its buildings now survives in recognisable form.

The present magnificent appearance of Trinity owes much to the generosity of the Tudor monarchs and to the vision of Thomas Nevile, appointed Master by Elizabeth I in 1593. Described as 'splendid, courteous and bountiful', he incorporated the mid-16C chapel and some of the buildings of King's Hall, including the two gatehouses, into a vast new court (the Great Court) larger than any other in either Oxford or Cambridge, demolishing in the process the scattered older buildings which encumbered the site. He also laid out a new court (Nevile's Court) to the west, enclosed on the west side by a wall which was replaced in 1676–95 by the Wren Library, the finest library building in either of the two universities. Since then there have been numerous alterations and expansions. Meanwhile the college developed a formidable accademic reputation both in the arts and in mathematics and the sciences (Sir Isaac Newton was a Fellow in the 17C), which it has preserved down to the present day, with a roll of famous alumni that cannot be matched by any other Oxford or Cambridge college.

The **Chapel** (choral services Tues/Thur 18.15, Sun 10.00 and 18.15 in term-time) was begun in 1555 at the instigation of Mary Tudor (and therefore one of the rare buildings of her reign), but was completed in the reign of her Protestant half-sister Elizabeth in 1567. It was mainly built of materials acquired through the demolition of Ramsey Abbey (Huntingdonshire) and the Franciscan friary which stood where Sidney Sussex College is now. Externally a late example of Tudor Gothic, with Perpendicular tracery and pinnacles, it owes its internal appearance to alterations carried out in 1706–17, when the controversial and disputatious Master of the time, Richard Bentley, put in the Classical organ screen, panelling and magnificent arched reredos. His tomb-slab is on the north (left) side of the altar rails, but does not record his Mastership, of which he was deprived but which he never relinquished.

In the **antechapel** are statues of great Trinity men, including Francis Bacon (1845, inspired by his monument in St. Michael's church at St. Albans), the historian Thomas Babington Macaulay (Woolner, 1868), the poet Tennyson (Hamo Thornycroft, 1909, with his pipe, partly concealed in laurel leaves), and, in

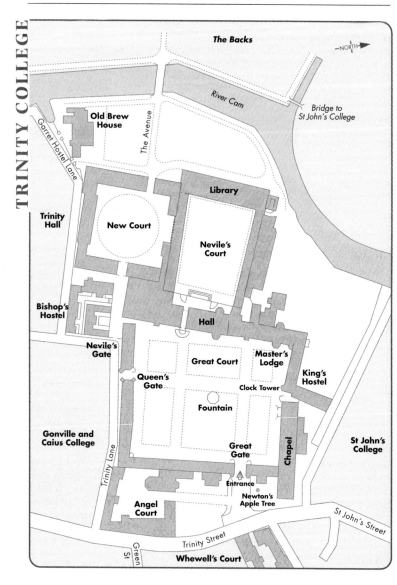

TRINITY COLLEGE

The Backs

—NORTH→

River Cam

Bridge to
St John's College

Old Brew House

The Avenue

Garret Hostel Lane

Library

Trinity Hall

New Court

Nevile's Court

Bishop's Hostel

Hall

Nevile's Gate

Great Court

Master's Lodge

King's Hostel

Queen's Gate

Clock Tower

Fountain

Gonville and Caius College

Trinity Lane

Great Gate

Chapel

St John's College

Entrance

Newton's Apple Tree

Angel Court

St John's Street

Green St

Trinity Street

Whewell's Court

splendid isolation at the west end, Sir Isaac Newton (Roubiliac, 1755); it inspired Wordsworth's famous lines: 'The marble index of a mind for ever/Voyaging through strange seas of thought, alone.' Sorrowfully impressive in their seeming endlessness are the names of the 1000 sons of the college killed in the two World Wars, those of the first at each side of the altar, those of the second in the antechapel.

Near the centre of the Great Court is the **fountain** (1601–15), enclosed within an Ionic arcade surmounted by a richly carved entablature and a profuse display of strapwork; the water was supplied from a pipeline laid by the Franciscans in the early 14C from springs over a mile away across the river (Conduit Head Rd, beyond Churchill College). On the south side, opposite the Chapel, is **Queen's Gate** (1597) with a statue of Nevile's royal patron Elizabeth I.

The west side of the court is dominated by the **Hall** (usually open 15.00–17.00), built and probably designed by the local master mason Ralph Symonds. It is closely modelled on the Hall of the Middle Temple in London, and is notable for its huge mullioned and transomed windows and splendid hammerbeam roof topped by a hexagonal lantern. Over the dais is a portrait of Henry VIII after Holbein, gazing over the expanse of tables and benches towards the carved wooden screen with its exuberant riot of Jacobean decoration.

Trinity College fountain

The screens passage leads into **Nevile's Court**. The north and south ranges (right and left), with their arched Renaissance loggias, date for the most part from 1605–12, but their Classical effect was accentuated by James Essex in a remodelling of 1755–58. They represent an important stage in the introduction of Classical architecture into Cambridge, and in 1676–82 they were extended westward. At the same time the then Master, Isaac Barrow, invited his friend and fellow-scientist Sir Christopher Wren to design the Library which closes the court on the west side.

The Wren Library

Built of Ketton stone under the supervision of Robert Grumbold, the library was begun in 1676 and completed in 1695. Here Wren's style reaches its maturity. To preserve the books from damp and to allow the best possible natural lighting, the library is raised above ground level, resting, in Wren's own words, on rows of Tuscan columns 'according to the manner of the ancients, who made double walks ... around the forum'. It is lit by huge semicircular-headed windows, and along the roof balustrade are statues symbolising Divinity, Law, Physic and Mathematics (by Cibber); the floor is cunningly placed at the level of the springing of the arches of the lower arcade.

The spacious **interior** (open Mon–Fri 12.00–14.00, Sat 10.30–12.30 in term-time), entered from the northwest corner of the court, breathes the spirit of late 17C rationalism and 'touches the very soul of any one who first sees it' (Roger North, 1695). The bookcases are embellished with lime-wood carvings, by Grinling Gibbons, of the coats of arms of donors, and are surmounted by plaster busts of Classical and modern writers; the busts on plinths in front of the bookcases, by Roubiliac and Scheemakers, are of eminent Trinity men. The window at the far end (by Cipriani, 1774–75) depicts the Muse of the College presenting Newton to George III, who sits enthroned among lightly draped nymphs, cherubs and clouds, while Bacon looks on, somewhat askance, notebook in hand. Underneath is the life-size statue of the poet Byron (by Thorvaldsen,

1831), rejected by Westminster Abbey in disapproval of his morals. The larges surviving portion of Newton's personal library is housed in the adjacent shelves
Displayed in covered glass cases down the centre aisle are some of the library' many treasures, which include an 8C copy of St. Paul's epistles, illuminated MS of the 11C and later, works by Bertrand Russell, Housman's *A Shropshire Lad*, on of Wittgenstein's notebooks, and A.A. Milne's *Winnie-the-Pooh*. Letters of othe writers including Robert Louis Stevenson, George Eliot and Anthony Trollope ar also sometimes displayed.

Beyond the library are the college Backs, and from here there is a good view c the 19C Gothic New Court of St. John's College (see below), framed by willows with the river flowing tranquilly in front. A path over the stone **bridge** (Jame Essex, 1765), a little to the south, leads to a gateway in Queen's Rd, from which the college's grounds can also be entered; the austere but powerful west front c the Library can be best seen from the bridge. None of the college's later building begins to match it in grandeur, least of all William Wilkins's feeble Tudor-Gothi **New Court** (1823–25), to the south of Nevile's Court. Here Arthur Hallam, t whom Tennyson was so devoted, had rooms; he had wished to go to Oxford, an in an early letter referred to Cambridge disparagingly as 'this college-studde marsh'.

In the 19C and 20C Trinity spread over Trinity St to take in a large and het erogeneous group of buildings stretching as far east as Sidney St (see p 213 Facing the Great Gate is the rather dull **Whewells Court** (Salvin, 1859–68 named after one of the college's most energetic and generous Masters; the bru talist ziggurat-like **Wolfson Building** (Architects' Co-Partnership, 1968–72 squeezed into an adjacent site, can be glimpsed from the former churchyard fac ing the east end of the college Chapel. Nearby—and only visible from Green St is **Blue Boar Court**, by MacCormac, Jamieson and Pritchard (1990), inge niously inserted behind the facades of older buildings.

Famous members

John Dee, alchemist, 1527–1608
Francis Bacon, philosopher and statesman, 1561–1626
Robert Devereux, Earl of Essex, favourite of Queen Elizabeth I, 1566–1601
George Herbert, poet and divine, 1593–1633
Andrew Marvell, poet, 1621–78
John Dryden, poet and dramatist, 1631–1700
George Jeffreys, judge at the 'Bloody Assizes', 1645–89
Richard Bentley, classical scholar, Master, 1662–1742
John Montagu, 4th Earl of Sandwich, inventor of the

sandwich, 1718–92
Lord Byron, poet, 1788–1824
Thomas Babington Macaulay, historian and poet, 1800–59
W.H. Fox-Talbot, pioneer photographer, 1800–77
Alfred, Lord Tennyson, poet, 1809–92
W.M. Thackeray, novelist, 1811–63
J.M. Neale, hymnologist, 1818–66
Charles Villiers Stanford, composer, 1852–1924
A.E. Housman, poet and classical scholar, 1859–1936
Bertrand Russell, philosopher and mathematician, 1872–1970
Ralph Vaughan Williams,

composer, 1872–1958
G.M. Trevelyan, historian, 1876–1962
Lytton Strachey (1880–1932), writer and member of the Bloomsbury Group, as were two other Trinity men, **Clive Bell** (1881–1964) and **Leonard Woolf** (1880–1969), Virginia's husband
A.A. Milne, creator of *Winnie-the-Pooh*, 1882–1956
Ludwig Wittgenstein, philosopher, 1889–1951 (he is buried in the Ascension Cemetery in All Soul's Lane of Huntingdon Rd)
Guy Burgess, spy (1910–63) was at Trinity, as were two of the other notorious spies for the Soviet Union, **Kim Philby** (1912–88) and the art historian **Anthony Blunt**, 1907–83

Politicians: **Spencer Perceval**, the only British Prime Minister to be assassinated, 1762–1812
Earl Grey, PM at the time of the 1832 Reform Act, 1764–1845
Lord Melbourne,1779–1848
Sir Henry Campbell-Bannerman, 1836–1908
Arthur Balfour, 1848–1930
Stanley Baldwin, 1867–1947
The Conservative politician **R.A. (Lord) Butler** (1902–82) became Master on his retirement
Jawaharlal Nehru (1889–1964), first Prime Minister of India, was also a Trinity man

Scientists and Nobel Prizewinners (a selection only): **Isaac Newton**, 1642–1727

George Airy, astronomer, 1801–92
Arthur Cayley, mathematician, 1821–95
Francis Galton, explorer and eugenicist, 1822–1911
James Clerk-Maxwell, physicist, organiser of the Cavendish Laboratory, 1831–79
George Darwin, astronomer, 1845–1913
J.W.S. Rayleigh, physicist, Nobel Prizewinner, 1842–1919
J.J. Thomson, mathematician and nuclear physicist, Nobel Prizewinner (as were seven of his assistants), 1856–1940
F.G. Hopkins, biochemist (vitamins), Nobel Prizewinner, 1861–1947
William and **Lawrence Bragg**, father and son, physicists, Nobel Prizewinners, 1862–1942 and 1890–1971
Lord Rutherford, atomic physicist, Nobel prizewinner, 1871–1937
Sir James Jeans, astronomer, 1877–1947
Arthur Eddington, astronomer, 1882–1944
A.V. Hill, physiologist, Nobel Prizewinner, 1886–1977
Sir George Thomson, physicist, Nobel Prizewinner, 1892–1975
Lord Adrian, physiologist, Nobel Prizewinner, 1889–1977.

Other old members of the college include **Edward VII**, **George VI** and **Charles, Prince of Wales**

Facing Trinity Chapel is a triangular open space which was once the churchyard of All Saints church, demolished in the 19C. On the north side is the red-brick Tudor-Gothic Selwyn Divinity school (Basil Champneys, 1878–79), opposite which is the entrance to St. John's College.

St. John's College

Plan 2, E; open all year exc. Christmas, weekdays 10.00–17.00, weekends 09.30–17.0; adm. charge Mar–Oct; ☎ 01223 338688, ✉ www.joh.cam.ac.uk.

History

Until overtaken by Trinity, St. John's was the largest college in Cambridge, and it is still second only in size and grandeur to its immediate neighbour. It was founded in 1511 according to the last wishes of Henry VII's mother, Lady Margaret Beaufort (d. 1509), but the proposal for a new college originated with John Fisher, Bishop of Rochester, and it was he who carried out her intentions, as at Christ's College. It replaced the late 12C Hospital of St. John the Evangelist and rebuilding began at once, only the chapel of the old hospital remaining (it was replaced by the present chapel in 1863–69). Fisher's concern for the new college continued until his death on the scaffold in 1535; in his hands both its finances and its scholarship prospered. As an enthusiast for the New Learning and friend of Erasmus he introduced the study of Greek at an early stage.

Strongly Royalist in the Civil War, St. John's suffered during the Parliamentary occupation of Cambridge; the Master and many of the fellows were expelled and the First Court was used as a prison. During the 19C the college acquired a great reputation for athletic prowess. Its boat club (Lady Margaret Boat Club or LMBC), founded in 1825, floated the first college eight on the river and the challenge by one of its members to Oxford in 1829 was the forerunner of the famous Boat Race on the Thames. The word 'blazer' is said to derive from the scarlet jackets worn by LMBC members. The college is still the second largest in the university, with over 800 undergraduates and graduate students, and is second only to Trinity in the number of its famous and distinguished old members.

Main gateway

St. John's stands immediately to the north of Trinity and is entered through the magnificent **gate tower**, of red brick with stone dressings. It carries the emblems of Lady Margaret Beaufort, mythical 'yales' (see Christ's College, Walk 3) supporting the Beaufort arms—the portcullis and the Lancastrian rose—against a background sprinkled with daisies ('marguerites') and speedwells, known locally as 'remember me' ('souvent me souvient'—the Beaufort motto) growing out of a well-populated rabbit warren. Above is a statue of St. John the Evangelist (1662); the heavy linen-fold-panelled doors are mostly original (1515).

First Court, though built 1511–20, was much altered in 1772–76, when the south side (left) was refaced and heightened and sash windows inserted. Over G staircase an inscription 'Stag Nov 15 1777' records a stag finally brought to bay by the local hunt halfway up the stairs. Near here the young William Wordsworth had his rooms, in:

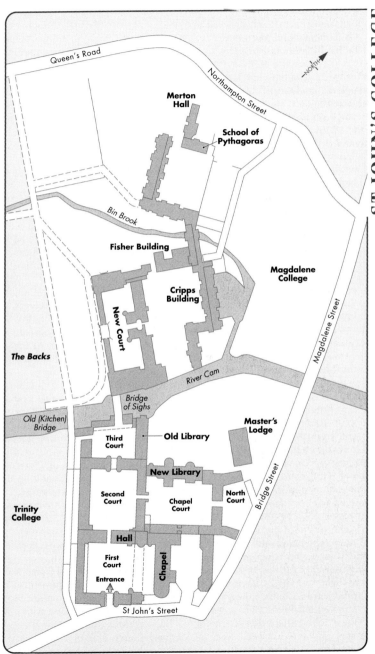

ST JOHN'S COLLEGE

'a nook obscure;
Right underneath, the College kitchens made
A humming sound, less tuneable than bees,
But hardly less industrious.'

On the west side of the court, straight ahead, is the **Hall** (no adm.), approached through a handsomely carved archway surmounted by a statue of Lady Margaret Beaufort. The hammerbeam roof, probably by the carpenter Thomas Loveday, dates from c 1516 and much of the linenfold panelling was introduced in the 1530s. When the present Chapel was built in the 1860s the Hall was extended to the north, taking in the former Master's Lodge, which was replaced by a much larger building on a new site in Bridge St, incorporating some of the old panelling. At the same time heraldic glass was installed in the Hall windows and heating was introduced to replace the ancient charcoal brazier.

The **Chapel** (usually open Mon–Fri 09.00–16.00, Sat 09.00–12.00) stands on the north (right-hand) side of First Court. It was built to the designs of Gilbert Scott in 1863–69, replacing the original chapel whose foundations can still be seen by the south wall. Like Scott's chapel at Exeter College, Oxford, it is a large apsidal Gothic building, owing something to French 13C models, and, like Exeter chapel, it dominates its surroundings in a way which the detractors of Victorian architecture have always found hard to forgive.

Uniquely for Cambridge (though not Oxford), it is planned in the shape of a T, with the antechapel at right angles to the main body of the church, and there is a huge tower, modelled on that of Pershore Abbey (Worcs), over the crossing; this is one of the most beautiful features of the Cambridge skyline, but it was not part of Scott's original design and its expense was a heavy financial burden on the college after the untimely death of the original donor. During this century it has become the custom on Ascension Day for a hymn to be sung from the top.

The noble **interior** is lit by large Decorated windows filled with good glass by Clayton and Bell (note especially the Last Judgement in the west window), and the same firm did the decorative painting on the ceiling of the main chapel; the Victorian furnishings fortunately survive intact. In the antechapel there are some monuments preserved from the previous building. On the south wall (left) are the three arches of Bishop Fisher's chantry (1525) and, set between two of them and protected by glass, is a fragment representing the hand of Christ. Opposite is the tomb of Hugh Ashton (d. 1522), one of Lady Margaret's officials, with a cadaver placed below as a memento mori, and Ashton's rebus of an ash-tree and barrel, or tun, on the tomb and railings. Note also the *Deposition from the Cross* of 1777 by Anton Raphael Mengs (south transept).

St. John's is one of the two Cambridge colleges with a full-scale choral foundation of men and boys, and the choir has a long tradition of excellence (choral services, during term time only, Sun 10.30 and 18.30; Tues–Sat 18.30).

Immediately to the west of the Chapel is **Chapel Court**. Opposite the Chapel is a neo-Tudor range by F.C. Penrose (1885), and projecting from it is the artfully contrived entrance to the **Library**, designed by Edward Cullinan and opened in 1994 (no adm.). To the right is **North Court** (Edward Maufe, 1939), with a carving of John Fisher's coat of arms by Eric Gill over the entrance archway.

A doorway next to the Hall leads into **Second Court**, built in 1598–1610 with the help of benefactions from Mary Cavendish, Countess of Shrewsbury, daughter of the great Derbyshire builder Bess of Hardwick. It is the work of Ralph Symonds—who also worked at Trinity, Emmanuel and Sidney Sussex—and Gilbert Wigge, and their plans, the oldest surviving in Cambridge or Oxford, are still preserved in the college library. As required in the contract, the style is similar to that of the Tudor-Gothic First Court before its 18C partial facelift; only the Elizabethan strapwork decorations give a clue to the real date. The gate tower on the west side is embellished with the Cavendish and Shrewsbury coats of arms (stag's head and dog respectively) and a late 17C statue of Lady Shrewsbury. Until 1859 its top storey was surmounted by an observatory. On the upper floor of the north side is the **Senior Combination Room** (no adm.), the former long gallery of the Master's Lodge and one of the finest such rooms to survive.

The west gateway leads into **Third Court**. On the north side (right) is the **Old Library** (no adm.) built in 1623–25 with a benefaction from John Williams, Bishop of Lincoln; the traceried Gothic shape of the windows was chosen because the donor believed that 'the old form of church window' was 'most meet for such a building'. The interior is largely unchanged, with the books in their original cases. The rest of the court was built in 1669–73.

The west side of Third Court overlooks the Cam, which is crossed by the **Old (Kitchen) Bridge** (Robert Grumbold, 1709), reached by a passageway on the south side of Third Court; it allows some of the most captivating views of the Backs. From here a path leads west through the college gardens to Queen's Rd.

Immediately to the north is the somewhat inappropriately named **Bridge of Sighs**, which leads directly from Third Court to **New Court**, on the opposite side of the river. Both were designed in 1826–31 by Thomas Rickman and Henry Hutchinson. They employed the Perpendicular, or Tudor, Gothic style which was so fashionable in the Cambridge of the 1820s; the vaulted cloisters, battlements and turrets successfully evoke the poetic spirit of romantic medievalism, although the planning is still essentially classical. The construction of New Court on its boggy riverside site was a formidable task; all the waterlogged soil had to be removed and replaced by a timber raft and huge cellars.

A passage through the north side of New Court leads to the **Cripps Building** (Powell and Moya, 1964–67), snaking along the Bin Brook onto open ground which, until 1959, belonged to Merton College, Oxford. It is perhaps the most successful of this firm's many commissions in Oxford and Cambridge: an engaging yet functional updating of the architectural language of the Modern Movement. To the left is the **Fisher Building** (Peter Boston, 1985–88), containing a concert hall and seminar rooms in a block which links the Cripps Building and New Court.

At the far (west) end of the Cripps Building stands one of the oldest buildings in Cambridge, the **School of Pythagoras**, a low stone house of the late 12C, altered in 1373; the reason for its curious name is unknown. It has been converted for use as a theatre and lecture room, and the picturesque timber-framed **Merton Hall** (16C) behind it now houses graduate students.

Famous members

Thomas Wyatt, poet, 1503–42
Roger Ascham, scholar and tutor
to Elizabeth I, 1515–68
William Cecil, Lord Burghley, chief

minister to Elizabeth I, 1520–98
William Morgan, Bishop of St.
Asaph and translator of the Bible
into Welsh, 1541–1604

Robert Herrick, poet, 1591–1674 (also Trinity Hall)	**Lord Palmerston**, statesman and Prime Minister, 1784–1865
Earl of Strafford, minister to Charles I, 1593–1641	**John Herschel**, astronomer, 1792–1871
Matthew Prior, poet, 1664–1721	**Louis Leakey**, anthropologist, 1903–72
Erasmus Darwin, scientific man of letters, 1731–1802	Nobel prizewinners **Sir Edward Appleton**, physicist, 1892–1965
William Wilberforce, politician and reformer, 1759–1833	**Sir John Cockcroft**, nuclear physicist, 1897–1967
Lord Castlereagh, statesman, 1769–1822	**Paul Dirac**, physicist, 1902–84
William Wordsworth, poet, 1770–1850	Also many bishops and eminent men of law

2 ~ SOUTH FROM KING'S

This walk, like Walk 1, starts at northern end of King's Parade outside the university church of St. Mary.

The east side of **King's Parade**, facing the chapel and screen of King's College (Walk 1), is made up of a row of former merchants' houses of varying dates. St. Edward's Passage leads from here to **St. Edward's church** (plan 2, G; usually open 13.00–15.00), surprisingly secluded in its churchyard among picturesque old houses, with a large fig tree to the north. The tower dates from the early 13C, but the aisled nave with its attenuated columns and tall pointed arches dates from c 1400; the chancel aisles were added in 1446 to serve as chapels for Trinity Hall (north side) and Clare College (south side), whose members had previously worshipped in the church of St. John Zachary, demolished when King's was founded.

The interior is light, spacious and pleasantly uncluttered. There is a good collection of floor slabs and wall tablets, and the wooden pulpit is made up of early 16C linenfold panelling; from here the Protestant reformers Hugh Latimer and Thomas Bilney preached. They are commemorated in stained-glass windows in the south aisle (by Sir Albert Richardson), installed in the 1940s, and nearby is a tablet to Frederick Denison Maurice (1802–72), theologian and social reformer, who founded the Working Men's College in London and also the first college for women (Queen's College, London); he was incumbent of the church in the last year of his life.

To the south of the church is the inconspicuous entrance to the **Arts Theatre**, built and presented to Cambridge by the economist John Maynard Keynes, a Fellow of King's College, and remodelled in the 1990s, with a café (open daily) on the top floor.

A left turn from King's Parade leads into Bene't St, on the north (left) side of which is the busy but congenial *Eagle Inn*, with a galleried courtyard (and good food and beer). It was extensively refurbished in 1992, when fragments of old wall paintings were discovered. Opposite is **St. Bene't's church** (i.e., St. Benedict's; plan 4, A), whose early 11C tower is the oldest surviving building in

Cambridge; the tower arch at the west end of the nave is a particularly good example of Anglo-Saxon work (note the carved beasts above the imposts). The rest of the church was rebuilt after a fire in the late 13C or early 14C, and the nave roof and clerestory date from c 1452. Until 1579 it served as the chapel of the adjacent Corpus Christi College, and a brick building was erected c 1490 with a gallery and gateway linking the chancel to the college.

Fabian Steadman, who perfected the art of change-ringing (ringing a set of bells in constantly varying order), and after whom various 'changes' are named, was parish clerk in the 17C, and is commemorated by a wall tablet. The nave aisles were widened in the 19C, and the interior has taken on a more cheerful appearance after a recent refurbishment.

The western side of King's Parade is dominated by the buildings of King's College. To the south of William Wilkins's 19C Gothic screen are the **King's Lane Courts** (James Cubitt and Partners, 1965–68), built with a bequest from John Maynard Keynes on the site of the former Bull Inn yard. They are shared between King's College and St. Catharine's, and include the latter college's dining hall (for the original hall, see below). The buildings are largely invisible from the street, but they cast a blight over the dismal passage known as King's Lane.

Further south in Trumpington St is the 1828 frontage of the Bull Inn, now part of St. Catharine's College.

St. Catharine's College

Plan 4, A; open daylight hours exc. May and June, ☎ 01223 338300, ✉ www. caths.cam.ac.uk.

History

Founded as Catharine Hall in 1473 by Robert Woodlark, Provost of King's, for the study of philosophy and theology, St. Catharine's College—as it has been known since 1860—originally contained only a Master and three Fellows, and in the 16C it was the smallest of all the Cambridge colleges. Numbers expanded in the 17C, and the present buildings were begun in 1673, during the Mastership of John Eachard, described on his monument in the college chapel as 'the second Romulus of this Rome'. The greater part of the present Main Court had been completed by the end of the 17C, leaving only the east end of the south range to be built by James Essex in 1757, in a style almost indistinguishable from that of the earlier buildings. In the 20C the college has expanded to fill the whole of its confined site, and, like many of the older colleges, has had to build on a new site on the opposite side of the Cam (St. Chad's Hostel, see p 263) in order to house the ever-increasing numbers of students.

St. Catharine's was originally entered from Queen's Lane, and for the first two centuries of the college's existence the Trumpington St frontage was occupied by private houses. These were cleared away in the 18C to reveal the plain but attractive late 17C brick architecture of the **Main Court**, which is closed on the east (entrance) side by an iron grille and gates dating from 1779; the original intention was to build a gatehouse and library range here, but, fortunately perhaps, the project never came to anything. In framing the design the college consulted an otherwise unknown Mr Elder from London and also the local master mason Robert Grumbold, who was probably the builder.

The college lies well back from the street, and the approach is flanked by the restrained and well-mannered **Hobson** and **Woodlark Buildings** of 1930 and 1949–51, the former named after the famous Cambridge carrier whose George Inn once stood here (see Hobson's Conduit, p 234). Inside the main court, the main point of interest is the **Chapel** in the north range (right). It was built by Grumbold between 1694 and 1704, possibly with the advice of William Talman, Comptroller of the King's Works. The light interior retains its original fittings intact, including the splendid carved wooden reredos and organ gallery. The former **Hall** (now the Senior Combination Room and Library: no adm.) lay immediately to the west, and was incongruously remodelled in the neo-Tudor style in 1868–69. The remaining elevations to the court retain their original hipped roofs, white-painted dormers and windows with single mullions and transoms of the type which immediately preceded the adoption of the sash window; at the centre of the west range is a stone frontispiece with Corinthian columns supporting a curved pediment.

Famous members

James Shirley, dramatist,
1596–1666
John Ray, naturalist, 1627–1705
(also Trinity)
Adam Buddle, botanist, after
whom the *Buddleia* is named,
d. 1715
John Addenbrooke, founder of
Addenbrooke's Hospital, d. 1719

John Bacchus Dykes, composer of
hymns, 1823–76
G.G. Coulton, medieval historian,
1858–1947
Sir Peter Hall, theatre director,
b. 1930
Sir Ian McKellan, actor, b. 1939
Jeremy Paxman, broadcaster,
b. 1950

Opposite St. Catherines' is Corpus Christi College.

Corpus Christi College

Plan 4, A; open daily 14.00–16.00 exc. May and early June, ☎ 01223 338000,
✉ www.corpus.cam.ac.uk.

History

The college, founded in 1352, is a monument to the Black Death of 1349: the worst known epidemic ever to hit England. It was established, uniquely for a Cambridge or an Oxford college, by a town guild, dedicated to the Body of Christ (Corpus Christi), which incorporated the depleted assets of the existing guild of the Blessed Virgin Mary, to which extra subscriptions were added by the survivors of the plague. The college combined chantry functions—the commemoration of deceased guild members—with the teaching of students; among its ancient treasures is an auroch's horn inherited from the guilds. The original 14C buildings survive largely intact as the oldest complete collegiate court in Cambridge, and, with Mob Quad at Merton College, Oxford, one of the two oldest in the ancient universities.

The college expanded substantially to the south in the early 19C, acquiring a new frontage to Trumpington St and a new set of buildings designed by William Wilkins, who is buried in the Chapel crypt. As student numbers grew after the Second World War, it expanded further to incorporate rooms in Botolph Lane and Eagle Yard, and a new graduate annexe was built in the grounds of Leckhampton House, to the west of the Cam (See Walk 4). It nevertheless remains one of smallest of Cambridge's undergraduate colleges.

The entrance leads into **New Court**, built to the designs of William Wilkins in the then-fashionable Tudor-Gothic style in 1823–27; it was, according to his monument, his favourite building, but its appearance was not improved when attics were added in the 1920s. The **Chapel** (usually no adm., but interior visible through a glass door), is conspicuously placed immediately opposite the entrance, its west front flanked by pointed turrets. The stalls, dating from c 1590, were taken from the Elizabethan chapel which it replaced, and there is some early 16C Flemish glass, given by Wilkins, in the side windows; the chancel and east window, by Arthur Blomfield, date from 1870. The **Hall**, to the left (no adm.), has a richly decorated plaster roof and stained glass windows, mainly of the 1820s.

On the south side of New Court (right on entering) is the **Library** (no adm.), housing the priceless collection of MSS and books bequeathed by Matthew Parker (Master 1544–53, and later Archbishop of Canterbury), many of which were rescued from monastic libraries dispersed after the Dissolution. Among its treasures are a MS of the *Anglo-Saxon Chronicle*, the 6C *Canterbury Gospels*, the *Peterborough Psalter*, the *Bury Bible* and Chaucer's *Troilus and Criseyde*. Parker left strict instructions for the care of the collection, including an annual surveillance by Gonville & Caius College and Trinity Hall.

Old Court is reached by a passage in the far left (northeast) corner of New Court. It was completed c.1377 and was until the 19C the college's sole court. It is built of rubble stone and faced with Barnack limestone, largely plastered over in 1919; though buttressed in the 15C and 17C, it retains its 14C appearance to a remarkable degree. The Hall (now the kitchen) was in the south range, and the residential accommodation, originally unheated, was arranged on two floors, the rooms lit by small one- and two-light windows. The dormers and chimneys date from the 16C, and there is a memorial tablet to Christopher Marlowe, one of the college's most famous old members, in the northwest corner.

An archway in the north range—the original entrance to the college—leads into St. Benet's churchyard; a brick building of c 1490 connects the college to the church, which served as the college chapel until 1579.

Famous members

Matthew Parker, Archbishop of Canterbury, 1504–75, and two other Archbishops of Canterbury, **Thomas Tenison**, 1636–1715 and **Thomas Herring**, 1693–1757 **Nicholas Bacon**, statesman, father of Sir Francis Bacon (Trinity), 1509–79

Christopher Marlowe, dramatist, 1564–93

John Fletcher, dramatist, 1579–1625

Stephen Hales, physiologist, 1677–1761 **Sir George Thomson**, physicist,	Nobel prizewinner, 1892–1975 **Christopher Isherwood**, poet and novelist, 1904–86

South of Corpus Christi is the **church of St. Botolph**, an aisled 14C and 15C building with a chancel rebuilt by G.F. Bodley in 1872. St. Botolph was a patron saint of travellers, and churches of this dedication were usually near city gates, in this case Trumpington Gate. The four bells date from 1460, and there is a particularly handsome font-case and cover (1637); note also the monuments to the theologian Dr Playfair (d. 1609) and to two men who did much to change the face of Cambridge: James Essex the younger (d. 1784) and Robert Grumbold (d. 1720; outer south wall of chancel).

From opposite St. Botolph's church Silver St leads west to the river alongside the south flank of St. Catharine's College. In the narrow Queens' Lane, leading off to the right, is the entrance to Queens' College.

Queens' College

Plan 3, B; open Apr–mid-May Mon–Fri 11.00–15.00, Sat–Sun 10.0–16.30; June–Sept daily 10.00–16.30, Oct Mon–Fri 13.45–16.30, Sat–Sun 10.00–16.30; Nov–March 13.45–16.30. Closed mid-May–mid-June. Adm. charge in summer months; ☎ 01223 335511, ✉ www.quns.cam.ac.uk.

History

Queens' traces its origins back to 1446, when Andrew Dokett, rector of St. Botolph's church and principal of St. Bernard's hostel—on the site of the present New Court of Corpus Christi College—made an abortive attempt to found a college dedicated to St. Bernard on a small site which now forms part of St. Catharine's College. In the following year, 1447, he acquired a new site on the west side of Queens' Lane and in 1448 the foundation came under the patronage of Margaret of Anjou, the young queen of Henry VI (who had just founded King's College, not far away). It was then renamed The Queen's College of St. Margaret and St. Bernard. Soon afterwards, the Wars of the Roses broke out; in 1461 Henry VI was deposed and the Edward IV became King. Four years later, in 1465, his queen, Elizabeth Woodville (a former lady-in-waiting to Margaret), became the college's new patron and 'true foundress by right of succession'; this explains the plurality of queens alluded to in the placing of the apostrophe in the college's name. The changes in royal patrons, who also included Richard III, account for the many elaborations of the college arms.

In 1506, and again c 1511–14, Queens' had the distinction of playing host to Erasmus, the great Renaissance scholar who introduced the study of Greek into Cambridge and Oxford. He was a friend of the former President, Bishop John Fisher, but was a most difficult guest, full of complaints, particularly about the college beer—'raw, small, and windy ... I am being killed with thirst'. Queens' is now one of the largest Cambridge colleges, only surpassed in numbers by Trinity and St. John's. This is not obvious, however, in the older parts of the college which have remained tranquil due to a shift in the 'centre

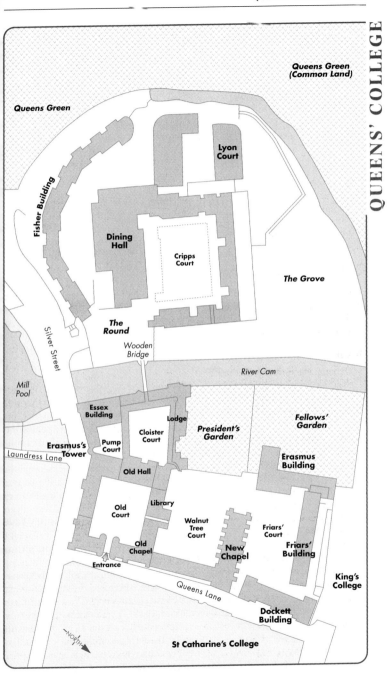

of gravity' to newer buildings on an island site over the Cam, erected o
ground first laid out by the college with walks and groves in the 16C.

The magnificent red-brick **gate tower** has a richly carved lierne vault and
flanked by tall turrets of the kind which later became normal in Cambridge co
leges. It leads into **Old Court**, the finest complete 15C architectural ensemble i
Cambridge. It was built in two stages in 1448–50, probably to the designs of th
master mason Reginald Ely. The large Perpendicular windows at the east end
the north range (immediately to the right on entering) light the former chap
and the rest of this range is occupied by the **Library** (no adm.), with a large su
dial of 1733 in the centre of the range at first-floor level, also telling moon-tim
The south (left) range contained most of the students' rooms.

Straight ahead, over the doorway opposite the gate tower, is the college coat
arms, carved in 1575 and showing quarterings of the many lordships to whic
Queen Margaret's father, Duke René of Anjou, laid claim; the bell turret above
dates from 1846. The door (original) leads into the screens passage, to the righ
of which is the **Hall**, with its restored oriel window lighting the high table en
Though structurally of the mid-15C, the dark, colourful interior has been rad
cally altered twice, first in 1732–34 by the elder James Essex and Sir Jame
Burrough, and secondly in the 19C. The 18C wood panelling and screen still su
vive, as does the 'reredos' behind the high table, richly embellished wit
Corinthian columns; on it, under the pediment and the college motto 'Florea
Domus' ('May the house flourish') is a portrait of Queen Elizabeth Woodvill
flanked on either side by portraits of Erasmus and of Sir Thomas Smith, the 16
scholar and diplomat, whose 'oratory and learning intermixed was so admirab
and beyond the common strain, that Queens' College carried away the glory fo
eloquence from all the colleges'.

The 18C plaster ceiling was removed in 1846, stained glass was inserted in th
windows in the 1850s, and in 1861 G.F. Bodley began a series of further altera
ations which involved restoring and painting the timber roof on which frag
ments of medieval painting had been discovered, tiling the floor, painting th
walls with a rich stencil decoration (1875), and uncovering the medieval fire
place on the west wall. On the overmantel above it is an attractive display of tile
by William Morris, Ford Madox Brown, Burne-Jones and Rossetti, representin
the months of the year, the saints of the college and the two queens.

Through the screens passage is the intimate and highly picturesqu

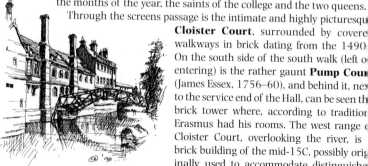

Cloister Court, surrounded by covere
walkways in brick dating from the 1490
On the south side of the south walk (left o
entering) is the rather gaunt **Pump Cou**
(James Essex, 1756–60), and behind it, ne
to the service end of the Hall, can be seen th
brick tower where, according to tradition
Erasmus had his rooms. The west range
Cloister Court, overlooking the river, is
brick building of the mid-15C, possibly orig
inally used to accommodate distinguishe
visitors, and now part of the President
Lodge (no adm.); over the north walk (righ

Queens' College, from the
River Cam

is the timber-framed **President's Gallery**, built at the end of the 16C, when long galleries were a fashionable feature of gentlemen's houses. The passage through the west range leads on to a wooden **Bridge** over the Cam (often, though wrongly, called the Mathematical Bridge); it was copied in 1904 from an original designed by William Etheridge and constructed by James Essex in 1749–50.

Beyond the bridge is a large complex of 20C buildings, with its own entrance from Silver St, and it is here that most of the college's activities now take place. Straight ahead is the concrete and glass **Cripps Court** (Powell and Moya, 1972–81), with a large dining hall (no adm.) and common rooms, and to the left is the neo-Tudor **Fisher Building** (G.C. Drinkwater, 1936), attractively laid out on a curved plan and best seen from Silver St. On the far side of Cripps Court is **Lyon Court** (Bland, Brown & Cole, 1986–89), clearly visible from the Backs. There is a short riverside walk (right) to the **Grove**—the only remnant of the once-extensive college gardens—from which the bridge and the buildings of Cloister Court form an attractive composition.

Back over the bridge in Cloister Court a passage under the President's Gallery (left on entering from the river side) leads into the open-ended **Walnut Tree Court**. It is dominated by the superb **Chapel** (G.F. Bodley, 1889–91), which replaced the original chapel in Old Court at a time when the college was expanding. It is a tall brick building in Bodley's favourite English late Gothic manner, with good woodwork, including the organ case, stained glass by Kempe (north side and east window), and a reredos containing three excellent painted panels of the *Agony in the Garden*, the *Resurrection* and *Christ Appearing to the Disciples*, attributed to the late 15C Brussels 'Master of St. Gudule'; some brasses from the old chapel are preserved in the antechapel.

To the west (left of the Chapel) is the Corbusier-inspired **Erasmus Building** (Sir Basil Spence, 1959), one of the first and best examples of the architecture of the Modern Movement in Cambridge; it forms one side of the unremarkable Friar's Court, named after the former Carmelite friary purchased by the college in 1538–44. The east side of Walnut Tree Court is occupied by a plain brick building of 1617–19, enlarged in 1778–82, and a passage through the south range a passage leads back under the Library into Old Court.

Famous members

Desidesrius Erasmus, scholar and humanist, 1466–1536

John Fisher, bishop and martyr, 1469–1535

Thomas Smith, statesman and scholar, 1513–77

John Whitgift, Archbishop of Canterbury, c 1530–1604

John Hall, physician and Shakespeare's son-in-law, 1575–1635

Thomas Fuller, antiquarian, author of *The Worthies of England*, 1608–61

Alexander Crummell, first black graduate of Cambridge, 1819–98

Charles Villiers Stanford, composer, 1852–1924 (also Trinity)

T.H. White, author of *The Once and Future King*, 1906–64

Abba Eban, foreign minister of Israel, 1915–2002

Graham Swift, novelist, b. 1949

Richard Hickox, music director, b. 1948

Stephen Fry, actor, b. 1957

A right turn out of Queens' College and another right turn into **Silver Street** leads to the River Cam. It is worth pausing on the bridge to look up river at the old mill-pool, the weir, the 'island' and, in the summer, the boats. On the east side (left) is **Laundress Green**, where much of the university's washing used to be hung out to dry. It is overlooked by the aggressively detailed **University Graduate Centre** (no adm.; designed by Howell, Killick, Partridge and Amis, 1964–67), to the south of which is the *Garden House Hotel*.

On the south side of Silver St are various university offices and lecture rooms, once part of the Cambridge University Press, whose **Pitt Building** (Edward Blore, 1831–33) looks out onto Trumpington St. Built with money left over from subscriptions collected for a memorial to William Pitt the Younger, Prime Minister during the Napoleonic Wars, the Tudor-Gothic architecture is so ecclesiastical in character that the building has been called the 'Freshmen's Church', from the old joke of directing newcomers to it on Sunday. Further south is a real church, **Emmanuel Congregational Church** (James Cubitt, 1875), whose chunky Gothic spire figures prominently in the Cambridge skyline; next to it is **Kenmare**, a very attractive late 18C house with no fewer than four Venetian windows enlivening its façade.

The very wide roadside channels on either side of **Trumpington Street** are the remnant of an open stream, constructed in 1610, which took water from the Cambridge New River to wash out the King's Ditch, which ran northeast from the long-vanished Trumpington Gate. Pipes also took supplies of drinking water to a conduit on Market Hill; the conduit-house was re-erected at the southern end of Trumpington St in 1856 (see below). Another channel was made in 1630, its water flowing east to St. Andrew's St to be piped to Emmanuel College and then to Christ's, whose pools still make use of it.

Pembroke St—a rather cheerless thoroughfare—leads east into a large complex of Science Faculty buildings (see p 248). It is flanked to the south by Pembroke College.

Pembroke College

Plan 4, A; open daylight hours exc. May–mid-June, ☎ 01223 338100, ✉ www. pem.cam.ac.uk.

History

The third oldest of the Cambridge colleges, Pembroke traces its origins back to 1347, when a site was acquired just to the south of the long-vanished Trumpington Gate. The founder was Marie de Valence, widowed Countess of Pembroke and a close friend of Lady Elizabeth de Clare, who had recently founded Clare College. Since her time the buildings have been greatly remodelled and extended, and they now provide a microcosm of the collegiate architecture of the last 650 years. The college housed some of the leading Protestant reformers of the 16C, and no fewer than three Pembroke men were martyred for their beliefs by Queen Mary Tudor. It later became noted for its poets, from Edmund Spenser in the 16C to Ted Hughes in the 20C.

The college is entered from Trumpington St. The 14C gateway leads into **Old Court** and on the left is the north range which, along with part of the west range, is a survival from the original 14C buildings. The crumbling clunch (chalk) walls were partly refaced in brick in 1633, and more extensively in pale ashlar stone in 1712–17, the first instance of this treatment in Cambridge.

The room with tall square-headed mullioned windows in the north range, immediately to the left on entering, was originally the Chapel, licensed in 1366 and the first in any Cambridge college. Now the **Old Library** (no adm.), it became a Library in 1690 after the building of the present Chapel and is now used for meetings; the plaster ceiling, by Henry Doogood, is of exceptional gaiety and charm, with scrolls and swags, open books and putti and flying birds.

The original intimacy of the court was unfortunately destroyed in 1874–75, when the east and south ranges were demolished. The south range was not replaced, and on the east side Alfred Waterhouse erected a new red-brick **Hall** (no adm.) which failed to please later generations and was remodelled in 1925 and again in 1949, with unfortunate external effect.

The south side of the enlarged Old Court (right on entering) is now occupied by the **Chapel**, built in 1663–65 to the design of the 31-year-old Christopher Wren. It was Wren's first building to be completed (he was also working at the same time on the Sheldonian Theatre in Oxford), and it represented a crucial landmark in the introduction of Classical architecture into Cambridge. The donor was Wren's uncle Matthew, Bishop of Ely, sometime fellow of Pembroke and former Master of Peterhouse. His High Church sympathies earned him 18 years in the Tower of London and his gift of the chapel was an expression of gratitude for his release and for the Restoration of the monarchy and the Established Church in 1660. The chapel originally formed part of a tiny court which was incorporated into Old Court in 1874–75. It was linked to the older part of the college by the arcaded Hitcham's Cloister, completed in 1666, and it is through this cloister that the chapel is now entered.

It is a plain building with tall round-arched windows of the kind later to be seen in the London City churches and a pedimented front to Trumpington St based on a plate in *L'Architettura* by the influential 16C Italian writer on architecture, Sebastiano Serlio. Inside, there is a 15C English alabaster carving of St. Michael and the Virgin Mary in the antechapel and beyond, in the main chapel, a beautiful plaster ceiling and some good contemporary woodwork in the stalls, reredos and organ gallery. The sanctuary, framed by massive Corinthian columns of Italian marble, was added by the younger George Gilbert Scott in 1880. On its south side (right) is the 14C piscina from the old chapel, and the chair of Nicholas Ridley, Bishop of London and one of the 'Oxford Martyrs', a former Master. Matthew Wren's cushions of turkey-work (made by the same method as an oriental rug) are still in use on the reading desks of the stalls, and over the altar is a painting of the *Deposition*, after Barocci.

To the south of the chapel, and flanking Trumpington St, is a range of red-brick residential buildings by Waterhouse (1871–72) in his strident though impressive French Renaissance manner, also to be seen at Caius. Admirers of Waterhouse's work will also enjoy his **Library** (1875–77), with its chunky, assertive clock tower, which faces north onto a lawn; the large bronze statue, by Richard Westmacott, is of William Pitt the Younger, one of the college's most celebrated old members and was originally made for the National Debt Office.

Opposite Pitt's statue is the south range of the three-sided **Ivy Court**, built in the 17C to the east of the Hall and closed on its eastern side by a wall and gateway. The north range is an attractive red-brick building of 1614 and the south range, mostly of 1659, is named after the donor, Sir Robert Hitcham of Framlingham (Suffolk). It carries his coat of arms in a pediment on the inner side, and on the first floor are the rooms occupied by the poet Thomas Gray from 1755 till his death in 1771 (no adm.). During restoration work, wall paintings were discovered behind the panelling here; there are two life-sized drawings of decorations on Wren's chapel, and a picture of a red-haired, bearded man, whose presence is an intriguing mystery.

The gateway on the eastern side of Ivy Court leads to the extensive and beautiful **gardens**; on a mound near the pond is a mulberry tree descended from one associated with the poet Edmund Spenser. To the north is a brick residential range by W.D. Caroe (1907), adjoining the **Old Master's Lodge**, by Waterhouse, and beyond, flanking Pembroke St, lies the richly detailed **New Court** (G.G. Scott the younger 1880–83). Its rather mannered elevations present a sharp contrast to those of the discreetly modernist **Foundress Court** (Eric Parry Architects, 1995–97), which occupies the south-eastern corner of the college and incorporates a new Master's Lodge together with spacious student accommodation.

Famous members

Nicholas Ridley, bishop and Protestant martyr, 1500–55

Edmund Spenser, poet, c 1552–99

Lancelot Andrewes, theologian and bishop of Winchester, 1555–1626

Richard Crashaw, poet, 1613–49 (also Peterhouse)

Roger Williams, founder of the state of Rhode Island, USA

Thomas Gray, poet, 1716–71 (also Peterhouse)

Christopher Smart, poet, 1722–71

William Pitt the Younger, statesman and Prime Minister, 1759–1806

George Gabriel Stokes, mathematician and physicist, 1819–1903

John Couch Adams, astronomer, discoverer of Neptune, 1819–92

Sir Arthur Bliss, composer, 1891–1975

Ted Hughes, poet, 1930–98

Peter Cook, actor and comedian, 1937–95

Clive James, writer and broadcaster b. 1939

Christopher Hogwood, conductor, b. 1941

David Munrow, conductor and promoter of early music, 1942–76

Opposite Pembroke College is the church of **St. Mary the Less**, or Little St. Mary's. It was built in 1340–52, and until 1632 it served as the college chapel for Peterhouse, which takes its name from the earlier church of St. Peter without Trumpington Gate which stood on the site. St. Mary's is a handsome, light, aisleless building, similar in character to Merton College chapel, Oxford, with large windows of flowing Decorated tracery; note the excellent glass by C.E. Kempe in the east window and elsewhere. On the north and south side of the nave are the remains of 15C and early 16C chantry chapels, that to the south leading into a Lady Chapel built by T.H. Lyon, architect of Sidney Sussex College chapel, in 1931.

The present vestry, to the south of the chancel, was at one time used as a chantry, and an oratory built over it connected with the adjacent Peterhouse by a covered gallery, like that connecting St. Bene't's church and Corpus Christi;

beneath the vestry is a tiny rib-vaulted crypt or ossuary (bone room). At the west end of the church, on the north wall, is a memorial to Godfrey Washington, vicar 1705–29, who from his coat of arms was evidently of the same family as the first President of the United States.

Peterhouse

Plan 4, C; open daylight hours exc. mid-Apr–late June, ☎ 01223 338200, ✉ www.pet.cam.ac.uk.

History

The oldest college in Cambridge, Peterhouse (never Peterhouse College) was founded by Hugh de Balsham, Bishop of Ely, in 1284, on much the same lines as Merton College, Oxford. His first attempt to found a college was in the Hospital of St. John (see St. John's College), but this project failed, and he eventually acquired two student hostels immediately to the south of St. Peter's church (now Little St. Mary's, above). A hall was erected in 1286, but the core of the college as it now stands, Old Court, was not completed until the 15C, and the college did not acquire its own chapel until the early 17C.

During the religious and political upheavals of the mid-16C the fortunes of Peterhouse were guided by Dr Andrew Perne (Master 1553–89), an early advocate of improved sanitation in the town and a forerunner of the celebrated Vicar of Bray. He so skilfully adjusted his opinions to the many changes of wind that the weather-vane he put up was regarded as something of an emblem; his initials 'A.P.', which formed part of its design, could be taken to signify 'A Protestant', 'A Papist' or 'A Puritan' (it is now in the church of St. Peter on Castle St). In the Civil War, Peterhouse plumped firmly for the King and paid dearly for its High Church and Royalist sympathies. Ever since it has remained, especially by Cambridge standards, notably conservative in outlook. It is also the smallest of the older Cambridge colleges.

Peterhouse is immediately to the south of Little St. Mary's. The college is entered from Trumpington St through the open-ended **First Court**. Immediately left of the 18C entrance gate, above the Porter's Lodge, is the brick-built **Perne Library** (adm. by written arrangement only), in which is housed the splendid collection of books, 'the worthiest in all England', bequeathed by Dr Perne. It was built in 1590–95, and lengthened in 1633; some of the fittings of 1641–48 survive. The restrained Classical **Burrough's Building**, on the opposite (right-hand) side of the court, was built in 1738–42 to the designs of Sir James Burrough, Master of Caius. On its top floor the poet Gray had rooms in 1742–56, and during this time he wrote his *Elegy in a Country Churchyard*; he had a morbid dread of fire, and the iron bar for his fire-escape can still be seen from the street, overlooking Little St. Mary's churchyard. Heartier members of the college made him the butt of practical jokes, and it was their raising of a false fire-alarm that eventually precipitated his departure to Pembroke. The story that he descended into a tub of water is, alas, fictional.

In the centre of the court is the **Chapel**, built in 1628–34 during the Mastership of Matthew Wren, who later gave Pembroke College its chapel. It is a fascinating mixture of Gothic and Renaissance architecture, the former predominating (note the blind arcade on the west or entrance side, with flattened

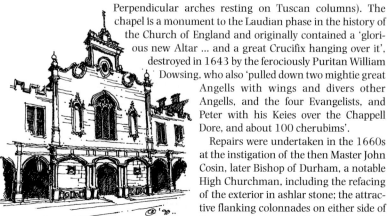

Perpendicular arches resting on Tuscan columns). The chapel is a monument to the Laudian phase in the history of the Church of England and originally contained a 'glorious new Altar ... and a great Crucifix hanging over it', destroyed in 1643 by the ferociously Puritan William Dowsing, who also 'pulled down two mightie great Angells with wings and divers other Angells, and the four Evangelists, and Peter with his Keies over the Chappell Dore, and about 100 cherubims'.

Repairs were undertaken in the 1660s at the instigation of the then Master John Cosin, later Bishop of Durham, a notable High Churchman, including the refacing of the exterior in ashlar stone; the attractive flanking colonnades on either side of the west end were rebuilt and Classicised by Robert Grumbold in 1709–11. The

Peterhouse Chapel

original stalls of 1628–34 survive, as does the east window of 1639, probably by Bernard van Linge, with a Crucifixion scene, but the other windows are filled with glass of 1855–58 from the Royal School of Glass Painting at Munich which casts a pietistic gloom over the interior. Over the altar is an early-16C German Pietà of wood, given in 1941 by the economic historian Michael Postan in memory of his first wife and fellow-historian Eileen Power.

The buildings of **Old Court** are for the most part much older than they appear, the 13C and 15C walls having been faced with ashlar on the inner side to Burrough's designs in 1754; the original medieval rubble-stone walling of the north range can still be seen from Little St. Mary's churchyard, and the late-medieval interiors of the rooms on B,C and D staircases survive behind the Classical façade to the Court. On the south side (left) is the late 13C **Hall**, virtually rebuilt by George Gilbert Scott the younger in 1870 and decorated by William Morris, who also designed the daisy-patterned tiles of the fireplace, first inserted in 1501. The fan-vaulted oriel window was designed by Scott, and the stained-glass windows both there and elsewhere were made by the William Morris firm, mostly from drawings by Ford Madox Brown (two are by Burne-Jones); they commemorate benefactors and distinguished members of the college, as do eighteen small painted portraits of the 16C and 17C, originally in the Combination Room but now on the wood panelling behind the high table and on the screen. On the right side of the high table a doorway, probably 16C, once led to a spiral stairway connecting with the Master's apartments.

A passage through the pedimented west range of Old Court leads to the grey brick Tudor-Gothic **Gisborne Court** (William Brookes, 1825–26); beyond is the flat-roofed **Fen Court** (H.C. Hughes & Peter Bicknell, 1939), one of the first intrusions of the Modern Movement into Cambridge collegiate architecture. The basement was designed as an air-raid shelter. To the south, a path leads through iron gates into the **Deer Park**, or **Grove**, once the grounds of the ancient Friary of the Penance of Jesus (Friars of the Sack), acquired by the college in 1307; the deer were banished in the 1930s. It is bounded to the east (left) by the Fitzwilliam Museum, and at the far end, in the Scholars' Garden, is the **William Stone**

Building, an eight-storey brick-faced tower by Leslie Martin and Colin St. John Wilson (1963–64), funded by and named after an old member of the college who died in 1958 aged 101.

Famous members

Sir John Paston of the Paston Letters, 1442–79 (also Trinity Hall)

Thomas Campion, poet and musician, 1567–1620

Richard Crashaw, poet, 1613–49 (also Pembroke)

Thomas Gray, poet, 1716–71 (also Pembroke)

Henry Cavendish, scientist, after whom the Cavendish Laboratory is named, 1733–1810

Charles Babbage, pioneer of computing, 1792–1871

William Kelvin, mathematician and physicist, 1824–1907

Frank Whittle, inventor of the jet engine, 1907–96

Sir John Kendrew, molecular biologist, 1907–97

James Mason, film star, 1909–84

Michael Portillo, politician, b. 1953

Sam Mendes, film director, b. 1965

Michael Howard, leader of the Conservative party (2004), b. 1941

The handsome brick house opposite the entrance to Peterhouse was built in 1702 by Charles Beaumont, a Fellow of Peterhouse, and became the **Master's Lodge** when he died in 1727. The gently curving stretch of Trumpington St to the south, facing the Fitzwilliam Museum, contains one of the best groups of houses in Cambridge. Some are timber-framed and plastered, others built of brick with Classically-inspired elevations, notably **Fitzwilliam House** (1727), the first home of Fitzwilliam College (see Walk 5); it now belongs, like much of the surrounding property, to Peterhouse.

Fitzwilliam Museum

Plan 4, C; open Tues–Sat 10.00–17.00, Sun 12.00–17.00, closed Mon (except BH Mon) 24, 25, 26, 31 Dec, 1 Jan, Good Fri, ☎ 01223 332900, ▨ www. fitzmuseum.cam.ac.uk.

George Basevi's monumental Roman **façade**, possibly inspired by the Capitolium at Brescia in northern Italy, provides a majestic foretaste of the wealth of antiquities and works of art inside the museum, one of the finest in England. At the centre is a massive Corinthian portico, deliberately placed at first-floor level to make the building appear more impressive from the narrow street, and in the pediment are carved figures of the Nine Muses from a design by C.L. Eastlake. The entrance leads directly into the **Staircase Hall**, sumptuously decorated in the richest High Victorian taste by E.M. Barry and lit from above by lunette windows and by Cockerell's glazed dome; on either side marble staircases rise to the Upper Galleries, with stairs under the galleries descending to the Lower Galleries.

Lower Galleries

The Lower Galleries are devoted to the Greek, Roman, Cypriot, Egyptian and Oriental collections, together with European decorative art. At the bottom of the stairs is the **Western Asiatic Gallery**, with Mesopotamian, Syrian, South

Arabian, Phoenician and Gandharan objects including ivories (9C–5C BC) and, on the stairs, the monumental figure of Ashurnasirpal II, King of Assyria (883–859 BC). In the **Egyptian Rooms** (right) are exhibits from the pre-Dynastic to the Ptolemaic periods; especially striking are the sarcophagus lid of Ramasses III, King of Egypt 1184–1153 BC, and several decorated mummy cases and sarcophagi of the first millennium BC.

The **Greek and Roman Room** contains statuary, grave reliefs, seals and vases, both black- and red-figure, some of them of outstanding quality (e.g., a black-figure vase of five satyrs dancing in a Dionysian frenzy, 6C BC). Especially noteworthy are the Pashley sarcophagus (2C AD), perhaps the finest Roman sarcophagus in England, showing the triumphal return of Bacchus from India; a child's sarcophagus (early 2C AD); and the monumental caryatid from Eleusis (1C BC). The refurbished **Leventis Gallery** (left) comprises a comprehensive display of ancient Cypriot art from the 3rd millennium BC to the 5C AD. Also refurbished are the two **Lower Roman Galleries**, presenting sculpture, textiles and small-scale antiquities from the eastern and western areas of the Roman Empire. The remainder of the ground floor of Basevi's building is occupied by the **Founder's Library** (adm. only by special appointment).

In the **Lower Marlay Gallery** the emphasis shifts from antiquities to the decorative arts, with excellent collections of Japanese and 18C European porcelain (Chelsea, Bow, Meissen, Sèvres, etc.), and of silver. At the far end is a marble figure of *Glory* by Giovanni Baratta (1715), made in Florence for the 1st Duke of Marlborough and for many years kept in the Senate House. The **Glaisher Gallery** is devoted mainly to **European pottery** from the 13C to the 20C, and includes a display of works by Morris & Co., and other Arts and Crafts designers.

In the first of the **Oriental Rooms** are displayed Chinese lacquer, bronzes, jade

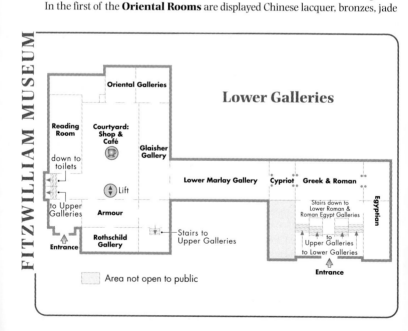

The story of the Fitzwilliam Museum

The museum was founded in 1816 by the bequest of the 7th Viscount Fitzwilliam, an old member of Trinity Hall, who left his priceless collection of MSS, pictures and books to the University, along with £100,000 for a building in which to house it. A narrow strip of land was purchased from Peterhouse and the museum was finally begun in 1837, to the designs of George Basevi, a pupil of Sir John Soane. He fell to his death from scaffolding in Ely Cathedral in 1845, three years before the official opening and the design of the unfinished Entrance Hall was modified by C.R. Cockerell and again by E.M. Barry in 1871–75.

Since then the collection has grown greatly through gifts, bequests and purchases, and the first major extension, the Marlay Galleries, was opened in 1924, followed in 1931–36 by the building of the Courtauld and Henderson Galleries, all of them designed by the firm of Smith & Brewer in a style which admirably complements the original building. Further extensions designed by David Roberts were built in 1966 and 1975.

A major rebuilding of the southern part of the Museum was completed in 2004 to the designs of John Miller & Partners, and has created a new glazed courtyard incorporating a shop, café, education rooms and temporary exhibition gallery.

One of the oldest and finest public art museums in Britain, the collection is remarkably comprehensive, with major European and Asian works of all epochs displayed with impeccable taste in spacious galleries which, appropriately enough, have something of the atmosphere of a great nobleman's town house in its palmiest days.

and ceramics. Next comes the **Gompertz Gallery of Korean Art**, opened in 1990 and mainly displaying ceramics. Among the exhibits in the **Near Eastern Gallery**, reached from the Glaisher Gallery, are a lustre-painted hawk from Iran (late 12C) and the 14C glass lamp cover of Emir Shaikhu from his mosque in Cairo. In an adjacent room is a collection of European and Oriental fans from the Messel-Rosse collection, acquired in 1985; from here stairs lead to the Upper Galleries.

The remaining lower floor galleries are the **Armoury**, with a varied collection of armour and 17C paintings of the long-demolished Tudor palaces of Nonesuch and Richmond (Surrey) on the walls, and the **Rothschild Gallery** of Medieval and Renaissance Art. It contains a diverse collection of manuscripts (including some 15C books of hours), sculpture, ivories, Limoges enamels, coins, and jewellery. There is also a good collection of miniatures, with works by Nicholas Hilliard and Isaac and Peter Oliver.

Upper Galleries

The Upper Floor houses the museum's collections of **European painting, sculpture and furniture**. Neo-classical sculptures from the 19C are displayed on the upper landing of the main staircase, and leading off from here to the right are galleries mainly devoted to the 19C and 20C British and French schools. **Gallery 1** contains important works by Sickert (*The Old Bedford Music Hall, Camden Town Nude* and *The Garden of Love*), Gwen John (*The Convalescent*),

Paul Nash (*November Moon*), Modigliani and Redon; there are also small pictures by Bonnard, Vuillard, Matisse, Braque and Picasso, and bronzes by Rodin and Epstein.

Gallery 2 is mainly devoted to 19C British art, with oil sketches by Constable (*Hove Beach*, *Hampstead Heath*, etc.), and paintings by the Pre-Raphaelites; they include a version of Ford Madox Brown's *The Last of England*, *The Bridesmaid* by Millais, and a portrait by Holman Hunt of his son.

The spacious, richly stuccoed **Gallery 3** contains a portrait of the founder of the museum by Wright of Derby; works by Hans Eworth; Van Dyck (portraits of the 4th Countess of Southampton and of Archbishop Laud); Hogarth (e.g., *Before and After*, and his portraits of George Arnold and his daughter); Richard Wilson (an Italian landscape); Reynolds; Raeburn (a magnificent portrait of William Glendonwyn); Gainsborough (the early *Heneage Lloyd and his Sister*), Stubbs (*Gimcrack on Newmarket Heath*) and Pompeo Batoni (*Lord Northampton*). There is also a superb long-case clock by Thomas Tompion.

In the upstairs gallery is a collection of smaller pictures of different dates and schools, including Blake's characteristically weird *Count Ugolino*.

Gallery 4, to the south of the main staircase, is devoted to the 17C and 18C French School, with works by Vouet (*The Entombment*), Poussin (*Eliezer and Rebecca*), Marguerite Gerard (*The Reader*), Corot, Delacroix (*Odalisque*) and members of the Barbizon School.

The French Impressionists and Post-Impressionists are well represented in **Gallery 5**, with paintings by Boudin, Fantin-Latour, Degas (*Au Café*), Renoir (*Le Coup de Vent* and *La Place Clichy*), Monet (*Le Printemps*, *Etretat*, *Rocks at Port-Coton* and one of his studies of poplars), Seurat (a study for *La Grande Jatte* in Chicago) and Cézanne (*L'Enlèvement*, on loan from King's), Gauguin, Pissarro,

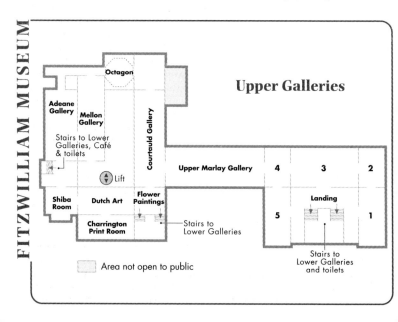

Sisley and Van Gogh; there are also waxes by Degas and bronzes by Rodin.

The **Upper Marlay Gallery** displays early Italian paintings, notably three panels from a 14C polyptych by Simone Martini showing *SS. Geminianus, Michael and Augustine*, Domenico Veneziano, *Annunciation* and *Miracle of St. Zenobius*, and Pinturicchio, *Virgin and Child with St. John the Baptist*; there is also a good collection of Renaissance manuscript illuminations, bronzes, medals and maiolica. A selection from the museum's outstanding collection of Old Master drawings is also displayed in cases.

At the far end are the **Courtauld Galleries**, devoted mainly to the European Old Masters. In the **Italian 16C and 17C Gallery** there are works by many of the leading painters of the Venetian School, including Palma Vecchio (a langorous *Venus and Cupid*), Titian (his magnificently sensuous *Venus and Cupid with a Lute Player* and the dramatic *Tarquin and Lucretia*), Tintoretto (*Adoration of the Shepherds*), Veronese (*Mercury, Herse and Aglauros*), Jacopo Bassano (*The Journey to Calvary*) and Canaletto; other painters represented are Sebastiano del Piombo (*Madonna and Child*—a spectacular recent acquisition), Guercino (*Betrayal of Christ*), Guido Reni (*Ecce Homo*) and Salvator Rosa (a grisly fantasy on *Human Frailty*).

Beyond the Italian Gallery is a **Flemish and Spanish Gallery**, with works by Joos van Cleve (an exquisite *Madonna and Child*), Van Dyck and Murillo (*St. John the Baptist with Saints*), and oil sketches by Rubens. The **Octagon** houses changing exhibitions, and beyond the Octagon is the **Adeane Gallery**, in which the arts of the later 20C are normally displayed, including ceramics and glass. Notable among the paintings and sculpture are abstract works by European and North American artists. The new Mellon Gallery for temporary exhibitions adjacent to the Adeane Gallery opened in 2004.

The remaining rooms can be reached from either the Italian or Adeane Galleries. At the east end of the Italian Gallery (left) is a room devoted to furniture, silver and Dutch and Flemish flower paintings from the **Fairhaven Collection** (see Anglesey Abbey, p 280), and from here a staircase leads down to the Lower Galleries. In the **Dutch Room** are beautiful landscapes by Cuyp, Ruisdael, Hobbema and Van Goyen, genre scenes by Gerard Dou and others, and a lively male portrait by Frans Hals (the portrait long believed to be by Rembrandt is now doubted as autograph). The adjacent **Charrington Print Room** and **Shiba Room** house changing displays from the museum's prints and drawings collection, one of the finest in England, with strong showings of Dürer, Rembrandt, William Blake, J.M.W. Turner and much else, including Japanese prints and drawings.

Opposite the Fitzwilliam Museum are the ponderous buildings of the old Addenbrooke's Hospital, founded with a bequest from John Addenbrooke (d. 1719), a Fellow of St. Catharine's. The hospital was opened in 1766 and was greatly expanded by Matthew Digby Wyatt in 1863. It closed in the early 1980s (New Addenbrooke's Hospital is in Hills Rd, on the outskirts of Cambridge). The old hospital has been converted in recent years into the **Judge Institute for Management Studies** (architect John Outram) opened in 1994; inside (no adm.) there is a vast, almost Piranesian, top-lit atrium crossed by staircases and walkways. Outram's highly individual post-modernist manner can also be experienced in the profuse and colourful rear elevation, visible by walking down

Fitzwilliam St and turning right into Tennis Court Lane. Also in Tennis Court Lane are the more sober recent buildings of the university's **Department of Biochemistry** (RH Partnership 1997). **Fitzwilliam Street** has changed little since it was laid out with plain but pleasing brick houses in 1821–22; no. 22 was occupied by Charles Darwin from 1836–37.

At the junction of Trumpington St and Lensfield Rd is the fountain of **Hobson's Conduit**, moved here in 1856 from its original site on Market Hill, where it had been dispensing fresh water since its construction in 1614; with its strapwork cresting and ogee-shaped dome it is an engaging piece of Jacobean whimsy. It is named after Thomas Hobson (d. 1631), landlord of the George Inn and the 'University carrier', on whose death Milton wrote two semi-humorous poems; he is also immortalised by the expression 'Hobson's choice', from his insistence that clients hiring his horses should take the one that had been longest in the stable and not select their own mount. Hobson was one of the promoters of the Cambridge New River, or Hobson's Brook, which brought water into the town from springs about three miles south of here; its water still flows along the roadside channels of Trumpington St and the river itself can be seen running along the east side of **Trumpington Road**, its southern continuation.

On the west side of Trumpington Rd is the Leys School, founded for Methodist boys in 1875, and to the east, in Bateman St, in the area called Newtown, are the attractive neo-Tudor buildings of the former **Cheshunt Theological College** (Morley Horder, 1913–15), now occupied by several institutions. Opposite is the main entrance to the University's **Botanic Garden** (open daily, exc. 24 Dec–2 Jan, 10.00–16.00 winter, 10.00–16.00 summer: glasshouses open 10.00–15.45, ☎ 01223 336265, ✉ www.botanic.cam.ac.uk). Cambridge's first Botanic Garden was founded in 1762 on the much smaller New Museums site to the north (see p 2449). But the present Garden was founded in 1846 by John Henslow, Charles Darwin's tutor, on a 40-acre site acquired by the University in 1831. It retains much of its original layout, including a landscaped lake, made out of a gravel pit, near the main entrance, and a formal avenue leading from the original entrance in Trumpington Rd to a fountain. The first greenhouses were built in 1880–89 and house tropical plants; the rock garden, next to the lake, dates from 1945–58. The collection of plants and trees contains 10,000 species, and is of international importance. Near the fountain is a visitor centre, shop and refreshment room, the latter recommended by habitués.

3 ~ SOUTHEAST FROM MAGDALENE BRIDGE

This walk starts at Magdalene College, next to the oldest and most important of the bridges over the River Cam. It then proceeds, with digressions, along the ancient Roman road road to Colchester which pre-dates Cambridge and which now forms one of the two main routes through the city.

Magdalene College

Plan 1, F/2, E; open daily 09.00–18.30 exc. mid Apr–mid-June, ☎ 01223 332100, ✉ www.magd.cam.ac.uk.

History

Magdalene College (pronounced 'Maudlin') traces its origins back to 1428, when the Benedictine abbey of Crowland (Lincs) founded a hostel here where its monks could live while studying at the university. The Crowland monks were later joined by others from the nearby Benedictine houses of Ely, Ramsey and Walden, and in time the establishment attracted financial help from the 2nd and 3rd Dukes of Buckingham, acquiring the name Buckingham College during the 1480s. As a monastic college, it was dissolved by Henry VIII but was almost immediately refounded in 1542 by the Lord Chancellor Thomas Audley, an important courtier who had acquired the site of Walden Abbey (see p 287). He supplied the college's new name, its motto 'Garde ta Foy' ('Keep Faith', or less reverently, 'Watch out for your liver'), and also the proviso that its Master should be appointed in perpetuity by his heirs and successors. The spelling of Magdalene with a final 'e' distinguishes it from Magdalen College, Oxford; this usage dates from 1856, and the name was previously spelt both ways.

Magdalene has an interesting link with the United States. In the mid-17C, when it was something of a Puritan enclave, a number of its members settled in New England, where one of them, Henry Dunster, became the first President of Harvard University. The post of Master at Harvard had been intended for the Moravian educationist Comenius, though he never took up the appointment. Dunster, however, always regarded himself as Comenius's deputy and therefore used the title 'President' (usually at Cambridge, though not at Queens' College, the title of the Vice-Master).

The buildings were erected piecemeal from the 1470s to the 1580s, and in the 17C a new block was built on a detached site to the east in which the famous library of one of the college's most celebrated alumni, Samuel Pepys, is now housed. Following its completion there was no major building until the 20C, when the college greatly expanded on the opposite side of Magdalene St. One of the most influential Masters (1915–25) was A.C. Benson, a prolific author who penned the words of *Land of Hope and Glory*. He lavished his wealth on the college, being responsible for many of the 20C additions and alterations.

A gateway of c 1585 leads into the brick-built, domestic-looking **First Court**, which until the 17C comprised the whole college. The north (left) and south (right) sides survive from the old 15C Buckingham College; over the staircase doorways are modern versions of the coats of arms which indicated to which abbey the 'house' belonged (see Worcester College, Oxford), and on the first floor of staircase E (no adm.) there is a room which retains its original arrangement—once the norm in both Cambridge and Oxford—of a communal bedroom with three study cubicles leading off from it. The **Chapel** (north side), was built in 1470–72, but has undergone many changes; it was Classicised in the 18C, it was given a Gothic facelift in 1847–51, with good woodwork and stained glass, including an east window by A.W.N. Pugin.

In the east range, opposite the entrance gate, is the **Hall**, built in 1519 but completely remodelled internally in 1714, when a plaster ceiling was introduced, a huge painted Royal Arms (Queen Anne's) installed over the high table, and an unusual double staircase built on the inner side of the screen; it leads to a gallery and to the Combination Room, and includes older decorative woodwork on the lower level. There is a good deal of heraldic glass, mostly of the 19C and 20C, much of it selected and paid for by Benson. The hall is still lit only by candles.

At the far side of Second Court, reached through the screens passage, is the **Pepys Building**. Originally known as the New Building, it was begun some time after 1640 but was not finished until c 1700. The elevations are stylistically conservative, with Classicism making only a token appearance in the round-arched loggia and frontispiece of the stone-faced west or entrance front, dating from 1679 and in the design of which the scientist Robert Hooke, a friend of Sir Christopher Wren, may have been involved.

In his will of 1703 Samuel Pepys, an old member, bequeathed his Library to the college and it was finally installed here in 1724. The books were to be arranged 'according to heighth' in their specially made glass-fronted cases, no new books were to be added, and a periodical inspection was to be made by Trinity College (the other possible legatee). As well as superbly bound books, the **Pepys Library** (open Mon–Sat in full term 14.30–15.30, also beginning of Easter term to end Aug 11.30–12.30) contains the original MS of Pepys's famous diary, written in his own shorthand, and also an account of Charles II's escape after the battle of Worcester as dictated to Pepys by the King himself. Also on show are a MS translation of Ovid's *Metamorphoses* made for William Caxton, several incunabula and musical MSS, and reminders of Pepys's days as Secretary of the Navy Board, including the only known contemporary representation of Henry VIII's ship the *Mary Rose*.

South of the Library, facing the river, is Bright's Building (Sir Aston Webb, 1909), and to the north is the **Fellows' Garden** (open 14.00–16.00).

On the opposite side of Magdalene St is a collection of old timber houses cleverly adapted for college use by the architect David Roberts, a fellow of the college, in the 1950s. Together with some buildings of Roberts's own design, they form part of the attractively varied **Benson Court**, the south side of which is occupied by the handsome neo-Georgian Lutyens Building (Sir Edwin Lutyens, 1930–32)—the only Cambridge building by this architect. To the northwest is **Mallory Court**, largely made up of old timber buildings and a former brewery, and beyond is the red-brick **Buckingham Court** (David Roberts, 1970).

Famous members

Henry Dunster, first President of Harvard, d. 1659

Samuel Pepys, diarist, 1633–1703

Samuel Marsden, first missionary to New Zealand, 1765–1838

Charles Kingsley, novelist, 1819–75

Charles Stewart Parnell, Irish Nationalist, 1846–91

John Douglas, 8th Marquess of Queensberry, patron of boxing and persecutor of Oscar Wilde (who went to Magdalen College, Oxford), 1844–1900

G.L. Mallory, mountaineer, 1886–1924

Lord Tedder, Marshal of the Royal Air Force and Deputy Supreme Commander Allied Forces, Second World War, 1890–1967

I.A. Richards, literary critic, 1893–1979

P.M.S. Blackett, physicist, Nobel prizewinner, 1897–1974
Michael Ramsey, Archbishop of Canterbury, 1904–88

Sir Michael Redgrave, actor, 1908 85
John Simpson, broadcaster and journalist, b. 1944

Magdalene Bridge is a cast iron structure of 1823. The Quayside development on the far side of the river (Nicholas Ray Associates 1989) encloses a lively court-yard with shops, cafés, etc; punts can be hired here in season. On the left side of Bridge St is a row of attractive timber houses interrupted by the much-restored 13C **St. Clement's church** (usually locked), with its tower of 1821; to the right is the red-brick Gothic Master's Lodge of St. John's College (Gilbert Scott 1863), with Scott's chapel and its tower rising up behind (see p 214). At the end of Bridge St the road forks, with the left-hand fork—now Sidney St—following the line of the old Roman and the right fork—now Trinity St—following the medieval route parallel to the river (See Walk 1).

At the fork is the the Church of the Holy Sepulchre, usually known as the **Round Church** (plan 2, F). Dating from c 1125–50, it was built by the short-lived Fraternity of the Holy Sepulchre and is one of only five medieval churches in England with circular naves. It was much altered in the 15C, when the square-ended chancel was rebuilt and there was a sweeping restoration in 1841 after part of the nave collapsed. The restoration work was entrusted to Anthony Salvin, under the direction of the Cambridge Camden Society, and the present convincingly Romanesque appearance of the nave, including the conical roof, is due in large part to its scholarly efforts. The central

Church of St. Sepulchre, or the Round Church

rotunda is enclosed by two tiers of massive cylindrical columns and is free of pews, allowing the visitor to enjoy the sturdy proportions and the vistas through to the rest of the church. It is surrounded by a vaulted aisle, lit by small windows filled with good stained glass of the 1840s (by Thomas Willement and others). The 15C angel roof still survives in the chancel.

For many years a major focal point of Cambridge's vigorous Evangelical churchmanship, the church is now part of the Cambridge Christian Centre, most services being held in the larger St. Andrew's church (below). Most of the chancel is now occupied by an **exhibition** on the history of the city and university of Cambridge entitled 'Saints and Scholars'.

Lurking inconspicuously behind the Round Church in Round Church St is the **Cambridge Union Society**. Founded as a debating club in 1815, it was suppressed two years later for debating politics, but was restarted in 1821 on condition that no discussions took place on the politics of the last 20 years. It moved in 1866 from the Red Lion Inn in Petty Cury to its hard red-brick Gothic building

(Alfred Waterhouse at his most strident) in 1866. Debates are held regularly in term time.

From here Park St leads to **Jesus Lane**. At the corner is Little Trinity (no. 16), a beautiful brick house of c 1725, and a short distance along Jesus Lane to the left, past the dull modernist façade of Wesley House, a theological college, is the entrance to Jesus College.

Jesus College

Plan 2, F; open daily 09.00–17.30 exc. Apr–June and late Dec, ☎ 01223 339339, ✉ www.jesus.cam.ac.uk.

History

Jesus College was founded in 1496 by John Alcock, Bishop of Ely and former tutor of the murdered Edward V. It occupies the site of a nunnery established c 1133–38 and dedicated to St. Mary and St. Radegund, founder of a religious community at Poitiers in France in the 6C. The nunnery was suppressed by Alcock—by which time it had dwindled to two nuns, one of them of ill-repute—but he retained and adapted the nuns' church and many of the conventual buildings, and these form the core of the college, which was somewhat enlarged in the early 16C and again in the 17C. Set slightly apart from the crowded centre of Cambridge, Jesus College was fortunate to take over a spacious site from the nuns and in 1615 King James I said that, if he were given the choice, he would worship at King's College and dine at Trinity, but would study and sleep at Jesus. Known in the 17C and 18C as a nursery of clergymen, the college did not expand significantly until the 19C and 20C, when many new buildings were erected, but even today it remains unusually spacious and secluded.

The college is approached by a passage known as 'The Chimney', with high brick walls on either side. At the end is the three-storeyed brick **Gate Tower**, built by Bishop Alcock c 1500, with his rebus of a cock perched on a globe over the central niche. It leads into **First Court**, which is open on the west side; a bronze horse, by Barry Flanagan, stands in the middle of the lawn. Until 1570 the early 16C range to the left of the gate housed a grammar school attached to the college; to the right is the Master's Lodge. Both parts of the range were heightened in 1718–20. The north range, opposite the gate, was built in 1638–41, but was deliberately designed to harmonise with the surprisingly plain buildings on the east (right) side, built by Alcock in front of the former nuns' cloister.

The entrance to Jesus College

A carved ogee-headed doorway in the east range, again surmounted by a cock, leads into **Cloister Court**. This was the heart of the old nunnery, to which Alcock added the third storey, the timber ceiling of the cloisters and his ubiquitous rebus. On the north side is the **Hall** (no adm.), the first in Cambridge to be placed upstairs. It was created by Alcock out of the nuns' refectory, and has a splendid

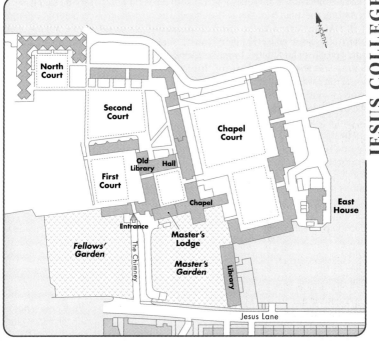

hammerbeam roof and a large and richly carved early 16C oriel window lighting the dais, filled with heraldic glass by the William Morris firm (1875). Outside the Hall, steps lead up to the **Old Library** (no adm.), which retains the original wooden ceiling of Alcock's time and also bookcases of c 1670.

Beyond the Hall entrance, in the east cloister walk, is a row of beautifully carved Gothic **arches** of c 1230 which mark what was originally the entrance to the nuns' Chapter House. Concealed for 350 years by Alcock's alterations, they were rediscovered during restorations in the summer vacation of 1840; only one undergraduate, Osmond Fisher, and one don were in residence, but orders were given for the arches to be plastered in, and it was not until 1893, when Fisher was an honorary fellow, that they were again revealed.

The nuns'church, on the south side of Cloister Court, survives as the **Chapel** of the college. It is a cruciform building with a central tower, begun c 1150 but extensively remodelled in the 13C, since when it has undergone many changes. Bishop Alcock removed the nave aisles and south transept chapels and converted the west end of the nave into rooms and part of the Master's Lodge; he also installed new Perpendicular windows and furnishings. In the late 18C the interior was Classicised, but of this phase virtually nothing remains, for in 1845, under the influence of the Cambridge Camden Society, a complete restoration began with the object of returning the chapel to its 13C state; the original architect was Anthony Salvin, but he was superseded in 1846 by A.W.N. Pugin. A second phase of restoration began in 1864, this time under the supervision of G.F. Bodley, with windows and fittings by the William Morris firm. As a result of these two restorations the chapel is now a superb repository of Victorian church art.

Among the main beauties of the chapel are the delicate and colourful ceilings by the Morris firm and the series of **stained-glass windows** by Burne-Jones (there is also one by Ford Madox Brown). Some of the finest windows are in the nave (prophets and scenes from the Old Testament); others are in the transepts (saints and angels); and some of Burne-Jones's cartoons are displayed on the south nave wall. An altar frontal by Pugin is preserved in a glass case in the south transept, and below it is the tomb-slab of a 13C benefactor of St. Radegund's; a slab to the left commemorates Thomas Cranmer, the first Anglican Archbishop of Canterbury.

The richly carved wooden screen, on the east side of the crossing, was designed by Pugin in 1846–49, as were the floor tiles, stalls and brass lectern; the stalls incorporate some carved figures and bench-ends from Alcock's time, sold to Landbeach church (about 5 miles northeast of Cambridge) during the 18C alterations. Pugin also replaced Alcock's east window with one made up of tall lancets in the Early English style of the original monastic church, matching the genuinely 13C windows on the side walls, and filled the windows with glass (by Hardman) inspired by the windows of Chartres Cathedral, to which he made a special visit; while there he purchased a sackful of fragments from a window under repair, and incorporated these with his own work. Some 13C columns (part of the north aisle) can be seen in the south cloister wall, exposed when the War Memorials were installed.

Most of the extensions to the college have been consistent in style with the original early Tudor buildings. **Second Court**, to the north of First Court, has a north range by Waterhouse (1869–70), with a characteristically assertive gate tower. Further west is **North Court**, a jagged, modernistic composition by David Roberts (1963–66), ingeniously planned though somewhat harsh and angular in appearance. To the east of Cloister Court is the spacious **Chapel Court** (east range by Carpenter & Ingelow, 1884–85; southeast and south ranges by Morley Horder, 1931), with a coat of arms by Eric Gill over the south gateway. Approached by a gateway in the wall to the south of the chapel is the new **Library Court** (1996–2000) (architects Eldred Evans and David Shalev, best known for their Tate Gallery at St. Ives, Cornwall), comprising library and computer centre and a range of student rooms.

The **grounds** of Jesus are open and extensive and contain several works of contemporary sculpture, enhanced by loans during the summer months. Sadly, the pleached limes which were such an attractive feature of Chapel Court were cut down in 1979, but the college still possesses a mulberry tree planted for James I and the great plane trees, from the Vale of Tempe in Greece, planted in 1801 in the Master's and the Fellows' gardens. Round the latter are massed crocuses, and in spring the gate into Jesus Lane is left ajar so that passers-by can look in.

Famous members

Thomas Cranmer, Archbishop of Canterbury, compiler of the English prayer book, 1489–1556 (he lost his fellowship after marrying the niece of the landlord of the Dolphin Inn, but regained it when she died)

Fulke Greville, poet and politician, 1554–1628

John Eliot, 'apostle of the

American Indians', 1604 90
John Flamsteed, first
Astronomer Royal, 1646–1719
Laurence Sterne, novelist,
1713–68
Thomas Malthus, economist,
1766–1834
S.T. Coleridge, poet, 1772–1834
A. Quiller-Couch, man of
letters, 1863–1944 (also Trinity
College, Oxford)
Alistair Cooke, broadcaster,
b. 1908
Raymond Williams, writer and
critic, 1921–88
David Hare, playwright, b. 1947
Nick Hornby, novelist, b. 1957

Opposite Jesus College in Jesus Lane is **All Saints church** (1863–71), one of the most important buildings of the Gothic Revival in England (Churches Conservation Trust: if closed, see notice outside for whereabouts of key). It was designed by G.F. Bodley, and marked a return to the English 'Middle Pointed' (Decorated) style after the supposed excesses of the 'High Victorian' period. The spire provides a memorable landmark on Jesus Lane and the interior has painted decoration by William Morris and C.E. Kempe, recently restored, an east window by Morris, Burne-Jones and Ford Madox Brown, and other windows by Kempe. Next door are the attractive red-brick neo-Tudor buildings of **Westcott House**, a Church of England theological college (Grayson & Ould, Temple Moore, Morley Horder, 1899, etc.) arranged around a cloistered courtyard. From here Jesus Lane leads west to Sidney St. On the left is the boundary wall of Sidney Sussex College, with an impressive Classical archway (Sir James Burrough, 1762), moved from the main entrance in Sidney St in 1831, and a little further along on the right is the miniature Ionic portico of the **Pitt Club** (Matthew Digby Wyatt, c 1865)—now well-restored as a *Pizza Express* restaurant—with the unmistakeable profile of the Younger Pitt in a roundel in the pediment.

A left turn from Jesus Lane into Sidney St leads to the entrance of Sidney Sussex College.

Sidney Sussex College

Plan 2, E; open daily 09.30–17.30 exc. mid-Apr–mid-June, ☎ 01223 338800, ✉ www.sid.cam.ac.uk.

History

The college was founded in 1594 under the will of Lady Frances Sidney, wife of the Earl of Sussex and aunt of the poet and soldier Sir Philip Sidney; the head of the Sidney family (of Penshurst, Kent) is still the Visitor, and the family crest, a porcupine, appears in various places on the buildings. The buildings occupy the site of the Greyfriars' (Franciscan) convent, dissolved in 1538; the church was demolished soon after the Dissolution, the materials being used for Trinity College chapel, and by the end of the 16C the remaining buildings had almost vanished too.

The purpose of the new foundation was to ensure the training of a 'godly preaching ministry' for the Church of England, and its statutes were closely modelled on those of the recently-founded Emmanuel College. During the religious controversies of the 17C the college was strongly Puritan but, despite the fact that Oliver Cromwell was an old member (he was only at the college for a year), it remained loyal to the King during the Civil War. The buildings, dating from the late 16C and early 17C, were transformed externally in the style of the Gothic Revival, starting in 1821, and in the late 19C and 20C there were major extensions, latterly stretching over Sussex St to the south.

The present external appearance of Sidney Sussex is almost entirely due to the restoration and alterations carried out in the Tudor-Gothic style by Sir Jeffry Wyatville (best known for his remodelling of Windsor Castle) in 1821–32. The college was made up of two parallel open-ended courts facing Sidney St; Wyatville covered the old brick buildings with Roman cement, added battlements and stepped gables, and created a new entrance on the street side of the central block separating the two courts.

Hall Court, to the left, stands on the site of the conventual buildings and was originally constructed by Ralph Symonds in 1598. Wyatville's loggia on the east side marks the entrance to the **Hall** (no adm.), completely remodelled inside in 1747–50, possibly to the designs of Sir James Burrough. A plaster ceiling masks the old hammerbeam roof, and the panelled walls have the usual display of portraits of college worthies, along with a superb full-length portrait of the Foundress and one of three of Oliver Cromwell owned by the college; this may be the one that he instructed should be a true likeness, 'warts and all'.

To the south (right) of Hall Court, beyond the Porter's Lodge, is **Chapel Court**, also transmogrified by Wyatville. The south range was originally built in 1628, and to the east (left) is the **Chapel**, which stands on the probable site of the warden's lodging of the friary. It runs north and south instead of the usual east and west—possibly a deliberate Puritan disregard of tradition. The simple chapel of 1600 was replaced in the late 18C by one designed by James Essex, and this in turn was extended and totally remodelled internally in 1912–23 (architect T.H. Lyon), making it in effect the third chapel on the site.

In the antechapel windows are fragments of 13C–14C glass from the medieval church of the Greyfriars, dug up in the college garden in 1959; a tablet records the burial of Oliver Cromwell's head, which after many vicissitudes found a resting place here in 1960. The interior of the main chapel, concealed behind Wyatville's Regency Gothic exterior, is an unexpected example of Edwardian Baroque architecture and craftsmanship, with excellent woodwork, plasterwork and marble floors. Over the bronze and marble altar hangs a fine painting of the *Holy Family* by the Venetian artist Giovanni Battista Pittoni, acquired in 1783.

A passage in the left-hand corner of Hall Court leads to **Cloister Court**, overlooked by ornate brick buildings by J.L. Pearson in a neo-Jacobean style (1891). From here a path gives access to to the beautiful **gardens**, landscaped in the late 18C and originally bounded to the east by the King's Ditch. To the south looms **Blundell Court** (Howell, Killick, Partridge and Amis, 1969), in purple brick and dark grey aggregate, also visible from King St; nearby is the friendlier neo-Georgian **Garden Court** (T.H. Lyon, 1923).

> ### Famous members
> **Oliver Cromwell**, Lord Protector, 1599–1658
> **Thomas Fuller**, author of *The*
> *Worthies of England*, 1608–61
> **C.T.R. Wilson**, physicist, Nobel prizewinner, 1869–1959

Facing Sidney Sussex on the west side of Sidney St is the gloomy façade of Trinity College's Whewells Court (see p 210). Immediately to the south of Sidney Sussex is **Sussex Street**, an attractive red-brick neo-Georgian ensemble of the inter-war period (E.R. Barrow, 1928–39), with student housing above and shops below; the arch over the far end was added in 1991. Further south in Sidney St, at the corner of Market St, is **Holy Trinity church** (plan 2, G), a 14C building remodelled and extended in the 15C. Historically it is linked with the Evangelical movement, a leading protagonist of which, Charles Simeon, was vicar from 1782 until his death in 1836; he is buried in the church, and the gallery in the south transept was erected during his incumbency.

Here academe gives way to commerce, with the chain stores and crowds of shoppers found in any English town above a certain size. A right turn along Market St leads to **Market Hill**, where trading has been uninterruptedly carried on since long before the first scholar ever set foot in Cambridge. Though it does in fact slope slightly down from west to east, the word 'hill' is used here to denote the open space rather than a hill as normally understood. The open space is filled with market stalls, and the university church of Great St. Mary (see p 193) rises up to the west. On the south side is the neo-Georgian **Guildhall** (C. Cowles Voysey, 1936–37), and in Guildhall St, to the east, is a small sculpture (*Talos*) by Michael Ayrton. Behind the Guildhall, in Wheeler St, is the **Tourist Information Centre**, housed in the former city library with its attractive domed interior of the 1890s. Opposite is the crazily-detailed polychromatic **Corn Exchange** (R.R. Rowe, 1874), Cambridge's best example of a 'Ruskinian' building, though Ruskin would no doubt have disowned it had he ever deigned to comment on it. It is now an arts centre.

Petty Cury leads back from Market Hill to Sidney St through an urban landscape transformed for the worse by the 'comprehensive redevelopment' of the 1960s and 1970s. The centrepiece of this scheme was the creation of **Lion Yard**, a large shopping development on the site of the yard of the Red Lion Inn to the south of the street; its existence is recalled by the large red lion on a white pole in the central square gazing down onto the shoppers and visitors to the Public Library. Opposite the junction of Petty Cury and Sidney St is the magnificent **Lloyd's Bank** (A.& P. Waterhouse, 1891), with a riotously ornate interior covered in glazed tiles.

Here Sidney St becomes St. Andrew's St, and just to the south is **St. Andrew's church** (Ambrose Poynter, 1842–43; usually locked), a Perpendicular Gothic preaching house on the site of a medieval church destroyed by fire; it contains monuments to the explorer Captain Cook (d. 1779) and his family, transferred from the previous church on the site.

Opposite the church is the entrance to Christ's College.

Christ's College

Plan 2, G; open term time Mon–Fri o9.30–16.30, Sat–Sun 12.00–16.30; vacation daily 9.30–12.00. Closed May–mid-June, ☎ 01223 334900, ✉ www.christs.cam.ac.uk.

History

The college was originally founded as God's House c 1436 by William Byngham, rector of St. John Zachary church in London. The intention was to provide a supply of trained teachers for schools, and the studies were secular rather than theological. Established near Clare College, which gave it some assistance, it moved to the present site in the 1440s, when the whole area south of Clare was cleared to make way for King's College; a royal charter was granted in 1448. In 1505 it was refounded, as Christ's College, by Lady Margaret Beaufort, mother of Henry VII, a great patron of scholars. The site was a spacious one on the edge of the town, and this has enabled the college to expand over the extensive gardens, part of which (the Fellows' Garden) has nevertheless been retained as one of Cambridge's more attractive enclaves.

The statutes were probably drawn up by Lady Margaret's friend, confessor and adviser John Fisher, the saintly Bishop of Rochester and former Master of Michaelhouse, President of Queens' and Vice-Chancellor of the University (he was executed in 1535 for refusing to recognise Henry VIII as supreme head of the Church). Both Lady Margaret and Fisher were also involved in the foundation of St. John's College and both were deeply interested in the New Learning. Classical studies formed an important part of the academic regime in the early years, and in the early 17C the college tended towards Puritanism (John Milton is one of the most famous of its old members). Like some other colleges in both Cambridge and Oxford, Christ's stagnated in the 18C, but it enjoyed a revival in the late 19C and 20C, the latter reflected in the impressive array of post-Second World War buildings.

The original buildings of 1505–11 still survive, though they were much altered in the 18C, when the brick façades were refaced in Ketton stone. The **Gate Tower**, through which the college is entered from St. Andrew's St, resembles that of St. John's, also founded by Lady Margaret, but the display of her insignia is even richer and more complicated. The Beaufort arms are supported by yales: fabulous creatures similar to antelopes, but with the great asset of being able to move their horns independently (as made clear by the curious angles at which they are set). Around them are the Beaufort portcullis and coronet, the Tudor rose and royal crown, and at the sides the Welsh dragon and greyhound, supporters of the Royal Arms; daisies, forget-me-nots and plentiful rabbits fill in the background. The linenfold-panelled doors are the originals, but have several inches cut off at the bottom to adjust them to the changed street-level.

The oldest buildings are picturesquely grouped around **First Court**, and the north range (left on entering) may incorporate some of the masonry from the late 15C God's House. If so, it is not at all obvious from the outside, because of the refacing by James Essex in 1766; Essex also refaced the rest of the court between 1758 and 1770, replacing the old battlements by plain parapets, inserting sash windows and supplying the doorways with trim Georgian architraves and pediments.

The **Chapel**, entered through the north range, was Classicised internally in 1701–03 and still retains its excellent carved woodwork of that date by John Austin. But some older features remain, including the original early 16C open timber roof (restored by Bodley and Garner in 1899 after being hidden for nearly two centuries), and some 15C and early 16C stained glass on the north side, some of which was probably in the chapel of God's House; the larger figures may represent St. Gregory and Henry VI, the smaller ones Henry VII, Lady Margaret and Edward the Confessor. The magnificent brass lectern also dates from the early 16C, and behind hinged panels on the north and south sides are doorways of the same period formerly leading to a side chapel and to the Master's Lodge; a small oriel window in the south wall allows views into the chapel from the oratory in the Lodge. On the north wall is a very fine monument to two close friends, Sir John Finch and Sir Thomas Baines (Joseph Catterns, 1684), their faces immortalised in oval medallions. An arresting metal sculpture of the *Deposition from the Cross* by Anthony Caro, an old member of the college, has recently (2001) been placed in the ante-chapel immediately facing the entrance.

The **Master's Lodge** is in the east range, with an oriel window over the doorway carrying the same Beaufort emblems as the gatehouse. The **Hall** (no adm.), to the right, was remodelled in 1723 and totally rebuilt by the younger George Gilbert Scott in 1876–79, using some of the older materials, including the roof and screen.

The screens passage, to the right of the hall, leads into **Second Court**. Opposite is the **Fellows' Building** of 1640–45, its balanced symmetrical elevations in Ketton stone reflecting the new taste for Classicism in Cambridge, though there are certain stylistic solecisms which would have offended the purists. The gateway in the centre opens into the **Fellows' Garden** (open termtime 14.00–16.00, vacation 10.30–12.00). At the far end is a mulberry tree (one of several in the grounds) vaguely associated with the poet John Milton. These trees are descendants of some of the 300 planted in 1608 at the request of James I, who wished to encourage silk manufacture; unfortunately the wrong species was chosen and all the silkworms died.

To the right at the far end of the garden is an outdoor **bathing pool** dating from the 18C, its water still supplied by Hobson's Brook; the Classical summer house and the busts of Milton and other luminaries bestow the appropriate note of philosophical contemplation.

To the left of the Fellows' Building is the large, open-ended **Third Court**, with the north range (J.J. Stevenson, 1888–89) flanked by well-proportioned neo-Georgian blocks by Sir Albert Richardson, chosen in preference to designs by Walter Gropius in the 'International Modern' style submitted in the 1930s. But the college atoned for its earlier timidity in 1966–70 by commissioning the modernist architect Denys Lasdun to design **New Court**, behind the Stevenson building; this is a monumentally impressive, though somewhat stark, agglomeration of rooms arranged in terraces, built in concrete and glass (and undergoing extensive repair at the time of writing). A new residential building, designed by the Architects' Design Partnership from Oxford, was erected on an adjacent site fronting onto King St, and was opened in 1994.

Famous members

John Leland, antiquary, 1506–52	**Lord Mountbatten of Burma**,
John Milton, poet, 1608–74, and	last Viceroy of India, 1900–79
his friend Edward King, lamented in	**C.P. Snow**, novelist, 1905–80
Lycidas	**Lord Todd**, scientist, 1907–97
Charles Darwin, scientist,	**J.H. Plumb**, historian, 1911–2000
1809–82	**Anthony Caro**, sculptor, b. 1924
Jan Smuts, South African states-	**Lord Irvine of Lairg**, former Lord
man, 1870–1950	Chancellor, b. 1940

A left turn out of Christ's College leads into the busy St. Andrew's St, from which a dingy passageway on the left gives access to Drummer St **Bus Station**: an unimpressive introduction to the city. Beyond it is **Christ's Pieces**, one of Cambridge's many commons, to the east of which there are several interesting developments of early 19C **artisan housing**, notably in Orchard Terrace and New Square (1834–35). Beyond, on the site of the working-class area formerly known as The Kite, is the **Grafton Centre**, a large modern shopping centre built in 1981–83.

From the Bus Station and Christ's Pieces Emmanuel St leads back to St. Andrew's St. A little to the south of the junction is the entrance to Emmanuel College.

Emmanuel College

Plan 2, H; 4, B; open daily 09.00–18.00, exc. May–mid-June, ☎ 01223 334200, 🖾 www.emma.cam.ac.uk.

History

Known familiarly as 'Emma', the college was founded in 1584 by Sir Walter Mildmay, one of Queen Elizabeth's courtiers and a former member of Christ's College. He was a staunch Puritan and his intention was to train men for a preaching ministry in the church. Questioned about his 'Puritan foundation' by Elizabeth I, whom he served as Chancellor of the Exchequer, Mildmay replied: 'No, Madam, far be it from me to countenance anything contrary to your laws; but I have set an acorn, which, when it becomes an oak, God alone knows what will be the fruit thereof.' Perhaps significantly, his acorn was planted on the site of a Dominican friary, dissolved in 1538, whose chapel, correctly oriented, became the college dining hall, while another building, which ran north and south, became the chapel. This may have been a deliberate demonstration of Puritan disregard for ritual and religious tradition (see Sidney Sussex College).

During the 1630s, when Puritans were in great disfavour under Archbishop Laud's regime, many Emmanuel men sought religious liberty in America; of the first hundred graduates who settled in New England a third were from this college. New Town, Massachusetts, was renamed Cambridge in honour of one of them—the preacher Thomas Shepherd—while another, John Harvard, who graduated in 1632, was the major benefactor of the first university in America, which bears his name. The link between Harvard and Emmanuel is preserved in the Lionel de Jersey Harvard Studentship, awarded each year to a graduate of Harvard to study at Emmanuel, and a graduate of Emmanuel to study at Harvard.

Emmanuel's Puritanism found favour during the Civil War and the Interregnum, when it supplied no fewer than 11 heads of colleges to replace those Masters ejected for their High Church and Royalist sympathies. But with the Restoration and the Mastership of William Sancroft (later Dean of St. Paul's, and then Archbishop of Canterbury), it gradually lost its original character of religious nonconformity and became staunchly Anglican in churchmanship and Tory in politics. The buildings are an interesting collection of collegiate architecture of all dates, and include a chapel designed by Sir Christopher Wren. As in several of the other colleges built away from the town centre, there are also attractive gardens.

The job of converting and adding to the friary buildings was given to Ralph Symonds and was his first major undertaking in Cambridge (see St. John's, Trinity, and Sidney Sussex). Little is now visible of his work, due largely to the activities of the ubiquitous James Essex. The ashlar-faced **entrance** range was designed in a sober Classical style by Essex in 1769–75, and Essex also rebuilt the north range of **Front Court** (left on entering) in 1760–64. It contains the **Hall** (visible through a glazed screen), originally the friary chapel, with its timber roof of 1584 obscured by the handsome Georgian plaster ceiling. The panelling and the wrought-iron gates of the screen also date from the 1760s, but the tables and benches survive from an earlier remodelling in 1694.

In the centre of the east range, opposite the entrance gateway, is the **Chapel**, flanked by lower hipped-roofed buildings, with an arched loggia or cloister at ground-floor level affording glimpses of the garden beyond; above, on either side of the chapel, is a Long Gallery which originally formed part of the Master's Lodge. The promoter of this attractive group of buildings was William Sancroft, Master of the college, Dean of St. Paul's Cathedral and subsequently Archbishop of Canterbury, and the architect was Sir Christopher Wren, who was also working on the design of new St. Paul's Cathedral while building was going on from 1668 to 1677.

The exterior of the Chapel has an engagingly intimate, almost Dutch character, its central feature echoing the west front of Wren's earlier chapel at Pembroke College. The wide, spacious interior retains most of its original woodwork, carved by Cornelius Austin to the designs of Pearce and Oliver of London, as well as one of the finest and most exuberantly detailed plaster ceilings in Cambridge, made by John Grove in 1673. The altarpiece is Jacopo Amigoni's *Return of the Prodigal Son*, presented in 1734, and the 19C stained-glass windows commemorate famous members of the college.

The south range of Front Court (right on entering) is occupied by the **Westmorland Building**, named after the 6th Earl of Westmorland, a descendant of the founder, who largely paid for its construction in 1719–22. It is an impressive if slightly forbidding example of the 'English Baroque' style, more often found in the larger country houses of the period than in Cambridge colleges, and incorporates some of the original brickwork of Symonds's Founders Range in its internal construction.

Running south at right-angles to the east end is the plain but dignified **Old Court** or Brick Building of 1633, with a Dutch gable at the south end; next to it is **South Court** (T. Hancock, 1965–66), in the brutalist idiom of that period, overlooking an attractive garden.

To the east is the **Library**, built as a lecture room to the designs of Leonard Stokes in 1909–10 and extended in 1972–74. It looks out onto the **gardens**, among the most beautiful in Cambridge. They were landscaped in the 18C, and make good use of water brought from Hobson's Brook; the herbaceous borders are especially fine. Near the Great Pond in the Paddock, to the east of the Chapel, is a bronze figure, *The Jester*, by Wendy Taylor, and further east, on Parker St, are the 'Queen Anne' **Hostel building** (W.M. Fawcett, 1886–94) and **Emmanuel House** (J.L. Pearson, 1894).

Returning to Front Court, a passage to the left of the Chapel leads to **New Court**: actually the oldest part of the college, through which it was originally entered. On the eastern side (right) is the **Old Library** (no adm.), originally the college chapel. It became the library when the Wren chapel was built and is now used for concerts and social gatherings. Behind a hinged panel can still be seen the ancient clunch and rubble of the medieval wall, and between the anteroom and main room is the screen of 1588. Further east is the stone-clad **Queen's Building** (Michael Hopkins & Partners, 1996), best seen from Emmanuel St; oval in plan, it has a rounded end to the street and a performance space in the centre.

From the dull neo-Tudor north range of New Court (Arthur Brown, 1824–25) a subway leads under Emmanuel St to **North Court** (also clearly visible from Emmanuel St), an impressive set of buildings of 1910–14 designed by Leonard Stokes in the inventive Edwardian 'free style' which he also employed in the Library.

Famous members

John Harvard, principal benefactor of Harvard University, 1607–38
William Sancroft, Archbishop of Canterbury and one of the 'Seven Bishops' who defied James II, 1617–93
William Temple, diplomat and essayist, to whom the *Letters of Dorothy Osborne* were written, 1628–99
William Law, author of *A Serious Call to a Devout and Holy Life*, 1686–1761
Thomas Young, physicist, Egyptologist and polymath, 1773–1829
Gowland Hopkins, biochemist, discoverer of vitamins, 1861–1947
R.G.W. Norrish, chemist, 1897–1978
Jonathan Swift's fictional **Lemuel Gulliver**, of *Gulliver's Travels* (published 1726) went to 'Emanuel College in Cambridge at Fourteen Years old, where I resided three years, and applied myself close to my Studies'.

Science area

Opposite the entrance to Emmanuel College, Downing St leads west into the heart of the University's Science Area, a motley collection of buildings in which functional considerations have generally triumphed over the dictates of beauty. To the south is the **Downing Site**, built up between 1904 and 1939 on land sold to the university by Downing College. It is dominated by a ponderous brick building in an eclectic style by T.G. Jackson (1904–11) which houses the School of

Earth Sciences and the **Sedgwick Museum of Earth Sciences** (open Mon–Fri 09.00–13.00, 14.00–17.00, Sat 10.00–13.00, ☎ 01223 333456, ✉ www.esc.ca.uk/SedgwickMuseum). The Museum, which is reached by turning left inside the archway from Downing St, is Cambridge University's oldest museum and contains Britain's oldest intact geological collection, amassed by John Woodward (1665–1728), given to the university after his death, and still displayed in its original cabinets. It was subsequently extended by Adam Sedgwick, Professor of Geology (1785–1873), and has recently been refurbished; it now contains important collections of fossils from both Britain and overseas, dinosaurs, minerals and gems, including rocks collected by Charles Darwin on the *Beagle*, displayed in a new mineral gallery, and a reconstruction of the Jurassic Sea, with fossils of marine reptiles.

In another part of Jackson's buildings (turn right from the archway to Downing St) is the excellent **Museum of Archaeology and Anthropology** (plan 4, A; open Tues–Sat 14.00–16.30, opens 10.30 Tues–Fri in summer: closed Sun, Mon, Easter week Christmas holiday period and public holidays; ☎ 01223 333516, ✉ http://museumserver.archanth.cam.ac.uk).

It is arranged on three floors, with the ground floor given over to prehistory and local archaeology, the first to anthropology and the second to changing exhibitions, all of them clearly and informatively displayed. Among the archaeological exhibits are objects from Celtic, Roman and Anglo-Saxon Britain, and objects from America and Africa, including Benin bronzes. Upstairs, in an impressive top-lit galleried room, there are items from the Pacific, South America, Canada (totem poles, etc.) and many other parts of the world. In the top gallery Jackson re-erected the central part of Inigo Jones's screen from Winchester Cathedral (c 1638), which he was restoring at the time.

On the opposite (north) side of Downing St, past Corn Exchange St, is the **New Museums** site, built over the site of the old Botanical Garden between 1863 and the First World War. Some of the discoveries made in the laboratories here have transformed the modern world, but the quality of the architecture does not, on the whole, match that of the scientific research. To the north of the ponderous late 19C buildings on the north side of Downing St (entrance through archway on the right) is the powerful but crudely detailed **New Museums Building** (Philip Dowson of Arup Associates, 1971), a monument of the 'New Brutalism' incorporating the Zoology and Metallurgy departments and a computer laboratory. It also houses the recently-refurbished **University Museum of Zoology** (open in university vacations Mon–Fri 10.00–13.00 and 14.00–16.45; termtime 14.00–16.45 only, ☎ 01223 336650, ✉ www.zoo.cam.ac.uk/museum), whose presence is marked by the skeleton of a whale over the entrance. The collections date back to 1814 and include specimens donated by Charles Darwin from his famous voyage on the *Beagle*, as well as important displays of fossils, skeletons, shells and wildlife (including a comprehensive display of British birds).

To the west of Tennis Court Rd, Downing St becomes Pembroke St. A right turn leads to Free School Lane, and immediately to the right is the entrance to the **Whipple Museum of the History of Science** (open Mon–Fri 13.30–16.30, ☎ 01223 330906, 01223 330906, ✉ www.hps.cam.ac.uk/Whipple: sometimes closed in university vacations: visitors requested to check beforehand). It is housed in the original schoolroom of the Perse or Cambridge Free School, founded in 1615, with a hammer-beam roof of 1618. The exhibits include microscopes, telescopes, astrolabes, calculators and other scientific and mathematical exhibits from the 16C to modern times, with an especially good collection of navigation and surveying instruments; two recently redesigned galleries contain displays relating to the sciences in 18C Cambridge and a reference collection of scientific instruments.

Further north in Free School Lane is the neo-Tudor frontage (W.M. Fawcett, 1874) of the world-famous **Cavendish Laboratories**, in which Rutherford, Cockcroft and others carried on their epoch-making research on atomic physics. Through the archway is the semicircular modernist façade of the **Mond Laboratory** (1931), decorated with a crocodile, by Eric Gill, in tribute to Lord Rutherford (nicknamed 'The Crocodile'), to the right of the entrance. Opposite is the back of Corpus Christi College's 14C Old Court, see p 219.

South of Emmanuel College, St. Andrew's St becomes **Regent Street**, infested by cars and buses and punctuated by trendy bars and restaurants. On the right, and south of the Downing Site, is the inconspicuous entrance to Downing College.

Downing College

Open daily in daylight hours, ☎ 01223 334800, ✉ www.dow.cam.ac.uk.

History

The college was founded in 1800 under the will of Sir George Downing of Gamlingay Park (1685–1749), great-grandson of Emmanuel Downing, one of the founders of the State of Massachusetts. George Downing was not an admirable character, and the provisions of his will were so complicated, and gave rise to so much litigation, that fifty years elapsed between his death and the establishment of his college, by which time the money available had greatly dwindled. The college was intended to have a much less clerical character than earlier Cambridge colleges, with only two fellows in holy orders, and in this respect it anticipated later developments both in Cambridge and Oxford.

The architecture was equally innovative. The original architect was William Wilkins, and the selection of his designs in preference to those of Lewis Wyatt in 1806 represented a notable triumph for the Greek Revival in England. Wilkins's plan, with the main buildings loosely arranged around a huge grassy quadrangle, anticipated Thomas Jefferson's design of the University of Virginaia at Charlottesville, U.S.A., by ten years, and even now Downing feels more more like an American university campus than a traditional Cambridge college. Financial problems ensured that Wilkins's scheme was not carried out in full, but the college retains the open, unenclosed character that he envisaged, with the main court opening out on the south to a long vista punctuated on the skyline by the spire of the Roman Catholic church (Wilkins had intended to close off this side of the court by a chapel and library flanked by colonnades). Despite the sale of the northern part of the site to the university in the late 19C, the spacious setting remains one of the most notable features of Downing, along with the consistently Classical tone of the architecture, down even to the most recent additions.

The first building to be seen, in front of the entrance gates, is the **Maitland Robinson Library**, a notable example of the work of one of England's leading modern Classicists, Quinlan Terry. Opened in 1993, it is faced, like many older Cambridge college buildings, in Ketton ashlar stone and has a Greek Doric portico on the south side, with a lantern on the roof based on the Tower of the Winds in Athens. Beyond is the **main court**, with Wilkins's east and west ranges (completed 1875 by E.M. Barry to a modified design) flanking the vista, and a more heavy-handed range on the north side (Sir Herbert Baker, 1929–32).

The Ionic portico in the centre of the north range gives access to the **Chapel**, which occupies the site of Wilkins's intended Grecian propylaeum through which the college would have been entered had his original designs been adhered to. Built in 1951–53 to the designs of A.T. Scott, the chapel is a plain and restful building of a somewhat Byzantine character with good neo-Georgian woodwork (open daily in term-time, vacations by appointment). In the apse windows is a semi-abstract depiction of the *Four Horsemen of the Apocalypse* (L.C. Evetts, 1963), and let into the floor on the south side of the altar is a small square of Greek marble from a Byzantine church in Sparta, the site of which was excavated by W.L. Cattle, Senior Tutor of the college.

Wilkins's **Hall** (1818–20: interior visible through glazed doors) is at the far end of the great court, on the west (right-hand) side. Like the Master's Lodge opposite, it has a noble Grecian Ionic portico facing inward to the court, and to the west, though not visible to the public, is a clever extension (by Howell, Killick, Partridge and Amis, 1966–70), housing the Senior Combination Room and echoing, albeit in a modernist idiom, the Grecian architecture of the original buildings.

Before leaving Downing it is also worth looking at Quinlan Terry's **Howard Building** (1987), to the northwest of the main court, its varied, crisply detailed elevations exhibiting a series of playful Mannerist variations on the Classical theme; to the south is **Howard Court**, also by Terry, opened in 1994.

Famous members

J.M. Neale, hymnologist, 1818–66 (Chaplain)	1847–1929
C.M. Doughty, explorer and poet, author of *Travels in Arabia Deserta*, 1843–1925	**F.R. Leavis**, literary critic, 1895–1978
E.R. Lankester, zoologist,	Also a number of distinguished lawyers, including **F.M. Maitland**, 1850–1906

Opposite the entrance to Downing College, though largely screened from Regent St by houses and shops, is another of Cambridge's commons, the much-frequented **Parker's Piece**. It belonged originally to Trinity College, and takes its name from an early tenant, Edward Parker, the college cook; in 1613 it was exchanged with the town for land which is now Trinity's part of the Backs. During the 19C it was much used as a games field, and pop concerts are now held here during the summer. On the northeast side is **Park Terrace**, a plain but handsome row of brick houses of 1831–38, acquired by Emmanuel College for student accommodation in 1982, and to the southeast, off Gonville Place, is **Fenner's**, the university cricket ground. Overlooking the cricket ground, off Mill Rd, a busy street lined with small shops and ethnic restaurants, is **Hughes Hall**, founded in 1885 as a women's teacher-training college, but now a full college of the University admitting both men and women graduates to study the usual range of subjects. The original buildings, by the local architect W.M. Fawcett, are in the red-brick 'Queen Anne' style pioneered at Newnham College.

A right turn into Lensfield Rd at the end of Regent St leads to the **Scott Polar Research Institute and Museum** (open Mon–Sat 14.30–16.00, ☎ 01223 336540, ✉ www.spri.cam.ac.uk, closed on some public holidays). Founded in 1920 in memory of Captain Scott and his companions who died on their expedition to the South Pole in 1912, the museum occupies a neo-Georgian building by Sir Herbert Baker (1933–34), behind which is a modern extension through which it is entered. Inside there are memorabilia of Scott and other polar explorers, including maps, watercolours of the Antarctic region by Edward Wilson—one of Scott's companions—tins of pemmican, and some of their poignant last letters. There are also displays of Arctic life and polar wildlife. The Latin inscription over the entrance front, facing Lensfield Rd, reads in translation 'They sought the secrets of the Pole and found God'; the room behind (the original entrance hall) has two shallow domes with painted maps of the Artic and Antarctic, and is separated from the rest of the building by a screen of columns with capitals of a bizarre 'polar order' invented by Baker, featuring penguins and polar bears.

Regent St continues in a southeasterly direction as Hills Rd and at the junction with Lensfield Rd, to the east of the the the Scott Polar Research Institute, is the large Decorated-style Roman Catholic church of **Our Lady and the English Martyrs** (Dunn & Hansom, 1885–90), whose spire makes a prominent contribution to the Cambridge skyline. In Union Rd, to the right of Hills Rd is the **Cambridge Crystalographic Data Centre**, completed in 1992 to the designs of the Danish architect Erik Sorensen; the austere but well-detailed brick façade has been cut away to reveal a crystalographic seam. Further south in Bateman St is the entrance to the Botanic Garden. Station Rd leads left from Hills Rd past Victorian villas to the **Railway Station** (Sancton Wood, 1845), an impressive brick structure in the simplified Classical style much admired in the early Railway Age; there is a massive arcade on the entrance side, and an unusually long single platform used by trains going in both directions. From here there are frequent buses to the city centre.

Some distance away to the south along Hills Rd, beyond the railway bridge, is **Homerton College**, whose students all read for degrees in Education. The college's origins go back to an 18C academy for training Congregationalist teachers which moved in 1894 from Homerton in east London to a set of institutional-looking red-brick buildings of 1876–89 (architects Giles & Gough) originally erected for Cavendish College, a defunct society for poor male undergraduates. Since then the college has become non-denominational, and there have been many additions to the original buildings, including a nursery school of 1940–41 by Maxwell Fry, one of the pioneer architects of the Modern Movement in England.

4 ~ NORTH AND WEST OF CASTLE HILL

Because of the rapid suburban growth to the east and south of the ancient city centre, Cambridge University expanded in the late 19C and 20C to the west and north of the river, and it is here that many of the students live and much of the University's teaching and research now takes place. This walk starts on the far side of Magdalen Bridge, in an area first settled by the Romans.

Just beyond Magdalene College (see Walk 3) at the junction with **Northampton Street**, is an attractive group of typically East Anglian timber-framed and plastered houses, not always easy to appreciate because of the incessant traffic. Opposite, at the corner of Castle St, is another picturesque 16C and 17C plastered building, once the White Horse Inn. It now houses the **Cambridge and County Folk Museum** (open Mon–Sat 10.30–17.00, Sun 14.00–17.00, closed Mon Oct–Mar, ☎ 01223 355159, ✉ www.folkmuseum.org.uk). Established in 1936, this is a fascinating collection of bygones relating to the lives of Cambridgeshire people from the 17C to the present. They are arranged thematically, with displays of local trades, cooking and lighting, domestic crafts, the City and University, children, farming, and life in the Fens; temporary exhibitions are also held.

   Immediately to the north is the tiny church of **St. Peter**, a mere fragment of a largely 14C church with a tower and spire whose chancel was demolished in 1781; the Norman font, decorated with mermen, survives in the truncated nave. The church is now cared for by the Churches Conservation Trust.

   Next to the churchyard is the inconspicuous entrance to Kettle's Yard, one of the best places in which to appreciate British avant-garde art of the first half of the 20C, and also the home of excellent temporary exhibitions.

Kettle's Yard

Plan 1, D/F; house and permanent collection open Tues–Sun, summer 13.30–16.30, winter 14.00–16.00; exhibition gallery Tues–Sun 11.30–17.30, ☎ 01223 352124, ✉ www.kettlesyard.co.uk).

History

The collection was amassed by Jim Ede, a former curator of the Tate Gallery who had been at school in Cambridge. In 1957 he bought and renovated four dilapidated cottages off Castle Hill and turned them into his home, filling it with the works he had collected over the previous 30 years and keeping open house for artistically-minded students: in his own words, 'a living place where works of art could be enjoyed, inherent to the domestic setting, where young people could be at home unhampered by the greater austerity of the museum or public art gallery, and where an informality might infuse an underlying formality'. The house and collection were conveyed to the University in 1966, and an extension was built in 1969–70 to the designs of Sir Leslie Martin, Professor of Architecture at Cambridge and a long-standing champion of the Modern Movement.

The **permanent collection** is housed in Ede's house (the former cottages) and in part of the purpose-built extension, itself an excellent example of modern gallery design. Among the artists represented are Henri Gaudier-Brzeska—one of the finest collections of his drawings and sculptures to be seen anywhere—David Jones, Alfred Wallis, Christopher Wood, and Ben and Winifred Nicholson, through whom Ede developed his enthusiasm for modern art; there are also small works by Joan Miró, Brancusi, Naum Gabo, Henry Moore and Barbara Hepworth, and pottery by Lucie Rie and Bernard Leach.

The works of art share the building with Ede's diverse collection of furniture (on which visitors are encouraged to sit) and *objets trouvés*, thus creating an unusually welcoming atmosphere. Changing exhibitions of 20C and contemporary art are also held in the **exhibition galleries** (extended 1994), which have their own entrance opposite St. Peter's church.

On the opposite side of Castle St is **Castle Hill**. On the south side is the impressive Victorian Gothic **St. Giles church** (T.F. & F. Healy, 1875; often locked), with a round arch from its 11C–12C predecessor at the end of the south aisle. From here Chesterton Lane leads along the north bank of the Cam, and on the left a lane gives access to Clare College's **Castle Hill Hostel**, consisting of two older houses and a more recent brick building by David Roberts (1957–58).

Castle Hill is the site of the medieval **castle** which overlooked the city of Cambridge from its eminence to the north of the river. There was a Roman camp here, and in 1068 William I made the artificial grassy motte, or mound, which was the main defensive feature of the castle. The earthworks extending eastwards are the remains of a second castle built by Edward I c 1285; there was some refortification by the Parliamentarians in 1643, but the last remaining building, the gatehouse, was pulled down in 1842 and now, apart from the mound, there is nothing to show for what must in its heyday have been a formidable collection of buildings and earthworks. But the site is still the centre of county administration, which is now conducted from a large neo-Georgian **County Hall** (1931–32), and the **mound**, approached from the southern edge of the car park, can be climbed to give an excellent view of the city.

At the top of Castle Hill Castle St becomes **Huntingdon Road**, and from here Mount Pleasant leads southwest (left) along the line of the ancient Roman fortifications to **St. Edmund's College**, a graduate college which began life in 1896 as a residential centre for Roman Catholic priests studying in Cambridge. It is now a full college of the University, with lay men and women members. The original red-brick buildings were erected as a graduate hostel in 1884, and have since been extended at various dates, most recently in 1987–93, when a six-storeyed entrance tower was built to the designs of Roderick Gradidge, adding a focus to a disparate and otherwise architecturally unremarkable set of buildings.

Back in Huntingdon Rd, a short walk leads to New Hall.

New Hall

Plan 1, C; for adm. times ☎ 01223 762100, ✉ www.newhall.cam.ac.uk.

History

Cambridge's third college for women, New Hall was founded in 1954. The society was first housed at The Hermitage in Silver St, now part of Darwin College (Walk 5), but it moved to its present site in 1964. The original buildings were erected in 1962–66 to the highly imaginative designs of Chamberlin, Powell and Bon, the architects of the Barbican in London, and they rank among the most interesting collegiate structures of that period. Lack of land inhibited the completion of the original project, but in 1994–96 new student accommodation, a new entrance court and new lecture rooms, seminar rooms, etc. were built to the designs of Frank Woods of Austin-Smith & Lord, a member of the team responsible for the original buildings; the work was carried out with the help of the Kaetsu Educational Foundation from Japan. The college continues to admit only women as students, but the Fellowship is mixed.

The college is entered through a new **entrance forecourt and rotunda** in Buckingham Rd, at the southern end of a spinal corridor or walkway which runs through the whole building. The original buildings are of white brick and concrete, now showing signs of weathering, and present a formidable face to the outside world. Inside, however, the atmosphere is one of cloistered enclosure, with two courts looking inwards over sunken pools and fountains, and bisected by the spinal corridor. **Fountain Court** (to the left of the corridor) is dominated by the massive bulk of the **Hall**, with its concrete dome surrounded by four half-domed staircase towers: a strange but memorable mixture of Byzantine and space-age imagery.

New Hall

The **Library** (no adm.), on the far side of the same court, is on two levels, and some undergraduates' rooms, most of which are around Orchard Court, are also on two levels, the upper one reached by ladder-like steps: a novel, if hardly very practical, idea. The **Kaetsu Centre** (no adm.) consists of an accommodation block attached to a striking rotunda faced in white Italian marble. Inside, are a lecture theatre, teaching rooms and a Japanese *tatami* room.

In 1992 the college became the home of a permanent **Collection of Contemporary Women's Art**, examples of which are hung in the Hall and throughout the college (viewing by appointment).

A short walk along Huntingdon Rd from New Hall leads to Fitzwilliam College.

Fitzwilliam College

For opening times, ☎ 01223 332000, ✉ www.fitz.cam.ac.uk.

History

Fitzwilliam began in 1869 as the Non-Collegiate Students Board, set up to administer the affairs of undergraduates who wanted to study at the university but who could not, or did not wish to, belong to a college (see St. Catherine's College, Oxford). The first premises were in Trumpington St, opposite the Fitzwilliam Museum, from which the society took its name, and as Fitzwilliam Hall, later Fitzwilliam House (see p 229), it became a centre for non-collegiate students, who always included a high proportion of graduates studying for higher degrees. It moved to its present site in 1963, and became a full college in 1966.

The first buildings (1961–67), by Denys Lasdun, architect of the National Theatre in London, consist of three long low ranges of dark-coloured brick with wide concrete bands, enfolding a **Hall** lit by clerestory windows, with an elegant roof of parabolic concrete hoods which would not look out of place in Dubai or Abu Dhabi. In 1985 a new residential block was added to the west to the designs of MacCormac, Jamieson and Pritchard; it is of the same height as Lasdun's buildings, and is also built of brick, but is detailed in a more interesting and lively way, reflecting the complex internal planning. Richard MacCormac was also responsible for the **Chapel** (1990–91), a highly successful circular building in the modernist idiom, not at all ecclesiastical-looking from the outside, but with a beautifully calm, light interior at first-floor level, and a dark, crypt-like lower chapel underneath. The clear glass window of the main chapel looks out onto a giant plane tree in the well-planted court, beyond which is a brick villa known as The Grove (William Custance, 1812–13), now containing the Senior and Middle Combination Rooms. The dark brick **Wilson Court** (van Heynigen & Haward, 1994) occupies the southern corner of the site, and represents a further step towards the reorientation of the college in that direction. A new building by Allies and Morrison with an entrance to Storeys Way was opened in 2003, and a new library by Edward Cullinan is also planned.

Beyond Fitwilliam College are two contrasting hostels for Trinity Hall: **Boulton House**, or Wychfield (Philip Dowson, 1967)—a cousin of his Leckhampton for Corpus Christi (see p 263)—and the **Herrick Houses** (MacCormac, Jamieson and Pritchard 1985). From here, enthusiasts for Victorian architecture, and those interested in the history of women's education, may wish to walk, or take a bus, a mile or so further along Huntingdon Rd to Girton College, which lies on the very outskirts of the city (also accessible by car from the M11 at junction 14).

Girton College

Visits by appointment with the Conference Officer, ☎ 01223 338975, ✉ www.girton.cam.ac.uk.

History

The first residential college in Britain to offer a university education for women, Girton was founded in 1869 by the educational pioneer Emily Davies, with the support and encouragement of such leaders of the women's movement as Barbara Leigh Smith (afterwards Mme Bodichon) and a number of liberal-minded Cambridge men. The first location was at Hitchin, a place discreetly removed from Cambridge yet accessible to visiting lecturers from the university; an indignant clergyman called it 'that infidel place'. In 1873 it moved to its present spacious site, where Alfred Waterhouse erected a set of red-brick buildings, which were subsequently extended by his son and grandson; an important innovation was the arrangement of rooms on corridors, instead of staircases as in the older colleges. Davies's insistence on women fulfilling exactly the same examination requirements as men, and the rigid discipline she imposed, led in time to conflict with both colleagues and students, and she resigned in 1904. Old members at the college include the historian Eileen Power, 1889–1940; the novelist Rosamund Lehmann, 1901–90, whose novel *Dusty Answer* was largely set in the college, and the social scientist Barbara Wootton, 1897–1988. Virginia Woolf's *A Room of One's Own* was based on the lectures she gave at Girton and Newnham in 1928. Men were admitted in 1979.

The approach from Huntingdon Rd leads to the formidable gate tower which gives access to **Cloisters Court**, designed by Waterhouse's son Paul in 1884–87 but displaying all the 'hard-edged' characteristics of his father's style. Paul Waterhouse's impressive, buttressed **Hall** (1900–02) is on the far side of the court; it is entered through a covered cloister, and portraits of successive mistresses of the college (including one by Stanley Spencer) are displayed on the walls. The smaller **Chapel**, of the same date, is to the right of the gate tower, and beyond it is **Woodlands Court**, with the Library, completed in a less assertive Tudor-Gothic style by a third member of the Waterhouse dynasty, Michael, in 1931.

Alfred Waterhouse's original buildings for the college are in the L-shaped **Emily Davies Court**, to the left of the main entrance. They were designed by in two stages in 1873–79 in a somewhat austere manner which set the tone for the rest of the college.

The beautiful **grounds**, of 46 acres, were originally laid out c 1900 by the then Mistress, Miss Elizabeth Welsh.

Returning towards the centre of Cambridge by the Huntingdon Rd, a right turn before Fitzwilliam College leads into **Storey's Way**, which contains some important early 20C Arts and Crafts houses by Baillie Scott (note especially no. 48, built in 1912–13). At the far end, after two right-angled bends, is the entrance to Churchill College.

Churchill College

Open daily during daylight hours: ☎ 01223 336000, ▨ www.chu.cam.ac.uk.

History

The college was founded in 1960 to promote scientific and technological studies, though it has never by any means been exclusively devoted to them. As a national memorial to Sir Winston Churchill—who never attended any university—it attracted gifts from all over the world, and it is now one of Cambridge's largest colleges. The buildings (by Richard Sheppard, Robson and partners 1959–68) are among the most impressive monuments of the Modern Movement in either Oxford or Cambridge. Built of brick and concrete, they are arranged around an intricate network of ten interconnecting courts, lending a sense of intimacy which does much to soften the brutalist harshness of the architecture.

By the entrance is a large bronze sculpture, *Diagram of an Object* (Second State) by Dhuva Mistry. From the massive, austere gatehouse, a wide corridor leads to the communal areas of the college. The **Hall**, the largest in Cambridge, is on the first floor, reached by a broad flight of stairs presided over by an impressive bust of Sir Winston Churchill (by Oscar Nemon); it is roofed by three concrete tunnel-vaults resting on exposed beams. To the south (left) of the corridor is a spacious, grassy court, from which the exterior of the Hall can be seen rising up impressively over the surrounding buildings.

On the west side of the court is the fortress-like **Bracken Library** (no adm.), built in memory of Churchill's Minister of Information, Brendan Bracken; the building also houses the **Bevin Library**, given by the Transport and General Workers Union in memory of Ernest Bevin, Minister of Labour in the wartime coalition and subsequently Foreign Secretary. Nearby is the **Churchill Archives Centre**, built to house a priceless collection of Sir Winston's papers, and also containing papers of many of his political, intellectual, military and scientific contemporaries; it was funded by US ambassadors to London, and other prominent American donors. Recent acquisitions include the papers of Margaret Thatcher.

To the west of the original complex of buildings is a large expanse of lawn, on which is Barbara Hepworth's monumental bronze *Four Squares* (1963), complementing the toughness of the architecture. Further west is the large postmodern, rather corporate-looking, **Maersk McKinney Moller Centre for Continuing Education** (Henning Larsen, 1992), looking out towards Madingley Rd, and beyond, at the end of the service road which runs along the north side of the site, are apartments providing accommodation for visiting scholars (Richard Sheppard) and graduate apartments and maisonettes (David Roberts).

Easy to miss at the western extremity of the extensive grounds is the **Chapel**, banished from the centre of the College because a religious building was not deemed appropriate in a community devoted to secular studies. Built by private subscription at the same time as the rest of the college, and designed by the same architects, it is a powerful statement of the 'brutalist' aesthetic, with a memorable roof-line composed of jagged concrete forms erupting from the plain brick walls.

The interior is laid out on a Greek-cross form, with a central altar and stained-glass windows by John Piper (made by Patrick Reyntiens) in memory of the first Master, the atomic scientist Sir John Cockcroft (d. 1967); the bell was given by the Admiralty, of which Churchill was First Lord in the First World War and at the beginning of the Second.

Churchill College looks out onto **Madingley Road**. On the north side beyond the college is the **University Observatory** (right), a Greek Revival building (J.C. Mead, 1822–23: no adm.) set well back from the road, with an impressive Doric portico and a diminutive (and visually not very effective) dome. In **Conduit Head Road**, further on, are some modernist houses of the 1930s (e.g. Salix, by H.C. Hughes, 1933). On the south of Madingley Rd are two large recent buildings by the RMJM (Robert Matthew Johnson Marshall) firm, both of them underlining Cambridge's central role in the creation of 'Silicon Fen': the **Microsoft Laboratory** (2001) and the **Department of Computer Sciences** (2000). More extensive building on what is now known as the West Cambridge site was going on at the time of writing. Further on is the extraordinary **Schlumberger Research Laboratory** (Michael Hopkins, 1984, 1992: no adm.), one of the most spectacular examples of the 'high-tech' style espoused by a number of the most creative British architects of this period; with its masts supporting the tent-like glass-fibre roofs, it looks like a massive spider perched on the hillside overlooking the city. On the opposite side of Madingley Rd is the well-landscaped and elegantly designed western **park and ride car park** (1996), from which there are very frequent buses to the city centre .

Returning towards Churchill College, a right turn leads south along Wilberforce Rd, and from here another turn into **Clarkson Road** gives access to one of Cambridge's most ambitious and impressive recent buildings, the **Centre for Mathematical Sciences** (Edward Cullinan, 2001). It adjoins the slightly earlier Newton Institute (Annand and Muscoe 1992) and consists of a group of low blocks with strange pagoda-like roofs rising up around a spacious grass-topped dining hall sunk into the ground and covered by a semicircular roof on concrete beams. Beyond is Girton College's domestic-looking **Wolfson Court** (David Roberts, 1969).

A left turn along Grange Rd leads back to **Madingley Road** and the centre of Cambridge. The complex of buildings at the corner of Lady Margaret Rd houses **Lucy Cavendish College**, approached from Lady Margaret Rd. Named after a Victorian pioneer of women's education, the college started life informally in the early 1950s in three large late 19C houses, one of them designed by J.J. Stevenson, promoter of the 'Queen Anne' style. It provided a social focus for senior women graduates working in the university and achieved full collegiate status in 1985; it now also admits some (mostly mature) women undergraduates. In 1995 a **dining hall** and two residential blocks were added (architects: van Heynigen and Haward), and a **Library** facing Madingley Rd was opened, to the designs of Freeland Rees and Roberts, in 1999. The new brick-built buildings blend attractively with the Victorian houses in the informal garden setting.

A little further east, at the junction of Madingley Rd and Northampton St, is **Westminster College**, a training college for Presbyterian ministers built in the 'free style' of the late 19C (H.T. Hare, 1899), its impressive tower effectively closing the vista north from Queen's Rd. This is very near the start of the walk, but those wishing to return to the centre of Cambridge via the Backs should turn right into Queen's Rd, from which there are several alternative routes.

5 ~ WEST OF THE CAM

This walk starts by the River Cam in **Silver Street** (see Walk 2) and explores more of Cambridge's 19C and 20C architecture, as well as some of the central institutions of the University.

To the right of the bridge are the buildings of Queens' College (see p 220), and immediately to the left after crossing the river is **Darwin College** (no adm.), a disparate collection of 19C and 20C buildings grouped in linear fashion along the river bank. Darwin is a graduate society, established in 1965 by Caius, St. John's and Trinity Colleges; at the core is **Newnham Grange**, the early 19C former home of the Darwin family, vividly described in the autobiographical *Period Piece*, by Charles Darwin's granddaughter Gwen Raverat. The neighbouring 19C house called the **Hermitage**, also part of the college, was the first home of New Hall (see p 255). The two houses are linked by a brick-faced building designed by Howell, Killick, Partridge and Amis in 1966–68, and there have since been further additions by David Roberts (1980) and Jeremy Dixon (1994), the latter taking the form of a sensitively detailed **Post-Graduate Study Centre**. This is best seen from Coe Fen, on the opposite side of the river, through which a footpath leads diagonally to Newnham Rd and Newnham College.

Newnham College is best approached by crossing Newnham Rd and walking along Malting Lane, which runs alongside an attractive former maltings. On the opposite side are the neo-Tudor buildings of **Ridley Hall**, an Evangelical Church of England training college (Charles Luck, 1879–81), and at the far end is the magnificent gate tower of Newnham College.

Newnham College

Plan 3, C; open daily in daylight hours, exc. May–mid-June, ☎ 01223 3357000, 🖾 www. newn.cam.ac.uk.

History

Newnham was founded as a women's college in 1871, largely under the aegis of Henry Sidgwick, a leading figure in the women's education movement in Cambridge. His ideas were more liberal and flexible than those of Emily Davies, the founder of Girton College (see p 257), and their differences of opinion led to the almost simultaneous establishment of the two separate foundations. Newnham's life began in 1871 with five students in a house in Regent St (Sidgwick's 'little garden of flowers') presided over by Miss A.J. Clough, who became the first principal; the college moved to the present site in 1875. Miss Clough was succeeded by Mrs Sidgwick, and the college became the Sidgwicks' home. It still admits only women; among the most distinguished old members are the Nobel prize-winning scientist Dorothy Hodgkin, 1910–94; the poet and novelist Sylvia Plath, 1932–63; and the X-ray crystallographer Rosalind Franklin, 1920–58, who worked with Crick and Watson on the discovery of DNA.

The liberal outlook and genial personalities of Miss Clough, the Sidgwicks and their Cambridge supporters have left their mark on Newnham, perhaps the most attractive of all the women's colleges in Oxford or Cambridge. The original buildings were planned on a deliberately domestic scale and were arranged in a series of self-contained houses, linked by passages, so that the students belonged to the smaller community of a house as well as to the larger community of the college.

The college announces its presence by a splendid red-brick **gatehouse** (1892–93) in the eclectic style known at the time as 'Queen Anne'. Like all the original buildings at Newnham it was designed by Basil Champneys, and his architectural vision is still omnipresent in the college, marred only by some mediocre extensions erected in the 1960s.

The main buildings face west and south onto a spacious, densely planted, garden: one of the most attractive in Cambridge. They include **Old Hall** (1874–75), to the left of the gatehouse, **Sidgwick Hall** to the right (1879–80), and beyond, to the west, the more elaborately detailed **Clough Hall** (1886–87), all of them displaying the pretty Dutch gables and white-painted sash windows which became the hallmarks of 'Queen Anne'. The **Dining Hall** (no adm.) adjoins Clough Hall and has two projecting oriel windows, a cupola, and a ceiling by Sir George Frampton, designer of the Peter Pan statue in Kensington Gardens. On the opposite side of the garden is the old laboratory, used by science students before they were admitted to university facilities; it was converted in 1997–98 into a Music and Performing Arts Centre.

The **Rosalind Franklin Building** (Allies & Morrison 1994–95) runs between Newnham Walk and Sidgwick Avenue, echoing the red brick and white woodwork of Champneys's buildings. The college is entered from Sidgwick Avenue through the **Fawcett Building** (1938), the first building in either Cambridge or Oxford to have been designed by a female architect (Elizabeth Scott, designer of the Royal Shakespeare Theatre at Stratford). Nearby on Sidgwick Avenue is the **Rare Books Room** library extension (Van Heynigen & Haward, 1984), a small two-storeyed building of blue and red brick; a further extension by John Miller and partners was under construction at the time of writing.

Sidgwick Avenue leads west into an area spaciously laid out in the late 19C for the prosperous houses of dons and professional people, but increasingly encroached upon in the 20C by the insatiable demands of the University, which has completely taken over the northern side.

The Arts Faculties

Immediately opposite Newnham is the University Arts Faculties complex (the 'Sidgwick site'; plan 3, B), an academic ghetto begun in 1956. Inconspicuously situated behind a block facing Sidgwick Avenue is the Faculty of Classics which contains the **Museum of Classical Archaeology** (open Mon–Fri 10.00–17.00, Saturdays in term-time 10.00–13.00, closed Christmas and Easter, ☎ 01223 335153, ✉ www.classics.cam.ac.uk). This is a collection of over 600 plaster casts of Greek and Roman sculpture, brought together in the late 19C in order to allow students, artists and lovers of antiquity to examine the most celebrated examples of Classical sculpture at first hand. The collection was housed from 1884 in a building in Little St. Mary's Lane—now the library of

Peterhouse— and were removed to their present well-lit setting in 1983. The casts are best viewed in anti-clockwise order, starting with the archaic works immediately in front of the entrance; they include the 'Peplos Kore'—a brightly-painted female figure from the 6C BC—the Delphi charioteer from Athens and the 'Farnese Hercules' from Rome, as well as many Roman portrait busts.

The raised **main court** of the Arts complex (Casson, Conder and Partners, 1958–64) is an example of the all-too-familiar modernist style found in many English academic institutions, with flat-roofed, sparsely detailed buildings (for the English, Moral Sciences, Economics and Languages faculties) elevated on stilts or 'pilotis' through which the East Anglian wind whistles inexorably for much of the year. More exciting from an architectural point of view is the **History Faculty Building** to the north of the main court (James Stirling, 1964–68; no adm.), made up of two six-storey blocks clad in fiery red tiles set at right angles to each other, evoking an opened book, with a receding pyramid of glass descending glacier-like between the two glazed inner walls to light the library. The aesthetic effect is startling, but the building has been so beset by practical problems—not all of them of the architect's making—that demolition was seriously considered by the Faculty a few years ago.

Stirling's building is upstaged by the adjacent—and, some would say, equally impractical—**Law Faculty Building** (Norman Foster, 1995: no adm.), its galleried interior clearly visible through a glazed semicircular-roofed screen. Turning its back on the fashionable post-modernism of the 1990s, it celebrates, like its neighbour, both the 'industrial aesthetic' of the 19C and the continuing appeal of its modernist idiom. On the other side of the History faculty is the rather more elegant glazed façade of the **School of Divinity** (Edward Cullinan, 2000), to the north of which is the zinc-roofed brick-clad **Faculty of Music** (Leslie Martin, Colen Lumley & Ivor Richards, 1975–77), incorporating a concert hall and rehearsal rooms. Next to Music Faculty, facing West Rd, is the minimally modernist **Faculty of English** (expected completion date 2004), designed by the firm of Allies & Morrison, who also designed the **Institute of Criminology** to the south. A right turn from here into **West Rd** leads to Caius College's impressive **Harvey Court** (Leslie Martin & Colin St. John Wilson, 1960–62), an inward-facing brick quadrangle with the rooms arranged in stepped-back terraced tiers overlooking a raised central space; the almost windowless street front is severe in the extreme, but well proportioned and powerful in its effect.

Returning along West Rd, a left turn into Grange Rd leads to **Selwyn College**. Plan 3, C; open all year in daylight hours, ☎ 01223 335846, 🖾 www.sel. cam.ac.uk.

History

Founded as a 'public hostel' in 1882 to provide a university education for young men of the Church of England unable to afford the fees of the older colleges (see Keble College, Oxford), the college was named in honour of the influential and greatly admired George Augustus Selwyn, first Bishop of New Zealand (d. 1878). It became an Approved Foundation of the university in 1923, and achieved full collegiate status in 1958.

The red-brick neo-Tudor buildings, set round a spacious court, were mostly designed by Sir Arthur Blomfield in 1882–95. They include the **Chapel**, a lofty and impressive Perpendicular Gothic structure whose west front, inspired by that of King's College Chapel, is placed directly opposite the entrance. Inside, there is good woodwork, and some stained glass by Kempe. On the south side of the court is the neo-Jacobean **Hall** (Grayson & Ould, 1908–09); the early 18C panelling behind the high table comes from the demolished English church in Rotterdam, and was presented in 1914 by A.C. Benson (see Magdalene College) in memory of his father, the former Archbishop of Canterbury. Nearby is the **Senior Combination Room**, built to the modernist designs of Stirrat Johnson-Marshall in 1963–64.

Opposite Selwyn, a private road leads to **Leckhampton** (no adm.), a graduate hostel for Corpus Christi College. Its interest lies chiefly in the modernist George Thomson Building (Philip Dowson of Arup Associates, 1963–64), attached to a red-brick house of 1880 and named after a Nobel Prizewinning scientist and former Master of the college. Dowson's buildings feature an exposed reinforced concrete frame—a system much used by this firm in their collegiate buildings in Oxford as well as Cambridge—and overlook a lawn with an enigmatic *Seated Figure* by Henry Moore.

From here a lengthy detour leads south along Grange Rd past large late-Victorian and Edwardian houses to Barton Rd, where a right turn gives access to **Wolfson College** (☎ 01223 335900, 🖳 www.wolfson.cam.ac.uk), one of the newer foundations in Cambridge. Founded in 1965 as University College, and renamed in 1973 in recognition of a large benefaction from the Wolfson Foundation, Wolfson is principally a graduate college, fostering connections with European and other overseas universities, and with business and administrative circles. The main buildings (A.M. Mennim, 1972–77) comprise two open-ended courts enclosed by low plain brick residential blocks, on either side of a larger open court (**Main Court**); the effect is welcoming and restrained, and free from the mannerisms of some Cambridge buildings of the previous decade. **East Court** incorporates the gabled Bredon House, formerly occupied by a professor of botany.

To the east of East Court is the **Lee Seng Tee Library** (David Williams of Brewer Smith & Brewer, 1992–93), with a bell tower over the entrance. Further north is the **Lee Seng Tee Hall** (R.H. Partnership, 1989–90); the Chinese-style garden adjoining it was laid out by P. Edwards.

Returning along **Grange Road**, at the corner of Cranmer Rd is Selwyn's **Cripps Court** (Cartwright, Woollatt & Partners 1966–68). Diagonally opposite, on the corner of West Rd, is **St. Chad's Hostel**, an outlier of St. Catharine's College, with a modern block (James Cubitt and Partners, 1976–81) next to a large Edwardian brick house.

A little further on in Herschel Rd (left from Grange Rd) is **Clare Hall** (plan 3, A; ☎ 012233 332360), a graduate college founded in 1966 by Clare College with help from two American benefactors and built on a confined three-acre site. The college, which is now independent, broke with tradition by providing both single and family accommodation, arranged not in traditional courts but on either side of two 'walks', the Family Walk and Scholars' Walk, with housing for fellows between. The densely packed buildings (by Ralph Erskine, 1966–69) show a marked Scandinavian influence, their brick walls, pitched roofs, timber balconies and narrow, intimate (and somewhat claustrophobic) courtyards also recalling the better English housing estates of the 1970s. There have been two recent additions: the striking **Brian Pippard Building** (Nicholas Ray Associates, 1997), with long sloping roofs, and the same firm's rather quieter **West Court**, built at the far end of Herschel Rd in 2000.

Opposite Clare Hall in Herschel Rd is the **Needham Institute** (Lyster, Grillet and Harding, 1986), an attractive example of architectural orientalism housing the East Asian History of Science Library, and making good visual use of the Bin Brook which flows underneath. Next to it, at the corner of Grange Rd, is **Robinson College**. Plan 3, A/1, G; open weekdays exc. May and early June 10.00–18.00, Sun 14.00–18.00, ☎ 01223 339100, ✉ www.robinson. cam.ac.uk.

This was the Cambridge college to be newly established for both men and women and the first to be planned with a view to conference use during vacations. It was entirely financed by a Cambridgeshire businessman, David Robinson, and the first students were admitted in 1977, four years before the formal opening. The college occupies a large site purchased from St. John's, and the buildings (by Gillespie, Kidd and Coia, 1977–80) are constructed around a concrete frame clad in deep red, hand-made bricks. Among the finest of all recent Cambridge collegiate buildings, they are imaginatively arranged on an L plan, looking out onto Grange and Herschel Roads and inwards to a large and beautiful garden bisected by the Bin Brook and shaded by mature trees, on the far side of which is a late 19C Tudor-style house, Thorneycreek, now used for student accommodation.

Externally, the college alludes to the castles and fortified towns of the Middle Ages, but inside the mood changes. An 'internal street' at first-floor level, reached by a ramp, for disabled access, leads to the **Hall** and also to the impressive **Chapel** (turn right from the entrance), lit by abstract stained glass in strong primary colours by John Piper; there is another window by the same artist in the side chapel, and the organ is by the Danish builder Erik Frobenius.

Opposite the entrance to Robinson College, Burrell's Walk leads back to the centre of the city. Immediately on the left is Trinity College's **Burrells Field Hostel** (Roberts & Clarke, 1978–79; no adm.), a group of linked brick pavilions with pyramidal tiled roofs, extended in 1995 by MacCormac, Jamieson and Pritchard to provide a series of residential courts interrupted by low towers overlooking the Bin Brook. This is one of the best examples of recent collegiate architecture in Cambridge.

The massive brick structure to the right of Burrell's Walk houses the **University Library**, built in 1931–34 to the designs of Sir Giles Gilbert Scott as replacement of the former Library on the Old Schools site. It is entered from the east under the huge central tower, which is flanked on either side by rows of tall narrow windows between sturdy brick-clad piers: an impressive, though somewhat forbidding, example of inter-war architecture from the designer of both Liverpool's Anglican cathedral and London's Battersea Power Station. The library is one of the most important in the country, with over six million books, a million maps of great beauty and historical, literary or scientific interest, and many MSS. Changing selections from the superb collections are displayed in the Exhibition Centre to the right of the entrance lobby (open Mon–Fri 09.00–18.00, Sat 09.00–12.30, ☎ 01223 333030, 🖂 www.lib.cam.ac.uk).

Immediately opposite the library entrance is Clare College's **Memorial Court**, commemorating members of the college killed in the First World War. It is a noble set of grey brick buildings in the neo-Georgian style, also by Giles Gilbert Scott (1923–34), but the original effect was, alas, somewhat spoiled when the college commissioned Philip Dowson to build the new **Forbes-Mellon Library** in 1985–86, inoffensive enough in itself, but blocking the axial vista through the court to the Library. On the lawn inside the court is Henry Moore's bronze *Falling Warrior*, and near the east front, close to Queens Rd, is Barbara Hepworth's *Two Forms* (*Divided Circle*).

From the end of Burrell's Walk a path leads across the Backs to a concrete bridge, allowing good views of the river, and from here Garret Hostel Lane leads past Trinity Hall to the city centre.

THE IMMEDIATE VICINITY OF CAMBRIDGE

The surroundings of Cambridge, though unspectacular, are attractive and surprisingly unspoilt. Four short excursions are recommended. They can be undertaken on foot, by car, or (in some cases) by public transport.

1 ~ To Grantchester and Trumpington

To the southwest side of the city centre there are numerous paths near the River Cam across **Lammas Land**, **Sheep's Green** and **Coe Fen**, beginning in Mill Lane (turn left, just before Silver St Bridge). At the end of Grantchester St, beyond the junction of Newnham Rd and Fen Causeway), a pleasant footpath runs parallel to the river to **Grantchester**, immortalised by Rupert Brooke in his poem *The Old Vicarage, Grantchester*.

> 'Ah God! To see the branches stir
> Across the moon at Grantchester!
> ... Stands the church clock at ten to three?
> And is there honey still for tea?'

The poet lodged for a time at the Old Vicarage (private), close to the river, where 'the chestnuts shade, in reverend dream/ The still unacademic stream.' He died at the beginning of the First World War and is commemorated both in the **church**, which has a fine mid-14C chancel with elaborate Decorated windows, and on the War Memorial in the churchyard. His name is also recalled by one of the four village pubs and his presence evoked in the tea-gardens which still flourish as the *Orchard Tea Rooms* (☎ 01223 845788).

About half a mile south, close to the river, is **Byron's Pool**, where 'his ghostly lordship' swam in his undergraduate days (reached by a footpath from the road to Trumpington); its poetic solitude is slightly vitiated by the close proximity of the M11 motorway. The parish church at **Trumpington** (1 mile from

CAMBRIDGE: surrounding area

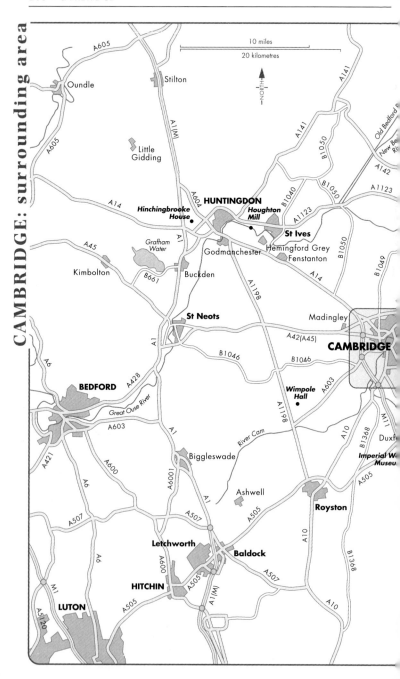

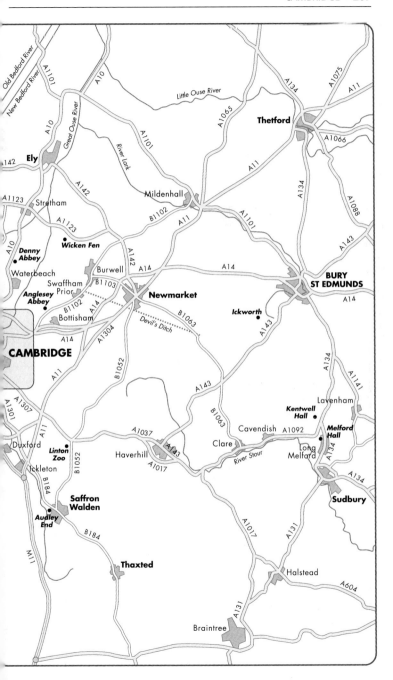

Grantchester or 2½ miles from the city centre via Trumpington Rd) is an impressive building with a 13C chancel and a spacious aisled nave of c 1330 lit by circular clerestory windows; under an ogee-arched canopy between the north aisle and the north chapel is a superb brass to Sir Roger de Trumpington (1289), the second oldest monumental brass in England.

There is a park-and-ride car park at Trumpington, and from here there are frequent buses back to the city centre.

2 ~ To Stourbridge Common and Fen Ditton

This walk starts at **Jesus Green**, which occupies the loop of the River Cam to the north of Jesus College. To the east of Victoria Avenue is **Midsummer Common**, where the old towpath beside the river, opposite the college boathouses, runs past the *Fort St. George* pub to Elizabeth Way (about 1 mile) and then along the path known as Riverside to the **Cambridge Museum of Technology**, housed in an old pumping station with a tall chimney (open Easter–Nov Sun 14.00–17.00; ☎ 01223 368650, ✉ www.museumoftechnology.com); the exhibits include working steam pumping engines, including a unique one of 1895, early wirelesses, scientific instruments and electronic equipment. Beyond is **Stourbridge Common**, site of a celebrated fair described in 1589 as 'by far the largest and most famous ... in all England', but long discontinued (the annual fair held each June on Midsummer Common is perhaps a pale reflection).

From here a footbridge leads across the river to **Chesterton**, a village with several attractive old houses, though now engulfed in suburban sprawl (also accessible from the city centre via Chesterton Rd). The 14C and 15C **church** (turn left along High St from footbridge) has a famous 15C *Last Judgement* painting over the chancel arch and two of the carved bench-ends portray young men in the fashionable costume of c 1430. For over 300 years the living was in the gift of the abbey of Vercelli in Italy, for whose representative **Chesterton Tower** was probably built, to the north of the church, in the mid-14C.

Returning to Stourbridge Common, a walk of about half a mile leads to the picturesque village of **Fen Ditton** (about 2 miles from Jesus Green), which stands at the western end of the ancient defensive earthwork known as Fleam Dyke. There is an attractive medieval church, a manor house of c 1637 and the *Ancient Shepherds Inn*, where good food can be obtained (also accessible by road via A1303 Cambridge–Newmarket and B1047).

From the towpath at Abbey Rd (also accessible from central Cambridge via Newmarket Rd) a detour can be made to the scanty remains of **Barnwell Priory**, founded by the Augustinians in 1112. The small aisleless church of **St. Andrew the Less**, on the north side of the road, was probably built by the canons in the 13C as a chapel outside the priory gates, and was extensively restored in the 19C. Just to the north, at the junction of Beche and Priory roads, is a small vaulted structure of clunch which is the sole survivor of the monastic buildings, possibly the kitchen.

About half a mile east, immediately beyond the railway bridge and opposite the Cambridge United football ground, is the tiny 12C **Stourbridge Chapel**, built as the chapel of a leper hospital maintained by the monks of Barnwell Priory. It consists of an aisleless nave separated from the chancel by a low arch enriched with chevron mouldings, and was given its present arch-braced roof in the 15C. After the Reformation it was used as a store, and as a beer-house during the Stourbridge Fair. It was restored in 1843–45 as a place of worship for railway labourers, and again in 1867, when Gilbert Scott inserted the Norman-style west window. It is now cared for by the Cambridge Preservation Society, and well worth a visit in spite of its drab surroundings (key at house near by).

3 ~ The American Military Cemetery and Madingley

The most attractive route to Madingley is by footpath, starting at the bridge over the Cam at the end of Garret Hostel Lane. From here the path runs west, skirting the University Library (Burrells Walk) to Adams Rd, which runs alongside Robinson College (signposted to Coton). From the far end of the road it is about 2 miles by footpath uphill to the village of **Coton**, from which a path to the right just after the medieval church crosses fields to the **American Military Cemetery** (☎ 01954 210350; also accessible from Madingley Rd park-and-ride: forms part of the bus tours operated by City Sightseeing). Created in 1944–54, it contains the remains of 3811 American servicemen based in Britain who were killed on operations during the Second World War, each grave marked by a stone cross or star of David; the beautifully landscaped gardens (by the Olmsted firm from Boston, Massachussets) overlook the flat Cambridgeshire countryside. To the right of the entrance is a long wall with the names of another 5127 servicemen whose bodies were never found, at the far end of which is the memorial chapel (architects Perry Stuart and Hepburn, Kehoe and Dean) with a mural map of the war in Europe and an impressive mosaic of the Resurrection and Last Judgment at the east end.

A little to the west of the cemetery another path crosses to the lane leading from Madingley Rd to **Madingley Hall**, now the home of Cambridge University's Department for Continuing Education. Built of brick in the 16C, it was remodelled in the 18C; at the entrance to the stable court is the elaborate 15C gateway to the Old Schools in Cambridge, removed to make way for the present east range in 1754. Next to the park entrance is the medieval **church**, with good furnishings and monuments to the Cotton family, owners of the Hall, and opposite is the popular *Three Horseshoes* inn, well-known for good food. The road to Madingley appears, along with other Cambridge locations, in E.M. Forster's novel *The Longest Journey*.

4 ~ The Gog Magogs

The **Gog Magog Hills**, about 4 miles southeast (leave Cambridge by Hills Rd), are the highest ground in the immediate vicinity of the city, rising to 222ft; for those without public transport the area is easily accessible from the Babraham Rd park-and-ride car park. The curious name may derive from a figure of a giant cut into the chalk, which has long disappeared. The hills are crossed by the old Roman Via Devana, now a grassy track, which ran from Colchester through Cambridge to Godmanchester near Huntingdon. On top of the hills is **Wandlebury Camp**, an Iron Age hill fort with the stable block of a vanished 18C house inside it; the area is maintained by the Cambridge Preservation

Society, and there are nature-trails, picnic places and a car park (fee payable) on the A1307 Haverhill road.

DAYS OUT FROM CAMBRIDGE
••

1~ Ely and the Fens

Ely (15 miles by road on A10, or by train or bus from Cambridge), on the River Great Ouse, is a small cathedral city and market town, described by the Venerable Bede in the early 8C as resembling 'an island surrounded by water and marshes ... it derives its name from the vast quantity of eels that are caught in the marshes'. It was the stronghold in which Hereward the Wake, 'the last of the English', made his final stand against the Normans (1070–71) after the Conquest. The city is dominated, as is the surrounding countryside, by the cathedral, one of the most impressive medieval buildings in England.

Ely Cathedral
Open all year, summer 07.00–19.00, winter 07.30–18.00, closes Sun 17.00; adm. charge. Choral Evensong weekdays, exc. Wed, 17.30, Sun choral services 10.30 and 15.45; ☎ 01353 667735, ▨ www.cathedral.ely.anglican.org.

The west end and the nave
The usual approach is from the west, and from here the dominant feature is the extraordinary late 12C **west tower**, 215ft high and carved all over with blind arcading of an almost oriental richness (the top storey dates from the late 14C and was originally surmounted by a lead spire, removed in 1801); the tower can be climbed during the holiday season (extra charge). To the south (right) is a **west transept**—a feature rarely seen in English churches—equally lavishly decorated; its counterpart on the other side of the tower fell down in the 15C, thus robbing the façade of its full dignity. At the base of the tower is the early 13C **Galilee Porch**, Early English in style, of two vaulted bays, with blind arcades on either side and an inner doorway of the utmost delicacy, flanked by shafts with stiff-leaf capitals.

Entering through the Galilee Porch, there is an impressive vista of the full length of the church, the architecture increasing in richness as the eye travels on to the stained glass of the east end lancets; until 1770 the view was blocked by a 12C stone screen, or pulpitum, which closed off the choir at the east end of the nave. To the left is Hans Feibusch's sculpture *Christus* and on the wall of the tower above it an abstract sculpture of *The Way of Life* by Jonathan Clarke, created as a Millennium project in 2000. Behind, and extending into the west end of the north aisle, is the cathedral **shop and refectory**, the latter providing snacks and lunches.

To the right is the southwest transept, adorned with interlaced arcading and opening into the apsidal **St. Catharine's Chapel**, rebuilt in 1848. An inconspicuous doorway in the corner of the transept gives access to the **Stained Glass Museum** (open Mon–Sat, 10.30–17.00, Sun 12.00–18.00, closes 16.30 in winter months; separate adm. charge, ☎ 01353 660347), housed in the south

Cathedral in the Fens

The first building at Ely was a Benedictine abbey for both monks and nuns, established by St. Etheldreda (or Audrey), Queen of Northumbria (d. 679), who retired from the world to the home of her girlhood, and became abbess in 673. Soon after her death miracles were being reported from the shrine set up to her and Ely became a goal of Anglo-Saxon pilgrimage. In 870 the Danes sacked the abbey, but in the 10C it was refounded by King Edgar (959–75) as a Benedictine monastery. William the Conqueror appointed as abbot a Norman, Simeon, who began the present structure in 1083, using stone from Barnack (Northants) transported here by water; the transepts and east end were completed by 1106 and three years later the church became the cathedral of a new diocese, while retaining its complement of Benedictine monks and the immense revenues derived from the lordship of the Isle of Ely.

The Norman nave and west tower were not finished until the end of the 12C and the Galilee (west porch) was added by Bishop Eustace (1198–1215). Bishop Hugh of Northwold (1229–54) lengthened the choir by six bays in the Early English style, which provided a worthy setting for St. Etheldreda's shrine. In 1322 the collapse of the central tower wrecked the Norman choir and gave the sacrist Alan de Walsingham and his team of craftsmen the chance to build the timber Octagon, one of the *tours de force* of English medieval architecture, and to rebuild the ruined west bays of thep-resent choir in an exquisite Decorated style; at the same time work began on the building of the equally sumptuous Lady Chapel, which was not com-pleted until 1353. The chantry chapels at the east end of the chancel aisles date from the late 15C and early 16C.

Many of the monastic buildings disappeared after the Dissolution, but the church survived in an increasingly dilapidated condition until the 1770s, when a major restoration was carried out by James Essex (see Emmanuel College, etc. in Cambridge). A second restoration by Gilbert Scott, starting in 1847, left the interior and exterior much in their present state.

triforium gallery. It traces the development of stained glass in England from the 13C—a small figure from the Lady Chapel—to the present day, using over 100 examples, most of them from demolished churches and secular buildings; the artists represented include Pugin, Burne-Jones and most of the famous 19C and early 20C manufacturers, as well as some interesting contemporary craftsmen. There are displays explaining the technicalities of glass-making, and from the gallery there are excellent views down into the nave.

The **nave**, one of the most satisfying works of Norman architecture in England, is nearly 250ft long and comprises 12 bays, with the triforium (gallery) arcade nearly equal in height to that of the main arcade, and a clerestory above; the wooden ceiling, depicting Old to the New Testament subjects, was painted in a convincingly medieval style by Henry le Strange, an amateur artist from Hunstanton (Norfolk) and Thomas Gambier Parry in 1858–64.

The aisles are vaulted in stone and the four east bays of the south aisle retain some of their original 12C colouring. The windows in the north aisle are Perpendicular insertions and those in the south aisle have been restored to their original Norman form; all are filled with Victorian stained glass by various artists including Henri and Alfred Gerente of Paris, much of it of very high quality. Near the east end of the nave lies Alan de Walsingham, builder of the Octagon, under a marble slab from which the brass has disappeared.

In the south aisle is the **Prior's Doorway** (c 1140), a superb example of English Romanesque sculpture; on the outside it is richly carved on the tympanum with Christ in Majesty, worshipped by angels, and on the imposts and shafts with fanciful figures of men and beasts. The capitals are carved with an interlaced pattern known as Solomon's Knot, symbolic of infinity.

Near the door is the base of a Saxon Cross, called '**Ovin's Stone**', erected to Ovinus, a leading East Anglian thegn (land-holder) and a vassal of Queen Etheldreda; the inscription on the pedestal reads: 'Lucem tuam Ovino da Deus et requiem amen' ('O God, grant Ovinus thy light and rest, amen'). He eventually renounced the world and joined St. Chad's brotherhood at Lastingham in Yorkshire.

The Prior's Doorway

The transepts and the Octagon

The aisled transepts are the oldest parts of the cathedral (1083–1106), their architecture plainer and less smoothly articulated than that of the nave (note the absence of the tall vertical shafts which give vertical emphasis to the nave); the timber hammerbeam roofs, adorned with brightly painted carved angels, date from the 15C. The attenuated bronze group of *Christ and Mary Magdalene* in the **south transept** is by David Wynne (1963); there is a virtually identical group at Magdalen College, Oxford.

At the heart of the cathedral is the **Octagon**, replacing the collapsed Romanesque central tower. It is lit by large windows with flowing Decorated tracery and is surmounted by a lantern which seems to be poised effortlessly in space. The lantern is of wood, and weighs 400 tons; the oaks for the corner posts, which are 63ft long, came from Chicksands (Bedfordshire). The weight is distributed by a wooden framework, on the principle of the hammerbeam, out of sight behind the vaulting: an unparalleled achievement. A model is displayed in the north transept, and tours are given during the summer months (extra charge).

The Octagon was the brainchild of the Sacrist, Alan de Walsingham, but the lantern could not have been carried out without the creative involvement of the master carpenter, almost certainly William Hurley, who worked for the King at Westminster and Windsor. High up on the angle shafts of the stone piers are carved **corbels** depicting incidents from the life of St. Etheldreda, and on the capitals of the arches are carved heads, reputedly of King Edward III and Queen Philippa, Alan de Walsingham and other worthies. The **lantern** was restored by Gilbert Scott in 1861–73, and the paintings, by Thomas Gambier Parry, date from that time, but the wooden boss of Christ in Judgment survives form the 14C.

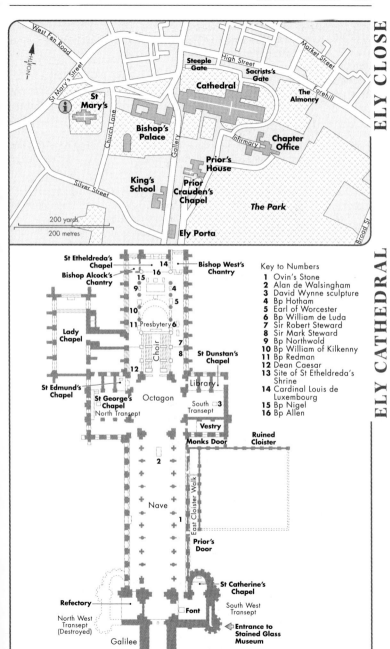

Map labels (Ely Close):

West Fen Road
High Street
Market Street
St Mary's Street
Steeple Gate
Sacrist's Gate
Cathedral
The Almonry
Forehill
St Mary's
Bishop's Palace
Gallery
Infirmary
Chapter Office
Church Lane
Prior's House
Silver Street
King's School
Prior Crauden's Chapel
The Park
200 yards
200 metres
Ely Porta
Broad St

Map labels (Ely Cathedral):

St Etheldreda's Chapel
Bishop Alcock's Chantry
14
16
15
Bishop West's Chantry
9
4
5
10
11 Presbytery 6
Lady Chapel
7
8
St Dunstan's Chapel
12
St Edmund's Chapel
Choir
St George's Chapel
Octagon
North Transept
Library
South Transept 3
Vestry
Monks Door
Ruined Cloister
2
East Cloister Walk
Nave
1
Prior's Door
St Catherine's Chapel
Refectory
Font
South West Transept
North West Transept (Destroyed)
Galilee
Entrance to Stained Glass Museum

Key to Numbers

1 Ovin's Stone
2 Alan de Walsingham
3 David Wynne sculpture
4 Bp Hotham
5 Earl of Worcester
6 Bp William de Luda
7 Sir Robert Steward
8 Sir Mark Steward
9 Bp Northwold
10 Bp William of Kilkenny
11 Bp Redman
12 Dean Caesar
13 Site of St Etheldreda's Shrine
14 Cardinal Louis de Luxembourg
15 Bp Nigel
16 Bp Allen

Until James Essex's restoration the choir stalls were under the Octagon, but they were then removed to the chancel; a recent re-ordering has introduced a nave altar at which services are regularly held.

On the east side of the north transept is **St. Edmund's Chapel**, with a 15C screen and a 12C wall painting of St. Edmund's martyrdom at the hands of the Danes, and next to it is **St. George's Chapel**, restored as a war memorial by Guy Dawber (1922). The northwest corner of the transept was restored by the Cambridge mason Robert Grumbold after damage from an earthquake in 1699, with advice from Sir Christopher Wren, whose uncle had been Bishop of Ely; the outer side of the north door is Classical in character.

The east end and Lady Chapel

The **choir** is separated from the Octagon by a wooden screen, designed by Gilbert Scott (1847–52). The bays immediately east of the screen were rebuilt after the fall of the central tower in 1322 and are lavishly embellished in the Decorated style, with copious carving around the arches, an elaborately traceried triforium and a complex lierne vault with some excellent carved bosses. The choir stalls are of the same date as the Octagon (completed 1342), beneath which they originally stood, and have an unusually good set of misericords; the front stalls are by Scott, as is the organ case and the sumptuous marble floor.

To the east is the **presbytery**, dating from 1234–52. It is a superb example of the first (Early English) phase of English Gothic, with the arcades supported on clustered shafts of Purbeck marble with stiff-leaf capitals, a beautiful tierceron vault sprouting from shafts which rest on lavishly carved corbels and a noble grouping of tall lancet windows at the east end. An inscribed slate slab in front of the high altar marks the site of St. Etheldreda's shrine; the reredos (1850–68) is by Scott and on the high altar a cross by Louis Osman (1964) stands between candlesticks of 1661. There is some particularly fine 19C glass (by William Wailes, 1851–57) in the east windows, admirably recapturing the style and colouring of medieval glass.

The aisles on either side of the chancel contain a number of important monuments, mostly to past bishops. Especially noteworthy in the **north choir aisle** are those to (west to east) Bishop Nigel, a carved slab of Tournai marble (c 1150) with the human soul represented by a naked figure held by an angel; Bishop Redman (d. 1506), an elaborate and much-restored confection dating from the last period of English Gothic and Bishop Hugh de Northwold, the builder of the east end of the cathedral (d. 1254), a recumbent figure in Purbeck marble. There is also a brass commemorating the architect George Basevi, the architect of the Fitzwilliam Museum in Cambridge, who died after a fall from the scaffolding at Ely Cathedral.

A newly-built passage leads from the north choir aisle to the **Lady Chapel**, one of the best examples of the Decorated phase of English Gothic architecture. Started c 1321 and completed c 1353, it was placed away from the more usual position to the east of the chancel, so as not to compete with the shrine of the patroness, St. Etheldreda. It is an aisleless building, lit by huge windows with flowing tracery and covered by a lierne vault of unusual flatness, the widest (46ft) vault in medieval England. Above and within the amazingly complex arcade of 'nodding' ogee arches under the windows are carvings of the utmost richness and delicacy, illustrating the Life of the Virgin. The Chapel served as a parish church from 1566 to 1938, when it was restored to its present form, and it has recently been cleaned and refurbished.

Most of the statuettes are badly damaged, partly due to the erosion of the clunch (soft chalky limestone) of which they are made, partly to the iconoclasm of the Duke of Somerset, Lord Protector during the reign of Edward VI, in the 1540s; the great Gothic Revivalist A.W.N. Pugin is supposed to have wept when he saw them for the first time, and he must also have lamented the virtual disappearance of the 14C stained glass, except for some fragments which survive in the window over the entrance. The interior now has a cold, even light, very different from the mysterious, almost magical luminosity intended by the medieval builders, but some colour has been introduced by a painted statue of the Virgin Mary by David Wynne over the altar, and works of art are sometimes displayed around the walls.

At the east end of the north choir aisle is **Bishop Alcock's Chantry**, a wild extravaganza of lace-like late Gothic ornament carved in clunch and commemorating the founder of Jesus College, Cambridge; as in the College, Alcock's rebus of a cock standing on a globe is omnipresent. In the corresponding position at the end of the south chancel aisle, beyond the retrochoir (St. Etheldreda'a Chapel), is **Bishop West's Chantry**, similar in its general character to Alcock's, but with Renaissance motifs (cherubs, etc.) creeping in, in accordance with the changing tastes of Henry VIII's court before West's death in 1534. In the **south choir aisle** is the much-restored canopied tomb of John Tiptoft, Earl of Worcester (d. 1470), along with several monuments to post-Reformation divines: an interesting contrast to those of their medieval predecessors.

The precincts

As one of the largest cathedral priories in England, Ely had many ancillary buildings clustered around the cathedral church and of these several still survive, especially to the south. They are approached from the cathedral through the **South Doorway**, or Monks' Doorway, at the east end of the south aisle, decorated on the cloister side with designs of great complexity. The **cloisters** themselves have largely disappeared, except for part of the east and north walks. A tombstone to William Pickering and Richard Edger (both died in 1845 in an accident during the building of the local railway) is inscribed with a naive poem called *The Spiritual Railway*, and another monument commemorates Humphrey Smith (d. 1743), who was 'eminent for his Superior Abilities in draining Fenny and Marsh lands'.

To the east, beyond the site of the chapter house, is a complex of 12C buildings which housed the monastic **Infirmary**. This was a large aisled stone structure of c 1175–85, the rounded arcades of which survive on either side of a lane leading to the former chapel, now the **Deanery** and Chapter Office; the miscellaneous buildings on either side of the lane date from after the 14C, when the aisles were cut off from the 'nave'. Looking back to the Cathedral, the intricate timber superstructure of the 14C Octagon, as restored by Gilbert Scott, can be clearly seen crowning the crossing, and a path leads from here around the east end of the cathedral to the Sacrist's Gate (see below).

To the southwest of the cloisters is a larger group of medieval buildings including the former Deanery, Prior's House and guest quarters. With the expulsion of the monks, the buildings were taken over by the **King's School**, founded by Henry VIII in 1539 as successor to the monastic school, and there have been many subsequent rebuildings and alterations. Of the buildings accessible to visitors, the least altered, and most beautiful, is **Prior Crauden's Chapel** (key at Chapter Office or from desk by south door of the Cathedral), attached to the largely 14C Priory, now part of the School. Built c 1324–25, over a 13C undercroft, the Chapel is a small but exquisite example of Decorated architecture at its most elaborate, with windows of elaborate flowing tracery, 'nodding' ogee arches like those of the Lady Chapel, fragmentary wall paintings and an original tiled pavement on which Adam and Eve are depicted.

The former Deanery to the north (now the **Bishop's Palace**: no adm.) was constructed in the 14C out of the old monastic guest-hall and retains some 13C and 14C work and remains of the 12C monks' kitchen; next to it is the much-rebuilt **Queen's Hall** (no adm.), built in the 14C as a hall for guests.

On the south side of the precinct is **Ely Porta**, the great gateway of the monastery, begun in 1397 and leading into a street called The Gallery from which it is a short walk back to the west front of the cathedral. To the east is a park, from which there are excellent views of the south front of the Cathedral, and on the south side of the park is **Cherry Hill**, the motte of the vanished 12C castle; at the summit is a column celebrating the local historian Canon James Bentham (1779).

The town

The former **Bishop's Palace** facing the cathedral is mainly late 17C, but retains the impressive brick tower built as a gatehouse by Bishop Alcock (d. 1501) and another tower and a long gallery built by Bishop Goodrich (d. 1554); it is now a Sue Ryder Home (no adm.). On **Palace Green**, in front of the cathedral, is a cannon captured from the Russians at Sebastopol and presented to Ely by Queen Victoria in 1860, and to the west is **St. Mary's church**, built in the Transitional style by Bishop Eustace (1198–1215), but with later alterations, including the 13C (Early English) chancel, 14C west tower and spire and 15C (Perpendicular) clerestory. The half-timbered **Oliver Cromwell House** nearby in St. Mary's St, is now the **Tourist Information Centre**. Cromwell's uncle leased property from the Dean and Chapter of Ely and the future Lord Protector lived here while he was Member of Parliament for Cambridge in the years before the Civil War. The house has recently been restored with appropriately furnished rooms (open Oct–Mar daily exc. Sun 10.00–17.15, Apr–Sept daily 10.00–18.00, ☎ 01353 662062). In the same street (no. 25) is the highly recommended *Old Fire Engine House* restaurant.

Returning along St. Mary's St to the town centre, a left turn into Market St by the *Lamb Hotel* (good food) leads to the former Bishops' Gaol, dating back to the 13C and housing the recently-restored **Ely Museum** (open daily 10.30–17.30, summer, 10.30–16.30 winter, ☎ 01353 666655); the displays illustrate local archaeology and Fenland crafts and trades, and the condemned and debtors' cells can be seen on the first floor. Further south, the High St flanks the cathedral close, which can be entered through **Steeple Gate** (16C timber-framing over a 14C undercroft). Beyond it to the east are the **Goldsmith's Tower** and the **Sacrist's Gate**, part of the sacristy rebuilt by Alan de Walsingham after 1322; it gives access to the east end of the cathedral. Next to the Sacristy is the **Almonry**, where the medieval monks distributed largesse to the poor; it is now a restaurant, with a vaulted undercroft of c 1200. Here High St changes its name to **Fore Hill**, which leads to the river, where there are boats for hire and pleasant walks; the Cambridge University trial eights practise here during Lent term. The old **Maltings** of 1868 has recently been turned into a cinema and restaurant complex.

Fens and Fenmen

Ely is in the heart of the Fens: an almost totally flat tract of land stretching north from Cambridge into Norfolk and Lincolnshire, criss-crossed by dykes and drainage channels, with huge skyscapes and a curious translucency of atmosphere. They are not beautiful in the conventional picturesque sense, but have a strange and compelling atmosphere, quite unlike that of any other part of England. Much of the land is below sea-level and was for centuries either under water, or waterlogged. Some drainage was carried out by the Romans and a few remains of their work still exist in the fragments of Carr Dyke, but after their departure the land was reflooded.

Determined attempts at reclamation, vigorously opposed by the local 'fen-slodgers' who earned their living by fishing and wild fowling, began in the 17C. Much of the work was carried out by the Dutch engineer Cornelius Vermuyden (d. 1677) under the aegis of the Earl of Bedford, after whom the Bedford rivers and Bedford Levels are named. The reclaimed land is extremely fertile and is now used for large-scale commercial market-gardening. The scattered towns and villages are always built on rising ground, to lift them above flood level and to provide a solid foundation. Ely in particular, on a slight hill, is visible from a great distance in this flat country.

The route back to Cambridge leads through flat Fen country. Just outside the village of **Stretham** on the A10 (12 miles north of Cambridge) is the **Old Pumping Engine** (turn right in the village onto A1123, then right again down a signed side road: open second Sunday of the month in summer, and bank holidays, ☎ 01353 649210). It is the sole surviving example of a steam-powered fen-drainage engine, built in 1831 to lift water from the surrounding channels into the river Ouse and last used in 1941. Its vast boilers, valves, pistons and flywheel give an impression of enormous power.

Just south of the A1123 and 3½ miles east of Stretham, lies **Wicken Fen National Nature Reserve** (National Trust, open all year daily exc. Christmas; ☎ 01353 720274, ✉ wicken.org.uk; adm. charge): 600 acres of primeval wetland, and the last surviving 'unimproved' remnant of the Great Fen. This is one of the most important nature reserves in Europe, providing habitats for a wide variety of flowers, birds, insects and butterflies; even the uninitiated can enjoy its quiet and mystery. Boardwalks give access to several hides; there is also an occasionally operating windpump and a Fen Cottage (open Sunday afternoons Apr–Oct, 14.00–17.00), as well as a visitor centre, where snacks can be obtained.

Denny Abbey

Returning to the A10, 9 miles north of Cambridge, is Denny Abbey, with its associated **Farmland Museum** (owned by English Heritage and the Farmland Museum: abbey and museum open Apr–Oct daily 12.00–17.00, ☎ 01223 860988; buses from Cambridge).

History

Founded c 1159 as a dependent cell of Ely, Denny Priory (as it then was) was transferred c 1170 to the Knights Templar and then, on the dissolution of that order in 1312, to the Knights Hospitaller. In 1327 it was granted by Edward III to Mary, Countess of Pembroke, the founder of Pembroke College, Cambridge. She established a community of Franciscan nuns here, one of only three such houses in medieval England, reserving part of the buildings for her own use and choosing to be buried there after her death in 1377. Most of the buildings were demolished after the Dissolution of the Monasteries, but the nave and transepts of the original Benedictine church survived as part of a farmhouse and the Franciscan refectory lingered on as a barn.

Recent restoration by English Heritage has made it possible to disentangle the complex and fascinating history of the **church**, whose oldest parts are the transepts, crossing and east bays of the nave dating from c 1160–70 (the west end of the nave and the south aisle were added by the Templars). The rounded late 12C crossing arches with their carved capitals are now embedded in later masonry, following the Countess of Pembroke's decision to turn the nave and transepts into residential accommodation for herself, the nuns and guests, and to build a new church immediately to the east (now entirely vanished); there were further alterations in the 16C and 18C, when sash windows were introduced. To the north is the spacious **Refectory**, dating from the mid-14C, and giving an idea of the grandeur of the Countess's foundation.

The recently restored **farm buildings** house displays of village life and farming in Cambridgeshire in the early 20C, including a reconstructed farm-worker's cottage and a fenman's hut; special exhibitions and activities for children are often arranged.

2 ~ Newmarket and the Fen Edge

Newmarket
Newmarket, the capital of English horse-racing, lies 13 miles to the northeast of Cambridge on the edge of chalk downland. It can be quickly reached from Cambridge by the fast A45 road, or by bus or train.

History

The small town stands on the edge of a chalky upland or Heath whose light, well-drained soil has for over 300 years provided conditions ideal for racing. James I was Newmarket's earliest royal patron and it was especially favoured by Charles II. There was a disastrous fire in 1683, but the precipitate departure of the royal party frustrated the plans which were being hatched to assassinate the King and his brother James as they returned to London (the Rye House Plot). The town later prospered through the coaching trade as well as from horse racing.

Newmarket was largely rebuilt in brick in the 18C and 19C, but there are few buildings of special architectural distinction. For lovers of the Turf, however, their absence is more than compensated for by the **National Horseracing**

Museum (open Apr–Oct Tues–Sun, also bank hol. Mon and Mon in July/Aug, 10.00–17.00, ☎ 01638 667333, ✉ www.nhrm.co.uk), housed in the elegant Old Subscription Rooms in the broad, spacious High St.

All aspects of horse racing and its history are lucidly explained and illustrated here, from royal patronage to the sign-language of the tick-tack man, bloodstock breeding to famous racecourse entertainers. Exhibits include old prints, paintings belonging to the British Sporting Art Trust, blown-up press photographs, racing trophies and memorabilia, a weighing-in room and a horsedrawn ambulance, and such curiosities as the telegram sent by Queen Alexandra to the royal jockey Herbert Jones after he and his horse were brought down in the Derby of 1913 by the militant suffragette Emily Davidson, described as 'that lunatic brutal woman' (she was killed, the horse and jockey recovered). Brave visitors can even gallop on a simulated racehorse aptly known as 'Long Legs'. The displays are varied from time to time and are constantly being added to. Tours to see horses training, etc, leave daily at 09.20, but must be booked in advance (extra charge).

Next door is the handsome neo-Georgian **Jockey Club** (Sir Albert Richardson, 1933), and nearby in Palace St is **Palace House**, a restored fragment of Charles II's house and now the **Tourist Information Centre** (☎ 01638 667200). At the end of the Avenue (right, just short of the Jockey Club) are **Tattersall's Sales Paddocks**. Regular horse sales were started by Richard Tattersall in 1776 at Hyde Park Corner in London. In 1865 they were moved to Knightsbridge (where sales were held until 1939) and the firm established itself at Newmarket in 1870. One reminder of the London days is the Fox Rotunda in the Park Paddocks Lower Parade Ring; the base was originally a fountain at Hyde Park Corner supporting a bust of the Prince Regent, who was a friend of Mr Tattersall. Another is the Arch (Victorian) at the top of the driveway, which was formerly the entrance to the Knightsbridge sale yard. On top of the Sales Ring (Sir Albert Richardson; completed 1966) is a beautiful copper weathervane of Pegasus, over 200 years old. The Classical 'lead' plant holders round the outside of the ring are modern imitations.

The **racecourses**, where many of the classic flat races take place, notably the Cambridgeshire and the Two Thousand Guineas (both October) and the Cesarewitch (spring), and the **National Stud**, lie between the A45 bypass and the Cambridge road (A1303); tours of the Stud are arranged from March to September and on race days in October (☎ 01638 666789, ✉ www.nationalstud. co.uk: booking advisable). There are many other studs and training stables in the vicinity, and horses may be seen on the gallops (mostly northeast of the town, on each side of A1304) in the early mornings.

An interesting route leads back by road from Newmarket to Cambridge along the edge of the Fens. Two miles from Newmarket at the junction of the B1103 and B1102 roads is **Burwell**, a large village which, like others in this part of Cambridgeshire, once profited from a flourishing trade along the navigable waterways to the sea. The magnificent mid-15C **church**, built of flint and locally quarried clunch, is flooded with light and is rich in stone and wood carving; the master mason may have been the Reginald Ely who worked at Queens' College, Cambridge and on the chapel at King's.

Next to the church are the earthworks of a Norman castle and a little to the north in Mill Close is a splendid windmill, complete with sails. Next to it is **Burwell Museum of Fen Edge Village Life** (open Easter–Oct, Thur, Sun & bank hol. Mon 14.00–17.00, ☎ 01638 741933), housed in a group of old farm buildings. It contains exhibits and artefacts relating to local farming, industries and fenland trades, as well as a blacksmith's forge and wheelwright's shop.

About half a mile south of Burwell the B1102 road crosses the line of the **Devil's Ditch**, one of the three great defensive earthworks of Cambridgeshire, built some time between the withdrawal of the Roman legions (c 420) and the Anglo-Saxon wars of the 7C and 8C (the others are Fleam Dyke and Bran's Ditch). It extends southeast in a straight line from Reach on the edge of the Fens, across Newmarket Heath to Stetchworth, 7½ miles away; a footpath along the top provides wide views in all directions, and in the spring a rich variety of wild flowers flourishes in its chalky soil.

A little further on along the B1102 is **Swaffham Prior**, an attractive village with the unusual feature of two churches of medieval origin standing side by side in the same churchyard. They originally served separate parishes, which were united in 1667. One of the churches, St. Cyriac's, was then demolished with the exception of the 15C flint tower, notable mainly for its unusual octagonal upper storey. The adjacent church, St. Mary's, then served the united parishes, but in 1767 its mainly 12C tower—also octagonal in its upper stages—was struck by lightning, and the parishioners later decided to move to St. Cyriac's, which was rebuilt in a plain 'churchwarden Gothic' style in 1809–11. This subsequently fell into disrepair, and in 1878 St. Mary's was restored, leaving St. Cyriac's to fall into ruin; the mainly Perpendicular interior has an interesting series of windows, showing inter alia First World War scenes, Wicken Fen and the Statue of Liberty. St. Cyriac's was renovated in the 1970s and now serves as a parish hall.

From here the B1102 continues through Swaffham Bulbeck to the village of Lode (6 miles from Cambridge) and Anglesey Abbey.

Anglesey Abbey
Open Apr–Oct, Wed–Sun and bank hol. Mon 13.00–17.00; gardens open same days 10.30–17.30, also daily in July, Aug; 'winter walk' open Nov–March Wed–Sun 10.30–16.00; ☎ 01223 811200, ✉ www.nationaltrust.org.uk. Buses from Cambridge.

History
There was a house of Augustinian Canons here from 1135 until the Dissolution of the Monasteries, but of this only the vaulted Parlour (the present Dining Room) survives in anything like its original form. The monastic remains were incorporated into a house in the 16C and in about 1630 this was given a new south front which survives largely intact today (the gables are a 20C replacement); it was probably built by Thomas Parker, son-in-law of Thomas Hobson, the famous (or notorious) Cambridge carrier. The Parker family were succeeded by Sir George Downing, founder of Downing College, but the present splendour of the house and grounds is due to Huttleston Broughton, 1st Lord Fairhaven, a wealthy collector who bought the property in 1926. The son of an Englishman who had made a fortune in American mining and railways and had married a New York heiress, he remodelled and enlarged the interior the house and created the extensive gardens for which Anglesey is mainly famous. When he died in 1966 both house and grounds passed to the National Trust.

The richly decorated **interior** exudes an aura of luxurious connoisseurship. There are fine pieces of furniture (eg, a late 18C French bureau made for Tsar Paul I), tapestries, sculpture (an early 16C German limewood figure of St. Christopher), bronzes, clocks, jewelled crosses, armour, ceramics and silver (e.g., a 'Shield of Achilles' by Flaxman). The paintings include works by Gainsborough, Bonington, Wilson, Sandby, Etty and Constable (a version of his *View of the Thames with the opening of Waterloo Bridge*). There is also a gallery full of views of Windsor Castle.

But the highlight of the collection, seen at the very end of the tour, is the pair of pictures known as 'Altieri Claudes' (*The Father of Psyche sacrificing at the Temple of Apollo* and *The Landing of Aeneas*). They were deemed to be of such importance that when first brought to England (by William Beckford, another famous collector) in 1799 they received a naval escort. In the library are over 9000 books, many of them specially bound.

The **gardens** were laid out by Lord Fairhaven between 1926 and the 1960s on what must have seemed a most unpromising 100-acre fenland site. They are on a magnificent scale, recalling the great country-house gardens of the Baroque era. Huge quantities of trees were planted (some, alas, flattened in gales or destroyed by Dutch Elm Disease), and avenues and formal enclosures created, enhanced by excellent examples of 18C statuary and Classical ornaments, notably in the Emperors' walk, east of the main drive. To the west of the house there are flower gardens, enclosed by clipped beech hedges, and to the east is an arboretum with several examples of rare trees. In the northeast corner of the grounds, near the Quarry Pool, is the weatherboarded **Lode Mill**, on what may be a Roman drainage ditch; it has been restored, and corn is ground there regularly (opening times as for house, also weekends Nov–March 11.00–15.30).

3 ~ Bury St. Edmunds and West Suffolk

Bury St. Edmunds

Bury St. Edmunds (27 miles from Cambridge on A45: also accessible by bus and train) is the county town of West Suffolk, and one of the most attractive market towns in the east of England.

History

Bury owes its foundation and its initial prosperity to the Benedictine abbey built on the site of the martyrdom of Edmund, king of the East Angles, in 869. The Abbey was rebuilt by the Normans and became one of the most important in England, vying locally with the Benedictine cathedral priory of Ely. But the church was virtually razed to the ground after the Reformation, leaving only two magnificent gatehouses as witnesses to its past glory. The town, however, laid out on a grid plan just after the Norman Conquest, continued to flourish and was extensively rebuilt in the 18C and early 19C, when it became a fashionable place of resort for the local gentry. The ecclesiastical importance of Bury returned in the 20C, when one of the two surviving medieval churches, St. James, became the cathedral of a new diocese. An Arts Festival is held here each May.

A tour of Bury should begin in the **Abbey Gardens**, created in the 19C as a public setting for the forlorn stumps of flint which are all that remain of the once magnificent Norman abbey church, 100ft longer than Ely Cathedral. On the northwestern side is the **Abbey Gate**, begun after its predecessor was destroyed by riotous townspeople in 1327; the western side has good carving in the Decorated Gothic style. It looks out onto **Angel Hill**, an open space of largely 18C character, with the town's main inn, the *Angel*, dating from 1779, on the west side and the **Tourist Information Centre** (☎ 01284 764667) to the east at no. 6. On the south side are the assembly rooms or **Athenaeum** (Francis Sandys, 1804), with a superb Neo-classical ballroom behind the stuccoed Classical façade.

Crown St leads out of Angel Hill, and on the east side, close to the Athenaeum, is the **Cathedral** (☎ 01284 754933), built as the parish church of St. James on the edge of the Abbey precincts in 1503 and raised to cathedral status in 1914. It is a typical East Anglian town church, Perpendicular Gothic in style, and was probably designed by the master mason John Wastell, a local man who was also responsible for the fan vault in King's College Chapel, Cambridge. The impressive chancel and crossing were designed by Stephen Dykes Bower in a style which complements that of the medieval nave without imitating it; they were completed in 1970, and a new central tower, also by Dykes Bower, is expected to be finished in 2004.

Immediately to the south of the cathedral is the massive **Norman Gateway** to the abbey precincts, built between 1120 and 1148 and embellished with Romanesque arches. It looks out onto Chequer Square, another attractive open space of largely 18C character. A little further south in Crown St is **St. Mary's church**, another splendid Perpendicular Gothic parish church, less altered than the Cathedral. It dates largely from the mid- to late 15C, and has a particularly fine hammer-beam roof embellished with angels. There are also several notable brasses and other monuments, including a cadaver figure of a clothier, John Baret, who endowed a chantry in the former Lady Chapel in the south aisle in 1467; its painted roof still survives.

Turning left into **Honey Hill** from St. Mary's is a handsome and well-preserved brick house of 1736-8 now serving as the **Manor House Museum** (open Wed–Sun 11.00–16.00, ☎ 01284 757072). It was built for Elizabeth, Lady Hervey, of Ickworth (see below), to the designs of Sir James Burrough, the guiding spirit behind the restoration of several Cambridge colleges in the 18C. Used for some years as local government offices, it became a museum in 1993 and now contains a good collection of pictures and costumes and an outstanding collection of clocks and watches, some of them dating from the 16C. The rooms retain much of their original decoration, including some excellent plasterwork.

To the south of the museum is the old **Greene King brewery**, recently relocated to a more spacious site on the edge of the town, and still a major local employer; tours of the old brewery are available (☎ 01284 714287). Opposite it in Westgate St is the sober façade of the **Theatre Royal**, built in 1819 to the design of William Wilkins, another architect much represented in Cambridge (open June–Aug Tues & Thurs 11.00–1300, 14.00–16.00, Sat 11.00–13.00, ☎ 01284 769505). The building, with its perfectly preserved auditorium, was used for many years as a storage place for beer barrels, but was restored in 1965 and plays are performed there regularly.

Returning along Crown St, a left turn into **Churchgate St** opposite the Norman gateway leads into the heart of the medieval planned town, where some late-medieval timber houses survive alongside others rebuilt in brick in the 18C. On the right, after Hatter St, is the richly detailed red-brick front of the **Unitarian Meeting House** (1711–12), testifying to the important part played by Nonconformity in the town's history. A right turn into the largely 18C Guildhall St, at the end of Churchgate St, leads to the much-rebuilt **Guildhall** of the medieval Candlemas Guild, still entered through a 15C porch.

The medieval market place was at the far (north) end of Guildhall St, and, although reduced in size by 'encroachments', it is still the commercial centre of the town. At the end of Guildhall St is the impressive Classical **Corn Exchange** (1861), and behind it, in a narrow street called The Traverse, is the *Nutshell*, claimed to be the smallest pub in England. Beyond it is **Cupola House**, built by an apothecary in the late 17C, and now also a pub (good food); the 'pleasing prospect' from the turret which gives the house its name was mentioned by the traveller Celia Fiennes in 1698. On the opposite side of the Traverse, facing Cornhill—the present market square in which open-air markets are regularly held—is the **Market Cross**, an accomplished Classical building by Robert Adam (1774–80); the upper floor, originally a theatre, became a concert hall in the 19C, when Franz Liszt, *inter alia*, performed there. It is now an exhibition room.

On the far side of Cornhill is **Moyses Hall**, dating from c 1180 and one of the most complete English town houses of its date. Having undergone many vicissitudes—including use as a gaol and a railway parcels office—and several restorations, it became a museum in 1899 and now houses collections relating to the history of the town (open Mon–Fri 10.30–16.30, Sat–Sun 11.00–14.00, ☎ 01284 706183). From here a short walk leads along Buttermarket and Abbeygate St to Angel Hill and the beginning of the walk.

Ickworth

Southwest of Bury 3 miles along the A143 at Horringer is Ickworth, one of the most impressive Neo-classical houses in England (National Trust: open late Mar–Oct Fri–Tues 13.00–17.00, 16.30 in Oct. Park open all year; ☎ 01284 735270, ✉ www. nationaltrust.org.uk. Accessible by bus from Bury).

History

The estate was acquired by the Hervey family in the 15C, but although they were ennobled as Earls of Bristol in the early 18C their house was for many years surprisingly unpretentious. This defect was remedied in a spectacular fashion by Frederick Hervey, the notorious 'Earl Bishop' of Bristol, who began the present house in 1796 with the intention of filling it with works of art acquired on the prolonged foreign tours to which the numerous Hotels Bristol on the Continent bear witness. The architect was an Italian, Mario Asprucci, but the execution of the house was placed in the hands of Francis Sandys, who had already worked for the Earl Bishop on his Irish estates. The house was left unfinished at the Earl Bishop's death in 1803 and a large part of his art collection was seized by Napoleon and never reached Ickworth. The building was completed by the 1st Marquess of Bristol in 1824–29 and it remained a family home until recent times; it now belongs to the National Trust, which has recently refurbished the interior and has turned the east wing into a hotel.

Ickworth is a massive house of Neo-classical character set in the middle of an extensive park, with a 600ft long **façade** made up of a central rotunda containing the main rooms and two wings joined to it by curved corridors. It is built of brick and stucco, with terracotta plaques over the rotunda windows containing representations of scenes from Homer, from Flaxman's exquisite illustrations. There is sculptural group by Flaxman (*The Fury of Atamas*), commisioned in Rome by the Earl Bishop, in the staircase hall, and the main **reception rooms**, lavishly decorated in the Regency taste, contain excellent 18C furniture collected by the 1st Marquess of Bristol. There are also some Old Master paintings, including works by Titian and Velázquez, and a good collection of family portraits by Hogarth, Reynolds, the Suffolk-born Gainsborough, and Elisabeth Vigée le Brun, whose portrait of the Earl Bishop shows him enigmatically smiling with a smoking Vesuvius in the background. There is also a good collection of silver, and off the west corridor is a Pompeian Room of 1879: one of the best examples of this mode of decoration in England.

Further south, and only easily accessible by car (A131 south from Bury, then A1141), is **Lavenham**, one of the most attractive small towns in this part of England. It became prosperous through the cloth trade in the later Middle Ages, and has a magnificent 15C **church** constructed out of the munificence of local clothiers, including the Spring family, whose chantry chapel survives inside. Lavenham has remained little changed since the 16C, when it was the fourteenth richest town in England, and many of its timber-framed buildings survive virtually intact, notably the **Guildhall** of the Corpus Christi Guild, which contains fascinating displays relating to the history of cloth-making in the town (National Trust: **open** Mar and Nov Sat, Sun 11.00–16.00; Apr Wed–Sun 11.00–17.00; May–Oct daily 11.00–17.00, ☎ 01787 247646). Next to it to the left is an excellent National Trust tea-room, and on the other side is the Tourist Information Centre.

A couple of miles southwest of Lavenham, on the A134, is **Long Melford**, a large roadside village which also owed its medieval prosperity to the cloth industry. Facing the green at the northern end of the village is the magnificent 15C **church**, built by the Cloptons, another wealthy family of clothiers whose chantry chapel of c 1496 is virtually a separate building at the east end, containing an excellent set of memorial brasses and other fittings. To the right (east) of the green, at the southern end, is **Melford Hall** (National Trust: open Apr, Oct Sat, Sun 14.00–17.30; May–Sept Wed–Sun 14.00–17.30, ☎ 01787 880286, 🖾 www.nationaltrust.org.uk), a red-brick Elizabethan house built on the site of a country retreat of the Abbots of Bury by Sir William Cordell, a rich lawyer, in the late 1550s or early 1560s. The interior was much altered in 1813 by a later owner, Sir William Parker, son of an admiral, to the designs of Thomas Hopper, and the rooms contain a good collection of naval pictures and family memorabilia. Outside in the gardens there are remnants of Elizabethan terraces. Opposite, on the west side of the green, is **Trinity Hospital**, founded as almshouses by Sir William Cordell in 1573 but much rebuilt in 1847. To the north of the church, and reached by its own drive from the A134, is **Kentwell Hall** (open Sun–Fri late July & Aug, also Wed, Thurs, Sun Apr–June & Sept 12.00–17.00, ☎ 01787 310207), another large 16C brick house, built within a moat by William Clopton, who died in 1562. The impressive neo-Tudor interiors date from a remodelling by Thomas Hopper in 1826 and there are attractive formal gardens created by the present owners, who acquired the house when it was virtually derelict in 1969 and have subsequently restored it. 'Re-creations of Tudor life' are held here in the summer.

From Long Melford the quickest route back to Cambridge is via the A1092, passing through the attractive villages of **Cavendish** and **Clare**, and then the A1307.

4 ~ Saffron Walden, Audley End and Thaxted

This route explores the pleasantly undulating countryside to the south and southeast of Cambridge. Here, over the Essex border, East Anglia merges into the Home Counties and there are numerous villages and small towns which still bear witness to the area's medieval prosperity.

Next to the M11 motorway at junction 11, on the A505 10 miles south of Cambridge is the **Imperial War Museum Duxford** (open daily exc. 24–26 Dec, 10.00–16.00 winter, 10.00–18.00 summer; ☎ 01223 835000, ✉ www.iwm.org.uk; free buses leave Cambridge railway station hourly in summer months). There has been a military airfield at Duxford since the First World War. During the Second World War it served as a fighter base for the RAF and the US Air Force and it is now a major outpost of the Imperial War Museum.

More than 150 historic aircraft from both world wars are on view in six huge hangars, along with some modern civilian aeroplanes, including Concorde 01; there is also a land warfare hall, featuring tanks and artillery. An impressive semicircular-roofed building of 1997 by Norman Foster (see Cambridge Law Faculty) houses a display of American aircraft. Nearby is a memorial sculpture by Renato Niemis comprising 52 glass panels and entitled *Counting the Cost*: namely the loss of 7031 aircraft from the Eighth and Ninth US Army air force and the aircraft of the US Navy during the Second World War. Pleasure flights are available at weekends (☎ 1870 902 6146, ✉ www.classic-wings.uk.com), and there are also occasional air displays.

Just south of the A1307 Cambridge-Haverhill road, on the B1052 10 miles southeast of Cambridge, is **Linton Zoo** (open daily winter 10.00–16.00, spring and autumn 10.00–17.00, summer 10.00–18.00, ☎ 01223 891308, ✉ www.stedmunds.co.uk/lifestyle/linton-zoo.html). Set in 16 acres of gardens, the zoo specialises in conservation and houses an exotic collection of creatures including tigers, tapirs, zebras, parrots, giant tortoises and tarantula spiders.

Continuing 5 miles south of Linton, just over the Essex county boundary, is Saffron Walden (15 miles from Cambridge via A1301 and B 184; buses from Cambridge), with the great house of Audley End immediately to the west.

Saffron Walden

History

Saffron Walden is one of the most attractive small towns in the east of England. Originally known as Chipping ('Market') Walden, it grew up to the south of a Norman castle built by the powerful de Mandeville family, who also founded an abbey not far away to the west on the site of the great house now known as Audley End (see below). In the late Middle Ages Walden's prosperity was based on the cloth trade and on the cultivation of the autumn-flowering saffron crocus; this was used for dyeing, and for medicinal purposes, and from it the town derives its present name.

There are many well-preserved timber-framed houses dating from the 15C to the 17C, most of them plastered and some 'pargetted' (covered in fanciful plaster patterns) in the typical East Anglian manner. The town was prosperous in the 18C and early 19C, but was bypassed by the main railway line and has suffered little from the ravages of modern industry and commercialism, preserving the character of a small but busy market town to a surprising degree, especially given its relative proximity (only 40 miles) to London.

The centre of the town is **Market Square**, where an open market is still regularly held. On the west side is the former Corn Exchange, an Italianate building of 1847–48 which now houses the **Library**, and facing it to the east is the impressive, red-brick **Barclay's Bank**, designed by W.E. Nesfield in 1874 in a free adaptation of the Tudor style for the Gibson family, prominent local brewers and bankers. The **Town Hall**, to the south, contains the **Tourist Information Centre** (☎ 01799 510444). At the far side of the wide **Common** to the east are traces of a medieval (or older) earth-cut maze, one of some half-dozen surviving in Britain; it was recut for the sum of 15 shillings in 1699.

The most interesting buildings are to the north and west of Market Square. At the corner of Market Hill and Church St is the former **Sun Inn**, now largely occupied by an antique shop; it dates back to the 14C, and is embellished externally with a splendid display of 17C pargetting, including the Saffron crocus and a battle between a local man Thomas Huckathrift and the 'Wisbech Giant'. The **parish church**, to the north, is one of the most magnificent of the many fine churches of East Anglia. It dates almost entirely from c 1450–1525, and has certain similarities to King's College Chapel, Cambridge, not surprising in view of the fact that the same master masons, Simon Clerk and John Wastell, worked on both buildings; the tall spire (193ft), admirably in keeping with the rest of the building, was added in 1831 by Rickman and Hutchinson (see St. John's College, Cambridge, New Court).

The aisled interior is lofty and light, with large Perpendicular windows and roof-timbers richly carved with bosses and heraldic badges, among which the Tudor Rose and portcullis are prominent; the saffron flower is carved in the spandrel of an arch in the south aisle of the church, facing the south door. The north chancel chapel contains an 18C copy of Correggio's *Madonna and Child with St. Jerome*, and in the south chancel chapel is the austere black Belgian slate tomb of Henry VIII's Chancellor Lord Audley (d. 1544), who bought Walden Abbey after the Dissolution and converted it into a house (see Audley End, below); Thomas Fuller thought that the slate was not blacker than the soul, or harder than the heart, of the man commemorated.

On the higher ground to the east of the church are the scanty remains of the 12C **castle**, and in the former castle precinct or bailey is the excellent **museum**, established in the present building in 1832 (open Mar–Oct Mon–Sat 10.00–17.00, Sun 14.00–17.00; Nov–Feb Tues–Sat 10.00–16.30, Sun 14.00–16.30, closed 24–25 Dec; ☎ 01799 524282.)

The remarkably varied and well-displayed collections include ethnography,

Egyptology, ceramics, glass, woodwork and costumes; there is also a natural history gallery. In the section on the ground floor devoted to local archaeology is the famous 9C Saffron Walden necklace, unearthed in the nearby Saxon cemetery; the Local History display illustrates many local houses which can still be seen, with specimens of woodwork from demolished or altered houses. Other displays are of dolls and toys, and there is also a stuffed lion, 'Wallace', from a 19C menagerie.

The ground falls away to the north of the church, and in the valley, reached from Castle St or through an inconspicuous gateway in Bridge St, are the **Bridge End Gardens**, first conceived by the local banker Atkinson Gibson c 1790, and enlarged by his son Francis Gibson in the 1830s; secluded and mysterious, they contain formal layouts, topiary, ornamental buildings and a recently replanted maze. On the south side, reached also from Castle St, is the **Fry Art Gallery** (open Easter–Oct, Tues, Sat, Sun and bank hol. Mon 14.00–17.00, ☎ 01799 513779), purpose-built in 1856 to house the collection of Francis Gibson and now containing a collection of works by locally resident artists including Edward Bawden and Eric Ravilious; special exhibitions of 20C British art are also held.

Bridge St contains several 14C and 15C timbered houses, their plaster lavishly adorned with pargetted birds, swags of foliage, and figures; the Youth Hostel, on the corner of Myddleton Place, and the *Eight Bells Inn* (good food) are especially noteworthy. Bridge St continues south as **High St**, lined with prosperous 18C and 19C houses, and from here and from **Gold St**, which runs parallel to the east, there are attractive views across the town to the church. At the end of Abbey Lane (west of the High St) are the lines of the **Pell** (or Battle) **Ditches**, which indicate a 13C extension of the town; over 200 Roman and Saxon graves have been found here. From here a footpath leads west across the park to Audley End, one of the greatest country houses of Jacobean England.

Audley End

Open Apr–Sept Wed–Sun and bank hol. Mon 12.00–16.00, Oct Sat, Sun 11.00–15.00, ☎ 01799 522842, ▓ www.english-heritage.org; can be reached by car via B1383, by bus from Cambridge or by train to Audley End Station, from which it is a 1-mile walk.

History

The house stands on the site of of the abbey of Walden, which was granted in 1538 to Sir Thomas (later Lord) Audley, Speaker of the House of Commons, in recompense for his part in the Dissolution of the Monasteries (see also Magdalene College, Cambridge). The builder was Sir Thomas Howard, Earl of Suffolk and Lord Treasurer to James I, who is said to have remarked that the house, which spread around two large courtyards, was 'too big for a king, but might do very well for his treasurer'. But in 1618, convicted of embezzlement, Suffolk fell into disgrace and in the 18C the house was reduced to its present more practical, but still substantial, dimensions.

In 1762 Audley End descended to Sir John Griffin Griffin (later Lord Howard de Walden and 1st Baron Braybrooke), who engaged Robert Adam to remodel the interior of the south wing and Capability Brown to landscape the park; he also collected many of the pictures now on view. Further internal alterations were carried out in the neo-Jacobean style by the 3rd Lord Braybrooke, an enthusiastic antiquarian who inherited in 1825. Since then there have been relatively few changes. The house passed into the care in of the government in 1948 and is now managed by English Heritage, but it retains its original contents, many of which still belong to the family, who live locally.

The house

The **entrance front**, of Ketton stone, is the central Hall range of the 17C house, from which two taller blocks extend back on either side to form an open courtyard (the original inner courtyard); the foundations of the outer courtyard lie underneath the lawn which extends to the lake. Inside is the **Great Hall**, entered through a richly carved Jacobean oak screen and lit by large mullioned windows. Portraits of Sir Thomas Audley and his family hang on the walls and at the far end is a Classical stone screen probably designed by Sir John Vanbrugh, who advised the 6th Lord Suffolk about alterations in 1708, from which staircases lead to the main reception rooms on the first floor. They include the **Saloon**, originally the King's Great Chamber, with a fine Jacobean plaster ceiling and a set of portraits introduced in 1784 celebrating Sir John Griffin Griffin's descent from Sir Thomas Audley. Most of the remaining rooms in the **south range** were remodelled in 1825–35, though retaining some of the original early 17C craftsmanship along with vestiges of subsequent Georgian alterations. They contain a good collection of pictures, including works by Canaletto and Holbein, and of 18C French and English furniture. A corridor or gallery, lined with cases of stuffed birds, leads across the back of the hall to the **Chapel**, an extravagant example of the Georgian Gothick taste, carried out in 1768–71 and still intact. Beyond, in the **north range**, is a set of bedrooms, some with their original Jacobean plaster ceilings and friezes, containing 18C furnishings, notably magnificent silk-hung bed made for an anticipated royal visit in 1786.

The **North Staircase** leads down to a lobby in which one of Lely's finest double portraits is displayed, showing the artist posing elegantly with his friend Hugh May, Comptroller of the King's Works under Charles II. From here another Gallery—until 1863 an open arcade—leads to the ground floor of the south range, embellished by Robert Adam in the 1760s and 70s in the delicate Neoclassical style of which he was a master, with furniture and wall hangings to match. The exquisite **Little Drawing Room** has an alcove for a sofa or day-bed screened off by attenuated columns, and delicate Roman-inspired paintings of 'grotesques' by Biagio Rebecca on the walls. Next comes the **Great Drawing Room** with its deep red colour scheme and richly embellished plaster ceiling, and at the far end is the **Dining Parlour**, largely empty of furniture as it would have been in Adam's time (the table was removed after meals). From here a lobby leads back into the Great Hall. The **kitchen** and laundry have recently been restored, and other rooms in the former servants' quarters on the north side of the house have been converted into a restaurant and shop.

The grounds

On the east side of the house, surrounded by a ha-ha, is a recently re-created 19C **Parterre** and **Flower Garden**, and on the hill top is the roofless Corinthian **Temple of Concord**, built in 1791 to the designs of R.W.F. Brettingham in celebration of the recovery of George III from his first attack of madness. It is well worth climbing the hill to this temple, both to enjoy the view east to Saffron Walden and to see the east front of the house, relatively little changed since the 18C.

The **park** still retains the calm, Arcadian character imparted by Capability Brown. Starting in 1762, he laid down lawns, interspersed with clumps of trees, and widened the river to the west of the house, creating a lake which is crossed by a stone bridge designed by Adam; Adam also designed the circular **Temple of Victory** on the wooded hill to the west of the London road. The much-restored Jacobean **stables** house a display of wagons and farm equipment, and to the north is the late 18C **Elysian Garden**, a tree-shaded grove with a cascade and a covered bridge designed by Adam in 1782. There is also an organic walled **kitchen garden**, opened in 2000. Open-air concerts and other events are held in the grounds during the summer (☎ 0870 333 1181).

A few miles south of Saffron Walden on the B184 is the equally attractive, though smaller, town of **Thaxted**. It derived its late medieval prosperity from the cutlery trade, but subsequently settled into a bucolic obscurity from which it has emerged only in the late 20C (it is only a few miles from London's third airport at Stansted). The 14C and 15C **church** is one of the finest in eastern England, its spacious interior bathed in light from the large Perpendicular windows, and its exterior dominated by a tall spire, built in 1822 to replace the original spire, struck by lightning a few years earlier. The composer Gustav Holst lived at Thaxted, and the hymn tune 'I vow to thee my country' (also used in the 'Jupiter' section of his most famous work, *The Planets*) was composed in, and named after the town. During the inter-war incumbency of the left-wing High-Church vicar, Conrad Noel, Thaxted became a well-known centre of Morris dancing and a Morris festival is still held there annually on the first weekend after the spring bank holiday. There is also a music festival in late June and early July, many of the concerts taking place in the church (☎ 01371 831421). South of the church are two rows of almshouses and a brick **windmill** of 1804.

Among the many old timber-framed buildings in the town, the 15C **Guildhall** in the market place is particularly noteworthy, with its open ground floor and jettied upper storeys (open Easter–Sept Sun and at some other times 14.00–18.00, ☎ 01371 851153). The finest post-medieval building is **Clarence House**, north of the church, built of brick in 1715 by a local apothecary.

5 ~ Wimpole Hall and beyond

This route explores the country to the southwest of Cambridge, taking in Wimpole Hall, the largest house in Cambridgeshire, and extending over the Hertfordshire border to Letchworth, the world's first Garden City. Leaving Cambridge by the A603, shortly after Barton village is a striking group of white dish **radio telescopes** belonging to Cambridge University's Cavendish Laboratory, and a few miles further on (8 miles from Cambridge), in empty countryside (but accessible by Whippet buses from Cambridge–Biggleswade), is Wimpole Hall.

Wimpole Hall
Open Apr-Oct daily exc. Mon, Fri, also Fri in Aug, 13.00–17.00; park open daily all year; ☎ 01223 207257, ✉ www.wimpole.org.

History

The history of Wimpole Hall begins in 1640, when Sir Thomas Chicheley, the descendant of wealthy London merchants, inherited the estate and built a brick house which was enlarged after 1713 by Edward, Lord Harley (later 2nd Earl of Oxford), one of a brilliant intellectual circle of poets, writers and artists, and the owner of the largest private library ever assembled in England. His architect was James Gibbs, the architect of the Senate House in Cambridge and the Radcliffe Camera in Oxford, and at the same time Charles Bridgeman was employed to lay out the park. But in 1740 Wimpole was sold to Philip Yorke, 1st Earl of Hardwicke, who engaged the Palladian architect Henry Flitcroft ('Burlington Harry') to re-face the central block, remodel the interiors and rebuild the parish church. The gardens were also 'naturalised', and in 1791–1806 further alterations were made to the house by Sir John Soane, who also designed a model farm which now provides one of the main attractions of a visit to Wimpole. The extravagant life-style of the 5th Lord Hardwicke (nicknamed Champagne Charlie) forced him to sell in 1894, but the house was later rescued by Captain and Mrs Bambridge (the daughter of Rudyard Kipling), and it now belongs to the National Trust.

The house is approached from the large mid-19C red-brick stable block. Slightly to the west is the **parish church**, rebuilt in 1749 by Flitcroft; despite some rather unfortunate changes in the 19C much of the original craftsmanship survives and there is a good collection of 18C and early 19C monuments, including work by Scheemakers, Bacon, Banks, and the elder and younger Westmacott, in the 14C Chicheley Chapel. Nearby is the Old Rectory, now the National Trust restaurant.

The red-brick neo-Palladian front of the **house** looks south onto a formal **Avenue**, now being replanted, the only survival of Bridgeman's early 18C lay-out; it leads to the octagon pond (beyond the A603 road). The **interior** reflects the changes in taste and ownership which characterise the history of Wimpole. Many of the contents were brought here by Mrs Bambridge in the 20C, but the architectural framework is largely of the 18C. Among the most notable rooms are the Gallery, created under Flitcroft's direction in 1742 to house the 1st Lord Hardwicke's pictures, and still retaining the splendid side-tables and pier-glasses made for the room; the Book Room, largely the creation of Soane; the spacious Library, designed by Gibbs, with plasterwork by Isaac Mansfield, one of the craftsmen working on the Cambridge Senate House; Soane's domed, top-lit Yellow Drawing Room, reminiscent of his now-destroyed interiors at the Bank of England; his highly original Bath House, upstairs, and contrived within the innermost recesses of the building; and finally Gibbs's **Chapel** (1723–24), in which Lord Harley worshipped from the raised family pew at the west end with the help of a private orchestra—the exuberantly Baroque *trompe l'oeil* paintings are by Sir James Thornhill, and the beautiful wrought-iron communion rails are by Thomas Warren, who also made the gates at Clare College, Cambridge. Visitors can also explore the extensive Servants' Quarters in the basement.

The **grounds** are very extensive. A **formal garden** was created to the north of the house in Victorian times, and has recently been restored. Beyond it is the **Park**, laid out by Capability Brown, with clumps of trees and an enclosing 'belt' of woodland. Some distance to the north, but accessible by footpath to the left of the house, are Brown's lakes, crossed by a **Chinese Bridge**; further north on a hilltop is the **Gothic Tower**, built by Brown and James Essex in 1768 to earlier designs by the Gothic enthusiast Sanderson Miller.

To the northeast of the house, beyond the 19C shrubbery and the 18C Walled Garden, is the **Home Farm** (open mid-Mar–Oct, Tue–Thur, Sat–Sun, also bank hol. Sun/Mon and Fri in Aug 10.30–17.00; Nov–mid-Mar Sat, Sun exc. Christmas/New Year 11.00–16.00; separate fee), a working farm and centre for rare breeds of farm animals. The buildings, of timber, brick and thatch, date from 1794 and are by Soane, and the magnificent barn houses a museum of farm equipment; there is also a well-preserved Victorian dairy.

The route can be prolonged beyond Wimpole along the A1198 to Royston and then along the A505 over the Hertfordshire border to Hitchin; the removal of hedgerows in this area has contributed to the creation of a broad, open land-scape in which the sky figures prominently. To the north of the A505 is **Ashwell**, an attractive village with a largely 14C **church** whose tall tower is topped by a needle spire of the characteristic Hertfordshire type; there are also several attrac-tive timber-framed houses, some of them plastered and pargetted, one of which houses a small museum, and a good pub (the *Three Tuns*). There is another good late medieval church at **Baldock** (22 miles), a market town at the junction of the A505 and the former Great North Rd (now superseded by the A1 which bypasses the town); evidence of 18C and early 19C prosperity can be seen in sev-eral red-brick coaching inns.

Those interested in the history of urban planning should continue to **Letchworth Garden City** (also accessible by frequent trains from Cambridge), immediately to the west of Baldock. This was the first Garden City to be built according to the principles of Ebenezer Howard's influential *Garden Cities of Tomorrow*. It was laid out, starting in 1903, by Barry Parker and Raymond Unwin, and it still survives largely intact, with its broad, tree-lined streets and restrained neo-vernacular and neo-Georgian housing; Parker's own office, a thatched build-ing at 296 Norton Way South, is now the **First Garden City Heritage Museum**, with exhibits tracing the history of the Garden City movement and a collection of Arts and Crafts furniture (open Mon–Sat exc. Christmas 10.00–17.00, ☎ 01462 482710). Walking tour leaflets and other information can be obtained here, and also in the **Tourist Information Centre** at 33–35 Station Rd.

From here the A505 leads back to Royston, from which Cambridge can be quickly reached along the A10.

6 ~ Into Huntingdonshire

The busy A14 road follows the Roman Via Devana northwest from Cambridge to **Fenstanton**, once the the home of Lancelot (Capability) Brown, the great land-scape-gardener, whose monument in the church commemorates him in an appropriate manner:

'Ye Sons of Elegance, who truly taste
The Simple charms that genuine Art supplies,
Come from the sylvan Scenes his Genius grac'd,
And offer here your tributary Sigh's ... '

Just after the village a right turn leads north to **St. Ives** (13 miles: buses from Cambridge) a small market town on the north bank of the Ouse whose old quay and wharves still bear witness to a once-busy river trade. Named after a legendary 6C Bishop Ivo, the town grew up in the Middle Ages in consequence of a vanished priory and the great Easter Fair (one of the four most important in England) granted by Henry I in 1110: hence, perhaps, the origin of the nursery-rhyme 'As I was going to St. Ives, I met a man with seven wives...'. The fair was later superseded in popularity by the Stourbridge Fair near Cambridge, but open-air markets are still held. Oliver Cromwell, Huntingdonshire's most famous resident, lived here for five years from 1631–36, and his **statue** (1901) is in the Market Place.

St. Ives is famous for its early 15C stone **bridge** carrying a small chapel, one of only three remaining bridge chapels in England. The history of the town, and of the old county of Huntingdonshire, is well told and illustrated in the **Norris Museum** on the south side of Broadway, the wide main street which runs through the town from east to west (open May–Sept daily 10.00–13.00 and 14.00–17.00, closed Sun mornings; Oct–Apr Mon–Fri 10.00–13.00 and 14.00–16.00, Sat 10.00–12.00, ☎ 01480 465101). Fossil and archaeological finds are on display, along with Civil War armaments and the products of local crafts. Close to the river at the western extremity of the old town is the mainly Perpendicular **church** (sometimes locked).

On a minor road to the west of St. Ives along the River Ouse is the village of **Hemingford Grey**, whose riverside **Manor House** has a 12C first-floor hall, making it one of the oldest inhabited houses in England. This is the house featured in Lucy Boston's children's book *The Children of Green Knowe*; the garden, laid out by Lucy Boston, has an excellent collection of roses and topiary (house open throughout year by appointment only; garden most days of the year, ☎ 01480 463134).

On the opposite side of the river, reached by the A1123 St. Ives–Huntingdon, is the pretty village of **Houghton**, and on the banks of river is the **mill**, one of the last surviving flour mills on the Ouse (National Trust: open Apr–Oct Sat, Sun and bank hol. Mon, also Mon–Wed June–Sept, 14.00–17.30). It is a large and impressive 19C building of brick and timber, and has been restored to its original state, with milling once again carried out each Sunday in summer, using the original machinery; there is also a tea room and an Art Gallery.

Just to the south of Huntingdon on the A14 is **Godmanchester**. It grew up in Roman times at the river-crossing of three important roads and the foundations of Roman buildings have been unearthed. Though now not much larger than a village, it was a chartered town in the Middle Ages, and achieved borough status in 1604, retaining its prosperity into the 18C when some impressive houses were built for the professional gentlemen of Huntingdon.

The mainly Perpendicular **church** has a west tower and spire of 1623; the 15C stalls, their misericords richly carved with animals both real and mythical, may have come from the great Benedictine abbey of Ramsey, 10 miles north in the Fens. Besides the river, at the junction of the main streets, lined with timber and brick houses, is the diminutive brick **Queen Elizabeth Grammar School** (1559) and the Flemish-gabled **Town Hall** of 1844; from here a wooden **Chinese Bridge** (1827) leads across the river to a series of islands and backwaters which give the town much of its character.

On the north side of the river Ouse is Huntingdon (16 miles: buses from Cambridge).

Huntingdon

History

Huntingdon is linked to Godmanchester by a bridge 'lately built' in 1327; differences in the cutwaters on the north and south sides indicate that it was jointly constructed by the two communities, each following its own ideas. In the past it was the administrative capital of the county of Huntingdonshire (merged with Cambridgeshire 1974), and in the early Middle Ages it was a major river port, with no fewer than 16 churches. It later declined, but in coaching days it became an important staging post on the old Great North Rd (not the present A1, which is about 3 miles west). In recent years the town has been greatly expanded, but the old centre retains much of its low-key 18C character, despite the inevitable encroachments of mass shopping.

The centre of Huntingdon is **Market Sq**, with the Town Hall (1746), All Saints Church (Perpendicular) and Walden House (late 17C) all facing onto the triangular open space. To the south in Princes St is the **Tourist Information Centre**, and to the north is the *George Hotel*, refronted after a fire in the mid-19C, but still retaining its original 17C courtyard and surrounding gallery, used from time to time as a setting for Shakespearian productions. On the east side is the late 12C Infirmary Hall of the suppressed Hospital of St. John, later the Grammar School, where Huntingdon's most famous resident, Oliver Cromwell, was educated, as was Samuel Pepys, the diarist; it is now the **Cromwell Museum** (open Apr–Oct daily exc. Mon 11.00–13.00 and 14.00–17.00, closes 16.00 Sat/Sun; Nov–Mar Tues–Fri 13.00–16.00, Sat 11.00–13.00 and 14.00–16.00, Sun 14.00–16.00, closed bank hols exc. Good Friday, ☎ 01480 425830, ✉ edweb.camcnty.gov.uk/ cromwell/). It contains a splendid collection of Cromwell memorabilia (hats, walking sticks, etc, and his powder flask of mother-of-pearl), letters, documents, books, coins, medals and portraits, well displayed and intelligently interpreted.

Cromwell was born in **Cromwell House** (virtually rebuilt in the 19C), on the site of an Augustinian friary in the northern part of High St; in All Saints Church is the register of the old church of St. John (now demolished), which records his birth. Further down the busy **High St**, which runs southeast towards the river, are **Cowper House** (early 18C) where the poet William Cowper lived with his friends the Unwins in 1765–67; St. Mary's Church, with an ornate Perpendicular tower; and the *Old Bridge Hotel* (18C), where there is a good restaurant. The mound of the Norman castle stands to the west of the bridge, rather too close to the ring-road for comfort.

West of the centre of Huntingdon, off Brampton Rd (A604) beyond the A14 flyover, is **Hinchingbrooke House** (open some summer Sunday afternoons, ☎ 01480 451121). It was built on the site of a small 12C nunnery acquired in 1538 by Richard Cromwell, nephew of Thomas Cromwell, Henry VIII's chief minister at the time of the Dissolution of the Monasteries. His son Henry (d. 1604), and his grandson Oliver (uncle of the future Lord Protector) greatly enlarged the house and re-erected the impressive Gatehouse of c 1500 from Ramsey Abbey, another of their possessions. But they were ruined by their vast expenditure, and in 1627 the estate was sold to the Montagu family, later Earls of Sandwich, who carried out more alterations and remained in possession until 1962. Much of the present building dates from a neo-Elizabethan remodelling by Edward Blore after a fire in 1830, when the finest rooms created by the Cromwells were burnt down. The house is now the sixth-form centre of the local comprehensive school.

The old Great North Rd (A1) runs to the west of Huntingdon, and along its route lie a number of attractive small towns and villages. At **Buckden**, 4 miles southwest by the A141, next to the Early English and Perpendicular church, there are the substantial remains of a **palace** of the medieval Bishops of Lincoln, now occupied by the Roman Catholic Claretian Missionaries. The red-brick buildings date from c 1475–90, and include an impressive keep-like Great Tower (restored) in which Henry VIII's discarded queen, Catherine of Aragon, spent a year of her lonely banishment before her final move to Kimbolton Castle (below). This forms part of an inner court, originally surrounded by a moat, with an inner gatehouse, which still survives, along with some of the outer curtain wall alongside the old Great North Rd.

A few miles west of Buckden, in the more hilly country of the Northamptonshire border, is **Kimbolton** (11 miles southwest of Huntingdon; take B661 from Buckden along the side of Grafham Water reservoir, and at Great Staughton turn right on A45). Though now a village, it grew up as a small town at the gates of the 12C castle and still retains its medieval layout of a broad main street with long 'burgage plots' serviced at the rear by back lanes; there are several attractive houses along the main street, some of them timber-framed and plastered, with the characteristic mansard roofs of Huntingdonshire and Cambridgeshire, others refronted in brick in the 18C.

At the west end is the very attractive **church**, Early English and Decorated, but enlarged and remodelled in the Perpendicular style in the 15C. The 14C west tower has a broach spire, and inside the church there is some excellent late 15C carved woodwork, especially in the aisles with their wooden roofs and in the screen of the south chapel, which retains some of its original painted figures of saints; there are also monuments to the Dukes of Manchester, and in the south chapel is the only English church window made by the famous Tiffany firm of New York (1902).

At the opposite end of the street is the monumental gatehouse (by Robert Adam c 1765) to **Kimbolton Castle**, now a school (occasionally open on summer bank holidays, ☎ 01480 860505.). Originally a fortified manor house, it was rebuilt by Sir Richard Wingfield early in the 16C, and Queen Catherine of Aragon was confined here from 1534 until her death in January 1536. In 1615 it was bought by Sir Henry Montagu, later Earl of Manchester, and it descended in this family until 1950. Between 1690 and 1720 it was entirely remodelled for the 4th Earl, and 1st Duke, of Manchester, a prominent supporter of William III who introduced Handel to England. Sir John Vanbrugh was largely responsible for the crenellated **exterior**, an important landmark in the medieval revival in English architecture, but the magnificent Doric portico on the east front has usually been attributed to Alessandro Galilei, the architect of the façade of St. John Lateran in Rome, and the late 17C brick elevations to the courtyard were probably designed by Henry Bell of Kings Lynn. Inside, there are magnificent **mural paintings** of c 1710 by the Venetian artist Antonio Pellegrini, along with portraits of the Dukes of Manchester by Lely, Pellegrini and others.

From Kimbolton a detour north along the winding B660 leads through quiet countryside to **Little Gidding**. Here there is a small, isolated church restored in 1625 by the Cambridge-educated Nicholas Ferrar (d. 1637), founder of an Anglican religious community which captured the imagination of T.S. Eliot in his poem *Little Gidding* in the *Four Quartets*. It retains some of the fittings of c 1625, and the inward-facing college-style seating may date from then, but there was a major rebuilding in 1714, and the plain façade is of this date. In the 20C Little Gidding has become a significant focus of Anglican spirituality.

From here country lanes lead southeast to the A1 at Alconbury, from which Cambridge can be quickly reached along the A14.

Glossary

Alien Priory A religious house belonging in the Middle Ages to another monastery on the Continent

Antechapel The liturgically western part of a college chapel, separated from the main body of the building by a screen

Ashlar Stonework cut to present a smooth appearance, with the joints scarcely visible

Barrel vault An inner ceiling of stone or plaster, semicircular in profile, running the full length of a church or gallery

Boiserie A French term for the decorative wood panelling of a room, usually 18C or 19C

Broach spire An octagonal spire on a square base of a tower with inclined masses of stone at the four corners of the base

Clerestory A row of upper windows placed over an arcade in an aisled building in order to bring light into the interior

Clunch Chalk used as a building stone

Crenellation The regular indentation of a parapet in medieval or medieval-inspired buildings, derived initially from fortified buildings. Also called battlements

Decorated Gothic The period of English Gothic architecture lasting from c 1250 to c 1350

Diocletian window *See* lunette window

Early English The earliest phase of English Gothic, lasting from c 1170 to c 1250

Encaustic tiles Decorative floor tiles, especially popular in the 19C

Entablature The stone superstructure of a colonnade in classical architecture, divided into architrave, frieze and cornice

Grisaille glass Silvery-grey glass arranged in decorative patterns in the windows of a medieval church

Grotesques Curvy decorative designs, often with bizarre heads, foliage and other naturalistic features, inspired by fragments of ancient Roman decoration widely used as painted decoration in Renaissance-inspired buildings

Ha-ha A sunken fence or ditch separating the garden of an 18C or later country house from the surrounding parkland

Hammer-beam roof A wooden roof in a late-medieval or Tudor hall or church with the main arched supports resting upon the ends of beams cantilevered out from the tops of the walls

Hipped roof A roof sloping up from all four sides of a rectangular house to a ridge or platform (as distinct from a gabled roof)

Impost A bracket-like moulding on which an arch appears to rest

In antis The recession of a portico or colonnade into the body of a building

Incunabula Books published before 1500

Jacobean From the time of King James I (1603–25), not to be confused with Jacobite

Jettied, jettying The outward projection of the upper storey or storeys of a timber-framed building

Lantern In architecture, a tower or dome whose windows allow light into the body of a building (usually a church)

Lierne vault A stone ceiling in late-medieval architecture where ribs are linked by mouldings on the stonework so as to create ornamental net-like or star-shaped patterns

Linenfold panelling Wood panelling in early 16C buildings carved in such a way as to imitate the folds of linen hangings

Loggia A covered space or passage in Renaissance architecture which is open on one side and demarcated by an arcade or colonnade

Lunette window A semicircular or half-moon shaped window in a classical or Renaissance-inspired building; if the window is divided by two evenly-spaced mullions it is sometimes called a 'Diocletian' window

Misericord A shelf underneath a hinged wooden seat in a medieval church, enabling the occupant to rest in a half-standing position during a long service. The underside of a misericord is often carved in a fanciful manner

Oriel A projecting bay window in a medieval building often, but not invariably, on an upper floor

Paterae Small circular ornaments in classical or Renaissance architecture, sometimes decorated with acanthus leaves

Perpendicular Gothic The final phase of English Gothic, popular from c 1350 onwards and lasting into the 16C

Pietà A representation of the dead body of Christ after the Crucifixion with the Virgin Mary and attendants

Piscina A drain for water near an altar in a medieval church, placed in a recess some way up a wall and usually surmounted by an arch

'Queen Anne' An eclectic style in late 19C English architecture drawing on 17C and 18C English, Dutch and Flemish sources and characterised by the use of red brick with white-painted windows, doors, etc

Rebus The representation of a surname in punning visual form in a medieval carving

Reredos A carved screen behind the altar of a church

Rustication The practice of leaving stonework in a deliberately rough state, or of deeply scoring the joints between stones, in order to convey an effect of strength and massiveness in a Renaissance or Renaissance-inspired building

Screens passage A passage across the service end of a hall of medieval type, demarcated from the main body of the hall by a wooden screen and allowing access both to it and to the kitchen, etc

Strapwork A form of decoration, ultimately Renaissance in origin, which became popular in Flanders in the second half of the 16C and spread to Elizabethan and Jacobean England by means of pattern-books

Tierceron vault A medieval stone ceiling with a profusion of ornamental ribs

Tractarian A term referring to High-church sympathies or practices in the 19C

Transom A stone or wooden horizontal bar in a window

Triforium A passageway or gallery in a medieval church situated above an aisle and below a row of clerestory (qv) windows, and demarcated by an arcade

Tripos An examination for an honours degree in Cambridge

Tuscan The primitive form of the Doric order found in ancient Italy and incorporated into Renaissance architecture as the simplest and most sturdy of the Five Orders

Tympanum The space between the top of a doorway and an arch in Romanesque architecture, often carved

Visitor The person to whom an appeal is ultimately lodged in the affairs of a college, often a leading ecclesiastic, a nobleman or even the sovereign

Sovereigns of England

Anglo-Saxons

827–836	Egbert
837–858	Ethelwulf
866–871	Ethelred I
871–899	Alfred the Great
899–925	Edward the Elder
925–940	Athelstan
940–946	Edmund I
946–955	Edred
955–959	Edwy
959–975	Edgar
975–978	Edward the Martyr
978–1016	Ethelred II (the Unready)
1016	Edmund Ironside
1016–1035	Canute
1035–1040	Harold I
1041–1042	Hardicanute
1042–1066	Edward the Confessor
1066–	Harold II

Normans

1066–1087	William (the Conqueror)
1087–1100	William II (Rufus)
1100–1135	Henry I
1135–1154	Stephen

Plantagenets

1154–1189	Henry II
1189–1199	Richard I
1199–1216	John
1216–1272	Henry III
1272–1307	Edward I
1307–1327	Edward II
1327–1377	Edward III
1377–1399	Richard II

Lancastrians

1399–1413	Henry IV
1413–1422	Henry V
1422–1461	Henry VI

Yorkists

1461–1483	Edward IV
1483–	Edward V
1483–1485	Richard III

Tudors

1485–1509	Henry VII
1509–1547	Henry VIII
1547–1553	Edward VI
1553–1558	Mary I
1558–1603	Elizabeth I

Stuarts

1603–1625	James I
1625–1649	Charles I
[1649–1660	Interregnum]
1660–1685	Charles II
1685–1688	James II
1688–1694	William III & Mary II
1694–1702	William III
1702–1714	Anne

Hanoverians

1714–1727	George I
1727–1760	George II
1760–1820	George III
1820–1830	George IV
1830–1837	William IV
1837–1901	Victoria

House of Saxe-Coburg (later Windsor)

1901–1910	Edward VII
1910–1936	George V
1936	Edward VIII
1936–1952	George VI
1952–	Elizabeth II

Index to people

A

Abrahams, Harold 205
Acland, Henry 128
Adam de Brome 79
Adam, Robert 125, 165, 287, 288
Adams, John Couch 226
Addenbrooke, John 218, 233
Addison, Joseph 95, 99, 100
Adrian, Lord 211
Ahrends, Burton & Koralek 31, 128
Airy, George 211
Aitchison, Craigie 198
Akroyd, John 58, 84
Alcock, Bishop of Ely 238, 276
Aldrich, Dean Henry 23, 76, 91
Alex French Associates 135
Alfred, King 103, 153
Alison & Peter Smithson 101
Allies & Morrison 256, 261, 262,
Allori, Alessandro 123
Amigoni, Jacopo 247
Amis, Kingsley 112
Amis, Martin 90
Andrewes, Lancelot 226
Annand & Muscoe 259
Anne, Queen 161
Antolinez, José 123
Appleton, Sir Edward 216
Architects Co-Partnership 111, 210
Architects Design Partnership 136, 245
Arnold, Matthew 80, 109, 144
Arnold, Thomas 80
Arnold, William 64
Artari, Giuseppe 56, 194
Ascham, Roger 215
Ashley-Cooper, Anthony 90
Ashmole, Elias 58, 63, 119
Asprucci, Mario 283
Asquith, H.H. 109
Atkinson, Rowan 95
Attlee, Clement 104
Aubrey, John 106, 107, 110
Audley, Thomas 235, 287
Auden, W.H. 78
Aung San Suu Kyi 136
Austin, Cornelius 247
Ayrton, Michael 243

B

Babbage, Charles 229
Bacon, Francis 207, 210
Bacon, John 135
Bacon, Nicholas 219
Bacon, Roger 15, 85
Badew, Richard de 200
Baker, Sir Herbert 130, 252
Bakst, Leon 169
Baldwin, Stanley 211
Balfour, Arthur 211
Balliol, John de 108
Balsham, Hugh de, Bishop of Ely 227
Baltimore, Lord 107
Bambridge, Captain & Mrs 290
Banks, Gerald 135
Bannister, Sir Roger 101
Baring, Thomas Charles 69
Barrow, Isaac 209
Barry, E.M. 229, 231, 251
Barry, Sir Charles 104
Basevi, George 28, 231, 229
Bassano, Francesco 56, 79
Bassano, Jacopo 233
Bateman, William, Bishop of Norwich
  201, 203
Bathurst, Ralph 106
Batoni, Pompeo 124, 232
Bawden, Edward 287
Beale, Dorothea 101
Beaufort, Lady Margaret 137, 196, 212,
  244
Beaumont, Frances 87
Beecham, Sir Thomas 65
Beerbohm, Max 83, 85
Bell, Charles 117
Bell, Clive 211
Bell, Henry 295
Bellini, Giovanni 123
Belloc, Hilaire 109
Benn, Tony 69
Benson, A.C. 235, 263
Bentham, Jeremy 95
Bentley, John 58, 84
Bentley, Richard 207, 210
Berchet, Pierre 107
Berkeley, George, Bishop of Cloyne 72
Berlin, Sir Isaiah 81, 93
Bernini, Gianlorenzo 123
Besse, Antonin 27, 135
Betjemen, John 100

Beveridge, William 104, 109
Bevin, Ernest 258
Bhutto, Benazir 138
Bicknell, Julian 98
Bilney, Thomas 19, 216
Bird, Francis 62, 76
Birt, John 133
Blackett, P.M.S. 199, 237
Blackstone, Sir William 87, 93
Blair, Tony 112
Blake, Robert 65
Blake, William 232
Bland, Brown & Cole 223
Bliney, Thomas 19
Bliss, Sir Arthur 226
Blomfield, Sir Arthur 134, 219, 263
Blomfield, Reginald 30, 138
Blore, Edward 63, 64, 111, 224
Blunt, Anthony 211
Bobart, Jacob 102
Bodley, G.F. 10, 30, 61, 72, 75, 199, 220, 223, 239, 241
Bodley, Sir Thomas 60, 84, 85, 100
Boleyn, Anne 198
Bolton, Thomas 64
Bomberg, David 123
Bonnard, Pierre 232
Borgnis, Giuseppe 172
Boston, Lucy 292
Boston, Peter 215
Botticelli, Sandro 78
Boudin, Eugène 124, 233
Bowra, Sir Maurice 64, 69
Boyle, Robert 21
Bracken, Brendan 258
Bragg, Lawrence 211
Bragg, Melvyn 65
Bragg, Sir William 211
Brancusi, Constantin 254
Brangwyn, Frank 86
Braque, Georges 124, 232
Bridgeman, Charles 166, 171
Bridges, Robert 81
Bronzino, Agnolo 123
Brooke, Rupert 199, 265
Brookes, William 228
Broughton, Huttleston 280
Brown, Arthur 248
Brown, Ford Madox 159, 222, 228, 232, 240, 241
Brown, Lancelot (Capability) 24, 164, 165, 289, 290
Browne, Sir Thomas 87
Bruton, E.G. 137
Bucer, Martin 19, 193

Buchan, John 58
Buckeridge, Charles 136
Buckland & Haywood 136
Buckler, J.C. & C.A. 88
Buddle, Adam 218
Bullock, Alan 133
Burges, William 114
Burgess, Guy 211
Burne-Jones, Edward 72, 73, 90, 96, 118, 130, 131, 138, 159, 222, 228, 240, 241
Burrough, Sir James 23, 200, 205, 222, 227, 282
Burton, Richard 90
Burton, Robert 58, 73
Butler, R.A. 211
Butterfield, William 29, 108, 127, 128, 145
Byngham, William 244
Byrd, William 22
Byron, Lord 209, 210

C

Campbell-Bannerman, Sir Henry 211
Campion, Edmund 86, 110, 112, 150
Campion, Thomas 229
Canaletto, Antonio 124
Canning, George 78
Canova, Antonio 124
Caro, Anthony 245, 246
Caroe, W.D. 226
Caroline, Queen 94
Carr, John 148
Carracci, Annibale 79
Carroll, Lewis 75, 78
Cartwright, Woollatt & Partners 263
Casson, Conder & Partners 262
Castle, Barbara 136
Castlereagh, Lord 216
Catherine of Aragon 294
Cavendish, Henry 229
Cavendish, Mary 214
Cayley, Arthur 211
Cecil, Lord David 69
Cecil, William 215
Cézanne, Paul 233
Chamberlin, Powell & Bon 255
Chambers, William 164
Champneys, Basil 30, 65, 68, 80, 84, 103, 104, 117, 130, 131, 133, 138, 261
Chantrey, Sir Francis 75
Charles I 20, 60, 61, 110
Charles II 63, 110, 278

Charles, Prince of Wales 211
Chavasse, C.M. 117
Chavasse, F.J. 117
Cheere, Henry 72, 93, 166
Cherbury, Lord Herbert of 104
Chesterfield, Lord 203
Chichele, Archbishop Henry 69, 92, 110
Chipperfield, David 149
Christopher, J.T. 87
Churchill, Carol 138
Churchill, John, 1st Duke of Marlborough 161
Churchill, Lord Randolph 85
Churchill, Sir Winston 160, 161, 258
Cibber, C.G. 209
Cipriani, Giovanni 201
Clare, Elizabeth de 200
Clarendon, Lord 62
Clark, John 58
Clarke, George 23, 76, 93, 94, 113
Clarke, Jonathan 270
Clarke, T.G. 138
Claude Lorrain 79, 123
Clayton & Bell 74, 90, 136, 214
Cleere, Richard 63
Clerk-Maxwell, James 211
Cleve, Joos van 233
Clinton, Bill 33, 104, 130
Clough, A.H. 80
Clough, Miss A.J. 260
Cobbe, Alec 107
Cobham, Thomas 56
Cockcroft, Sir John 216, 250, 258
Cockerell, C.R. 28, 119, 121, 205, 231
Cockerell, S.P. 167
Coddrington, Christopher 93
Coke, Humphry 81
Coleridge, S.T. 241
Colet, John 19, 100
Colt, Maximilian 205
Combe, Thomas 134
Comper, Ninian 126
Constable, John 124, 232, 281
Cook, Captain James 243
Cook, Peter 226
Cooke, Alistair 241
Cookes, Sir Thomas 113
Cornwallis, Lord 201
Corot, J.B. 124
Cosin, John 228
Cottingham, L.N. 98
Coulton, G.G. 218
Courbet, Gustave 124
Cowper, William 293
Cranmer, Thomas 20, 61, 71, 105, 110, 240

Crashaw, Richard 226, 229
Crick, Francis 205
Critz, Emanuel de 121
Cromwell, Oliver 60, 158, 242, 243, 276, 292, 293
Cromwell, Thomas 19
Crossman, Richard 69
Crowe, Sylvia 102
Crummell, Alexander 223
Cubitt, James 224
Cullinan, Edward 32, 214, 259, 256, 262
Curzon, Lord 93, 109
Cuyp, Aelbert 169, 233

D

Danby, Lord 102
Darwin, Charles 234, 246, 249
Darwin, Erasmus 216
Darwin, George 211
Dashwood, Sir Francis 166
Davenant, William 91, 105
Davies, Emily 257
Day Lewis, Cecil 65
de Quincey, Thomas 114
de Stanton, Hervey 206, 207
de Valence, Marie, Countess of Pembroke 224, 278
Deane, T.N. 71, 129
Dee, John 210
Degas, Edgar 124, 233
Delacroix, Eugène 232
Derby, Lord 76
Destailleur, Hippolyte Gabriel 169
Devereux, Robert, Earl of Essex 210
Dirac, Paul 216
Dixon, Jeremy 115, 260
Dixon Jones Partnership 115
Dodgson, C.L. 75, 78
d'Oilly, Robert 13, 115
Dokett, Andrew 220
Donne, John 70
Doogood, Henry 225
Domenichino 79
Dou, Gerard 169, 233
Doubleday, John 64
Doughty, C.M. 251
Douglas, John, 8th Marquess of Queensbury 236
Douglas, Keith 85
Downing, Sir George 250
Dowsing, William 21, 204, 228
Dowson, Philip 111, 126, 133, 134, 249, 256, 263, 265

Drinkwater, G.C. 223
Dryden, John 210
Duchêne, Achille 161, 164
Dughet, Gaspard 124
Dunn & Hansom 236
Duns Scotus 15
Dunster, Henry 235, 236
Dyke, Sir Anthony van 79, 123
Dyke, John Bacchus 218

E

Eachard, John 217
Eastlake, C.L. 229
Eban, Abba 223
Eddington, Arthur 211
Ede, Jim 31, 253
Eden, Sir Anthony 78
Edgar, King 271
Edmund, King 281
Edward I 254
Edward II 79
Edward III 207
Edward IV 60, 220
Edward VII 78, 104, 211
Edward VIII 100
Edward the Confessor 151
Effingham, Lord Howard of 203
Eglesfield, Robert de 94
El Greco 68
El-Wakil, Abdul Wahid 100
Eliot, John 240
Eliot, T.S. 85, 295
Elizabeth I 20, 88, 110, 161
Elizabeth II 75
Ely, Reginald 222
Ely, Robert 196
Epstein, Jacob 67, 76, 232
Erasmus Desiderius 19, 117, 220, 223
Eric Parry Architects 226
Erith, Raymond 95, 138
Erskine, Ralph 264
Essex, James 23, 194, 209, 210, 217, 222, 242, 247, 271, 291
Evans, Sir Arthur 121
Evans, Daniel 87
Evans, Lewis 63
Evans & Shalev 32
Evelyn, John 77, 109
Evetts, L.C. 251
Eworth, Hans 232

F

Fantin-Latour, Henri 233
Fawcett, W.M. 248
Fell, Dean 75
Ferrar, Nicholas 201, 295
Fischer, H.A.L. 69
Fisher, Edmund 133
Fisher, John 19, 212, 223, 244
Fitzwilliam, Richard 203, 231
Flamsteed, John 241
Flanagan, Barry 238
Flaxman, John 103, 284
Flecker, James Elroy 108
Fleming, Robert 90
Fletcher, John 219
Flitcroft, Henry 290
Flower, Barbard 197
Foot, Michael 65
Ford, Onslow 103
Forster, E.M. 199
Fortnum, Charles 119
Foster, Norman 32, 132, 262
Fowles, John 69
Fox, Charles James 70
Fox-Strangeways, W.T. 78, 119
Fox-Talbot, W.H. 210
Foxe, John 58
Foxe, Richard 80, 100
Frampton, George 261
Franklin, Rosalind 260
Fraser, Lady Antonia 138
Freeland, Rees & Roberts 202
Freibusch, Hans 270
Freud, Lucien 124
Frogley, Arthur 96
Froude, J.A. 80
Fry, C.B. 65
Fry, Maxwell 252
Fry, Roger 199
Fry, Stephen 223
Fuller, Isaac 93
Fuller, Thomas 223, 243

G

Gabo, Naum 254
Gaddi, Taddeo 138
Gainsborough, Thomas 75, 232
Gaitskell, Hugh 69
Galsworthy, John 69
Galton, Francis 211
Garbett, E. 70
Gardiner, Stephen 203
Gaudier-Brzeska, Henri 254

Gauguin, Paul 233
Geoffrey of Monmouth 116
George I 194
George III 110, 112
George IV 65
George V 104
George VI 211
Gerard, Marguerite 232
Gerente, Henri & Alfred 272
Gertler, Mark 123
Getty, J. Paul 133
Gandhi, Indira 133
Ghirlandaio, Domenico 123
Giambologna 124
Gibbon, Edward 21, 77, 100
Gibbons, Grinling 107, 162, 209
Gibbons, Orlando 88
Gibbs, Alexander 127
Gibbs, James 23, 56, 111, 165, 196, 290
Gibbs family 127
Giles & Gough 252
Gill, Eric 67, 111, 240, 250
Gillespie, Kidd & Coia 31, 64, 65, 264
Gilman, Harold 124
Giorgione 123
Giovanni da Bologna 76
Giovanni di Paolo 78
Girolamo da Treviso 79
Gladstone, W.E. 78
Goes, Hugo van der 78
Gogh, Vincent van 233
Golding, William 58
Goldsmith, Oliver 145
Gonville, Edmund 203
Gore, Spencer Frederick 124
Goyen, Jan van 233
Gradidge, Roderick 254
Grahame, Kenneth 131
Grandison, Viscount 75
Grant, Hugh 69
Graves, Robert 112
Gray, Thomas 226
Gray, William 108
Grayson & Ould 263, 202
Green, Dr & Mrs Cecil 27, 134
Green, J.R. 89
Greenbury, Richard 98
Greene, Graham 109
Gresham, Thomas 205
Gresswell, Richard 114
Greville, Fulke 240
Grey, Earl 211
Grey, William 108
Grocyn, William 19, 69
Grosseteste, Robert 15

Grove, John 247
Grumbold, John 200
Grumbold, Robert 22, 209, 215, 218
Grumbold, Thomas 200
Guardi, Francesco 124
Guercino 233
Guise, John 78
Gwynn, John 88

H

Hague, William 100
Haig, Field-Marshal Earl 58
Hailsham, Lord 93
Hales, Stephen 220
Halifax, Lord 78
Hall, John 223
Hall, Sir Peter 218
Hallam, Arthur 210
Halley, Edmund 65, 95
Hals, Frans 79, 233
Hampden, John 100, 150
Hancock, T. 248
Hansom & Sons 133
Hare, H.T. 30, 70, 259
Harrington, John 199
Harris, Renatus 198
Harrison, Austen 116
Harvard, John 246, 248
Harvey, J.W. 87
Harvey, William 205
Haveus, Theodore 205
Hawke, Bob 104
Hawking, Stephen 104
Hawksmoor, Nicholas 23, 56, 58, 62, 92,
    93, 94, 113, 161, 162, 164
Hayward, John 87
Heath, Sir Edward 109
Henrietta Maria, Queen 84
Henry I 112
Henry II 147, 161, 164
Henry VI 18, 92, 195
Henry VII 193
Henry VIII 18, 19, 20, 73, 151, 196,
    207, 276
Henry, John 80
Hepworth, Barbara 124, 132, 254, 265
Herbert, George 210
Herrick, Robert 203, 216
Herring, Thomas 219
Herschel, John 216
Hervey, Frederick 283
Hervey, Lord 201
Hervey, William 85
Heseltine, Michael 87

Hickox, Richard 223
Hill, A.V. 199, 211
Hitcham, Sir Robert 226
Hobbema, Meindert 233
Hobbes, Thomas 100
Hodder Architects 132
Hodgkin, Dorothy 260
Hogarth, William 232
Hogwood, Christopher 226
Holliday, W.G. 114
Holman Hunt, William 125, 127
Holst, Gustav 289
Hone, Gaylon 197
Hooche, Pieter de 169
Hooke, Robert 21, 236
Hooker, Richard 81
Hopkins, F.G. 211
Hopkins, Gerard Manley 109, 142
Hopkins, Gowland 248
Hopkins, Michael 32, 259
Housman, A.E. 112, 210
Howard, Ebenezer 291
Howard, Thomas, Earl of Arundel 118
Howard, Sir Thomas, Earl of Suffolk 287
Howe, Lord 203
Howell, Killick, Partridge & Amis 135,
    136, 242, 251, 260
Hughes, H.C. 228, 259
Hughes, Ted 224, 226
Hughes, Thomas 80
Hullier, John 20
Humfrey, Duke of Gloucester 15, 60
Hutchinson, Henry 215
Huxley, Aldous 109
Huxley, Thomas 129
Hyntner, Nicholas 203

I

Ireton, Henry 107
Irvine of Lairg, Lord 246
Isherwood, Christopher 220

J

Jackson, John 55
Jackson, T.G. 29, 57, 65, 69, 70, 82, 91,
    92, 102, 106, 117, 129, 133, 248
Jacobsen, Arne 31, 132
James I 64, 110, 238, 278
James II 103
James, Clive 226
James Cubitt & Partners 217, 263
James, John 204
James, M.R. 199

Janyns, Robert 82
Jeans, Sir James 211
Jeffreys, George 210
Jenkins, Sir Leoline 89
Jenkins, Roy 109
Jervais, Thomas 66
John, Gwen 232
John, King 112
John Miller & Partners 231
Johnson, Dr Samuel 21, 87
Jones, David 254
Jones, Walter 165
Jones, Sir William 103
Jowett, Benjamin 26, 108
Juxon, William 111, 112

K

Kandinsky, Wassily 123
Keble, John 26, 55, 81, 127
Keene, Henry 108, 113, 134
Kelvin, William 229
Kemp, Thomas, Bishop of London 60
Kempe, C.E. 57, 87, 226, 241
Kempster, Christopher 151
Ken, Thomas 69
Kendrew, Sir John 229
Kendrick Associates 31
Kent, William 166, 171
Kettell, Ralph 106
Keys (Caius), John 203
Keynes, John Maynard 199, 216, 217
Khan, Imran 127
Kilvert, Francis 65
King, Robert 75, 86
Kingsley, Charles 236
Kingsley, Mary 129
Kohn, Pedersen & Fox 32, 130
Koninck, Philips de 123

L

Laguerre, Louis 162
Lancaster, Osbert 91
Landor, Walter Savage 78
Lanfranco, Giovanni 123
Lankaster, E.R. 251
Lankaster, Jack 134
Larkin, Philip 112
Larsen, Henning 258
Lasdun, Denys 245, 256
Latimer, Bishop 19, 20, 61, 105, 110,
    201, 216
Laud, Archbishop William 20, 55, 110,
    112

Law, William 248
Lawrence, D.H. 150
Lawrence, Sir Thomas 75, 123
Lawrence, T.E. 89, 93
Le Carré, John 91
Le Sueur, Hubert 60, 61, 111
Leach, Bernard 254
Leadbetter, Stiff 135
Leakey, Louis 216
Leal, Valdes 99
Leavis, F.R. 251
Legge, Thomas 204
Lehmann, Rosamund 257
Leland, John 246
Lenthall, William 158
Lewis, C.S. 100, 104, 126
Liddell, Edith 74
Lightfoot, Luke 170
Linacre, Thomas 19, 93, 130
Linge, Abraham van 22, 72, 95, 103, 109
Linge, Bernard van 22, 64, 74
Lily, William 19
Lippi, Filippino 78
Locke, John 21, 78
Lorenzo di Credi 123
Lotto, Lorenzo 79
Loudon, John Claudius 162
Loveday, Thomas 214
Lovelace, Richard 114
Lubyns, John 75
Luck, Charles 260
Lutyens, Sir Edwin 30, 76, 86, 236
Lyell, Charles 90
Lyon, T.H. 226
Lyster, Grillet & Harding 264
Lytton, Bulwer 203

M

Macaulay, Thomas Babington 207, 210
MacCormac, Jameson & Pritchard 31, 65, 112, 114, 210, 256, 264
Macmillan, Harold 109
Macneice, Louis 85
Maguire & Murray 85, 107
Maillol, Aristide 137
Maine, Jonathan 107
Maitland, F.M. 251
Mallory, G.L. 236
Malthus, Thomas 241
Mamesfield, Henry de 84
Mandelson, Peter 133
Manet, Edouard 124

Manning, Cardinal 85, 109
Mansfield, Isaac 162
Manzuoli, Tomaso 202
Margaret of Anjou 220
Marlowe, Christopher 219
Marsden, Samuel 236
Marshall, Edward 170
Martin, Sir Leslie 31, 130, 132, 134, 253, 262
Martini, Simone 233
Marvell, Andrew 210
Mary I, Tudor 20, 207
Mary II 103
Mason, James 229
Mather, Rick 119, 128
Matilda, Queen 115, 151
Matisse, Henri 124, 232
Maufe, Edward 113
Maurice, F.D. 203, 216
McKellan, Sir Ian 218
Mead, J.C. 259
Melbourne, Lord 211
Mellon, Paul 201
Mendes, Sam 229
Mengs, Anton Raphael 93, 214
Mennim, A.M. 263
Merton, Walter de 82
Michael Hopkins & Partners 248
Michelangelo 79, 123
Mickelthwaite, J.T. 127
Middleton, John 58
Middleton, Thomas 95
Mildmay, Sir Walter 246
Millais, Sir John Everett 75, 125, 232
Miller, Sanderson 291
Milne, A.A. 211
Milner, Lord 109
Milton, John 244, 246
Miró, Joan 254
Mistry, Dhuva 258
Modigliani, Amedeo 232
Monet, Claude 124, 233
Monk, George 199
Montagna, Bartolomeo 68, 123
Montagu, John 210
Monet, Claude 233
Moore, Dudley 100
Moore, Henry 254, 263, 265
More, Sir Thomas 19
Morgan, William 215
Morley, David 136
Morley-Horder, Percy 133, 240
Morrell family 100
Morrell, Lady Ottoline 150
Morris, Jane 160

Morris, William 29, 90, 107, 118, 154, 159, 222, 228, 241
Mountbatten of Burma, Lord 246
Munrow, David 226
Murdoch, Iris 133
Murdoch, Rupert 114
Murillo, Bartollomé 233
Murray, Gilbert 69, 112

N

Naipaul, V.S. 104
Nash, Paul 232
Nash, Richard 'Beau' 89
Neale, J.M. 210, 251
Nehru, Jawaharlal 211
Nemon, Oscar 258
Nesfield, W.E. 286
Nevile, Thomas 207
Newbolt, Sir Henry 81
Newdigate, Sir Roger 104, 119
Newman, Cardinal John Henry 26, 55, 107, 108, 143
Newton, Sir Isaac 21, 206, 207, 211
Nicholas Ray Associates 237
Nicholson, Ben 124, 254
Nicholson, Winifred 254
Nicoll, W.G. 114
Nightingale, Florence 164
Nollekens, Joseph 124, 194
Norrish, R.G.W. 248
North, Lord 107
Nuffield, Lord 24, 148116

O

Oglethorpe, General 81
Orchard, William 60, 74, 97
Orley, Bernard van 80
O'Shea Brothers 128
Ostade, Adriaen van 123
Outram, John 32
Owen, Morgan, Bishop of Llandaff 55
Oxford Architects Partnership 85, 109, 133
Oxford Martyrs 61

P

Pace, George 68
Paddy, Dr William 111
Palin, Michael 58
Palma Giovane 79
Palma Vecchio 233
Palmer, Samuel 125

Palmerston, Lord 216
Paolo de Matteis 123
Parker, Barry 291
Parker, Edward 251
Parker, Matthew 19, 219
Parnell, Charles Stewart 236
Parry, C.H. 90
Pasmore, Victor 124
Paston, Sir John 203, 229
Pater, Walter 57, 58, 95, 131
Patten, Chris 109
Pattison, Mark 91
Paxman, Jeremy 218
Pearson, J.L. 68, 136, 201, 242, 248
Peckitt, William 68
Peel, Sir Robert 75, 78
Peisley, Bartholomew 22, 100, 111, 126
Pelham-Holles, Thomas 201
Pellegrini, Antonio 295
Pembroke, Earl of 60
Penn, William 78
Penrose, F.C. 214
Pepys, Samuel 235, 236
Perceval, Spencer 211
Perne, Dr Andrew 19, 227
Perse, Stephen 204
Peter Yiangou Associates 131
Peto, Harold 160
Petre, Sir William 89
Philby, Kim 211
Philippa, Queen 94
Phillips, John 77
Phillips, Tom 132
Picasso, Pablo 124, 232
Pierce, Edward 123
Piero di Cosimo 123
Pietro da Cortona 70
Pinturicchio, Bernardino 233
Piper, John 31, 116, 124, 139, 258, 264
Pissarro, Camille 124, 233
Pitt, Thomas, Earl of Camelford 171
Pitt, William the Elder 107
Pitt, William the Younger 224, 226
Pittoni, G.B. 242
Pitt-Rivers, A.H. Lane-Fox 129
Plath, Sylvia 260
Plowman, John 116
Plumb, J.H. 246
Pomfret, Countess of 56
Pope, Alexander 148
Pope, Sir Thomas 106
Porphyrios, Dmitri 96
Portillo, Michael 229
Portman, Sir John 64
Poussin, Nicolas 123, 232

Powell & Moya 31, 57, 77, 78, 82, 137, 215, 223
Power, Eileen 257
Poynter, Ambrose 243
Pré, Jacqueline du 101
Preti, Mattia 123
Price, Hugh 88Price, William 68
Priestly, J.B. 203
Prior, Matthew 216
Pugin, A.W.N. 28, 56, 235, 239
Pusey, Rev. E.B. 74, 78, 126
Pym, John 87

Q

Quiller-Couch, A. 108, 241

R

Radcliffe, Dr John 56, 91, 103, 104, 135
Raeburn, Henry 232
Raleigh, Sir Walter 80
Ramsey, Archbishop Michael 237
Rantzen, Esther 133
Raphael 79, 123
Rattigan, Terence 108
Raverat, Gwen 260
Ravilious, Eric 287
Ray, John 218
Rayleigh, J.W.S. 211
Redgrave, Sir Michael 237
Redman, Henry 75
Redon, Odilon 232
Rembrandt van Rijn 79
Reni, Guido 89, 233
Renoir, Pierre Auguste 124, 233
Revett, Nicholas 166
Reynolds, Bainbridge 109
Reynolds, Sir Joshua 66, 75, 124, 162, 169
Rhodes, Cecil 33, 80, 104
Ribera, Jusepe 172
Ricci, Marco 79
Ricci, Sebastiano 79
Riccio, Andrea 124
Richard I 112
Richard III 187
Richards, Ceri 96
Richards, I.A. 236
Richard Sheppard, Robson & Partners 31, 258
Richardson, Sir Albert 216, 245
Rickman & Hutchinson 28
Rickman, Thomas 215
Ridley, Bishop Nicholas 19, 20, 61, 105, 110, 226
Rie, Lucy 254
Robert Matthew Johnson Marshall Partnership 130, 259
Roberts & Clarke 264
Roberts, David 136, 231, 236, 240, 254, 258, 260
Roberts, Thomas 56, 76, 95
Robertson, Daniel 80
Robinson, David 27, 264
Robinson, Richard, Bishop of Armagh 75
Robinson, Sir Thomas 170
Robsart, Amy 56
Rodin, Auguste 124, 232, 233
Rogers, Annie M.A.H. 136
Romney, George 75
Rosa, Salvator 172, 233
Rossetti, Dante Gabriel 118, 159, 222
Rothschild, Ferdinand 169
Roubiliac, Louis François 123
Rowe, R.R. 243
Rowney, Thomas 126
Rowse, A.L. 93
Roysse, John 152
Rubens, P.P. 79, 123, 198
Ruisdael, Jacob van 123, 169, 233
Runcie, Archbishop Robert 58
Ruskin, John 29, 78, 118, 128, 143
Russell, Bertrand 210
Rutherford, Lord 211, 250
Rysbrack, John Michael 56, 163

S

St. Birinus 145
St. Edmund of Abingdon 96
St. Etheldreda 271, 274
St. Frideswide 12, 72, 73
Salisbury, Lord 78
Salviati, Antonio 205
Salvin, Anthony 110, 205, 239
Sandcroft, William 247, 248
Sandys, Francis 283
Sargent, John Singer 123
Savile, Sir Henry 84
Sayers, Dorothy 133
Scheemakers, Peter 209, 290
Schmidt, Bernard 193
Scorel, Jan van 79
Scott, Baillie 257
Scott, Elizabeth 261
Scott, Sir Giles Gilbert 30, 63, 111, 135, 138, 200, 225, 226, 228, 245, 264, 265
Scott, Gilbert 29, 65, 68, 72, 82, 90, 92,

103, 104, 110, 145, 214, 237, 271, 274
Scott, Robert Falcon 252
Sebastiano del Piombo 233
Seckham, Samuel Lipscombe 137
Selden, John 61
Selwyn, George Augustus 262
Seth, Vikram 81
Seurat, Georges 233
Seuss, Dr 91
Shakespear, George 77
Shakespeare, William 105
Sheldon, Archbishop Gilbert 62, 107
Shelley, Percy Bysshe 103, 104
Shenstone, William 87
Shepherd, Thomas 246
Sedgwick, Adam 249
Seurat, Georges 233
Shirley, James 218
Sibthorpe, Dr 101
Sickert, Walter 123, 232
Sidgwick, Henry 260
Sidney, Lady Frances 241
Sidney, Sir Philip 78
Simeon, Charles 243
Simpson, John 237
Sisley, Alfred 233
Smart, Christopher 226
Smith, Adam 109
Smith, Barbara Leigh 257
Smith, F.E. (Lord Birkenhead) 65
Smith, Sydney 21, 69
Smith, Thomas 223
Smithson, James 87
Smuts, Jan 246
Smythe, William, Bishop of Lincoln 57
Snow, C.P. 246
Soane, Sir John 290
Soddy, Frederick 85
Solomons, Sir David 205
Somerville, Mary 133
Sorensen, Erik 256
Southey, Robert 109
Spence, Sir Basil 223
Spenser, Edmund 224, 226
Spenser, Gilbert 131
Spenser, Stanley 124
Spooner, W.A. 69
Stainer, Sir John 131
Stanford, Charles Villiers 210, 223
Stanley, Charles 56
Stanton, Hervey de 206
Stapledon, Walter de 89
Steadman, Fabian 217
Steer, Wilson 123

Sterne, Laurence 241
Stevenson, J.J. 259
Stirling, James 31, 100, 262
Stokes, George Gabriel 226
Stokes, Leonard 113, 117, 248
Stone, Nicholas 84, 98, 102
Stonor family 150
Strachey, Lytton 211
Stradivarius, Antonio 122
Strafford, Lord of 216
Street, G.E. 89, 117, 136
Streeter, Robert 63
Strozzi, Bernardo 79
Stubbs, George 232
Sutherland, Graham 75, 103
Sutton, Sir Richard 57
Swift, Graham 223
Swinburne, Algernon 109
Sydenham, Thomas 64
Symonds, Ralph 209, 215, 242, 247

T

Talbot, Dr E.S. 137
Talman, William 217
Tanfield, Sir Lawrence 158
Taylor, Jeremy 93, 205
Taylor, Sir Robert 119
Taylor, Wendy 248
Tedder, Lord 236
Temple, Archbishop William 109
Temple, William 248
Tenison, Thomas 219
Tennyson, Lord Alfred 207, 210
Terborch, Gerard 123, 169
Terry, Quinlan 31, 251
Tesdale, Thomas 86
Thackeray, W.M. 210
Thatcher, Margaret 133, 258
Thelwall, Sir Eubule 88
Thomas, Edward 91
Thomas, John 100
Thomson, Sir George 211, 220
Thomson, J.J. 211
Thornhill, Sir James 62, 92, 95
Thornycroft, Hamo 207
Thorvaldson, Bertel 209
Tiepolo, G.B. 124
Tintoretto, Jacopo 79, 123, 233
Titian 79, 123, 233
Todd, Lord 246
Tolkien, J.R.R. 85, 90, 126
Toulouse-Lautrec, Henri 124
Townesend, William 23, 81, 87, 94, 111, 113

Townshend, Charles 'Turnip' 199
Tradescant, John the Elder 119
Traherne, Thomas 58
Trevelyan, G.M. 211
Trevor-Roper, H.R. 78
Trott, Adam van 109
Tull, Jethro 112
Turing, Alan 199
Turner, J.M.W. 124
Turner, William 124
Tye, Christopher 199
Tynan, Kenneth 131
Tyndale, William 100

U

Uccello, Paolo 123
Udall, Nicholas 81
Underwood, H.J. 90
Unwin, Raymond 291

V

Valence, Marie de 224
Vanderbilt, Consuelo 161
Vanbrugh, Sir John 23, 161, 162, 164,
     171, 294
Van Heynigen & Haward 101, 119, 256,
     259, 261
Vaughan, Henry 89
Velázquez, Diego Rodriguez da Silva 284
Veneziano, Domenico 233
Venn, John 205
Vermuyden, Sir Cornelius 277
Verney family 164
Veronese, Paolo 233
Vigée le Brun, Elisabeth 284
Vouet, Simon 232
Voysey, C. Cowles 243
Vuillard, Edouard 232

W

Wadham, Dorothy and Nicholas 64
Wailes, William 274
Walker, Obadiah 103
Waller, Edmund 199
Walpole, Horace 199
Walpole, Robert 199
Walsingham, Alan de 272
Walsingham, Francis 199
Warren, Thomas 200
Wastell, John 194, 282, 286
Waterhouse, Alfred 29, 108, 109, 118,
     204, 205, 240, 257

Waterhouse, Paul 257
Watteau, Antoine 124, 169
Watts, G.F. 75, 128
Waugh, Evelyn 70
Waynflete, William 69, 97
Webb, Sir Aston 205, 236
Webb, E. Doran 126
Webb, Philip 159
Wesley, John 55, 78, 91
Westley, John 200
White, Gilbert 80
White, Sir Thomas 110
White, T.H. 223
Whitefield, George 87
Whitgift, John 223
Witham-Smith, Andreas 127
Whittle, Frank 229
Wightwick, Richard 86
Wilberforce, Samuel 80, 129
Wilberforce, William 216
Wilde, Oscar 100
Wilkins, John 64
Wilkins, William 28, 113, 137, 196, 199,
     219, 250, 282
Wilkinson, William 113
Willement, Thomas 143
William I 13, 254
William of Durham 103
William of Ockham 15
Williams, David 293
Williams, Eric 133
Williams, John, Bishop of Lincoln 215
Williams, Ralph Vaughan 210
Williams, Raymond 241
Williams, Roger 226
Williams, Archbishop Rowan 201
Williams, Shirley 133
Williamson, Benedict 101
Wilmot, John 65
Wilson, C.T.R. 243
Wilson, Colin 31, 132
Wilson, Edward 205, 252
Wilson, Harold 89
Wilson, Richard 124
Winchcombe, Richard 166
Winde, William 154
Winterson, Jeanette 133
Wittgenstein, Ludwig 211
Wolsey, Thomas 72, 73, 97, 100
Wood, Anthony 82, 85, 115
Wood, Charles 205
Wood, Christopher 254
Wood, Sancton
Wood, Thomas 63
Woodlark, Robert 217

Woodville, Elizabeth 220
Woodward, John 249
Woodward, Benjamin 29, 72, 118, 128
Woolfe, Leonard 211
Woolfe, Virginia 257
Wootton, Barbara 257
Wordsworth, Elizabeth 136
Wordsworth, William 21, 212, 216
Worthington, Sir Hubert 68, 86, 129
Worthington, Thomas 131
Wren, Sir Christopher 21, 22, 62, 65, 71, 76, 93, 107, 209, 225, 247
Wright of Derby 232
Wright, Stephen 23, 153, 195
Wyatt, Matthew Digby 233
Wyatt, James 23, 75, 78, 80, 114, 134, 149
Wyatt, Thomas 215

Wyatville, Sir Jeffry 242
Wycherley, William 95
Wyck, Jan 70
Wyclif, John 15, 85, 95, 109
Wykeham, William, Bishop of Winchester 66, 166
Wyliott, John 82
Wynford, William 66
Wynne, David 272

Y

Young, Thomas 248

Oxford index

A

Abingdon 150
Adderbury 172
Addison's Walk 99
Alice's Shop 86
All Saints Church 91
All Souls College 92
Ardington House 153
Ashdown House 154
Ashmolean Museum 118

B

Balliol College 108
Banbury 166
Banbury Road 136
Bartlemas Chapel 101
Basildon Park 148
Bate Collection of Historical Instruments 86
Beam Hall 82
Beaumont Street 112
Bibury 159
Binsey 142
Blackfriars 126
Blackwell's Bookshop 63, 106
Bladon 160
Blenheim Palace 160, 161
Bloxham 168
Boar's Hill 144
Boarstall Duck Decoy 174
Bodleian Library 58
Bonn Square 116
Botanic Garden 102
Brasenose College 57
Brill 173
Broad Street 106
Broad Walk 85
Broughton Castle 167
Buckinghamshire Railway Centre 170
Bulwarks Lane 116
Burford 157
Bus Station 113
Buscot Park 160

C

Campion Hall 86
Carfax 88
Castle 115

Catte St 69
Centre for Islamic Studies 100
Chalgrove 150
Chapel of our Lady 70
Chastleton House 165
Chemistry Research Laboratory 130
Cherwell Boathouse 137
Chiltern Hills 148
Chipping Campden 165
Chipping Norton 164
Christ Church Cathedral 71
Christ Church, the College 75
Christ Church Meadow 84
Christ Church Picture Gallery 78
Christmas Common 150
City Information Centre 110
Clarendon Building 62
Claydon House 170
Codrington Library 93
Cogges Manor Farm Museum 155
Convocation House 61
Cornmarket Street 105
Corpus Christi College 80
Cotswold Wildlife Park 158
County Hall 116
Covered Market 88
Cowley Road 101
Cumnor 144

D

Dead Man's Walk 85
Departments of Zoology and Psychology 130
Didcot Railway Centre 153
Divinity School 60
Dorchester 145
Duke Humfrey's Library 61
Durham College 106
Dyke Hills 146

E

East Hendred 153
Ewelme 146
Examination Schools 102
Exeter College 89
Eynsham 155

F

Fairford 159
Faringdon 154
Fawley Court 150
Florey Building 100
Folly Bridge 70, 85
Frewin Hall 117
Fyfield 155

G

Garsington 150
George Street 117
Gloucester College 113
Gloucester Green 113
Godstow Abbey 142
Golden Cross 105
Goring Gap 147
Great Coxwell 154
Great Tew 168
Green College 134
Greyfriars 101
Greys Court 148

H

Harcourt Arboretum 145
Harris Manchester College 131
Hart Hall 65
Headington Hill Park 100
Henley-on-Thames 149
Hertford College 69, 85
High Street 13, 88
History Faculty 65
Holywell Manor 131
Holywell Music Room 65
Holywell Street 65, 133

I

Icknield Way 147
Iffley 139
Iffley Lock 139

J

Jacqueline du Pré Music Building 101
Jarn Mound 144
Jericho 134
Jesus College 88
John Parsons Almshouses 104
Jowett Walk 131

K

Keble College 127
Kellogg College 125
Kelmscott Manor 159
Kemp Hall 104
King Edward Street 104
Kingston House 154

L

Lady Margaret Hall 137
Lechlade 159
Linacre College 130
Lincoln College 90
Little Clarendon Street 133
Littlemore 143
Lockinge 153
Long Crendon 174
Longwall Street 96
Lord Berners' Folly 154

M

Magdalen Bridge 100
Magdalen College 97
Magpie Lane 82, 104
Maison Française 137
Mansfield College 130
Mapledurham 148
Martyrs' Memorial 110
Merton College 82
Merton Street 80, 82
Milton Manor 153
Minster Lovell 156
Mitre Hotel 88
Modern Art Oxford 117
Moreton-in-Marsh 165
Museum of Oxford 70
Museum of the History of Science 63
Music Faculty 86

N

Nettlebed 148
New Bodleian Library 63
New College 66
New College Lane 69
New Inn Hall Street 117
New Road Baptist Church 116
Nissan Institute for Japanese Studies 136
Norham Manor Estate 137
North Hinksey 143
North Parade 136
Northleach 159

Nuclear Physics Laboratory 126
Nuffield College 116
Nuffield Place 148
Nuneham Courtenay 145

O

Old Ashmolean 63
Old Fire Station Arts Centre 113
Old Marston 143
Old Palace 86
Oriel College 79
Osney Abbey 142
Otmoor 168
Oxford Brookes University 100
Oxford Canal 115, 142
Oxford Centre for Mission Studies 136
Oxford Movement 26
Oxford Playhouse 113
Oxford Story 110
Oxford Union Society 117
Oxford University Press 62, 134

P

Painted Room 105
Pangbourne 148
Park End Street 115
Park Town 137
Pembroke College 86
Pitt-Rivers Museum 129
Plain, The 100
Port Meadow 142
Postmasters' Hall 82
Prison, former 116
Pusey House 126

Q

Quainton 170
Queen Elizabeth House 126
Queen's College 94
Queen's Lane 95

R

Radcliffe Camera 56
Radcliffe Infirmary 135
Radcliffe Observatory 134
Radcliffe Science Library 129
Radcliffe Square 56
Randolph Hotel 113
Regents Park College 125
Rewley Abbey 142

Rewley House 125
Rhodes House 130
Ridgeway 154
Rollright Stones 165
Rothermere Institute for American Studies 130
Rousham House and Gardens 166
Ruskin College 115
Rycote Chapel 174

S

Sackler Library 125
Saïd Business School 115
St. Aldate's Street 70, 86
St. Aldate's Church 87
St. Aloysius 133
St. Anne's College 135
St. Antony's College 135
St. Barnabas church 134
St. Benet's Hall 126
St. Bernard's College 110
St. Catherine's College 132
St. Clement's Church 100
St. Cross Building 131
St. Cross Church 131
St. Cross College 126
St. Ebbe's Church 116
St. Edmund Hall 96
St. George's Tower 115
St. Giles 110
St. Giles Church 126
St. Giles House 126
St. Hilda's College 101
St. Hugh's College 136
St. John's Church 101
St. John's College 110
St. John Street 125
St. Mary and St. John Church 101
St. Mary Hall 104
St. Mary Magdalen Church 110
St. Mary the Virgin Church 55
St. Michael's Church 105
St. Michael's Street 117
St. Paul's Church 134
St. Peter's College 117
St. Philip and St. James 136
St. Stephen's House 101
Schools Quadrangle 58
Science Area 129
Sheldonian Theatre 62
Shelley Memorial 103
Ship Street 105
Shotover Country Park 143

Sir Geoffrey Arthur Building 85
Slaughters, Upper and Lower 165
Social Studies Faculty Centre 132
Somerville College 133
South Park 100
Stanton Harcourt 155
Steventon 153
Stone's Almshouses 100
Stonor Park 150
Stow-on-the-Wold 165
Stowe 171
Swinbrook 157

T

Tackley's Inn 104
Taylor Institution 118
Templeton College 144
Thame 173
Town Hall 70
Trinity College 106
Turl Street 88

U

Uffington Castle 154
University College 103
University Museum of Natural History
   128
University Offices 134
University Parks 138
University Sports Ground 101

V

Vale and Downland Museum 153

W

Waddesdon Manor 168
Wadham College 64
Wallingford 147
Walton Street 134
Wantage 153
War Memorial Garden 71
Waterperry Gardens 174
Wesley Memorial Church 117
West Wycombe 172
Westgate Centre 116
White Horse, Uffington 154
Widford 157
Windrush Valley 156
Witney 156
Wittenham Clumps 146

Wolfson College 137
Wolsey Almshouses 86
Woodstock 164
Woodstock Road 133
Worcester College 113
Wycliffe Hall 138
Wytham 144
Wytham Woods 144

Cambridge index

A

Addenbrooke's Hospitals 233
All Saints Church 241
American Military Cemetery 269
Anglesey Abbey 280
Arts Faculties 261
Arts Theatre 216
Ashwell 291
Audley End 287

B

Backs, The 199, 215, 251, 259, 265
Baldock 291
Barnwell Priory 268
Botanic Garden 234
Buckden 294
Burrells Field Hostel 264
Burwell 279
Bury St. Edmunds 281
Bus Station 246
Byron's Pool 268

C

Cambridge and County Folk Museum 253
Cambridge Camden Society 28
Cambridge Crystalographic Data Centre 252
Cambridge Museum of Technology 268
Cambridge Union Society 237
Cambridge University Press 224
Castle 254
Castle Hill 254
Castle Hill Hostel 254
Cavendish Laboratories 250
Centre for Mathematical Sciences 259
Cheshunt Theological College 234
Chesterton 268
Christ's College 244
Christ's Pieces 246
Churchill College 258
Clare College 199
Clare Hall 263
Clarkson Road 259
Coe Fen 265
Corn Exchange 243
Corpus Christi College 218
Coton 269
County Hall 254

D

Darwin College 260
Denny Abbey 277
Department of Computer Sciences 259
Devil's Ditch 280
Downing College 250
Duxford 285

E

Eagle Inn 216
Ely 270
Emmanuel College 246
Emmanuel Congregational Church 224

F

Fen Ditton 268
Fenner's 251
Fens, The 277
Fenstanton 291
Fitzwilliam College 256
Fitzwilliam House 229
Fitzwilliam Museum 229
Fitzwilliam Street 234

G

Garret Hostel Lane 203
Girton College 257
Godmanchester 292
Gog Magog Hills 269
Gonville and Caius College 203
Gonville Hall 203, 204, 207
Grafton Centre 246
Grange Road 263
Grantchester 265
Guildhall 243

H

Hemingford Grey 292
Hinchingbrooke House 293
Hobson's Conduit 234
Holy Trinity Church 243
Homerton College 252
Houghton 292
Hughes Hall 251
Huntingdon 293
Huntingdon Road 254

I

Ickworth 283
Imperial War Museum Duxford 285

J

Jesus College 238
Jesus Lane 238
Judge Institute for Management Studies 233

K

Kenmare 224
Kettle's Yard 253
Kimbolton 294
King's College 195
King's Lane Courts 217
King's Parade 193, 216

L

Lammas Land 265
Laundress Green 224
Lavenham 284
Leckhampton 263
Lee Seng Tee Library 263
Letchworth Garden City 291
Linton Zoo 285
Lion Yard 243
Little Gidding 304
Little Trinity 238
Long Melford 284
Lucy Cavendish College 259

M

Madingley Hall 269
Madingley Road 259
Maersk McKinney Moller Centre for Continuing Education 258
Magdalene Bridge 237
Magdalene College 235
Market Hill 243
Microsoft Laboratory 259
Midsummer Common 268
Mond Laboratory 250
Museum of Archaeology and Anthropology 249
Museum of Classical Archaeology 261

N

National Horseracing Museum, Newmarket 278
Needham Institute 264
New Hall 255
New Museums Building 249
Newmarket 278
Newnham College 260
Newnham Grange 260
Northampton Street 253

O

Old Court of King's College 201
Old Schools 195
Our Lady and the English Martyrs Church 252

P

Park Terrace 251
Parker's Piece 251
Pembroke College 224
Peterhouse 227
Petty Cury 243
Pitt Building 224

Q

Queens' College 220

R

Railway Station 252
Regent Street 250
Ridley Hall 260
Robinson College 264
Round Church 237

S

Saffron Walden 285
St. Andrew's Church 243
St. Bene't's Church 216
St. Botolph Church 220
St. Catharine's College 217
St. Chad's Hostel 263
St. Clement's Church 237
St. Edmund's College 254
St. Edward's Church 216
St. Giles Church 254
St. Ives 292
St. John's College 212

St. Mary the Great 193
St. Mary the Less 226
St. Michael's Church 206
St. Peter's Church 253
Schlumberger Research Laboratory 259
Science Area 248
Scott Polar Research Institute and
    Museum 252
Sedgwick Museum of Earth Sciences 249
Selwyn College 262
Senate House 194
Senate House Passage 203
Sheep's Green 265
Sidgwick Avenue 261
Sidney Sussex College 241
Silver Street 224, 260
Storey's Way 257
Stourbridge Chapel 269
Stourbridge Common 268
Stretham 277
Sussex Street 243
Swaffham Prior 280

T

Thaxted 289
Tourist Information Centre 243
Trinity College 206
Trinity Hall 201
Trinity Lane 206
Trinity Street 206
Trumpington 268
Trumpington Road 234
Trumpington Street 224

U

University Graduate Centre 224
University Library 264
University Museum of Zoology 249
University Observatory 259

W

Wandlebury Camp 270
West Cambridge 259
Westminster College 259
Whipple Museum of the History of Science
    249
Wicken Fen National Nature Reserve 277
Wimpole Hall 289
Wolfson College 263